D0820261

Schemas in Problem Solving explores a new theory of schema development and its ability to serve as a unified basis for understanding learning, instruction, and assessment. The theory's prescriptions for teaching are direct, and its application to assessment suggests new directions for tests.

After examining the roots of the theory in earlier work by philosophers and psychologists, Marshall illustrates the main features of her theory with experimental evidence from students who are learning to recognize and solve complex arithmetic story problems. She describes individual performance with traditional empirical studies as well as computer simulation. The computer simulation reflects a new approach in modeling cognition. Marshall's model links neural networks with symbolic systems to form a hybrid model that uses pattern matching of sets of features as well as logical step-by-step rules.

Schemas in problem solving

SCHEMAS IN PROBLEM SOLVING

Sandra P. Marshall
San Diego State University

Published by the Press Syndicate of the University of Cambridge
The Pitt Building, Trumpington Street, Cambridge CB2 1RP
40 West 20th Street, New York, NY 10011-4211, USA
10 Stamford Road, Oakleigh, Melbourne 3166, Australia

First published 1995

Printed in the United States of America

Library of Congress Cataloging-in-Publication Data
Marshall, Sandra P.
Schemas in problem solving / Sandra P. Marshall.
p. cm.
Includes bibliographical references.
ISBN 0-521-43072-0
1. Schemas (Psychology) 2. Problem solving 3. Learning,
Psychology of. 4. Word problems (Mathematics) 5. Educational tests
and measurements. I. Title.
BF395.S34M37 1995
153.4'3 – dc20   94-17590

A catalog record for this book is available from the British Library.

ISBN 0-521-43072-0 Hardback

Contents

Preface

"There can be no doubt that all our knowledge begins with experience." With these words Immanuel Kant began his account of reason (*Critique of Pure Reason*, p. 41). I concur with his view; it is in the accumulation of experiences that we learn about our environment. Initially, each experience is unique and may be stored in memory separately. However, we eventually amass a great many experiences that are highly similar, and evidence abounds that we do not store each one completely and in isolation. Instead, we seem to clump together the common elements of experiences and retrieve from memory only selected highlights of those instances which are in some way unusual or atypical.

Similar experiences come together under the broad umbrella called a schema. The schema is the means by which similar experiences are assimilated and aggregated in such a way as to be quickly and easily remembered. It is a mechanism in human memory that allows for the storage, synthesis, generalization, and retrieval of similar experiences. In short, it is an essential ingredient of learning and remembering. A distinctive feature of a schema is that when one piece of information associated with it is retrieved from memory, other pieces of information connected to the same schema are also activated and available for mental processing. A second important feature is that many different kinds of knowledge are linked through the schema, including conceptual information, discriminating features, planning mechanisms, and procedural skills. A well-formed schema will have all of these.

This book is about schemas. As such, it touches on important issues such as learning and remembering, misunderstanding and forgetting, and merging old memories with new experiences. The central topic here – the schema – is not neatly confined to a single discipline such as cognitive psychology or cognitive science. Rather, it pops up in many areas, and its richness is that it makes contributions not only to the cognitive fields but also to other areas such as anthropology and philosophy. Not insignificant is its importance also for instructional design, diagnostic assessment, and computer modeling. There are important practical issues to be considered as well as intriguing theoretical ones.

This book is about schemas, but it is more than that. It is also about how we can use what we know of schemas to improve people's learning, how schemas can direct the assessment of learning, how understanding schemas can lead to better understanding of memory, and how we can use this understanding to create more satisfactory models of learning and performance. These endeavors have both theoretical and practical consequences.

From the theoretical point of view, schemas have great value because they join together two great schools of thought about how people think and organize knowledge. These two perspectives have recently been called symbolic processing and connectionist learning. One views cognition as a rational, sequential process following clear and concise rules. The other sees it as a complex series of pattern matches in which all pieces of the pattern are processed simultaneously. The schema theory described here incorporates both perspectives and is truly a hybrid theory of cognition. The learning studies of part III and the models of part V contain important details about the role of the schema for learning.

On the applied side, the fundamental idea is very simple. Much of an individual's learning takes place in a classroom, and it seems foolish to consider learning outcomes without looking also to the instruction intended to promote that learning. A similar argument can be made for assessment. To study learning, we must have some way of interpreting the outcomes we observe, and, again, it seems only reasonable that the theory which explains the learning be applied also to the interpretation of the outcomes. Thus, if schemas are a basic mechanism for learning, then instruction ought to help individuals develop strong schemas, and assessment ought to identify specific strengths and deficiencies in their schemas. Schema theory seems to be an ideal vehicle for providing the needed theoretical structure to look at both instruction and assessment. At a time when the restructuring of education is part of the national agenda, it seems likely that schema theory will be important and will play an essential role. As I show in part II, schema theory can guide instructional design. And, as I illustrate in part IV, it also plays a role in assessment.

The notion of the schema has been with us for a very long time, at least as far back as Plato and Aristotle (see part I). Over that time, its meaning has shifted and evolved in a number of interesting ways. A quick perusal of the current psychological literature yields a host of different ideas about what constitutes a schema. Some of the differences in formulation are relatively trivial but others are critically important. If we are to progress in understanding the schema, we need to reconcile the differences, recognize the many similarities, and embrace a common meaning for the term. What is needed is a baseline definition that can be examined in detail, applied to a number of different domains, and evaluated for its success or failure in describing human cognition. This book serves as a starting point.

My goals here are to explore what is meant by the term *schema*, to formalize its definition, and to lay out the rudiments of a theory of schema development. Much of my research derives from the domain of arithmetic story problems, and this domain is emphasized in the following pages. In the context of the selected domain, I examine a number of important issues that are related to schema representation in memory, schema retrieval, schema-based learning, and schema-based assessment. I also describe several competing approaches to modeling the use and acquisition of schemas. Within a single domain, a continuity can be developed to illustrate and tie together many different facets of schema theory. This continuity allows me to look at schema identification, instructional design, assessment of learning, and cognitive modeling, all within the common framework of arithmetic story problems.

Although I present only one domain, I do not consider the schema theory described here to be limited to arithmetic story problems. I have applied the theory with some success to the assessment of rational numbers (Marshall, 1993a), and I have recently completed a preliminary application to decision making, focusing on the decisions made in ambiguous and rapidly changing situations by commanding officers of United States Navy ships (D. E. Smith & Marshall, 1993, in press). The decision-making model has been enthusiastically received by a number of researchers and practitioners. It seems to me that schema theory has considerable potential for application to many disparate domains.

The outline I have adopted in this volume is simple. The five parts each focus on a different theme of importance to schema theory. Each part opens with a brief introduction, describing its theme and summarizing the chapters contained in it. The first chapter in every part lays out the important issues associated with the part theme, and the subsequent chapters describe my research on arithmetic problem solving that is pertinent to the theme. Although the results on problem solving are important in themselves, I have tried throughout to emphasize the critical features of schema theory and ways we may test them.

I expect that various parts of this book will have differential value for readers, depending upon their interests and expertise. For instance, the sections on instruction and assessment might be most pertinent to those most concerned with instructional design. Similarly, the sections on learning and modeling could be of greatest interest to those who are developing models of cognition. For all readers, part I provides the essential fundamentals of the theory and the necessary specifications of the domain.

As the noted psychologist Donald Hebb once commented, "A good theory is one that holds together long enough to get you to a better theory" (1969, p. 27). It is my hope that the schema theory laid out in the following pages will serve in such a manner.

Acknowledgments

The research reported here was funded by the Cognitive Science Program of the Office of Naval Research under Contracts N-00014-K-85–0661 and N00014–90-J-1143, and I am grateful for both the monetary and the intellectual support of that program. The program officers, together with the other ONR contractors whom I frequently met, provided challenges and questions that (almost) always advanced my thinking about schemas. I wish especially to acknowledge the contributions of the program manager, Dr. Susan Chipman. During the years in which this research was carried out, she provided constructive criticism and theoretical insights that have been immensely valuable to the project. She also provided many useful comments on an earlier draft of this book.

I also want to thank my graduate and undergraduate research assistants for their valuable contributions to the project: Kathryn Barthuli, Margaret Brewer, Pam Gee, Fred Rose, Patti Scott, and Julie Smith. Finally, I would like to acknowledge the programming contributions of my son, John P. Marshall. He developed much of the *Problem Solving Environment* as well as substantial parts of the connectionist models, and it was a unique and lasting pleasure working with him.

I

Fundamentals

The three chapters in part I present my view of the integral formulation of schema development and usage in problem solving. These chapters provide an overview of the historical importance of the schema, review contributions from various disciplines, lay out the basic theory that guides the research presented in this book, and describe the specific schemas that are the focus of the research reported in later chapters. A central goal of part I is the formulation of an operational definition of a schema. The word *schema* is widely used, it often appears with little or no definition, and it frequently takes on a slightly different meaning for every researcher who uses it. In part I, I describe very specifically what I mean when I use the term *schema*.

Chapter 1 looks at the history and meaning of the term *schema*. It summarizes how schemas have been defined and described, beginning with ancient Greek philosophy and closing with modern cognitive science. Most striking is the extent of our debt to the ancient Greeks. Many of our current debates have roots in their philosophical discussions.

Chapter 2 contains the basics of schema theory as I see it. The definition of a schema is more complex here than in the earlier research described in chapter 1, although as I point out, the current framework encompasses many of the existing usages already described. Chapter 2 is a foundational chapter, because all the experimental studies and modeling that follow in subsequent chapters derive from the theory laid out here. This chapter paints a broad picture of the schema. It has become the norm in psychological research to focus on small, specific hypotheses about particular cognitive mechanisms and to avoid sweeping statements that cannot be substantiated by experimentation. This, after all, is the way that careful scientific theory usually develops. For the purpose of aligning schema theory with a more expansive vision of cognition, however, I take some liberties with the norm. I consider it important to reflect on ways that other areas of research, such as motivation and attention, support and are supported by schema theory. My approach is consistent with recent suggestions that more attention be given to unified theories of cognition than to discrete models of isolated phenomena (Newell, 1990; Johnson-Laird, 1988). I use this chapter to point out some of the important linkages.

Chapter 3 presents the specific schemas of arithmetic story problems. Most of my research has been done in this area, and the remainder of the chapters in this book center on the five schemas described here. The situations that underlie the schemas were identified through an examination of existing texts and other curricular materials currently in use in today's classrooms. As shown in chapter 3, this method of identifying schemas depends on meaningful ways of characterizing the problems that occur in the existing environment and reflects the underlying assumption that this environment, or at least the problems within it, are likely to remain much the same over time. The means of identification and verification are explained in some detail. Chapter 3 is essentially a case study of how one can go about pinpointing essential schemas and their characteristics. It concludes with an appendix describing alternative classifications of story problems.

1

Schema roots

In current cognitive science and psychology, one encounters little consensus about what constitutes a schema. The term has been loosely used for some time, and it lacks a common and well-specified definition to which we all can turn. Even dictionaries are not of much assistance, because, for the most part, they give only vague synonyms such as *shape* or *form* for the word *schema*. My intention in this chapter is to clarify our understanding of the concept by identifying the important and lasting attributes that have been attached to the term over the history of its use, first in philosophy and then in psychology. These attributes will be incorporated into an expanded definition of the schema in chapter 2, resulting in a formulation having sufficient detail to allow the development of explicit cognitive models.

The term *schema* has a long and rich background. Both the word and the concept it reflects are prominent in the writings of the ancient Greek philosophers. It permeates the philosophy of Immanuel Kant. It guided the research of many early psychologists. And now it has a place in cognitive science. As one might expect, *schema* has not carried exactly the same connotations over this long period of usage, although there are important continuities. Even more important for the study of modern schema theory are the differences and the unresolved issues that vexed our predecessors. A look at a few instances of its previous application sheds light on our modern understanding and use of the term.

All of us have some notion of what schema means because we have encountered the term in a number of well-known places.

Unfortunately, its meaning is not particularly consistent in these many occurrences, as we shall see. Even its origin in philosophy and psychology is frequently argued. The introduction of the schema as an important construct is attributed variously to (a) Piaget in his many works such as *The Origins of Intelligence in Children* (1952), (b) Bartlett in *Remembering* (1932), and (c) Kant in *Critique of Pure Reason* (1787/1968). Actually, its usage is a great deal older and may be traced at least to the ancient Greek philosophers.

The ancient Greeks' σχημα

The word *schema* comes from the Greek language and, in fact, is a letter-for-letter transliteration from the Greek word, σχημα.[1] Thus, a linguistic and semantic investigation must begin with the ancient Greeks. In modern and ancient Greek, σχημα means "form," "shape," or "figure."[2] It is an everyday word whose concrete, commonplace meanings fail almost completely to capture either the richness of the term as it was used by Greek philosophers long ago or the precision of the term as psychologists use it today. Much like our own word *form,* σχημα has several meanings, many of which are evident in Plato's dialogues and Aristotle's *Metaphysics.* The original Greek texts reveal numerous occurrences of σχημα in several denotations, which depend upon the context of the example.

Two central meanings predominate in Plato's dialogues. First, *schema* (translated variously as "form," "shape," "figure," or "fashion") often occurs, along with "color," "sound," or "music,"[3] in discussions about the intrinsic nature of objects; for example, "in the case of letters, we both see and know the form [schema] and color."[4] A second use occurs with abstract concepts, as in "the form [schema] of a law,"[5] the "shapes [schemas] of lives,"[6] or the "fashion [schema] of a legend."[7] In both contexts, *schema* indicates the essential commonality of a broad category.

A large part of the dialogue of Plato's *The Meno* is a discussion of what is meant by σχημα. The highly respected translation of W. R. M. Lamb renders σχημα as "figure" in this context. Socrates and Meno are discussing virtue and Socrates asks Meno to tell him what "figure" is (i.e., schema). Socrates points out that there are many types of figures, such as round and straight. What he asks of Meno is the nature of the category "figure" that describes both round and straight: "We are always arriving at a variety of things, but let me have no more of that: since you call these many things by one single name, and say they are figures, every one of them, even when they are opposed to one another, tell me what is that which comprises round and straight alike, and which you call figure."[8] Clearly, "figure" (or schema) is the common, essential feature of the numerous examples of geometric shapes.

Similarly, in the *Laws,* book 2, where the translator uses "posture" for σχῆμα, one finds: "But in fact, while postures and tunes do exist in music, which deals with rhythm and harmony, so that one can rightly speak of a tune or posture being 'rhythmical' or 'harmonious,' one cannot rightly apply the choirmasters' metaphor 'well-coloured' to tune and posture; but one can use this language about the posture and tune of the brave man and the coward, and one is right in calling those of the brave man good, and those of the coward bad. To avoid a tediously long disquisition, let us sum up the whole matter by saying that the postures and tunes which attach to goodness of soul or body, or to some image thereof, are universally good."[9] Schema as "posture" refers here first to the movements of dance, a concrete instance of schema as essence. Then through analogy and abstraction, it refers to the essential characteristics that attach to "goodness" or "badness."

Plato's usage, it seems to me, is entirely in keeping with the way we use *schema* today. Consider, for instance, as Plato did, what constitutes a schema for a good man. What does this mean? Typically, it refers to those characteristics that taken together and functioning as a group allow the observer to decide whether a particular person is good, that is, whether this schema applies to him. I will not attempt here to flesh out this particular schema – it is a philosophical question quite beyond my scope. Its relevance here is that it begins to show how a schema takes on a meaning of stereotype. In using *schema* repeatedly in different contexts, Plato is reaching for broad generalizations, not specific details.

In his *Metaphysics*, Aristotle maintains some of the same meanings as Plato. There are numerous instances of σχημα in the sense of geometrical figure and physical shape.[10] Aristotle, however, introduces a second meaning of σχημα in the *Metaphysics*, a meaning that relates directly to his fundamental categories. In general, he uses the Greek word κατηγορια to refer to the categories, and, indeed, κατηγορια is the title of his widely known treatise on that subject. (One notes in passing that transliterated *categoria*, κατηγορια, has also passed into English nearly unchanged.) In English translations of Aristotle's work, κατηγορια is often rendered as "predicates." There are ten of them: "what (or Substance), how large (that is, Quantity), what sort of thing (that is, Quality), related to what (or Relation), where (that is, Place), when (or Time), in what attitude (Posture, Position), how circumstanced (State or Condition), how active, what doing (or Action), how passive, what suffering (Affection)."[11] According to Aristotle, these are the primitive characteristics by which everything can be classified. He does not use σχημα to describe any particular category. Rather, there are many instances in which he refers to the categories as a whole as σχηματοσ, that is, forms or figures of predication.[12]

Both Plato and Aristotle wrote a great deal about the σχημα, and, as noted, it has routinely been translated as "form." Thus, we find Aristotle discussing essential forms and Plato describing ideal forms. In fact, they are talking about schematos (or σχηματοσ, as the plural is written in Greek).[13]

In the *Metaphysics*, Aristotle is concerned frequently with form. "By form [schema] I mean the essence or very nature of the thing . . . . It is according to form [schema] that we know all things."[14] Aristotle frequently uses *nature, essence,* and *form* almost interchangeably, as in "The very nature of a thing is the essence of the thing."[15] If we understand the translated word "form" to be schema (and, indeed, the original Greek text often is the word σχημα), then we have the essence of the thing is its schema.

Clearly, *schema* was an important term in the works of Plato and Aristotle, although the two disagreed on several fundamental points. The underlying meaning for both of them seems to be that it is through the schema that we understand what we see. That is, according to Aristotle, the importance of *schemas* or *categories* is that they allow recognition and understanding of basic properties. From Plato, we have *schema* in the sense of a general framework or basic outline, so that we can talk about a schema of a king or a schema of a good man. Together, these two usages of *schema* provide us with a rough foundation upon which to build our own definition of *schema*. We can conceive of a schema as a means of organizing characteristics about something (deliberately vague) in such a way that the resulting framework can be useful in categorizing other instances that have the same or similar structure.

An interesting side note here is that very few (if any) translators of Plato's and Aristotle's works retain the word *schema* in the English translation. Translators often select more common English words rather than opting for a literal translation,[16] and as noted, almost always *schema* is rendered "shape" or "form." From our perspective this is unfortunate because some of the original meaning is lost in the translation. Readers of the original Greek texts will encounter the word σχημα. Readers of an English translation will not. And "shape" or "form" does not capture the full meaning of *schema* as used today.

Kant's concept of schema

Plato and Aristotle used *schema* widely in their philosophical writings. Immanuel Kant also frequently employed the term but with a different purpose. To the Greek philosophers the schema was primarily a vehicle for describing an object or concept. Interest was squarely on the thing being described. Kant, too, was interested in describing concepts but he extended the notion of schema by also describing the schema itself. Thus, it is important for us to look at what he had to say.

Kant dealt at length with the notion of a schema in his *Critique of Pure Reason* (see particularly chapter 1 of the "Transcendental Doctrine of Judgment"), and his views have been widely quoted. Essentially, Kant believed that there are pure concepts or categories of understanding that exist a priori in the mind. The difficulty is to apply these abstract categories to perceived real-world objects, thus linking the concept (the innate understanding) and the percept (the perceived phenomenon). For Kant, the schema was that link. He postulated the existence of three things: the a priori categories, or pure concepts of understanding, the empirical information derived through sensory perception, and the schema, which links sensibility and understanding (1787/1968, pp. B176–180).[17] The schema provides the representation of the perceived phenomenon which can then – and only then – be interpreted under the general restrictions of the innate categories.

Certainly, psychologists today have adopted a great deal of Kant's formulation, especially with respect to the link between concept and percept. Almost every modern usage of *schema* draws upon the person's application of knowledge found in memory to make sense of some experience or event taking place in his or her world.

However, much of current cognitive psychological research would challenge the premise that schemas reflect innate knowledge. This issue will be addressed later in this chapter. Modern usage also quarrels with the assertion that the pure concepts "ought to apply to things in general, *as they are*, and not, like the schemata, represent them only *as they appear*" (Kant, 1787/1968, p. B186, italics in original). In fact, as I will point out shortly, most modern theories attribute to the schema such generality. One interesting and fruitful arena of schema research is the investigation of the extent to which a current perceived instance can deviate from the memory's somewhat idealized schema and still be interpreted by it. Such a view is at odds with Kant's theory.

It is somewhat difficult to pin down a precise definition of the schema in Kant's writing. Among its characteristics are the following (see Kant, 1787/1968, pp. B179–180):

"The schema is void of all empirical content. . . ."
"The schema is in itself always a product of imagination. . . ."
"[T]he schema has to be distinguished from the image. . . . "
"The schema of the triangle can exist nowhere but in
       thought. . . ."

"No image could ever be adequate to the concept of a triangle in general."

"It [the schema] would never attain that universality of the concept which renders it valid of all triangles. . . . "

It is clear from Kant's work that he draws heavily upon the Greek meaning of the term *schema*. As remarked earlier, Plato also was concerned with how we understand what we see. His position may well be the origin of Kant's a priori categories. In contrast, Aristotle described how form exists in matter and how we extract the form from things. In our terms, this would be extracting the schema or general structure from multiple experiences, a notion very contrary to Kant's premise but perhaps more consistent with current cognitive science theories.

It is worthwhile noting that Aristotle, Plato, and Kant were all concerned primarily with concepts (e.g., both Aristotle and Kant devoted many pages to the nature of number and to describing what makes a triangle a triangle).[18] Modern psychological usage moves beyond this scope and looks at events, experiences, and situations as well. However, much of what these philosophers observed about schemas for concepts is equally valid for our topics as well.

Psychological study: Bartlett and Piaget

The study of schemas remained for a long period of time in the purview of philosophy, only gradually penetrating into the work of a few psychologists. The schema was largely ignored by early psychologists (especially American psychologists), who focused most of their attention on physiological and behavioral issues. It re-emerged in the work of two outstanding scholars, the British psychologist Frederic Bartlett and the Swiss biologist and genetic epistemologist Jean Piaget. Bartlett focused his attention on how individuals remember and what they remember. Piaget studied, among other things, the development of scientific reasoning. The schema is a cornerstone of both men's theories, although in considerably different ways.

Bartlett's "effort after meaning"

In his treatise on remembering, first published in 1932, Bartlett postulated that memory is organized around schemas containing summaries of familiar stories or situations. The schemas are activated when an individual tries to comprehend a new story. Abnormal or strange elements of a new story that do not fit the schemas are changed and adapted so that the story conforms more closely to an existing schema. This adaptation takes place during the encoding of the story in memory so that, upon later recollection, some of the original elements are lost and only their adaptations are recalled.

Bartlett used schemas to explain why subjects altered or ignored unfamiliar parts of a story when they attempted to recall it. His most famous study (1932) centered on the following story:

The War of the Ghosts

One night two young men from Egulac went down to the river to hunt seals and while they were there it became foggy and calm. They heard war cries, and they thought, "Maybe this is a war party." They escaped to the shore and hid behind a log. Now canoes came up and they heard the noise of paddles and saw one canoe coming up to them. There were five men in the canoe, and they said,

"What do you think? We wish to take you along. We are going up the river to make war on the people."

One of the young men said, "I have no arrows."

"Arrows are in the canoe," they said.

"I will not go along. I might be killed. My relatives do not know where I have gone. But you," he said, turning to the other, "may go with them."

So one of the young men went, but the other returned home.

And the warriors went on up the river to a town on the other side of Kalama. The people came down to the water, and they began to fight, and many were killed. But presently the young man heard one of the warriors say, "Quick, let us go home; that Indian has been hit." Now he thought, "Oh, they are ghosts." He did not feel sick, but they said he had been shot.

So the canoes went back to Egulac, and the young man went ashore to his house and made a fire. And he told everybody and said, "Behold, I accompanied the ghosts, and we went to a fight. Many of our fellows were killed, and many of those who attacked us were killed. And they said I was hit and I did not feel sick."

He told it all, and then he became quiet. When the sun rose he fell down. Something black came out of his mouth. His face became contorted. The people jumped up and cried.

He was dead. (p. 65)

Bartlett presented this story to a number of individuals and examined their later remembrances of it. He found that people tended to misunderstand the story and to distort the parts that were misunderstood. For example, the story generally was short-ened in the retelling, and the language made more modern. Sub-jects typically had trouble dealing with the ghost theme and fre-quently changed the story substantially to resolve the problem (e.g., changed the ghosts to a warring tribe or clan). Of interest is the fact that the line "Something black came out of his mouth" was remembered by almost all subjects whom Bartlett quotes, although its context was frequently altered (1932, chap. 5). One might speculate that although this image may not be part of a person's schema, it is so dramatic and salient that it becomes encoded nevertheless.

Bartlett hypothesized that these modifications result from the story schemas that his subjects had previously developed about Indians, ghosts, wars, death, and so forth. When story elements did not fit the memory schemas, the story details were altered, in Procrustean fashion, until they did.

In defining the schema, Bartlett was influenced by the physiolo-gist Sir Henry Head, who used the term *schema* in a completely different context. Head was interested in real and imagined body postures, in how individuals move and in how they imagined the positions of their limbs.[19] Head used *schema* to mean the imagined posture. Although the sense of *schema* as a universal or ideal is lacking, the application is strikingly parallel to the Greeks' usage of *schema* as posture described earlier.

Bartlett (1932) adopted Head's term but chafed at the lack of precision that already characterized it:

> I strongly dislike the term "schema." It is at once too definite and too sketchy. The word is already widely used in controversial psychological writing to refer generally to any rather vaguely outlined theory. It suggests some persistent, but fragmentary, "form of arrangement," and it does not indicate what is very essential to the whole notion, that the organized mass results of past changes of position and posture are actively *doing* something all the time; are, so to speak, carried along with us, complete, though developing, from moment to moment. (pp. 200–201)

Thus, Bartlett was clearly bothered by the imprecision of the term. He goes on to comment that, although he would prefer to use the term *organized setting,* he would continue to use *schema,* and he attempted to make his usage more precise:

> "Schema" refers to an active organisation of past reactions, or of past experiences, which must always be supposed to be operating in any well-adapted organic response. That is, whenever there is any order or regularity of behavior, a particular response is possible only because it is related to other similar responses which have been serially organised, yet which operate, not simply as individual members coming one after another, but as a unitary mass. Determination by schemata is the most fundamental of all the ways in which we can be influenced by reactions and experiences which occurred some time in the past. (p. 201)

Bartlett's key contributions to the study of the schema are his emphasis on organization and his view that a schema necessarily entails an element of expectation, that is, of anticipation of what ought to occur or be present if the schema is appropriate to the situation. His work reflects consistently his view that individuals strive to impose order or detect meaning in a novel situation by using past experiences organized in schemas, a characteristic he referred to as "effort after meaning" (1932, p. 44).

Bartlett's goal was a theory of remembering. He hypothesized that memory was not composed of a fixed set of remembered episodes that would be recalled one by one in their entirety as needed. Rather, he postulated that memory consisted of an active reorganization or reconstruction of events, with the reconstruction built on the accumulated experiences of the individual. These accumulated experiences were organized so that the total mass, rather than isolated elements, influenced the reconstruction. In his theory, the schema holds and organizes these past experiences and consequently guides their recollection. This suggests a highly specific and selective memory structure.

Although Bartlett complained about the vagueness and looseness of prior definitions of schemas, his definition is prone to the same weakness for our purpose of building a cognitive model of the schema. His definition gives considerably more structure to the term than was previously available, but it is nonetheless insufficient. One cannot use it to test the hypotheses suggested by his theory that are of concern to us. For example, do schemas exist, how do they form, do they comprise different types of knowledge, and do failures or faulty modifications occur? Further, the definition does not suggest how an individual concludes that one schema fits a situation better than another.

Bartlett's work was largely ignored during the reign of behaviorism in American psychology. However, it was rediscovered in the 1960s and 1970s and directly influenced most of those who turned their attention to schema knowledge. These individuals for the most part worked in the areas of artificial intelligence or cognitive psychology. Depending on their field of interest, they tended to emphasize different aspects of what we call a schema.

Piaget's accommodation and assimilation

Bartlett focused on a single aspect of cognition, remembering. For one of the best-developed theories of schema-based learning, we look to Jean Piaget. Piaget's view of the development of cognition profoundly influences today's thinking about cognitive and developmental psychology, and it has had an impact on the development of cognitive science. Although many psychologists have rejected his stage theory of development, they nevertheless acknowledge his immense contribution to our understanding of how learning comes about, particularly children's understanding of space, time, logic, and mathematics. His detailed clinical studies of individual children remain landmark single-subject studies.

Piaget's notion of schema is spread throughout a large number of books and scholarly papers and is consequently rather difficult to pin down. In general, he described the schema as a completely coordinated set of physical actions and cognitive functions, a set that worked together in its totality to respond to every perceived experience that could be related to the schema (Piaget, 1952, p. 237). What is new in this description is the emphasis on action. Schemas govern action as well as cognition and consequently are tied to behavior. To function in these capacities, schemas must of necessity be both cohesive and flexible.

Piaget made a key contribution to schema theory with his focus on how schemas develop and change. Schemas develop only for those situations or events or patterns that occur over and over again. In the course of these many repetitions there will undoubtedly be differences in the characteristics of the situation. These may need to be perceived in an altered way if they are to "fit" the characteristics that are already part of the schema. Thus, the experience is altered to fit the schema and its altered characteristics are subsequently incorporated. This modification corresponds to Piaget's *assimilation*. On the other hand, when the situation features cannot be realistically altered, the schema itself may need to be modified. This is *accommodation:* The schema must adapt itself to accommodate the situation it is trying to assimilate. In Piaget's theory, assimilation and accommodation are the two operative principles, both adopted from biological study and adapted to the cognitive realm.

To Piaget, a schema is the result of three important aspects of assimilation: repetition, recognition, and generalization (1952, p.

241). In the course of multiple repetitions of situations, individual schemas of necessity become altered. As a greater number of events or behaviors become associated with the schema, their particular or idiosyncratic details become less important. Thus, the schema becomes generalized and can be applied to a broader range of experience. At the same time, these larger numbers of stimuli also lead to discrimination, so that recognition and discrimination among them become part of the schema as well.

One of the most enduring and influential of Piaget's beliefs about cognition is that individuals actively construct their world. Individuals are not passive creatures acted upon by the environment, automatically encoding experiences into memory as they occur. Rather, individuals operate with and on the environment, constructing their own perceptions as they assimilate new experiences into existing schemas and adapt the schemas to accommodate the constraints of the experiences. As George Mandler once commented in a discussion of Piaget's influence, the schema both structures our experience and is structured by it (1985, p. 36).

It should be obvious that both Piaget and Bartlett have departed substantially from the a priori schemas set forth by Kant and Plato. The a priori structures are ahistorical. That is, their development does not depend upon past experiences of the individual. In contrast, both Piaget and Bartlett define schemas as products of interactions with the environment in which similarities in the experiences are generalized and retained in memory. In the thinking of Piaget and Bartlett, an individual is actively seeking to understand the environment. Bartlett terms this effort after meaning. Piaget calls it the search for equilibrium. The content of the search is more detailed in Piaget's view, continually involving the processes of assimilation and accommodation.

From these two theorists, then, we have a view of the schema as a memory structure that develops from an individual's experiences and guides the individual's response to the environment. Both scholars argue a holistic view, stressing that the schema influences the individual not sequentially through its component pieces but simultaneously as a total mass.

Piaget and Bartlett arrived at their similar views of the schema from extraordinarily different paths. Bartlett, on the one hand, was studying how adults remember and what they remember; for him, schemas were a way of explaining how and why individuals distort and ignore particular features in a new experience. Piaget, on the other hand, studied the development of reasoning in infants and children, and he looked to the schema as their means for making sense of the environment. He, too, perceived schemas as key memory structures, but he was more concerned with explaining how they develop than with how they influence retrieval or recall.

Together, Bartlett's and Piaget's ideas provide the skeleton of schema theory. It begins to be understandable but does not yet have sufficient substance. Several recent researchers have sought that substance by performing more-detailed empirical investigations about the nature of a schema and by developing sophisticated computer models that simulate schema instantiation.

Recent research

The nature of a schema

From Plato, Aristotle, Kant, Bartlett, and Piaget, we have a conceptual outline of a schema. It is a mental structure centered on an event, situation, experience, or object. It may or may not require action (Piaget says yes, but the philosophers seem to say no). It organizes past experiences in such a way that their features are noted and retrieved to interpret a current instance. It has some definite form or shape, because it can contribute to distortions of recollection, but very little has been said about what that shape might be. We now look at additional characteristics that have been explored in more recent research.

In the history of schema research, 1975 was a very good year. A number of schema-related papers appeared in a fairly short period of time, and they have had strong and lasting influence. Three individuals are frequently cited as primary instigators of the resurgence of schema theory: Marvin Minsky, Roger Schank, and David Rumelhart. Each represents a unique viewpoint, uses different terminology, and has distinctly influenced the growth of schema investigation.

In 1975, Marvin Minsky wrote "A Framework for Representing Knowledge" to be included in a volume about current research in computer vision. In that chapter, he sketched a new theory about data structures that could be used to represent knowledge in human memory. He called these structures *frames*. Minsky himself acknowledged the ties between frame theory and schema theory, noting that frames originated in Bartlett's notion of schemas. Although frame theory was developed to deal with issues of visual processing, it is equally relevant to a much broader range of cognitive processing.

Minsky hypothesized that frames are structures for storing large interrelated chunks of knowledge. Each frame describes a stereotyped situation. His initial example is the situation of a birthday party. A bit later he develops the theory for the situation of recognizing a cube. Virtually anything qualifies as a situation; there are no restrictions.

Minsky's theory articulates the components of the frame. An important contribution to the development of schema theory as we understand it today is Minsky's (1975) recognition of anticipatory knowledge in the knowledge structure. "Attached to each frame are several kinds of information. Some of this information is about how to use the frame. Some is about what one can expect to happen next. Some is about what to do if these expectations are not confirmed" (p. 212). Not only is there a component dealing with anticipation, but there is also knowledge about how to take action, reminiscent of Piaget's theory.

A second important characteristic of the schema as we see it today was introduced by Minsky. This is the distinction between fixed and variable content. Some information associated with a frame is fixed; that is, some features must occur in a specified way if the frame is to be used. Other features are inconstant and may change with the situation. The frame typically contains default characteristics to describe these. Minsky speculated that the frame normally has a number of default characteristics in place. As details from the current situation are observed, they replace the defaults. He refers to these pieces of the frame as *slots*. Slots may also be filled by default values if situation details are lacking.

Minsky identified five important issues that need to be addressed if we are to have a useful theory of frames (or schemas). These remain important – and largely unaddressed – issues today.

1. *How a schema is selected.* This issue hinges on how we use specific pieces of data from a situation to select an appropriate schema. It is, as Minsky says, "a matter of finding the right memory" (1975, p. 248).
2. *How additional schemas are called as needed.* Once the initial schema is selected, one may need to call on additional schemas to embellish and add further detail. It is a matter of investigating how schemas are interrelated.
3. *How a schema is modified.* When a selected schema does not fit the given situation adequately, a new one must be found or the current one must be adapted. The means of adaptation are important to discern. (Note the similarity to Piaget's assimilation and accommodation.)
4. *How a new schema is created.* If no existing schema is sufficient, a new one may be required. (Again, this is reminiscent of accommodation.)
5. *How the memory store changes as a result of learning.* Following the use and modification of an existing schema, some changes may be made in what is stored in memory for the schema.

Minsky does not solve the problems associated with these issues. His paper is designed to present a rough outline of a theory and to suggest future topics of research. To a large extent, these issues guide the research described later in this book, where I offer solutions to some of the problems – and raise a few new ones as well.

Minsky approached schema theory from the field of artificial intelligence. A second and somewhat different perspective from the same field comes from Roger Schank. Schank reached his theory about *scripts* by way of studying how computers can engage in natural language processing. His research led him to explore the structure of episodes of experience and how they are stored in memory. Much of Schank's work builds directly on Bartlett's earlier work with stories, and Schank continues Bartlett's method of investigation by using stories to study the script/schema.

Schank (1975) introduced the script as a special data structure containing a specific sequence of events in a well-understood context. It is clear that this is a restricted subset of the allowable topics of frames or schemas. Although working in a computer environment with the explicit goal of developing computer models of discourse and comprehension, Schank also initially argued that scripts were equally appropriate in describing human memory. And certainly many (but not all) aspects of script theory have been adopted by cognitive psychologists in describing human cognition.

What Schank meant by a script can best be understood by looking at an example. In fact, Schank himself often used a particular example, the experience of eating in a restaurant, to describe what he meant by a script (1975; Schank & Abelson, 1977). Scripts have several key features. For one thing, they are causally organized. One event comes after another, in a predetermined sequence. Consider that in the restaurant script, one does not expect to be served a meal before one orders from the menu. Scripts, like frames, have variables. The restaurant script does not dictate the type of food one orders or the companions who share the meal.

One aspect of note is that scripts typically describe common social events and have very similar structure from individual to individual. Thus, my script for a particular event looks much the same as yours. We can share understanding of an event because we have similar scripts. Again, the restaurant example is apt. Most of us have common expectations, and we can converse about a restaurant situation by drawing on our similar knowledge, which represents many repeated experiences for each of us.

Researchers studying scripts soon encountered the same problems that beset those who were examining schemas: namely, the concept is too vague. As Schank himself later noted, scripts were used to describe a wide variety of things, and many users of the term disagreed on the structure of the concept (Schank, 1982, p. 7). *Script* developed into a catchword for any high-level knowledge associated with inferences, some of its original specificity was lost, and, consequently, rigorous studies of it became very difficult.

The most obvious difference between a script, as Schank originally described it, and a schema, as it is defined here, is the greater rigidity of the script. A script is not a general knowledge structure. It is a data structure containing specific details about a specific event. The script was originally conceived as a structure that joined a multitude of different episodes into a recognizable stereotype and that controlled inferences about the specific situation underlying the stereotype. Its usefulness is in matching exactly the pattern of details of a new instance of the event. It appears to be less useful in making sense of a new somewhat related event that does not yield a precise pattern match. Indeed, this is a central reason that Schank turned to larger structures in his subsequent work (see Schank, 1982, chap. 1).

Of the three researchers influencing schema theory in 1975 – Minsky, Schank, and Rumelhart – David Rumelhart has probably contributed the most to our current understanding of schemas. He has written a number of important articles about the nature of schemas, beginning with the one in 1975 and culminating with his work on parallel distributed processing (PDP) in 1986. Whereas Minsky introduced the *frame* and Schank the *script*, Rumelhart retained the word *schema* in his research. However, it takes on a substantially different meaning from that in earlier schema studies.

Rumelhart's 1975 paper, a chapter in a book about representations in memory, is surprising in a number of ways. Perhaps most surprising is that it receives so much credit for the resurgence of schema study. Its title, to be sure, is "Notes on a Schema for Stories." However, the word *schema* appears only in the title and nowhere else – it does not occur even a single time in the text. Why then has this paper received such recognition? I think it is because Rumelhart uses *schema* much as the ancient Greeks did; that is, he expects his readers to have a vague idea of what he means by *schema* and he is not particularly interested (in this paper) in describing the general nature of a schema. What he is interested in is a set of rules that can be used to develop a paraphrase or summary of a story (i.e., a story grammar), and he focuses his attention on the specification of these rules. The fact that he called the whole thing a schema is almost incidental.

In hindsight, with the advantage of 20 years of additional research on schemas, one can regret that Rumelhart's work was taken so literally. Nowhere in the paper does he argue that every schema is a story grammar per se. Rather, the particular schema (or form) he studies happens to be a story grammar. The impact of his work, however, was a proliferation of studies about details of story grammars. Schema research was temporarily displaced by story and reading studies, and one frequently had the feeling that the formalisms by which the rules were produced were more important than the general structures they were intended to model. So strong was the influence of Rumelhart's work that we are only now beginning to see schema studies focused on topics other than stories and fables.

Rumelhart's later work turned explicitly to the nature of the schema. In 1977, he and Andrew Ortony published a speculative study about what constitutes a schema. Rumelhart, as noted, approached the study of schemas through his work on story grammars (1975). Ortony arrived by way of studying the metaphor (1975). In their joint endeavor, they outlined four essential characteristics of the schema, and most of their chapter addresses these issues. However, the essence of their position can be found in a brief paragraph that precedes the discussion of these four characteristics. In that small paragraph (Rumelhart & Ortony, 1977, p. 101), they lay out a number of important points:

"[Schemas] are data structures for representing the generic concepts stored in memory."
"They exist for generalized concepts underlying objects, situations, events, sequences of events, actions, and sequences of actions."
"[Schemas] are not atomic. A schema contains, as part of its specification, the network of interrelations that is believed to

generally hold among the constituents of the concept in
    question."
"[Schemas], in some sense, represent stereotypes of these con-
    cepts."

The first point of interest is that a schema is a *structure* for
organizing data. The implication is that we should pay attention
to its form. This is a key issue. Unless we can create exact hypotheses about the nature of the structure and how it serves memory,
we will be unable to create viable models of the schema. Together
with Minsky and Schank, Rumelhart and Ortony pushed the
notion of schema away from a purely conceptual or interpreta-
tional construct toward one whose form could be specified. This
approach moves well beyond Kant's speculations and foreshadows
the importance of formal models.

Not only is a schema a structure, but it is a structure that contains a *generalized concept*. The statement is somewhat vague, but
one assumes that a generalized concept contains the commonalities that exist in a number of replications of the concept around
which the schema developed. This interpretation, in turn, suggests
that a schema is not a record of all instances of a particular concept but rather emerges when some abstraction occurs, abstraction that captures the essential features of the multiple episodes.

A second point has to do with the focus or theme of a schema.
Notice the emphasis on actions. This, of course, concurs with the
theory developed by Piaget, and again, it is an important observation. Many examples in early works about schemas (or their coun-
terparts, frames and scripts) use objects such as a room (Minsky,
1975) or a story such as a fairy tale (Rumelhart, 1975) or a particular setting such as a restaurant (Schank, 1975). The restriction to
these examples suggests incorrectly that actions are not essential
to schema knowledge and, in some instances, implies a strict tem-
poral sequence and relatively rigid format.

Rumelhart and Ortony's third point is that there are a number
of *interrelations* in a schema. A schema is not simply a list of features but rather is a collection whose parts are linked together. The
nature of these linkages remains unspecified, but this notion is an

important premise about the underlying structure of the schema and must surely be explicated in any usable schema theory.

And, finally, a schema is in some ways a *stereotype*. I find this a good metaphor, much better than the extended one that immediately follows in the Rumelhart and Ortony chapter, where they compare a schema to a stage play. Underlying the stereotype is the notion that many things can be identified under this very general description. These different things may be varied on a number of dimensions so long as they retain the general features of the stereotype. The play metaphor suggests a different analogy. Coupled to the play metaphor is the implication that there is a fixed script that will occur for every presentation (instance) of the play. We know from experience that in plays deviations from written scripts are rather small. Thus, the analogy leads to the expectation that schemas also have fixed scripts and are therefore relatively inflexible. The schema-as-play idea is misleading.

As mentioned earlier, Rumelhart and Ortony (1977, p. 101) postulate four key characteristics, which, taken together, combine into the powerful structures we call schemas. The first of these asserts that schemas have variables and corresponds directly to Minsky's idea of the slots of a frame (Minsky, 1975). For any particular instance to which a schema applies, we expect to find several attributes specific to that instance. That is, certain attributes will vary from instance to instance. In large part, it is this variability that gives the schema its flexibility. The second and third characteristics emphasize that schemas can be nested within other schemas and may exist at a number of different levels of abstraction, some very simple and some elaborately complex. Also, the same concepts may participate in multiple schemas with varying levels of complexity. Finally, the last characteristic distinguishes between the type of knowledge contained in a schema and the type of knowledge that defines a concept. This is an important point, because a number of researchers seem to equate schemas and concepts. One may have some knowledge of a concept that is just barely adequate to distinguish it from other concepts. This knowledge is approximately equal to a dictionary definition, but its use is generally restricted to identification. The dictionary analogy is an apt one, for it also conveys the sense that one can readily "look up" a concept but will not find much more than the definition. So, too, are concept definitions often easily retrieved from memory. One may also have other knowledge about the concept that enables one to reason about the current instance. If so, that additional information would be schema knowledge. Rumelhart and Ortony liken the difference between definitional knowledge and schema knowledge to the difference between a dictionary and an encyclopedia.

Although the papers just described are frequently cited as critical in schema research, others from that general period also made important contributions. One that took as its subject the nature of discourse also offers some insight into the structure of a schema (Winograd, 1977). It makes a number of the same arguments about the nature of a schema as do Rumelhart and Ortony. Like many researchers at that time, Winograd distinguishes between declarative and procedural knowledge. In contrast to others who were beginning to use the term *schema*, he suggests that the schema is composed primarily of declarative knowledge but also serves as a guide for procedural knowledge. This is a substantive point, because it captures some of the essence of schema knowledge. A schema is not just a static collection of facts about a concept. It is an active structure that has procedural components. Winograd merely hints at how this union of procedural and declarative knowledge comes about. I will have more to say about this issue in chapter 2 when I present the schema theory underlying this volume.

Minsky, Schank, Rumelhart and Ortony, and Winograd made important hypotheses about the nature of the schema. However, a limitation in their presentations is that they were confined to hypothesis or speculation. Brief hints appear of how models might be constructed or how individuals might use schemas, but they are not elaborated. We are left at this point with several good ideas but no evidence of whether schemas provide a viable means of describing human cognition. We must look elsewhere for such evidence.

Individual differences and schema content

Let us turn now to a different question, namely: Do individuals actually have knowledge structures that function as the above theorists have suggested? Pieces of confirming evidence can be found in Bartlett's and Piaget's studies. Both of these researchers attempted to establish the existence of schemas through empirical study.

As noted, Bartlett asked individuals to read stories such as "The War of the Ghosts" and to recollect the story as accurately and completely as possible. Most of his discussion in *Remembering* refers only to this story, although he mentions that others were used as well. In the basic experiment, he asked 20 subjects (7 women and 13 men) to read the story and to recall it at various (unplanned and unequal) later intervals, ranging from 15 minutes to 10 years (!) after the initial reading. One objective of the study was to determine what subjects recalled and to examine when and if they tended to develop a stereotype of the story. He does not give a statistical summary of his experiment, relying on verbal summaries, individual descriptions, and anecdotal material to convey the results. Nonetheless, his arguments are persuasive. Subjects did tend to distort the story and to reshape it to conform to their own expectations. Moreover, there were substantial individual differences in the modifications that his subjects made to the original story.

Piaget's method of study differed from Bartlett's. Piaget carried out intense longitudinal studies of single subjects, frequently his own children. He formulated hypotheses about a child's development and carried out careful experiments, observing and recording the child's actions and reactions. He repeated his small experiments again and again at different times to gain insight into the child's changing responses.

Neither Bartlett nor Piaget offers us strict experimental evidence that schemas exist. Although persuasive, their studies lack the precision we expect in scientific inquiry. What types of experiments could be used to provide evidence? How would we determine if schemas were or were not playing a role in learning and remembering? One possibility would be to investigate the influence of previous experience, contrasting the performance of subjects having a particular type of experience with the performance of subjects lacking this experience. If previous experiences have no influence, all subjects should perform similarly. A second approach would be to set up situations and manipulate the circumstances to trigger inappropriate schemas by subjects. A specific manipulation should elicit the implementation of a predetermined incorrect schema. Both of these experimental paradigms have been fruitful.

Story comprehension. An example of the first type of study – looking at the influence of previous experience – was undertaken by R. C. Anderson (1984) using the following story:

> Tony slowly got up from the mat, planning his escape. He hesitated a moment and thought. Things were not going well. What bothered him most was being held, especially since the charge against him had been weak. He considered his present situation. The lock that held him was strong but he thought he could break it. He knew, however, that his timing would have to be perfect. Tony was aware that it was because of his early roughness that he had been penalized so severely – much too severely from his point of view. The situation was becoming frustrating; the pressure had been grinding on him for too long. He was being ridden unmercifully. Tony was getting angry now. He felt he was ready to make his move. He knew that his success or failure would depend on what he did in the next few seconds. (p. 245)

This story usually activates one of two schemas, a schema for breaking out of jail or a schema for wrestling. Not surprisingly, only those individuals with strong background in wrestling view this as a sports story. Almost everyone else initially sees Tony as a criminal planning his escape. Richard Anderson and his associates have used this story to provide evidence that the prior knowledge of the individual determines which schema will be activated and guide the interpretation of the story.

The same design was used in a cross-cultural study by Steffensen, Joag-dev, and Anderson (1979). This experiment contrasts two cultural schemas for a wedding, a social event well understood by nearly everyone. Two groups of subjects, Americans and Indians, were asked to read two descriptions of a wedding. One described a typical American wedding, and the other described an Indian one. These two types of weddings are very different and provide rich grounds for the contrasting of schema knowledge. Steffensen et al. compared reading times, amount of recall, detail of recall, and text modifications for subjects' same-culture passage versus cross-culture passage. Distinct group differences were observed. On the American passage, American subjects read more quickly, recalled more details, and made fewer distortions than they did on the Indian passage. The results were just the reverse for Indian subjects, who read the Indian passage more quickly and recalled more salient information from it. Much like Bartlett's subjects, Steffensen et al.'s subjects distorted details of the unfamiliar passage to fit their own cultural schema.

The above studies examined groups of individuals for comprehension as the result of different prior knowledge. A second design investigates comprehension as the result of activating the appropriate prior knowledge. This design relies on complex and somewhat incomplete stories such as that used by Bransford and Johnson (1972):

> The procedure is actually quite simple. First you arrange items into different groups. Of course one pile may be sufficient depending on how much there is to do. If you have to go somewhere else due to lack of facilities that is the next step; otherwise, you are pretty well set. It is important not to overdo things. That is, it is better to do too few things at once than too many. In the short run this may not seem important but complications can easily arise. A mistake can be expensive as well. At first, the whole procedure will seem complicated. Soon, however, it will become just another facet of life. It is difficult to foresee any end to the necessity for this task in the immediate future, but then, one never can tell. After the procedure is com-

pleted one arranges the materials into different groups again. Then they can be put into their appropriate places. Eventually they will be used once more and the whole cycle will then have to be repeated. However, that is part of life. (p. 722)

Most individuals have difficulty comprehending this passage and when asked to recall it can only provide a few details. However, if subjects are told *before* reading that the passage is about doing laundry, they have much greater recall than those who are not so informed. This result is taken as evidence that the schema for washing one's clothes provides a setting in which the details of the passage can be interpreted. In the absence of something to trigger the appropriate schema, the reader is left floundering.

Stories of these kinds are used to demonstrate that individuals do use prior experience to comprehend stories. However, as evidence of schemas, they are somewhat weak. What we have is confirmation that prior experience is stored in memory and that it influences recall. Studies such as these cannot provide evidence about the structure of the memory storage. Why not? We cannot make any such claims because the nature of the storage has not been specified nor have the specific contents. All that we can determine from these studies is that the prior knowledge does influence the subjects as they read and encode the story for later recall. However, these studies have made an important contribution to the overall understanding of schemas by expanding the focus of the research beyond the formal symbolism of the structural rule set to a more general conceptual framework.

Problem solving. A second approach to the study of whether individuals use schemas comes through problem solving. Hinsley, Hayes, and Simon (1977) provide the most evidence. They make the following claims: If schemas are important in problem solving, then individuals should (*a*) be able to categorize problems using schema knowledge; (*b*) be able to categorize problems without developing equations; (*c*) have a store of information about the general types of problems; and (*d*) use the category identifications in developing plans to solve the problems (p. 92). Each of these four claims is verifiable. Hinsley et al. present a series of experiments designed to evaluate each one. I describe these experiments here in some detail for two reasons. First, this is one of the few instances in which experimental data are available. More typically, schema research is based on very few subjects and extensive computer modeling. Second, the focus of their studies is algebra problem solving and closely akin to the focus of my own research presented in later chapters, arithmetic problem solving.

Consider a group of students who have studied algebra in a traditional class with a traditional text and thus have been exposed to a large number of algebra story problems. If we are correct about the nature of a schema, then it is reasonable to expect that, as a result of their many experiences with algebra story problems, these students will have developed a set of schemas about these problems. Hinsley et al. speculated that one aspect of that schema knowledge would be problem recognition. That is, students should be able to categorize problems, placing similar problems together. Moreover, given their common experiences with the problems (i.e., all read the same book, all heard the same lectures), one expects them to develop relatively similar schemas and to make highly similar categorizations. This was, in fact, the case.

However, classification alone does not imply schema instantiation. An alternative hypothesis is that instead of retrieving information from memory about the problem types, students were constructing equations for the problems as they read them and classifying the problems by placing similar sets of equations together. Such behavior would mean that students were using equation structure rather than schema memory as the basis for classification. To determine whether subjects were relying on equations, Hinsley et al. carried out a second, smaller experiment in which they read fragments of problems to subjects. Subjects were asked to make a classification as early as possible. If they were unable to do so, a second story fragment was read to them, and so on, until the entire problem had been presented. Subjects were very quick to make classifications on this task. Half of them made correct classifications on hearing only 20% of the text. Some could do so after only three words (e.g., "A river steamer . . .").

Hinsley et al. report several other experiments, but the findings are suspect because they involve only two subjects, both graduate students. It seems unwise to draw generalizations from such a small nonrandom sample. However, in a final study with a slightly larger group (six students), they examined whether subjects would be misled by including in a problem irrelevant information that pointed to an incorrect schema. They (1977) presented their subjects with the following problem:

The Smalltown Problem

Because of their quiet ways, the inhabitants of Smalltown were especially upset by the terrible New Year's Eve auto accident which claimed the life of one Smalltown resident. The facts were these. Both Smith and Jones were New Year's Eve babies and each had planned a surprise visit to the other on their mutual birthday. Jones had started out for Smith's house traveling due east on Route 210 just two minutes after Smith had left for Jones's house. Smith was traveling directly south on Route 140. Jones was traveling 30 miles per hour faster than Smith even though their houses were only five miles apart as the crow flies. Their cars crashed at the right angle intersection of the two highways. Officer Franklin, who observed the crash, determined that Jones was traveling half again as fast as Smith at the time of the crash. The crash occurred nearer to the house of the dead man than to the house of the survivor. What was the name of the dead man? (p. 102)

Subjects were equally divided in choice of problem schema. Some of the subjects accessed a "triangle" schema and some a "distance-rate-time" schema. Those who attempted to use the triangle schema were unable to solve the problem. The importance of this study is that it demonstrates the necessity of knowing which schema to use in problem solving. If individuals apply the wrong schema, they obtain the wrong answer.

Both the reading and the problem-solving studies provide positive, if not definitive, support for the existence of schemas. At the very least, these experiments are consistent with organized memory structures that allow discrimination and recognition.

Mechanisms of schema development and change: Learning

There are potentially three big areas in schema research: the investigation of how schemas influence memory recall, the specification of models to simulate schema instantiation, and the study of how schemas develop and change. All require substantial theoretical and empirical study, but the nature of the theories differ. A considerable body of research exists for the first two areas, as is evident from the preceding discussion, but the third is largely untapped. For the most part, researchers have taken schemas as given, and few have dealt with issues having to do with schema creation or modification.

Piaget was the exception, and his work on cognitive development has had a strong and continuing influence on recent cognitive science models of learning. His theory of schema development via the processes of assimilation and accommodation remains virtually the only attempt to describe in detail how this memory structure evolves and changes. However, much of his schema work centered on the very young child in what he called the sensorimotor stage, and the schemas he describes are centered on motor skills and behaviors rather than cognitive ones. More importantly, the level of detail he describes is insufficient for the intricate models of today's research.

If we look at research about schemas, we encounter some conflicting conclusions. For example, it is clear in studies of transfer that researchers may expect schemas to develop from a single experience (e.g., Kieras, 1991; 1992). A well-known example is given by Gick and Holyoak (1980, 1983), who document a number of experiments in which their subjects were expected first to create a schema for a "divide and conquer" strategy from a story about soldiers storming a castle and second to use this schema to solve a problem having to do with applying radiation therapy to a tumor. This one-instance learning contrasts with the 100 hours of practice hypothesized for learning a procedural skill (J. R. Anderson, 1982, p. 369) or the thousands of trials required in competitive learning models of connectionism. In the face of this conflicting evidence, one is left to wonder how schemas are acquired, how much and which knowledge is retained from a single exposure, and when the very important connections among knowledge elements are built. I will return to these topics when I describe the learning experiments with arithmetic problem-solving schemas in chapter 7.

A new approach to the study of learning has emerged with the growing acceptance of connectionist (or neural net) theories and with the development of new computer models to test them. Key to this development is the work of Rumelhart and his colleague J. McClelland, who elaborated a theory of parallel distributed processing (Rumelhart, McClelland, & the PDP Research Group, 1986; McClelland, Rumelhart, & the PDP Research Group, 1986). Their work has its roots in Rosenblatt's (1962) perceptron, a simple parallel processing machine. Basically, the perceptron is a system that generates an output response as a result of some pattern of inputs. The order of input is unimportant; the system responds to the accumulated activation resulting from all inputs. The perceptron model had certain limitations, which were pointed out so sternly by Minsky and Papert (1969) that it was virtually abandoned. Rumelhart and his associates developed a new form of the model that is not subject to the same criticisms, and their PDP model has given rise to a renewed interest in learning.

Learning in the PDP system consists of building up associations so that particular input patterns will elicit specific output results. At all times connections exist between the input and output (albeit these connections are frequently indirect). As learning takes place, the relevant connections become stronger and the irrelevant ones become weaker. Typically, a very large number of input patterns must be observed by the system for learning to occur.

Although Rumelhart maintains some interest in the schema, his current work does not strongly emphasize it. The learning he describes in the PDP volumes is largely pattern matching at a lower level of cognitive processing. Nevertheless, he and his colleagues have several interesting things to say about the learning of schemas and the use of connectionist models in representing them. The most important contribution, in my opinion, is the notion that a schema is much more flexible than any one had previously hypothesized and that connectionist models can capture that flexibility. What this means for learning is that individuals will develop unique schemas and will not necessarily create and attach the components in identical ways. Rumelhart's work provides the starting point for the modeling of schemas that is described later in chapters 13 and 14.

Educational applications

Work on educational applications of schema theory is even more sparse than the research on learning. Nonetheless, some important papers have addressed this issue.

Concerning the problem of learning to read, Richard C. Anderson has given the educational implications considerable thought, and he makes several instructional recommendations (R. C. Anderson, 1984). These mostly have to do with ways that publishers can improve reading texts, but they can be understood in a broader sense as well. Anderson calls for materials that will activate students' relevant prior knowledge. If students do not have such knowledge, then it becomes their teachers' responsibility to help them acquire it. He recommends an integration of lessons so that each one builds on what students already know. He suggests, for example, that before reading a specific story, students be encouraged to activate relevant schemas and make predictions from those schemas about possible outcomes. Anderson's suggestions are not idle speculations. They are based on an extensive body of research that he and his associates have carried out.

Richard Skemp also gives considerable attention to the schema in his *Psychology of Learning Mathematics* (1987). He attributes three functions to the schema: (1) It serves to integrate what is already known, (2) it provides the framework for further learning, and (3) it is the basis for understanding. In Skemp's (1987) words,

"To understand something means to assimilate it into an appropriate schema" (p. 29). He takes the position that it is possible and desirable to target specific schemas in instruction. Indeed, he suggests that a major responsibility of the instructor is the selection of appropriate schemas for learners to develop.

Skemp's suggestion that we can target specific schemas for acquisition by students is in direct contradiction to that of Rumelhart, McClelland, and the PDP Research Group (1986), who state: "There is no point at which it must be decided to create this or that schema. Learning simply proceeds by connection strength adjustment, according to some simple scheme" (p. 21). Can we reconcile these two positions? I think so. Although it is certainly true that each individual creates his or her own unique schemas, it is also true that many individuals have similar experiences that contribute to these schemas. It is this commonality of experience that allows us to have common scripts for something like eating in a restaurant. For each individual, a subtly different set of perceptual inputs may also help to characterize the situation (i.e., one individual might notice some additional features, whereas a second individual might attend to others). However, there is no need for all inputs to be the same in *every* person's schema. I will show later that we can follow Skemp's suggestion about using the schema to guide instruction while adopting Rumelhart's connectionist perspective to model the individual's schema acquisition.

Summary

The importance of the schema to the study of cognition should by now be evident. It has played a central role in many influential philosophical and psychological investigations of how we know what we know. What common threads bind the several views of schema that are apparent in these investigations?

First, of course, there is structure. We must remember that the word *schema* means "form" or "shape," and in most of the studies described above, there is an implicit, if not an explicit, assumption that schemas tend to have a common structure or form. The ancient Greeks simply took it for granted. Modern cognitive scientists question it by building detailed computer models.

A second common thread is organization. The notion of the schema that has emerged over time is one of an encompassing structure of memory, highly organized and containing a great deal of specific and interrelated information.

Still another thread is experience. Schemas arise from experience. The particular details of any single experience may or may not be part of schema knowledge. Certainly there is the implication that many of the details will fade over time, leaving only broad generalizations to characterize the schema.

And, finally, there is the thread of stereotype. Beginning with the ancient Greeks and continuing with today's cognitive scientists, we are told that it is the schema that captures the essence of a concept, event, or experience.

Thus, we have a fairly good idea of what constitutes a schema, broadly speaking, but we lack details about how the schema develops, exactly what it contains, how it is used, and what differentiates it from any other hypothesized memory structure. In most of the research and speculation described above, the schema is presumed to contain a great deal of detail. Up to now, however, research has not addressed the question of what constitutes this detail, so we know little about which knowledge is or is not part of a schema or whether different types of knowledge unite to form a schema. Moreover, as noted, some confusion exists about how the schema develops and whether it forms from a single instance or many repetitions.

The remainder of this book focuses on these critical issues. In the chapters that follow, I explain the theory and model of schema development that have guided my research, and I describe a number of experimental studies designed to test specific aspects of the theory in the domain of arithmetic story problems. Underlying these chapters are two important premises: First, the study of the schema will yield theoretical findings of value to the study of cognition, and second, the schema is the means by which theory can guide practice. With respect to the latter premise, the schema has the potential of being a theoretical construct with practical application in real-world activities such as creating a well-structured lecture or text or setting the stage for a new psychological theory of assessment. With respect to the former premise, the schema is, in fact, a key to understanding how people learn and the means by which we may enhance that learning.

2

The nature of a schema

In many fields, advances in tools and technology open new doors of investigation. As more sophisticated means of analysis become widely used, researchers are able to ask new and different questions. This has certainly been the case with the biological and physical sciences, and so it is with cognitive science. Now that hardware with expanded computational power is generally available to cognitive scientists, together with a variety of computer analyses and modeling procedures to take advantage of the speed and capacity of these machines, the types of questions addressed in research are changing.

One of the major contributions of cognitive science research to studies of cognition is the shift in the way that different cognitive processes are studied. The importance to schema theory is that the techniques of cognitive science facilitate the investigation of unobservable cognitive activity by allowing tests of hypotheses through simulation. In general, computer models are used to simulate various cognitive phenomena, and these models introduce several breaks with traditional practice. For one thing, they frequently focus on one individual at a time in great depth. For another, they require much more fine-grained detail than models used in the past.

Some of the limitations of the early work on schemas become strikingly evident when one faces the task of creating an explicit computer model of a particular schema. The characteristics of a schema, such as those illustrated in chapter 1, have not been determined at the detailed level required for computer modeling. They fail to tell us *exactly* what constitutes a schema or *precisely* how its components interact. Exactness and precision are missing and must be provided, both for the construction of cognitive models and for the practical application of schema theory to real-world issues. The original ideas are, for the most part, sound and have been recognized for a great many years. Modern researchers can and should build on them, but we must push further if we are to make progress in laying out the theory.

This book represents an effort to attain the needed specificity. One of the initial goals in my problem-solving research was the development of a computer model to simulate schema development and instantiation. Careful study of the schema literature suggested that it would first be necessary to reformulate the notion of a schema. I began – as I believe one must – with the substantive work described in the previous chapter, focusing on the two predominant perspectives that run through that body of research. One perspective seeks to explain important psychological issues surrounding schema formation and content, with primary emphasis on how individuals create and use schemas. Bartlett and Piaget exemplify this perspective. The second perspective addresses the issue of memory storage and is concerned with architectural details about the shape and form of the schema and its role in cognition. Rumelhart and Minsky typify this approach. The two perspectives are not necessarily conflicting points of view, but they have rarely been considered together, as they must be for a full model of the schema.

My purpose here is to join these two lines of thought in a single comprehensive theory. The theory is not a formal one of the type most frequently encountered in textbooks, with attendant definitions, axioms, postulates, and laws. Rather it is an informal theory of the sort that most often guides psychological research. At its heart is the premise that a schema consists of several different kinds of knowledge, as described later. A second and equally essential premise is that schema functioning involves both parallel and sequential processing. Both of these ideas have been noticeably absent from previous theories.

Also key to the theory are a number of general schema characteristics, some of which have to do with form and some with content. Many of these characteristics have been articulated before by myself and other researchers, several have been generally accepted without having been put into words, and a few are new to the study of schemas. This chapter pulls them all together.

The basic definition

To study the acquisition and use of schema knowledge, we must have a working definition that allows us to observe when such knowledge is present and when it is not. I propose the following:

> A schema is a vehicle of memory, allowing organization of an individual's similar experiences in such a way that the individual
> - can easily recognize additional experiences that are also similar, discriminating between these and ones that are dissimilar;
> - can access a generic framework that contains the essential elements of all of these similar experiences, including verbal and nonverbal components;
> - can draw inferences, make estimates, create goals, and develop plans using the framework; and
> - can utilize skills, procedures, or rules as needed when faced with a problem for which this particular framework is relevant.

This definition is the cornerstone of the schema theory set forth in this book. It assigns four functions to schema instantiation and use, each demanding its own type of knowledge. These types of knowledge may be defined and studied separately as well as compositely. My research about schema formation and schema assessment provides evidence that individuals have and use these four types of knowledge. On the basis of the outcomes they elicit, I have called the four knowledge types identification knowledge, elaboration knowledge, planning knowledge, and execution knowledge.

Identification knowledge

Identification knowledge is probably the most common gateway to schema activation. The central function of identification knowledge is pattern recognition. It is this knowledge that contributes to the initial recognition of a situation, event, or experience.

Identification knowledge is not a list of features that an individual can hypothetically scan and check off one by one in a prescribed order. Pattern recognition occurs as a result of the simultaneous cognitive processing of many features, and no single feature serves to trigger the recognition. Different configurations of several features present different patterns, and they must all be recognized as the same basic situation, depending on the specific characteristics that are noticed. Each schema will have its own distinct core of identification knowledge, although two schemas may share some common elements.

Elaboration knowledge

Elaboration knowledge contains elaborations about the main features of the situation or event around which the schema has developed. It is primarily declarative in nature. Typically, specific examples from the individual's experience will be found here, together with general abstractions that can describe these experiences. As some of my research indicates, both verbal and visual information is retained here, as is probably other sensory information.

Elaboration knowledge enables an individual to create a mental model about the current problem. Once the general situation or experience has been recognized by means of the identification knowledge, the details from the current experience will be fit onto a template about the situation. This is an interpretive step in using schema knowledge. The individual's understanding of the current experience comes from the way in which these details are fit to the schema template. As Bartlett showed in his research about stories, the exact details of the experience are more or less discarded in favor of the interpretation created by the individual. This interpretation cannot be made unless there are sufficient details and general descriptors in the schema's elaboration knowledge.

Together, identification and elaboration knowledge constitute a framework that allows the individual to form a tentative hypothesis about a situation and then to test it. The hypothesis forms as a result of the recognition of the situation, usually brought about through application of the identification knowledge. The evaluation of the hypothesis comes as the elaboration knowledge is used to determine whether or not sufficient evidence exists to warrant accepting recognition of the situation and adopting its concomitant schema.

Planning knowledge

Planning knowledge refers to the way in which the schema can be used to make plans, create expectations, and set up goals and subgoals. Use of the schema will not necessarily be straightforward. Recognizing that a schema may be used in a particular problem-solving situation does not necessarily mean that it can automatically be channeled into complex plans. This knowledge is acquired from experience in using each schema and is presumably updated steadily with such use.

The examination of planning knowledge helps us as researchers to determine whether or not an individual has a schema. It is quite conceivable that an individual could recognize a situation using identification and elaboration knowledge but have no planning knowledge. Such an individual would not be considered to have a working schema.

Execution knowledge

Execution knowledge is knowledge that allows the individual to carry out the steps of the plans. It consists of techniques that lead to action, such as performing a skill or following an algorithm. Execution knowledge will generally be shared among many schemas. It seems unlikely that each schema has its own set of distinct procedures to be executed, although that is undoubtedly the case for some. For example, all the schemas about arithmetic story problems (see chapter 3) use execution knowledge having to do with carrying out the four arithmetic operations of addition, subtraction, multiplication, and division. The particular choice and order of operation are determined by the planning knowledge.

We can add considerably to our understanding of the schema by studying the basic definition in light of the many characteristics that have been hypothesized about schema form and substance. The characteristics described in the following sections are organized so that those of form are grouped together and those of substance are similarly clustered. I present the central issues of each perspective separately and then, in the final section, discuss how they come together in mutual support in a single, unified schema theory.

Form: The architectural features

Storage

Although they have been the subject of a tremendous amount of psychological research, the mechanisms by which knowledge is stored in human memory remain unknown. A number of models of memory have been propounded to explain how storage transpires. What has emerged from the research is a general consensus that no single system will suffice, and most models now contain multiple forms of memory. Reasons for the multiple systems have been nicely expressed by a longtime memory researcher, E. Tulving, who articulated them in defense of his own three-system model (1985). Among his reasons are (*a*) the observation that no single system can explain all that we understand (so far) about memory and (*b*) neurological evidence increasingly shows that the brain exhibits a high degree of differentiation, suggesting different functioning.

Knowing that we *do not* fully understand how memory works, let me nevertheless put forth the following supposition: A schema is one means by which related information is retained in human memory. Thus, it can be thought of as a storage mechanism. This storage issue is a central one, and it is the crux of most cognitive models of schemas.

Networks

Most structural representations of schemas display them as networks of connected elements, which, of course, opens a wide door of possibilities for the actual form of the elements, the connections, and the networks themselves. Although researchers disagree about some of these issues, they are generally of one mind in adopting the network as the fundamental representation for schema knowledge.

Consider what memory would be like without such a mechanism. If things were not linked together in memory under some rationale, we would be faced with the situation of combing through unrelated memories every time we needed to remember something. Search time would be exorbitant and extremely inefficient, and would not reflect what we can observe of human information processing. We know that humans have access to a lot of information and are able to retrieve what they want quickly – more quickly than most computers can search and retrieve. There must be an efficient storage mechanism, but researchers of neuroscience have not yet determined precisely what it is and how it works. Thus, we theorize about what such a storage mechanism looks like. A tightly organized schema network is a plausible candidate, because its use contributes to the reduction of a number of things – such as search time, retrieval time, and strain on short-term memory (since a schema represents efficient chunking).

Connectivity

Several levels of schema connectivity exist. First, schemas from the same subject domain undoubtedly are connected to each other. Second, components within a single schema have many connections, else the schema could not hold together. And third, within each components there are connections among the elements. The number and strength of the various connections for each domain studied under the schema theoretic approach need to be ascertained.

The degree of connectivity is one of the most important characteristics we can determine for any given schema. It is the connections that allow the schema to function as a cohesive unit. In general, the more connections, the greater the cohesiveness and the stronger the schema. How do we assess the connectivity of a schema? One useful way is by means of techniques borrowed from statistical graph theory, as I have pointed out elsewhere (Marshall, 1990b). Another way, as I will show in future chapters, is through structured interviews with individuals.

For a schema to become fully active, there must be some initial probe to one or more of its constituent elements. This probe is usually externally based, either a part of the environment or an aspect of a posed problem or even a feature of a previously encountered problem. In a typical schema, the target element or elements will be linked to other elements. All the elements directly connected to the active ones themselves become active, and they in turn spread some of their activation to other elements to which they are connected. In this way, the excitation of a small number of elements may lead rapidly to the full activation of a great many interconnected units that work together as a single schema.

Connections may be excitatory or inhibitory. That is, some of the connections will promote the spread of activation from one node to another, and others will block it. In some cases, a schema may be compatible with others, and many schemas may be active at the same time. If a schema is incompatible with specific other ones, they will be inhibited.

Flexibility

One of the most interesting characteristics of a schema is its flexibility. In most cases, the schema in memory will contain a great deal more information than can be used in one particular instantiation. Thus, some of its contents may be only weakly activated by a specific problem. Some of its attendant procedures may not be needed at all. And certainly one instance will not demand all possible plans for goals and subgoals. In each case, only a subset of information is needed, and it is not a subset that can be predetermined. Most schema instantiations – beyond the trivial ones – will involve unique sets of schema elements, because each instance, with its own unique features, will activate slightly different elements. Many of the resulting patterns will be similar but not precisely identical.

Part of a schema's flexibility lies in the several ways in which the schema may be accessed. For instance, some piece of it may be tied to a particular sensory perception. It may be reached as a subgoal for another schema. It may be activated as a result of conscious memory search by the individual who knows that a situation with similar features fits it. Or it may be retrieved because of a remembrance of a particular procedure. Thus, any of the basic knowledge components can provide access to the entire schema.

Variability in size

Schemas can be large or small. Some are very broad and some are highly specific. One slot of a schema may be filled by another schema. As far as I know, no one has studied the optimal size of a schema. In models of schema performance, most restrictions on size have been made because of computing limitations rather than because of psychological necessity. It seems reasonable to speculate that there is an optimal size for a schema, and that when any schema exceeds the optimum, the individual tends to subdivide the schema, making several new ones. I give examples of how this may occur in story problems in the discussion of the schemas of that domain (see chapter 3).

Embedding

This point has been made indirectly in the discussion of several of the previous characteristics, but it deserves to be said forthrightly. One schema may be embedded in one or many others, and one schema may serve as a conduit to several others.

Summary

To summarize, the key issues of the structure and form of a schema are as follows:

- A schema is a basic storage device.
- A schema has a network structure.
- The degree of connectivity among the schema's components determines its strength and accessibility.
- A schema is a flexible structure, accessible through many channels.
- Schemas have no fixed size; they may be large or small.
- Schemas may embed and overlap.

Substance: The psychological features

Schema construction

The image of an individual *constructing* a schema is a powerful one. It invokes a building metaphor that entails deliberate choice, conscious unification, and purposeful creation. It suggests that many different things combine to produce the whole and that the strength of the structure rests on the solidity of its foundation. It also leaves the door open for future renovations and remodeling.

This notion of construction is important and has several far-reaching implications. An individual does not commit a schema to memory in the same way that he or she may memorize a formula or definition. One difference is that the latter may easily be done by rote with little or no understanding of what the memorized piece means. The schema demands understanding. A second difference is that such rote memorization frequently engenders isolated bits of knowledge that are unconnected to any other knowledge and that can only be accessed in memory by a direct probe. A third is that no construction is required of the individual who memorizes a formula. One does not memorize just one or two symbols and then construct the rest of the formula at a later time. The entire formula is learned as a fixed and relatively rigid unit.

The construction necessary for creating a schema rests on the foundation of prior knowledge. New, incoming information is linked to old, previously stored knowledge. This feature is particularly important in educational applications of schema theory. Educators have long stressed that students should have sufficient background knowledge before beginning new topics of learning. Thus, they have established prerequisites for various subject domains. A theoretical justification for this practice lies in schema construction: The appropriate background store of knowledge is a necessary, but not sufficient, condition for learning because it provides the foundation upon which the individual may construct for himself or herself the new schema.

Attention

Attention has been one of the more problematic areas of psychological research. For a great many years it was neglected because it, like consciousness, suggested too strongly the introspective approach, which behavioral psychology rejected. Attention, like a number of other important cognitive phenomena, has proven elusive to definition. We find ourselves falling back on William James's efforts in the late nineteenth century to characterize it. James said that we all know what attention is. To loosely paraphrase James, it is focused, concentrated, and conscious thought. Moreover, it results from what appears to be a competition (although James does not use this term) among different trains of thought (which is his term). The upshot is that one train of thought dominates to the exclusion of the others (see James, 1890, pp. 403–404). Thus, attention is not only conscious but selective.

Selective attention is an important characteristic of schema development. Two rival theories have been brought forward to explain it. The first is a filter or bottleneck theory, which proposes that the amount of incoming information is screened very early, before receiving much processing (see, e.g., Broadbent, 1958). In this theory, only a limited number of sensory inputs survive to be processed. The second theory suggests that all inputs receive initial processing but that differing amounts of attention are allocated to various pieces of information depending upon the circumstances (Shiffrin & Schneider, 1977). The latter is often called a theory of controlled attention. Much experimental evidence has accrued for both theories. With respect to schema formation, it may be that the two theories explain different things, with the first having greater application to the recording of an experience in memory and the second pertaining more to its incorporation into a schema.

In constructing a schema, an individual will perforce have available more information than he or she can comfortably process. Consequently, some of the information will receive attention and some will not. That which does will become part of the individual's schema knowledge. That which does not will be ignored.

It remains an unresolved issue whether an individual must consciously allocate attention to information for it to be incorporated into the schema. Certainly there is experimental evidence of incidental learning by subjects (Postman, 1964; Nelson, 1976). As we engage in further research about schema development and growth we may be able to answer this question.

Repetitions

Schemas do not spring into creation without prior experience, although there is a perspective in philosophy that advocates this position (see Gardner, 1987, for a cogent summary). How, then, do they develop? One might argue that humans have a predisposition to form schemas, that is, there is a hard-wiring in the brain that facilitates schema creation and use. I can offer no insight into this issue and concede willingly that it is a question for the neuroscientists. I regard it as a plausible premise, however, because we observe that individuals do exhibit signs of using schema knowledge to operate in their environments – no matter what the environment. Moreover, the similarities among signs exhibited by different individuals in the same experiment suggest that people very likely have common schemas that operate in essentially the same way.

Most of the studies on schema use and development suggest that a schema develops in response to repeated problem-solving experiences that have identifiable features in common. One experience does not generally create a schema. Rather, it lays down a sequential memory about what has happened and the order in which events have occurred. This is to some extent a linear stream. What makes a knowledge structure a schema is its networked form and the patterns of interconnections – not a linear flow.

Evidence that schemas do not emerge from one single experiential episode comes from several sources. For example, Dave Kieras has tried to teach schemas about electronics to students in one sitting, using materials developed quite a long time ago by the U. S. Navy. He found that students simply did not absorb the relevant information (Kieras, 1991, 1992).

Gick and Holyoak's (1980, 1983) work on transfer may also be looked at as an attempt to instill a schema with one experience. They asked students to read a complex story having a military plot. They hypothesized that students would form a story schema about the strategy employed by the protagonist of the story and then use it when reading another story having a surgical plot. Such behavior was rarely observed. Most of the time, students failed to see the underlying similarities in the two stories.

Finally, as will be described later in this volume, my own work on schema development provides strong evidence that individuals do not develop schemas without repeated experiences. As would be expected, the amount of repetition that is required varies from individual to individual and is an issue to be considered when we address the role of the schemas in instruction.

Uniqueness

It stands to reason that if schemas are constructed on the basis of personal experience, no two individuals will form identical schemas because they cannot have precisely identical experiences in life. Nevertheless, it is not the case that individuals form radically different schemas from relatively similar experiences. Rather, their schemas have roughly the same general form. Let me illustrate this point with an analogy about traveling. Most of us have taken a number of trips by airplane, although each of us will have had different experiences on those trips, including different points of departure, different destinations, different traveling companions, and different reasons for traveling. I would wager that we nevertheless have relatively similar schemas for how to purchase a ticket, what to do if our baggage does not arrive, how to find out about transportation to and from the airport, what to expect of airplane meals, and so on. Thus, although the details of our distinct experiences vary, the general knowledge found in our schemas is really quite similar and allows us to use our schemas in similar ways.

I will have more to say about similarities and differences in individuals' schemas in chapter 7–9, where I describe both intraindividual and interindividual differences for a group of students learning about arithmetic story problems. These variations have significance when we think of how individuals learn in group settings.

Abstractions

One result of the multiple repetition of experiences is that the individual tends to abstract general properties from the most relevant features of the situation. These abstractions become an essential part of the schema because they facilitate application of the schema to new experiences. The repeated experiences that contribute to schema formation are not exact duplicates of each other; otherwise, a single trace would do for memory retrieval, there would be little need for the power of a schema, and little abstraction would take place. Probably a schema develops most easily when the situation varies moderately and the procedures for resolving the problem remain essentially the same.

For example, as Hinsley, Hayes, and Simon (1977) found in their algebra studies, high school students apparently develop schemas grounded in algebra problem type. So, if a student had encoded the necessary abstract representation for a mixture problem, a schema could develop and be applied to any new mixture problem. Each instance would be slightly different (different parts of the problem would be unknown, and different settings would be represented in the problems), but the overall plan and procedures would take roughly the same form from instance to instance.

Content variability

Schemas typically develop around situations, experiences, ideas, or events. The focus of the schema may be as abstract as identifying an honest man (e.g., Socrates' discussion with Meno) or may be as specialized as finding a departure gate in an unfamiliar airport. Schemas are not created about specific people, such as one's mother, but they form instead around the general roles that people assume, such as motherhood. In the same way, one would not have a schema for one's house or one's office. Instead, one has a specific memory of such places, with unambiguous details that apply only to them. At the same time, one almost certainly has a number of schemas that can call on the information stored in these specific memories. One also has schemas associated with offices or houses in general.

Neither concept nor rule

At various times over the past 25 years, cognitive psychologists have found it convenient to postulate two kinds of knowledge: procedural and declarative.[1] For the most part, procedural knowledge means rule knowledge and has to do with skill acquisition and performance. Declarative knowledge is composed of concepts and facts. A schema does not exactly fit into either of these categories but instead transcends both of them.

Conceptual knowledge tends to be static, limited to a set of facts or features. As a number of researchers have documented, it quite likely has a hierarchical structure, with some concepts grouped together as a superordinate class of broader concepts and others grouped as a subordinate class (Collins & Quillian, 1969; E. E. Smith, Shoben, & Rips, 1974). Although it is possible to pose a problem requiring only the access of conceptual knowledge, as is done in concept identification experiments for example, such tasks are generally artificial. They do not call on the individual to plan a response and take action. Moreover, as much of the psychological research has shown, it is possible to have nonsense concepts. That is, concepts can be developed that have no meaning for the individual. Schemas without meaning cannot occur.

Similarly, rule knowledge is more limited than schema knowledge. Rule knowledge tends to be rigid: If *A* is true, then do *B*. Schemas have greater flexibility. Schemas also differ from rules by departing from a single sequence of decisions. Many of the decisions arrived at by means of schemas result from parallel, rather than serial, processing (which will be discussed further in the modeling chapters of part V). Both conceptual and rule knowledge are integral parts of a schema, as I show later, but neither alone suffices.

Purposeful versus spontaneous instantiation

A question of interest in schema usage is whether an individual invokes schemas consciously and purposefully or whether their use is automatic and occurs spontaneously. I can see no reason why this should be an either/or issue. There appears to be equal opportunity for both.

In support of conscious processing, one can make the following argument. Given the problem-solving function of a schema, it seems reasonable that recognition of a problem implies conscious attending to its nature and hence a conscious and controlled attempt to solve it. Thus, schema invocation is made deliberately, using selected pieces of information.

On the other hand, the same problem may present itself over and over again. It still must be solved, but the solution is routine. Herein, one surmises, lies the root of habit. Whenever this particular problem occurs, invocation of the appropriate schema is automatic and requires little conscious thought. If anything untoward occurs during the application of the schema, more attention is directed to the problem, and the processing may become controlled rather than automatic.

An example may be helpful to illustrate the difference between the routine and almost unconscious processing of information at a background level and the bringing to bear of direct attention to the experience at hand. This morning, when you awakened, you probably left your bedroom and eventually walked into your kitchen for breakfast. Did you have trouble finding the kitchen? Do you remember making conscious decisions to go through a doorway? to walk down the stairs? Probably not. In all likelihood you cannot even remember the particular experience without a great deal of thought, although you may be sure it occurred. The journey through your house did not present a problem to you. You know and recognize every step, and navigating is essentially automatic.

Now consider another scenario. You are staying at a friend's house for the first time. You awaken in the dark and decide you need to get a drink of water from the kitchen. But this is an unfamiliar house and you do not have routine memories about how to get from your room to the kitchen. You may never have been in the kitchen. Now you have a problem, and now you must use your conscious processing – and several schemas – to find a solution.

The point at which the schema becomes purposefully invoked is when there is something unknown in the situation – in short, a problem. It may be trivial: "Here I am in a strange place and I want to get something out of my briefcase. Where can I put it down safely?" Or it might be more complex: "Here I am in a hotel in an unfamiliar city and I'm hungry. How can I get a meal?" Simply having the concept of a tuna sandwich will not alleviate hunger pains. The successful traveler will have a schema for finding a meal in an unfamiliar city, and that schema may in turn involve many other schemas (e.g., how to use the Yellow Pages, where to get a city map, whom to ask in the hotel, how to call room service).

Problem-solving mechanism

A schema develops because it is a useful and efficient mechanism for solving problems. If there is no problem to be solved, there is no need to give conscious attention to the processing of information and consequently little need to establish memory links among salient features of the current experience. Another way of stating the same point is to say that a schema is a goal-oriented cognitive mechanism. The goal is to solve the problem.

A problem can take a vast number of shapes. It might be a standard problem of the type one commonly observes in educational settings ("find this" or "solve that"). It might be an internally created problem: "How can I get to the grocery, the bank, and the cleaners before 5 o'clock?" Or it might be rather mundane: "I need to look up an address but I've misplaced my address book." For each problem, some action needs to be taken, and in many instances, a set of goals or subgoals needs to be established and procedures need to be identified for achieving them. Obviously, some problems are more difficult than others and will require elaborate interfacing of multiple schemas. And, as mentioned earlier, a problem may be concrete or hypothetical.

The problem-solving function of a schema is supported by the componential structure of the storage mechanism. As reported by various researchers, there are many aspects to problem solving, and these include recognizing the problem, making a mental model that fits the problem to some internal representation, forming plans for solving the problem, and carrying out the solution. Not surprisingly, these aspects correspond to the four components of schema knowledge described earlier. To solve a problem, one usually must ask several questions, such as:

What exactly is the problem?
Do I have a frame of reference for it?
Is it unique?
Have I solved any problems that are similar to it?
Have I noticed all of its critical features?
What will I do first to solve it?
Do I know how to solve it?
How will I know when I have found a good solution?

Answers to these questions can be found in the four knowledge components. By focusing on one or another of the components, we begin to understand a great deal more about how a schema functions and about how individuals go about the business of problem solving.

Identification knowledge serves the recognition requirement. All of the stored details and abstractions come together to allow the individual to confirm that the schema might fit the problem. Elaboration knowledge works in the opposite direction; it serves to determine whether the problem fits the schema. That is, according to the identification knowledge, the schema might seem to be the most appropriate one, but critical elements required for instantiating the schema may be missing from the problem. Thus, the individual uses his or her schema to create a mental model of the problem. The elaboration knowledge of the schema determines the basic form of this mental model and specifies its key elements. The problem supplies the details that fit into these elements.

Not all pieces of the mental model will be completely known, of course, or there would be no problem. One important role for a schema is to supply, *where reasonable and appropriate,* the default characteristics that allow the schema to be used. Too many pieces may be missing, however, and the mental model will be on shaky ground because too much of it has been supplied by these default mechanisms. An individual may elect at this point to review the problem for additional details, to search for other possible schemas, or to continue with the present schema knowing its fit is problematic.

A key corollary of the problem-solving requirement for schema development and use is that the individual necessarily does something with schema knowledge. A new schema will not be created or an existing schema will not be activated unless some action is needed. Action does not necessarily mean physical movement. It may just as easily be mental activity.

Analogical reasoning

In order to make use of the abstractions and prior instances that make up a schema, the individual typically must engage in analogical reasoning. An elemental requirement for using analogical reasoning is that the pieces must fit together in a cohesive pattern. Thus, the cohesion and connectivity of the schema come into play.

Analogical reasoning allows the individual to map the current experience onto a template that has been derived from previous experiences. This template develops as part of the elaboration knowledge of the schema. The abstractions that are part of the schema make up a basic part of this template, and the individual either consciously or unconsciously will attempt to match each of these with some aspect of the current experience. If the abstractions are not well developed, some or all of the mappings may occur between the memory of a specific previous problem, rather than the more general abstract details, and the current problem.

Simultaneous versus sequential processing

Perhaps no single issue related to cognition is more visible today than the conflict between advocates of parallel cognitive processing and adherents of sequential cognitive processing. The debate is most often heard when the subject is cognitive modeling. This debate has carried over into models of schema instantiation and usage. On the one hand, one may argue that much of schema functioning must be simultaneous, such as the recognition of the situation. Just as strongly, on the other hand, one may also argue that there is clearly some logical, sequential processing carried out in the use of planning and execution knowledge.

I mentioned before that most psychologists now believe that no single theory of memory will suffice. Similarly, it appears that no single processing mode will explain all of cognition. The nature of the processing involved in some aspect of cognition will depend upon the topic of one's research. For areas involving pattern matching, the simultaneous processing described by connectionist or parallel distributed models appears best. For the sequential processing needed in structured or decision-making tasks, one turns instead to the symbolic models with conditional actions.

Schemas involve both types of processing. This is an essential and perhaps unique characteristic of schemas, and it is one with far-reaching implications. In particular, it has the welcome result of allowing the simultaneous/sequential debates about cognitive structure and function to be put aside in favor of more fruitful questions about the ways in which these processes interact.

There are many ways in which one might unite the different processing perspectives, and a few researchers are beginning to adopt the joint approach (e.g., Schneider & Oliver, 1991; Hendler, 1991; S. P. Marshall & J. P. Marshall, 1991). I expect many new and important developments to emerge as this approach becomes more central to cognitive modeling. I will return to this topic in a later chapter, at which point I will describe a hybrid model of schemas containing both connectionist and symbolic elements.

Summary

To reiterate the points of this section:

- A schema is constructed by the individual.
- Schema formation involves attention and selective processing.
- A schema results from a repetition of similar experiences.
- No two individuals will have precisely identical schemas.
- A schema contains abstractions of commonalities in experiences.
- Schemas may have as foci either abstract notions or concrete situations.
- A schema is neither a concept nor a rule.
- Schema instantiation may be purposeful or spontaneous.
- A schema is a problem-solving agent.
- Schema invocation involves analogical reasoning.
- A schema may involve both simultaneous and sequential processing.

These eleven characteristics of schema substance may be grouped into three primary areas of psychological investigation: schema formation (the first four), schema contents (the next three), and schema usage (the last four). The formation issues have to do with which cognitive processes are involved in schema creation. The contents questions center on the schema's similarity to known psychological constructs. And the usage questions focus mainly on how schemas are implemented.

Unification

To sum up, schemas develop after many similar and repeated experiences, each of which constitutes a problem for the individual. Schemas are used to interpret the problem and to apply to it as much as possible any relevant prior knowledge, using both parallel and sequential cognitive processing.

Let us return for a moment to the substance/form dichotomy and consider some of the overlapping issues. An obvious one emerges when we consider the importance of construction and memory storage. Naturally, the construction takes place in memory, else how could the individual build on previous knowledge stored there? Moreover, as part of the construction, the individual stores what he or she constructs, else how could the construction be used on subsequent occasions? From a purely structural point of view, one may care little about whether the individual constructs the schema piece by piece or somehow absorbs it in toto. The point to be made here is this: Whatever makes up the schema is stored so that it may be used again as a cohesive unit. Notice how consistent this position is with the substantive point of view, which rests upon the premise that whatever develops has precisely this cohesiveness. The major ideas about what goes into a schema, the ways that schemas are created, and the means by which these creations are retained do not contradict each other.

Furthermore, the presumption that the created schema has a network form blends nicely with the above assertions about particular content. The network develops from the many repetitions required for schema creation, with connections forming among the various parts of the situation being repeated. A great many connections may form, depending to some extent on the number of details found in the experience that is central to the schema. Each individual will create an idiosyncratic network, based on his or her experiences, the number of repetitions, and the demands for problem solving that exist. The degree of connectivity that develops in the network will also depend on just these aspects. Moreover, in the course of these repetitions, important features about the schema are abstracted from the details of the experiences. These become important characteristics of the schema, and as a whole they become the critically important identification knowledge, one of the four components of a schema.

One concludes that schemas are useful because they provide the individual with the means of responding to and interacting with the environment in some reasonable way. These responses and interactions may be the result of long deliberation, or they may be rapid and almost spontaneous. Hence, the schema must be a flexible structure, capable of triggering many different kinds of responses and able to reach activation through many differing initiations.

As I pointed out in chapter 1, Marvin Minsky set forth five issues that a schema theory should address (Minsky, 1975). If we construe them as questions, we can ask how the theory outlined here would answer them.

1. *How is a schema selected?* Schema selection occurs as the result of pattern matching that utilizes the individual's identification knowledge. Once the basic situation is recognized, the individual then accesses the necessary elaboration knowledge for additional details.
2. *How are additional schemas called on?* As plans are created, the elements within them become themselves the inputs to other schemas. This may occur by direct access to any knowledge component or by additional pattern matching.
3. *How are schemas modified?* Two kinds of modifications must be considered: enlarging the schema with new information and changing information that is already part of it. In the first case, the modification occurs as the result of repetition, although the precise amount of repetition remains unknown. The second type of modification has not yet been addressed by researchers.

4. *How are schemas created?* We have made a substantial beginning in understanding how schemas develop, primarily through the studies described in subsequent chapters. The schema development observed in experimental subjects progresses from a few details of examples to full abstract characterizations and strong mental models.

5. *How does the memory store change as a result of learning?* Perhaps the most important change resulting from schema development is the increased connectivity among schema elements. This suggests that as learning occurs, connectivity strengthens. We have a variety of experimental evidence from studies using connectionist models to support this position (Marshall, 1993b; McClelland & Rumelhart, 1989).

These five issues provide a useful yardstick against which the theory can be measured repeatedly as it continues to evolve. At this juncture, of course, neither schema theory nor any other cognitive theory is yet sufficiently developed to explicate them fully. However, schema theory does have something to contribute to each of them, and more importantly, it generates hypotheses about these issues that may be empirically tested and that have the potential of contributing to further theoretical advances.

To close the chapter, I repeat again its main thesis: A proper theory of schema acquisition and implementation requires that we integrate the two perspectives of form and substance which have long been present in philosophical and psychological thought. This is accomplished by focusing on two key characteristics that have been missing from previous schema theories: the componential nature of schema knowledge and the need for both parallel and sequential processing. These two features are essential because without them it is extremely difficult – and perhaps impossible – to formulate adequate and precise models of schema development, retrieval, or use. To construct adequate models, we need to be able to make a detailed, working representation of the schema's structure and to specify the components that make up this structure. To apply the model with any meaning we must also specify the nature of the schema's contents and how they depend upon the individual whose schemas we study. And, finally, we must specify the nature of the processing that occurs during schema instantiation. These are the central issues underlying the schema theory presented here. The remaining chapters in this book address them severally and collectively.

3

The schemas of arithmetic story problems

Let us begin with the premise that successful problem solving in a specified domain depends upon the schemas that a person possesses. It should be immediately evident that we need to ascertain which schemas and how many of them are needed to solve problems. Almost certainly, for any complex domain these questions can be answered in numerous ways. What we seek is a *basis set of schemas*, that is, a minimal set of schemas that is sufficient to solve all problems in the domain. Like the basis of a vector space – a minimal, spanning set – the basis set of schemas would be all that is needed to generate, through suitable combinations of its members, the entire space of problem-solving capabilities. Clearly, a basis set would consist of high-level schemas having strong interconnections to lower-level schemas and accessing these lower-level ones as needed.

The approach described here derives from the idea that in any problem-solving domain, only a limited set of basic situations will occur. The number of basic situations is presumed to be small, but many complex situations can arise because the basic ones can be logically combined in many ways. Given that there is but a small collection of basic situations, the objective is to delineate one and only one schema for each of them. Just as basic situations combine to create complex situations, the corresponding basic schemas are combined in solving complex problems.

In many domains, a person may develop a basis set of schemas quite naturally. In a number of educational domains, however, we have evidence that students are not developing powerful schemas with which they can reason about problems of the domain. One probable cause of students' failure to develop strong schemas is the instruction they receive. Consequently, it is worthwhile to consider new approaches that better blend cognitive theory with educational practice. I propose one approach here: Instruction should focus explicitly on the basis set, that is, on the important schemas of the domain to be studied. How this can be achieved is one theme of this book.

The present chapter serves a dual purpose: to outline a general procedure for identifying a basis set of schemas that can guide instruction and to describe a set for arithmetic story problems that ensued from implementing the procedure. The specific schemas described here are not the schemas that students today typically develop during instruction about problem solving. In fact, as I discuss later in some detail, I have yet to encounter a student with a preexisting, full set of schemas exactly as I have outlined them. This finding does not dismay me, however, because I do not discover many students having a good understanding of story problems either. Moreover, I would not argue that all individuals must have the same basis set of schemas for a domain or that only one basis set will lead to successful problem solving. Almost surely, there will be many ways to characterize a domain, and any hypothesized set will be only one of a number of viable alternatives. I will argue that we can improve learning by selecting one of these and focusing instruction appropriately. I am convinced that the schemas students now typically develop about story problems are *not* among the acceptable alternatives, because students' knowledge seems neither well structured nor sufficient.

The issue of how to identify an effective basis set of schemas for use in instruction is a thorny one for a number of reasons. At first glance, it might seem that one need only ask experts how they solve arithmetic problems and then extract or abstract their schemas from the responses. This approach has at least three limitations. The first limitation is endemic to all schema research: People are not very good at telling us how and what they think. Almost every researcher who studies expertise faces this problem. As Nisbett and Wilson (1977) illustrated in their research, individuals may not be aware of their own problem solving and thus cannot describe accurately what they are doing or thinking.

The second limitation also pertains to most schema research. Experts may not share a common set of schemas. To be sure, we would expect some consistent threads among their different configurations. But, for instruction and for cognitive models, it is necessary to identify a single set of schemas upon which to build. The problem is how to select an appropriate one given several alternatives. Which expert's perspective do we embrace?

The final limitation is specific to the study of arithmetic story problems. Two kinds of experts might be studied: "old" experts, who have advanced well beyond the study of arithmetic story problems, and "young" experts, who have just reached some measurable level of mastery of simple story problems. Neither one of these groups is actually appropriate for the level of investigation I want to make. The old experts no longer have simple schemas. Their original schemas have continued to develop and modify as these individuals studied other areas of mathematics. As a consequence, their problem solving is inextricably bound to all the problem solving of their experience, and their approach to story problems shows it. For example, old experts might reasonably use the framework of algebra or calculus to attack a complex story problem. It is quite difficult, if not impossible, to get back to their original schemas of arithmetic story problems. Moreover, their understanding of a simple story problem is almost instantaneous and virtually impossible for them to describe. All this poses a problem for my schema investigation because I focus on the initial form of story-problem schemas as children develop them, and instruction must be at the appropriate level. The knowledge and skills available to old experts are not initially available to children (or other novices) and cannot logically be part of their early schemas.

One is tempted to turn instead to young experts, i.e., children who have mastered simple arithmetic story problems but who have not yet studied other areas of mathematics. I initially attempted this approach but abandoned it after interviewing all sixth-grade children in two elementary schools. The difficulty with young experts is that they have not necessarily developed appropriate schemas that will be useful for more complex problems. We have abundant research to indicate that children are very successful on simple problems but unable to solve difficult ones. They have apparently developed one or more schemas that are too limited. The key-word strategy described later in this chapter is a prominent example.

What I would really like to know are the schemas of old experts that they used when *they* were young experts. It would be incredibly valuable to know which young-expert schemas will eventually develop into old-expert ones. This knowledge could be ascertained only by a longitudinal study of some years' duration, which has yet to be carried out. In its absence, we must use other means for selecting a basis set of schemas to guide instruction.

The strategy I have developed is given in some detail below. I began by focusing on existing instructional materials, namely, textbook items and test problems. These were used to define the universe of story problems to which the resulting basis set of schemas should pertain. The result is a set of epagogic domain schemas rather than expert-based schemas. The procedure consists of several distinct steps. In this discussion, for the purposes of separating the steps I have labeled them situation description, status quo appraisal, source evaluation, theoretical verification, and practicality check. Each has a unique objective.

The first step, *situation description*, lays the basic framework for the set of situations to which the schemas will pertain. At this point, one specifies the details of each major situation in the domain, paying particular attention to its identifying characteristics and discriminating features.

Next, one takes into account the knowledge organization that already exists in students' heads. This is the stage I call *status quo appraisal*. Students are not tabulae rasae; they already have a great deal of knowledge that they use in the domain. We ask here: What schemas do they already have? What principles of organization can be detected in their knowledge structures? What prior knowledge do they have and how do they bring it to bear in their problem-solving attempts?

The stage of *source evaluation* involves choosing instructional materials and determining how adequately the newly hypothesized situations overlay them. The issue is whether the situations sufficiently account for the bulk of experiences that an individual might routinely expect to have in the domain under study. Several choices of materials may be available for the analysis, and it is conceivable that they will lead to different analytical outcomes. It would be a waste of time to use sources that inaccurately reflect current curriculum or represent an extreme subset of the curriculum. Probably the best choice, as illustrated below, is a variety of different materials.

Then comes *theoretical verification*. This stage requires both the elaboration of the hypothetical schema structures and the corroboration that they conform to the strictures of general schema theory. One wants to establish that the chunks of knowledge hypothesized to be potential schemas are capable of functioning in the multiple and complex ways that are expected. Here, it is necessary to consider the four components of schema knowledge and how they may be manifested in the newly identified schemas.

The final stage is a *practicality check*. It is empirical in nature and requires that an assessment be made about whether individuals can actually acquire the knowledge pertaining to situations that is needed for schema development. Given the centrality of situations to the schemas, it is critical to determine that individuals can readily make the discriminations needed for solid schema formation.

In the following sections, I describe fully these stages with respect to formulating the schemas of problem solving. The detail is vital to this volume for two reasons: to present the methodology itself and to describe carefully these particular schemas. The procedures serve as a general methodology that may be applied to other domains, and as is often true with the introduction of a new methodology, the more detail, the better. Further, these schemas are themselves the subject of subsequent chapters, and an understanding of their composition is essential for comprehending future discussions of assessment and modeling.

The importance of knowledge about situations

As one would expect, my ideas about using schemas for instruction evolved slowly over time. They were the result of an increasing awareness first of the type of difficulties that students have in solving story problems and second of their lack of structured knowledge about story problems. Most scholars today share the first awareness. The second perception is, perhaps, less well understood and consequently not as widely held. It became evident to me only after many conversations with students during individual interviews about the strategies they used – and those they failed to use – to solve word problems (reported in Marshall, 1981). Close scrutiny of students' behaviors while solving problems and my subsequent analyses of their verbalizations about what they were trying to accomplish led me to the realization that a large number of students – who could compute correctly the answers to simple problems – lacked cohesive knowledge about story problems.

This realization generated a number of questions for me about the nature of students' problem-solving knowledge and its organization in memory. I developed hypotheses about the nature of schemas in general and of schemas for arithmetic story problems in particular, but at that point, of course, the conception of schemas as laid out in chapter 2 was not yet fully formed. It emerged during the course of my research efforts. My early ideas about problem-solving schemas were based on the concepts described in chapter 1 together with the current views of story problems described by researchers such as Kintsch (1988), Kintsch and Greeno (1985), Carpenter and Moser (1984, 1982), and Riley, Greeno, and Heller (1983).[1] As they have pointed out, the patterns of associations and relationships in story problems were clearly critical to making sensible choices about arithmetic operations. It seemed to me that schemas were the appropriate mechanism of memory to capture both the patterns of relationships as well as their linkages to operations. As I focused on the specific schemas presented later in this chapter – and especially on the way that instruction about them might be created – I became aware of the dual need for a more developed and elaborate conception of a schema in general as well as explicit descriptions of the situations that can occur in arithmetic story problems.

In an ideal world – such as Garrison Keillor's Lake Wobegon – all children would not only be above average but would also be able to solve story problems. In reality, story problems are strongly disliked by many people because they find the problems hard to solve. This distaste for story problems is not limited to children; adults experience it as well. The extent and longevity of the dislike are frequently surprising, and jokes about story problems are widespread and almost universally understood. A familiar example to mathematics educators is Gary Larson's cartoon depicting "Hell's Library" – which contains nothing but books of story problems.

Why do so many individuals have trouble solving story problems? Both children and adults apparently have adequate computational skills. If you give them some numbers and a specified arithmetic operation, they can readily carry out the appropriate steps of the algorithm. Much evidence supports this claim, including large-scale evaluations such as those carried out by the National Assessment of Educational Progress (NAEP) and the California Assessment Program (CAP). Troubles abound only when problems are couched in stories, as shown in many research studies (see, e.g., some of the research described in Silver, 1985). As Kintsch (1988) points out, a key aspect of the difficulty of story problems lies in the relational and situational details contained in them.

One surmises that the would-be problem solvers have failed to recognize the relevant relationships described by stories. They apparently lack the requisite knowledge for making decisions based on such recognition. Moreover, they rarely display evidence of creating problem-solving plans that use important relational information gleaned from the stories. For the most part, as students I interviewed often insisted, a number of the problems just do not make sense to them (Marshall, 1981). Moreover, the perceived senselessness of the problems does not seem to bother the students; they do not expect otherwise.

Table 3.1. *An imaginative story problem*

A Race at School.

The Race between Teacher and Beauchamp Reynolds, aged 11, is still remembered at our School (*school,* a word derived from the French, which derived it from the Latin, which derived it from a Greek word meaning rest, leisure: always seize every chance to acquire useful information). Champ was reciting in History.

Teacher: "In what year did Columbus discover America?"

Champ: "In 1492."

Teacher: "Wrong. Next."

Champ: "The book says – "

Teacher: "Do you compare a vile book with me? I give you one more chance. What's the date?"

Champ: "1492."

Of course, nothing remained for Teacher to do, except to chastise (*chastise,* a word derived from the French; it meant originally to make pure: always seize every chance to acquire useful information) Champ. She sprang down from the platform. Champ was already nearing the door. She gave chase . . . .

It was a beautiful day for a Race – a sunny, late-November afternoon, cool, bracing air, squirrels in the clumps of oaks, partridges in the fields.

Champ started with a lead of 9 feet. The beaten path around the schoolhouse measured 30 yards. As the chase swept over this path, the windows were filled with groups of happy children. Throughout the Race, Champ ran at a speed of $220\frac{1}{2}$ feet per 10 seconds. As for Teacher, she ran less rapidly along the two ends of the schoolhouse, where there were no windows, but made up for it while passing in front of the well-filled galleries. Her average speed was 13.333 rods per 10 seconds. How many rounds did the contestants make per half-hour, and what was their relative position at the close of the first hour?

Source: R. Weeks, *Boys' Own Arithmetic* (New York: E. P. Dutton, 1924)

An important assumption in the formulation of problem-solving schemas is that recognition and understanding of the situations expressed in story problems are necessary elements in schema formation and invocation. To explore this assumption, consider that a story problem is, in principle, meant to be a shorthand representation of a real-world situation. Sometimes the stories are elaborate, as in the imaginative problems of *Boys' Own Arithmetic* (Weeks, 1924), which can run from two to five pages (see Table 3.1). More often, the stories are terse, only one or two sentences in length, and students are expected to use their own prior knowledge of the world to fill in gaps about the situation depicted in the story. Thus, students are presumed to have and to use knowledge about situations. Failure to employ the appropriate knowledge contributes to, and in many cases causes, their observed difficulties in solving story problems. Under schema theory, the understanding of situations is essential.

If we consider that the solving of arithmetic story problems has two primary components – the recognition of the situation and the application of appropriate operations – it is clear from analyses of students' errors that the former bears more responsibility for individuals' difficulties than the latter. This two-component model of problem solving greatly oversimplifies the case, but it aids in our identification of a major source of students' shortcomings. What students need is a mechanism by which they can acquire knowledge about problem-solving situations to augment their knowledge about arithmetic operations. In short, what is needed is a set of schemas that reflect the basic situations.

Situation description

What is it about a situation that makes it different from or similar to others? Three distinct criteria come to mind. First, situations may vary in surface features, such as story context. Second, they may vary in syntactic features such as length, complexity of language, or number and type of operations. And third, they may vary in the relationships they express.

Surface features are perhaps the most obvious differences among story problems. However, they appear to be a poor basis for differentiating situations, as a number of novice-expert studies in mathematics and other domains have pointed out. What these studies have found is that experts rarely attempt to use surface features to understand problem situations. Such behavior is observed more often in unsuccessful solvers than in successful ones. This has been observed in domains such as physics (Chi, Feltovich, & Glaser, 1981) and eighth grade mathematics (Silver, 1979).

Syntactic characteristics have often been used to predict problem difficulty (e.g., Loftus & Suppes, 1972; Barnett, 1979), but no one seriously suggests that better recognition of syntactic features will improve students' abilities to make critical distinctions. What researchers do suggest, however, is that simplification of some syntactic features may make problems easier for children to comprehend (De Corte, Verschaffel, & De Win, 1985). Nevertheless, syntactic details seem to be of relatively little use to students as the basis for distinguishing situations.

The third criterion, based on common relational characteristics, seems to be the most relevant one for successful problem solving (Riley et al., 1983; Carpenter & Moser, 1982). The essence of a problem can be represented in terms of a general description of the situation that eliminates both surface and syntactic features while preserving the relational ones. Such a general description allows the solver to recognize a problem's similarity to a canonical situation that is already well understood.

It is this third approach that allows relevant distinctions to be made among situations in story problems. As shown in what follows, it requires identifying the key relationships and how they are expressed through stories.

I propose that five situations, taken alone or in combination, are sufficient to describe the relations within common arithmetic story problems. These situations I call Change, Group, Compare, Restate, and Vary. Each reflects a different relationship among its constituent elements. Examples of simple problems, each containing a single situation, are given in Table 3.2. More difficult problems may involve several situations at once.

A Change situation characterizes a problem in which there is a permanent alteration over time in a measurable quantity of a particular thing. Only one thing is involved, and it has a value at some point in time that is different from its value at a second point in time. Three numbers are of importance: the amount prior to the change, the extent of the change, and the resulting amount after the change has occurred. Multiple time periods are essential to a Change situation, and some comprehension of the ways that time

Table 3.2. *Examples of the five situations*

Change: Stan had 35 stamps in his stamp collection. His uncle sent him 8 more for a birthday present. How many stamps are now in his collection?

Group: In Mr. Harrison's third-grade class, there were 18 boys and 17 girls. How many children are in Mr. Harrison's class?

Compare: Bill walks a mile in 15 minutes. His brother Tom walks the same distance in 18 minutes. Which one is the faster walker?

Restate: At the pet store there are twice as many kittens as puppies in the store window. There are 8 kittens in the window. How many puppies are also in the window?

Vary: Mary bought a package of gum that had 5 sticks of gum in it. How many sticks would she have if she bought 3 packages of gum?

is ordinarily expressed is required for understanding the nature of the change.

A Group situation exists whenever a number of small groups are combined meaningfully into a large group. Sometimes the grouping is explicit, and the story spells out very directly that the larger group is formed by joining two or more smaller groups. More often, the grouping is implicit, and the solver is expected to use his or her own prior knowledge to understand that a new group is being formed and that it is logically feasible to make the grouping. The solver is expected to know that the subgroups mentioned in the problem form the entirety of the larger group, that is, there are no missing subgroups. Thus, in a story about dogs and cats, a reference to pets means the combined grouping of dogs and cats. Other animals that may potentially be pets, such as gerbils or parakeets, are not eligible in this scenario, and the skilled problem solver knows that they need not be considered. The solver also is expected to understand that the members of the subgroup retain their identity when combined in the large group. The cats remain cats, while at the same time they may be considered to be pets. Typically, three or more numbers are necessary in a Group situation: the number of members in each of the subgroups as well as the overall number in the combination.

A Compare situation exists whenever two things are contrasted to determine which of them is larger or smaller. The Compare situation relies heavily on students' prior knowledge about size relations. The most frequent occurrences call for the solver to determine whether the larger or smaller value is wanted when the operative relation is stated as a comparative adjective or adverb (e.g., quicker, longer, better buy, less costly). It is the nature of the expressed relationship that leads the student to know that *quicker* means less time and consequently the smaller, and not the larger, of two numbers. The Compare situation is found most often as part of complex problems involving two or more situations, but it may occur singly as well.

A Restate situation is present if a specific relationship is described between two different things at a fixed point in time. The relationship holds only for the particular time frame of the story; it cannot be generalized to a broader context. Two descriptions always occur in a Restate situation. First, there is a linkage of the two things by some relational statement, such as twice as great as, three more than, or one half of. Second, there is a restatement of this relationship using numerical values rather than the relational statement. It is not usually explicitly stated, but the numerical values must also fulfill the original relational statement. The student is supposed to understand that the second statement is just a restatement – or another way of saying – the first.

The Vary situation is the fifth and final one. A Vary situation exists when a specified relationship connecting two things can be generalized over other manifestations of those things. The two things may be two different objects or one object and a measurable property associated with it. The essential feature of the Vary situation is that the relationship is preserved whether the numbers of things increase or decrease. The situation derives its name from the fact that if one varies the amount of one thing, the amount of the second changes systematically as a function of the known relationship. There is a hypothetical flavor to this situation: One is asked to assume a relationship and then to hypothesize about its outcome if one of the elements involved in the relationship is modified. Frequently, one encounters the wording "if . . . then . . ." in Vary situations.

As often happens during conceptual development, my views on these situations matured as I carried out the research described in these pages. Initially, I began with only three situations, those described by Riley et al. (1983), which they called the semantic relations of Change, Combine, and Compare.[2] The Riley et al. work had its foundations in how children learn addition and subtraction. Thus, its scope was strictly additive. As I extended my perspective to look at the entire realm of story problems, it was necessary to define the Restate and Vary situations in order to encompass multiplicative situations as well as additive ones. Moreover, it was necessary to redefine the Compare relation and to rename the Combine one. As used by Riley et al. the Compare relation is just the simplest additive case of a Restate situation. That is, it has the form of one thing having a particular relationship to a second, with the critical relational statement being "some amount greater than" instead of a statement such as "twice as large as." The Compare situation described in these pages, whose problem form asks only that the solver compare two values and decide which satisfies the question of larger or smaller, was not included in the Riley et al. study. With respect to the Combine relation, I found that students who were instructed to use it as a situation label tended to focus on addition only. The name itself suggested the addition operation. Hence, I adopted the term *Group,* which appears to have a weaker association to the operation of addition.

Thus, I eventually settled on the five situations. This set of situations has three important characteristics. First, they are very simple. Formal arithmetic operations do not need to be mastered in order to comprehend and distinguish among them. In fact, understanding them requires prior world knowledge, not prior algorithmic knowledge.

A second characteristic of these situations is the ease with which they can be combined to form a wide range of problems, from very simple problems to diverse and complex ones, as in the following:

Alice had $50.00 when she went to the grocery store. She bought two quarts of milk at 95 cents each, 1 1/2 pounds of cheese at $3.50 per pound, and a loaf of bread for $1.39. How much money did she have after she made these purchases?

A visual representation of the situations in this problem is given in Figure 3.1. The overall problem is one of Change and may be re-phrased as: Alice had some money, she spent some, and she has a smaller amount remaining. Several other situations are embedded in this problem. There is a Group situation, reflecting the amount she spent on the various items. There are two Vary situations, one having to do with the cost of milk and the other having to do with the cost of cheese.

By looking at the problem in terms of its situations, a solver can develop goals and subgoals for solving the problem. It seems intu-itively easier to remember that one needs to focus on a grouping of several items to form the total cost and to determine the change

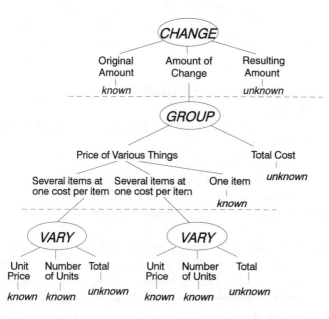

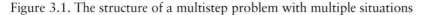
Figure 3.1. The structure of a multistep problem with multiple situations

that occurs in the amount of money Alice has than to try to keep track of a list of operations that should be carried out to solve the problem.

Finally, a third characteristic is that the repeated joint appearance of two or more of the situations can be the basis for defining additional and more elaborate situations. Thus, whenever two of the situations occur together with some frequency, an individual is likely to develop a new situation category to represent the joint occurrence.

Status quo appraisal

The key-word schema

If students do not use situational schemas to solve problems, what do they use? Evidence suggests that many students rely heavily on a single schema as they attempt to solve story problems (Marshall, 1981). That single schema is based on how to identify key words in a problem and how to use these key words to select an arithmetic operation. Students' own statements point to the key word schema:

"You'd subtract . . . because it says *left.*"
"*Of* means times."
" . . . because *full* usually means to add . . . . That's what our teacher told us."
"You add . . . 'cause it says *how many.*"
"Okay, you want to multiply. No, you want to add because it says *how many.*"
"I was taught that the word *of* means multiply."[3]

The key-word approach works moderately well for students so long as they are confronted only with very simple problems, that is, those requiring only one arithmetic operation. Thus, they can succeed with this strategy until they face more challenging problems, which usually happens about the time they reach middle school. At this point the key-word approach breaks down, usually because problems require that several operations be carried out and because key words occur less frequently in the problem text.

A specific example of failure of the key-word strategy appears with the following problem, one which I used in the interview study. Some of the students responded to this item during the interview, and some saw it as part of a paper and pencil exercise.

John had 12 baseball cards. He gave 1/3 of them to Jim.
How many did John have left?

To my surprise, a large number of the sixth graders gave the answer 11 2/3. If pushed to "identify" or label the answer, as many teachers require, they were happy to call it baseball cards. Not one reflected that two-thirds of a baseball card was odd. These students were apparently (and, in many instances, by their own verbal reports, very definitely) responding to the key words "have left" that appear in the problem. Moreover, only two numbers are explicitly stated, the number 12 and the fraction 1/3. Thus, they were confident that they needed only to subtract one of the numbers from the other, and they believed that they should always subtract the smaller number from the larger (again, this is one of the points made by many of them during the interviews). Both contextual cues and situational details were completely ignored.

What knowledge do individuals already have about situations?

Because students' knowledge about situations is of interest, it is prudent to examine not only the strategies that students currently use to solve problems but also the depth of their knowledge about different situations, even if it is not evident in their problem solving. To do so necessitates that the students' attention be focused on the situational features. They may not be using their knowledge of situations in solving problems, but they may nonetheless have it. This is an important issue for several reasons. First, students may have such knowledge easily accessible to them. Unifying already existing knowledge into a schema is quite different from having to acquire new information before the schema can be built. Second, students may have already tried to use knowledge about situations and rejected it. If so, we need to know why. Third, students may be attending to unusable aspects of their knowledge, paying heed to surface or syntactic features and overlooking the important relational ones.

To determine the nature and extent of individuals' knowledge, my research associates and I carried out four experiments. For these studies, we assembled a set of 20 simple story problems, each having a single situation embedded in it. The problems were similar to those presented in Table 3.2. We asked a large number of individuals to look at the set of problems. Each individual was given a deck of 20 cards, with the problems printed one to a card, and each was invited to rearrange the problems so that similar ones were grouped together. Any number of groups was permissible. In theory, this number could range from 1, indicating that the problems were all alike, to 20, indicating that there were no similarities. The instructions about how to form categories and how many categories to create were deliberately vague because we wanted to see which similarities the individuals perceived. It is interesting to note that no one ever found this to be a confusing or ambiguous task, and no one ever took more that 10 minutes to complete it.

The 20 problems used in the task contained 4 examples each of the five situations: Change, Group, Compare, Restate, and Vary. All four arithmetic operations were represented in the set of problems, and their content reflected several different contexts. Some of them were stories about games or sports, others were stories about families, some had to do with food, and others had money as a topic.

We studied the responses of four groups: three very different classes of students and a workshop of mathematics teachers. The first group of students was an accelerated class of sixth-grade children, many of whom were classified as "gifted and talented" as a result of high intelligence test scores (e.g., scoring two or more standard deviations above the mean). The second group was a group of less-able sixth graders who were classified by the school as slower learners than others at their grade level and who were performing at approximately fourth-grade level in arithmetic. Many of them spoke English as a second language. The third group was composed of students enrolled in a remedial mathematics course in a community college. Each of the students in this last group was paid a small amount to participate in the study. The final group was composed of teachers attending a workshop held for outstanding mathematics teachers. Both elementary and secondary teachers were participants in the workshop.

We made the task as similar as possible for all four groups. They all saw the same problems, and they all received the same instructions. The instructions for both sixth-grade classes and for the teachers participating in the workshop were given by an elementary mathematics teacher who was the regular math teacher for the accelerated group, was also well-known by the less-able group, and was herself a member of the teachers' workshop. The instructions for the community college students were given by a graduate research assistant.

The results of all four studies are displayed in Figure 3.2, which is a graphic representation derived from multidimensional scaling (MDS) and complete-link cluster analysis (CA). Each diagram in Figure 3.2 illustrates the similarities observed by one of the four groups of individuals. For these analyses, the four groups' responses were first analyzed using MDS. In MDS, items perceived as similar by most of the members of a group fall close together whereas those perceived to be dissimilar are spaced far apart. One advantage of using this representation is that recurring patterns of responses across groups of individuals can be identified very easily. For ease of comparison, each letter in all four diagrams in Figure 3.2 consistently represents the same problem. The coordinates of the letters in the diagrams derive directly from the MDS analyses.

Each group's responses were also analyzed by complete-link CA, a technique that forms a cluster of items only if each one is perceived to be similar to every other one in the cluster. The irregularly shaped closed figures around the letters in Figure 3.2 show the results of the CAs. In almost all cases, the items found to be

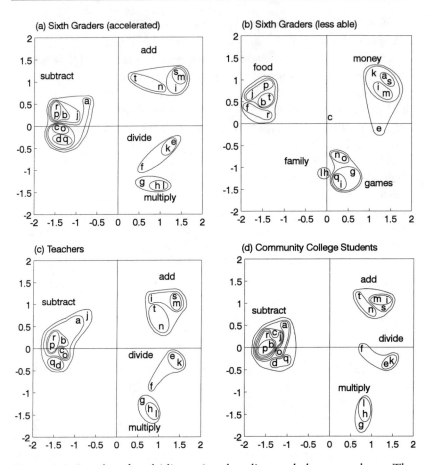

Figure 3.2. Results of multidimensional scaling and cluster analyses: The initial sorting task

similar under the MDS were also similar under the CA, providing confirming evidence of the underlying structure in the data.

Study 1: Accelerated sixth-graders. Overwhelmingly, these 21 students elected to group the problems according to arithmetic operation. Thus, they typically formed four clusters, one each for addition, subtraction, multiplication, and division. The results of their sorting task are given in Figure 3.2a. Both MDS and CA yielded the same pattern.

Study 2: Less-able sixth-graders. The results of this study are given in Figure 3.2b. Like the accelerated class, these 21 students formed distinct clusters of items, but their groupings are very different. They tended to form clusters according to surface structure, that is, the subject of the situation given in the problem. They put items about money into one group, items about games into another, items about food into a third, and items about family members into a fourth. The singleton item C not included in any cluster had as its subject a mountain and thus did not fit in any other group.

It is interesting to observe that arithmetic operations were seldom used by these students as a means of classification. We know this because the students were asked to write short descriptions of the bases for their groupings after they had completed the task. Almost all of them mentioned only surface features. As in Study 1, both the CA and the MDS yield consistent results.

Study 3: Elementary and secondary mathematics teachers.
A group of 30 teachers participated in the third experiment, and their results are given in Figure 3.2c. The pattern in the figure is quite similar to that of the accelerated sixth graders (see Figure 3.2a). Students and teachers sorted the problems according to arithmetic operation.

Study 4: Remedial mathematics students in a community college.
Twenty-five students enrolled in a remedial mathematics course in a community college completed the task. Their results are shown in Figure 3.2d. Once again, the clustering is according to arithmetic operation.

Conclusions. These four studies suggest that individuals do not classify story problems according to abstract situation. In fact, no one in any of these studies ever reported using situational features as a criterion for cluster formation nor did any individual's solution correspond to such a classification.[4] Essentially the same results were observed for students of differing levels of achievement as well as for teachers. In three of the studies, the individuals classified the items almost exclusively according to arithmetic operation. This is confirmed both by two multivariate analyses (MDS and CA) and by explicit labeling of the groups by many individuals at the end of each experiment. Only the less-able sixth-grade students used criteria other than arithmetic operation. As pointed out, most of them chose to focus on the surface structure of the stories.

We may reasonably conclude that students and teachers do not focus on critical and appropriate details of the situation given in the problem. However, the fact that the individuals in the 4 studies did not *choose* to use such knowledge as their criterion for sorting the problems does not necessarily mean that they did not perceive the situations. It is entirely possible that they saw the situational differences but chose to sort instead according to arithmetic operation or surface structure. This hypothesis was investigated further with the group of remedial community college students who participated in Study 4.

Study 4: Follow-up. The 25 students in this study were asked to carry out the experimental task three times, using a different criterion each time they created the groupings of items. At the conclusion of each task, they were asked to articulate the criterion they had used. The results given in Figure 3.2d reflect their responses the first time they carried out the task.

On their first attempt, 16 of the 25 students explicitly grouped the problems according to operation and made no errors in determining the correct operation. Several others made an attempt at such a grouping but generally had a number of misclassifications using the operation criterion. For their second attempt, 16 students gave answers corresponding to the surface structure of the less-able sixth graders. Many of the remaining students simply repeated their answers from the first response (i.e., they again responded with the four arithmetic operations) and were unable to sort the problems using a different criterion. They could find no similarity other than arithmetic operation. On their third attempt, a majority of the students could not find a third way to sort the problems. They tried unsuccessfully to use criteria such as "contains odd or even numbers," "easier and harder," or "boys and girls." No student reported using knowledge about situations.

Again, this is not conclusive evidence that the students did not understand the differences in the situations. It does indicate that they were unable to generate or retrieve the necessary knowledge from memory by themselves. In a last attempt to determine whether they could recognize the different situations in the problems, we asked these same students to carry out one final task. Each student was told to examine an arrangement of the 20 problems displayed on a nearby desk. The arrangement had five groupings, one for each of the five situations: Change, Group, Compare, Restate, and Vary. The student was told, "Another student sorted the problems in this way. Can you help me understand why these problems were put together?" The responses from the 25 students to this question were tape-recorded and transcribed.

Only two of the students were able to describe any of the situations. Both of these students first saw a pattern in the Compare items and then looked (unsuccessfully) for other patterns in the remaining groups of items. The other 23 students were unable to describe the rationale underlying any of the groups. They tended to focus only on the arithmetic operations. Gradually, they realized that the operations were not sufficient because they commented that most of the groups contained more than one operation.

Thus, once again, we were unable to detect any evidence that students relied on relevant knowledge about situations to make sense of story problems. This finding says nothing about whether students were trying to use schemas to solve problems. It suggests only that they have not developed knowledge of situations into a useful part of their problem solving.[5] The issue of whether they have such knowledge – in terms of easily being able to understand the situations when they occur in problems – is addressed later in this chapter as well as in future chapters. At this point, we move to the next stage of the evaluation of situations, which is an examination of the materials that students routinely see in the course of instruction. One possible reason for students' lack of knowledge about situations may be that they rarely encounter problems containing these situations. The only way to find out is to look at the materials directly.

Source evaluation

Two standard sources of problems were examined: problems in textbooks and problems on standardized tests. These are the curricular materials that have the greatest influence on students' experience with story problems, and they provide an impartial view of what is covered in a typical classroom. Multiple grade levels were evaluated in each analysis.

Textbook problems

Three levels of texts were examined: sixth grade, eighth grade, and remedial college. Textbook selection was made in the following way. At the sixth grade, only texts adopted for use in California schools as of 1985 were examined. Adopted textbooks tend to remain in circulation for several years. The eighth-grade texts were similarly selected from those adopted for use in California as of 1987. The remedial texts selected were used in at least two large junior colleges in California during this same time period. Thus, we can be reasonably sure that the texts chosen for analysis were not obscure or little-used materials.

Most of the selected textbooks were organized in roughly the same way. A brief examination of several other texts that did not meet California adoption criteria had the same organization as well. They all had chapters on various themes or topics, and at the end of each chapter were sets of exercises. Some texts also had short exercises interspersed throughout the chapters. Most of the time, the exercises began with several purely computational drills and culminated with a few story problems. A few textbook authors considered story problems to be so unique as to require isolation from the other problems under a separate heading or even in a separate chapter that contained most of the story problems for the entire book. At the end of each chapter there could usually be found one or more chapter tests. These rarely contained more than a single story problem, and many had none at all.

All story problems presented by the texts for students to solve were classified into three categories, according to whether they contained one, more than one, or none of the situations described above. Problems containing a single situation are the most common in arithmetic classes, and their number would be expected to be large. Problems containing more than one situation are the complex, multistep problems that are more typical of advanced arithmetic and pre-algebra classes. We hoped to see a relatively large number of them because they have the potential of forcing a student to formulate problem-solving goals and plans. The final category, none, indicates that something other than the five situations was required for solution. A large number of these would serve to weaken the claim that the hypothetical set of five situations is a useful basis of schema knowledge because it would mean that schemas derived from these situations would not be satisfactory for a substantial proportion of problems in the domain.

A simple procedure was adopted for making the classification. Each text was completely and independently coded by two coders trained to recognize the five situations. There were no disagreements between coders about category assignment. The sixth-grade texts were examined as part of a study presented to the American Psychological Association (Marshall, 1985), and the other texts were evaluated and reported in a later technical report (Marshall, Pribe, & Smith 1987). Tables 3.3–3.5 synthesize the findings from both studies.

The columns labeled 1-S in Tables 3.3–3.5 display the number of problems that expressed only a single situation. As mentioned before, these are the simplest and, one might add, the easiest to solve by inappropriate means, such as the key-word strategy. As can be seen in Table 3.3, 71% of the problems in the sixth-grade texts were of this type. Even at the eighth grade (Table 3.4), we still observed mostly these simple problems, with 65% of them

Table 3.3. *Classification of story problems in texts:*
Sixth-grade texts

Text		1-S	2-S	Geometry	Estimation	Other	Total
I	freq	229	30	18	8	2	287
	%	80%	10%	6%	3%	1%	
II	freq	134	21	21	0	2	178
	%	75%	12%	12%		1%	
III	freq	107	46	8	8	17	186
	%	57%	25%	4%	4%	8%	
IV	freq	134	62	16	0	10	222
	%	60%	28%	7%		5%	
V	freq	251	35	19	0	9	314
	%	80%	11%	6%		3%	
VI	freq	69	26	13	5	9	122
	%	57%	21%	11%	4%	7%	
Total	freq	924	220	95	21	49	1,309
	%	71%	17%	7%	2%	4%	

Note: 1-S = problems having one of the five situations; 2-S = problems having two or more of the five situations; geometry = problems involving area, volume, Pythagorean theorem, etc.; estimation = problems requiring estimation or rounding only; other = problems otherwise uncoded, including probabilities, range, maps, distance–rate–time formula.

Table 3.4. *Classification of story problems in texts:*
Eighth-grade texts

Text		1-S	2-S	Other	Total
I	freq	258	58	26	342
	%	75%	17%	8%	
II	freq	117	97	24	238
	%	49%	41%	10%	
Total	freq	375	155	50	580
	%	65%	27%	9%	

Note: Classification includes only arithmetic portions of text. Excluded are chapters of statistics, linear transformations, square roots, and coordinate geometry. 1-S = problems having one of the five situations; 2-S = problems having two or more of the five situations; other = problems otherwise uncoded, including probabilities, range, and geometry problems.

Table 3.5. *Classification of story problems in texts:*
Remedial texts

Text		1-S	2-S	Other	Total
I	freq	133	39	6	178
	%	75%	22%	3%	
II	freq	258	198	44	500
	%	51%	40%	9%	
Total	freq	391	237	50	678
	%	58%	35%	7%	

Note: 1-S = problems having one of the five situations; 2-S = problems having two or more of the five situations; other = problems otherwise uncoded, including probabilities, range, and geometry problems.

having a single situation. The remedial texts (Table 3.5) were lowest at 58%, but here too over half of the problems involved a single situation (and a single application of one arithmetic operation).

The columns labeled 2-S in the tables reflect the multistep problems. To fall into this category, a problem must involve two or more distinct and discernible situations or two separable instances of the same situation. There were substantially fewer of these than problems having a single situation, with averages of 17%, 27%, and 35%, respectively for the sixth-grade, eighth-grade, and remedial college texts.

The success of the classification scheme can be measured by the proportion of problems falling into the two categories. Altogether, the situations were sufficient to classify uniquely 88%, 92%, and 93% of the sixth-grade, eighth-grade, and remedial college-level problems, respectively. I consider this highly successful, especially in light of the nature of the problems that fell outside these two categories.

No classification failures occurred for "traditional" story problems, that is, problems in which students are expected to read the problem, understand the story, select appropriate computational procedures, and produce a numerical response. The problems that could not be categorized according to situation were problems that directly told the student what to do and how to do it. These included explicit directions for the use of a particular formula (e.g., "Use the formula for finding area to compute the following. . ."), problems of Euclidean geometry ("Use the Pythagorean formula to determine the length of C."), or problems involving mathematics vocabulary ("What is the median of the following set of test scores?"). One may argue – reasonably, I think – that these by definition are not really story problems. They are included here because they appeared together with story problems in the word-problem sections of the textbooks. Their inclusion in these sections suggests that, at least to the textbook authors, they were of the same nature as story problems. Many mathematics educators would disagree.

Test problems

A second common arena in which students encounter story problems is the standardized test. The analysis here is based upon the CAP tests given to every third-, sixth-, and eighth-grade student enrolled in California public schools in 1989. Each test had multiple forms and contained many arithmetic story problems. A full description of the tests can be found in the reports issued annually by the California Department of Education (e.g., California Assessment Program, 1986).

The problems of the CAP tests were analyzed in the same manner as were those in the textbooks. Table 3.6 contains a summary of the situations found in the test problems. Each of the CAP tests had a large number of test items: 360 items on the third-grade test, 480 items on the sixth-grade test, and 468 items on the eighth-grade test. Of these, story problems accounted for roughly 30% of the third-grade test items and about 40% of the other two tests.

Most of the story problems at all three levels could be distinguished by the situations depicted in them. In toto, over 80% of the items had unique situation classifications. All traditional items were classifiable by their embedded situations. Items not classifiable on the third-grade test were primarily of two types: items requiring the student to count (e.g., "What comes next?") and

Table 3.6. *Classification of story problems on standardized tests*

Grade		1-S	2-S	Other	Total
Third grade	freq	72	13	14	99
	%	73%	13%	14%	
Sixth grade	freq	109	50	23	182
	%	60%	27%	13%	
Eighth grade	freq	85	64	31	180
	%	47%	36%	17%	

Note: 1-S = problems having one of the five situations; 2-S = problems having two or more of the five situations; other = problems otherwise uncoded, including area and perimeter problems, series, odd/even, orientation, writing numbers in words, and rounding problems.

items requiring the student to translate a number into words or vice versa. At the sixth grade, items not identified by situation were rounding items or items requiring identification of odd/even numbers. At the eighth grade, such items reflected spatial orientation (north/south), geometry (e.g., Pythagorean theorem), rounding, and statistical knowledge (e.g., mode, median).

These three tests have extensive problem-solving components. Not all story problems are presented to the student as problems requiring numerical answers. Sometimes the student is asked to identify relevant or irrelevant information. Sometimes several different representations are given and the student is asked to indicate which best describes the problem. Regardless of the format, virtually all the problems reflect identifiable situations and could be classified in the same way as traditional items.

Summary

These analyses are based on a total of 3,027 story problems from textbooks and standardized tests. In both arenas the same finding was observed: Most problems (2,695) could be classified uniquely according to the situations depicted in them. The remarkable feature of this finding is that although story problems may appear highly diverse because of their surface features, the problems actually involve relatively few situations. Moreover, the studies of texts and tests reveal that the five situations described above are sufficient to categorize problems at very different levels of instruction, ranging from third grade to remedial mathematics at the college or junior college level.

What do we lose by failing to categorize the 332 items classified as "other" in Tables 3.3–3.6? Very little. Most of them are not story problems at all but have been erroneously placed with the story problems in the curricular materials. Instead of requiring the student to use his or her own prior knowledge about situations, they depend upon the student's ability to retrieve specific formulas (e.g., area, perimeter, volume) or to understand the mathematical definitions of specific terms (e.g., median, mode, probability). These terms are always used explicitly in the question directed to the student. It is clear from the wording of such problems that the situations (i.e., the stories) are relatively unimportant. On the other hand, for *all* cases in which the situation was important – because a problem solver must extract the meaning of the problem from the story situation and use that information to carry out necessary computations – the five situations served well.

Theoretical verification

From the above analysis we observe that five situations are sufficient to cover the realm of story problems. And, from the evidence presented earlier, we observe that students do not draw on their understanding of these situations. We may conclude that students have not created appropriate schemas that utilize relevant situation knowledge, that is, schemas that build on previous experiences, that contain relevant abstractions, and that facilitate analogical reasoning. We come now to the crux of the matter: If situation-based schemas develop, what will they look like?

The Change schema

Identification knowledge. It is important to keep in mind that the central function of identification knowledge is pattern recognition.

To recognize with certainty the pattern that characterizes a Change situation, the problem solver should perceive that the problem contains some or all of the three essential elements (i.e., starting amount, amount of change, and ending amount) as well as the passage of time and a central object whose value is shifting. As will be demonstrated by the experiments discussed in part III and the models described in part V, pattern recognition seems to occur as a result of a simultaneous cognitive processing of many features, and no single feature serves to trigger the recognition of a situation. Rather, different configurations of several features present different patterns, and they should all be recognized as Change situations, depending on the specific characteristics that are noticed. For example, a problem might emphasize the passage of time, using highly salient terms such as *before, during,* and *after.* These would probably cause the solver to consider the Change situation to be likely, even though other critical features might be absent or as yet undetected. Alternatively, the problem might minimize the time elements and highlight the action that causes a change. The resulting set of features as noticed by the solver would suggest to him or her that the situation was one of Change. Or the statement of the problem could highlight that the change taking place is permanent, which is another salient characteristic of this situation.

Elaboration knowledge. The elaboration knowledge for the Change situation enables the solver to construct the appropriate mental model of the situation. Here we find not only the general structure of the situation but also descriptions of its components: the details about what constitutes a starting amount and an ending amount, what is allowable as a change, and how all of these accommodate each other. Almost certainly the solver initially needs an example situation to serve as a baseline analogy, an analogy against which he or she can match the current problem components to evaluate the fit of the hypothesized situation as determined through the identification knowledge. The general form of the mental model may come from a specific example or may derive from a generalized description of a Change situation such as the following: X has some amount of something, X gets more of it (or loses some), and now X has a new amount.

Planning knowledge. The planning knowledge involved in a Change situation contains information about how to identify the unknown part(s) of the change, the direction in which the change occurs, and which arithmetic operation to use in obtaining the unknown value. Planning knowledge is frequently very difficult knowledge for individuals to acquire. It depends greatly on having the appropriate mental model of the problem and using that model comfortably.

Any of the three parts of a Change situation may be unknown, and the planning knowledge will be used to identify the correct one and also to determine the operation needed. Consider this very simple example:

> Joe had 6 marbles. Bob gave him 7 more. Then Joe had 13 marbles altogether.

This situation can be formulated as three distinct problems:

1. Joe had some marbles. Bob gave him 7 more. Then Joe had 13 marbles altogether. How many did he start with? [start unknown]
2. Joe had 6 marbles. Bob gave him some more. Then Joe had 13 marbles altogether. How many did Bob give to Joe? [change unknown]
3. Joe had 6 marbles. Bob gave him 7 more. How many did Joe have altogether? [result unknown]

Although the same general mental model applies to each case, the goals formulated for each one are quite different. In Problem 1, the solver must understand that the starting state is unknown, that it is to be augmented in the act of change (here the giving of marbles), and that the final state is known. Thus, the plan of finding the initial state must take into account the knowledge that one must *subtract* the amount of the gift from that which remains. Notice that this directly contradicts the key word of the problem, "altogether," which typically indicates addition. In Problem 2, the model also leads the solver to understand that subtraction is again required. Only for Problem 3 does the key word coincide with the desired operation.

Planning knowledge is especially critical for problems containing multiple situations and/or multiple unknowns. It is by means of this knowledge that the solver determines the priority with which he or she addresses each situation. Thus, for the Change situation, if more than one component of the mental model is unknown, the plans must shift to include a search for another situation (or a repetition of the current one) that will allow determination of one of the missing elements. This may necessitate, of course, a call to one of the other schemas.

Execution knowledge. The planning knowledge is used to determine which steps to take in solving a problem. The execution knowledge follows up on the plan by carrying out those steps. Thus, if the plan involves looking for the unknown, the solver will use his or her execution knowledge to scan the problem and pick out the question(s), tagging the unknown component(s) of the Change situation. As each piece of the plan is completed, the execution knowledge is called on to address subsequent ones. Part of the execution knowledge, of course, is knowledge about how to perform the relevant arithmetic operations associated with the Change schema.

The Group schema

Identification knowledge. The identification knowledge needed to recognize the Group situation centers on understanding the various ways that different things may be combined and renamed and, conversely, the ways whereby something may be meaningfully partitioned and labeled. Given the emphasis on combinations and partitions and the requisite dual labels of things (a label for the combination as well as a label for each partition), it is clear that a large part of the identification knowledge for this situation needs to be semantic. The problem solver who does not have a large

store of knowledge about class inclusion and hierarchical categories will be at a disadvantage.

A lack of action characterizes a Group situation, so an additional constraint will be the absence of any change. The awareness
of this static state may serve either as a corroborative constraint or
as the operative one which generates the initial hypothesis that a
Group situation is present.

Elaboration knowledge. Regardless of whether the problem solver is operating under the sole constraint of absence of change or
under the combination/partition recognition, he or she will need to
instantiate a mental model of a Group situation and to identify
elements of the problem that correspond to the different parts of
the model. The mental model here has at least three distinct parts,
and these have a hierarchical structure. At the top is the component representing the combination of all things pertinent to the
grouping. Below this level are the various partitions that make up
the total. There must be at least two of these, and there may be
many more than two. A further aspect of the mental model is the
conservation of the elements making up the partitions. That is, for
the duration of the situation, they must be unvarying.

Planning knowledge. As in all situation-based schemas, one aspect of the planning knowledge concerns identifying the un-
known(s) in the problem. A second aspect focuses on determining
whether one searches for the combination or for one of the partitions in the grouping. Very often, a Group situation is part of a
complex problem in which values for most or all of the partitions
must themselves be calculated. Typically, these arise from distinct
Vary situations, as in:

> As Christmas gifts for her family, Mary purchased five scarves
> at $15.00 each and three wallets for $20.00 each. How much
> did she pay for these gifts?

The mental model of this Group situation would have all unknowns: the amount of money associated with the combined set of
gifts, the amount associated with the scarves, and the amount

associated with the wallets. Before finding the first of these, one must successfully deal with the two Vary situations. Without adequate planning knowledge, the unwary solver will either be content to combine the amounts of money as specified in the problem (without regard for quantity) or will be misled by the second Group situation present in the problem – the grouping of numbers of items per category in contrast to cost per category – and will simply add 5 + 3.

Execution knowledge. As in the Change schema, the execution knowledge for the Group schema contains information about how to identify unknowns and how to perform the needed arithmetic operations. It also contains the rules that allow the individual to determine the hierarchical relationship among the objects in the problem.

The Compare schema

Identification knowledge. The principal constraint for the Compare situation is the presence of two comparable items. This usually means that there will be two very similar statements having the following form: X has property x and Y has property y. It is necessary that x and y be of the same unit (or be transformable by some operation into comparable units). One may not meaningfully compare dollars and hours, for example.

Like the Group situation, a Compare situation is static and reflects no change. Also like the Group situation, the elements of the problem maintain their identities throughout the situation.

Compare situations are almost certainly the most easily recognized by solvers because of the unique way they are presented: They not only require no computation but also always contain a comparative adverb or adjective.

Elaboration knowledge. The mental model here is faintly reminiscent of a balance scale. If two comparable statements can be found, they need to be weighed one against the other. There are only three possible outcomes: The first will be greater than the second, the second will be greater than the first, or they will be equal in weight. To activate the mental model, the solver must first identify the two things to be compared and then determine the nature of the desired comparison.

The comparison will be in terms of a stated quantifiable relationship, such as greater, smaller, higher, lower, faster, slower. Nonquantifiable relationships are not permissible. Frequently, relations that we might consider nonquantifiable, such as better or worse, may be scaled in the context of the problem in such a way that they can be valued. For instance, in a problem about gymnastics we might see:

> Robin achieved a 5.2 score for the balance beam and Rachel obtained a 5.05. Whose score was better?

Here, the solver needs to have the general knowledge that a higher score is a better score, making the assumptions that the desired goal of the competition is to win, that higher scores win, and that winning is somehow "good." This is not situation knowledge per se but world knowledge. One can imagine other activities in which a lower value is "better," such as a mile race or a game of golf. Thus, an added constraint of the Compare situation is that the individual must search his or her own experience to make a firm identification of the story context as well as of the general situation.

As with the Group situation, a great deal of semantic information is required. The most trivial cases of the Compare situation ask only for greater or smaller; but more-complex ones state the question in other ways, and the solver must understand the adverb or adjective reflecting the desired relationship.

Planning knowledge. Planning knowledge is particularly critical for the Compare situation because the situation most often occurs as the final stage of a multiple situation problem. Thus, the solver should recognize and order the various subgoals that must be satisfied before the comparison can be made. In many instances, the comparison is not directly stated and the solver must make several transformations just to get the problem components into comparable states. Key features of the planning knowledge include how and when to access other schemas in order to facilitate the comparison.

Execution knowledge. The arithmetic knowledge required to carry out the final comparison is rather trivial, consisting of the ability to compare two numbers and determine which has the greater or smaller value. More important is the ability to make transformations that may be needed prior to the comparison.

The Restate schema

Identification knowledge. The basic condition for a Restate situation is that a relationship be expressed between two distinct but analogous things. The things are usually of the same type; we typically find problems about two people, two automobiles, and so on. We rarely see problems relating unlike things (e.g., a person and a tree). On occasion, the two things are parts of the same whole, or a relationship between one part and the whole. A requirement is that each of the things involved in the relationship have a common property that is numerable, such as age, weight, or cost. Frequently, the relationship described will be a true statement only for a short period of time, and the story will emphasize that particular time (e.g., "In five years, Mary will be twice as old as Ann . . . "). Generally, Restate problems express the same relationship twice, so any repetition of the relationship is a strong pointer to this situation.

Sometimes a Restate situation resembles a Compare situation, and it is necessary to determine which one applies. In the Compare situation, the solver is not told which of two things has the greater or smaller value: This determination is the goal of the comparison. In contrast, in the Restate situation, the solver is explicitly informed that one or the other is greater and is asked to determine the size of that difference. Thus, the first asks "which one" and the second asks "how much more."

The essential understanding required for a Restate situation is that it is possible to describe some object in two different ways. Consider the following problem:

Mary is one-third as old as her mother. If her mother is 45 years old, how old is Mary?

There are two ways to look at Mary's age in this problem. First, she must be some number of years old. This is the unknown of the problem. Second, since both her age and her mother's age can be expressed as years, we can look at one as a function of the other. In this case, Mary's age is related to her mother's by the fraction 1/3. Thus, there are two statements about Mary's age and both are simultaneously true.

Elaboration knowledge. There are five basic parts to a Restate situation: the two things, the relationship that binds them, and the numerable properties associated with each one. As with the other schemas, an important part of the elaboration knowledge here is semantic: The solver must recognize and understand the relationship. It is usually given by expressions such as "twice as large as" or "one-third of," but it may also be stated as a percentage or a proportion.

One important function of the elaboration knowledge and its related mental model of the situation is to preserve the order expressed in the relationship from its first manifestation to the second. Consider again the age problem introduced above. The two "things" in this problem are readily identifiable as Mary and her mother. Their associated measurable properties are ages in years. The relationship of interest is that Mary's age is one-third of her mother's age. The importance of the mental model should be evident here. Without an adequate model, the solver might be tempted to apply a formulaic approach that depends on a sequential parsing of the problem, expecting the two statements of the relationship to maintain their order. In fact, as this simple problem illustrates, the order is often disrupted. In this problem, the initial statement is *Mary-related to-mother*. In the final statement, we have *mother-related to-Mary*. The sequential mapping strategy of the problem text yields a solution of the form:

If: Mary's age is 1/3 of Mother's age
Then: 45 years is 1/3 of ??

which, of course, will lead to an incorrect solution. The mental model aids the solver in making the appropriate realignments so that the relationship is accurately expressed in both statements.

A defining characteristic of Restate problems is that one answer to the question posed in the problem is explicitly stated. For the age problem, the question is "How old is Mary?" We already know from the problem statement that she is one-third as old as her mother. But this is not the desired form of response. An individual solving this problem is expected to know from previous experience that the solution will be expressed in years, even though an explicit question about *years* is not stated.

Planning knowledge. It should be evident by now that the four types of schema knowledge are interrelated, and this is clearly seen in the Restate schema. Much of the planning knowledge is interwoven with the elaboration knowledge, especially with the mental model. As with the other schemas, plans for solving the Restate problem depend on which elements of the mental model are known and which are unknown. It is especially important in the Restate situation to set the goal of verifying that the original relationship is maintained. Other planning knowledge involves knowing when and how to make transformations so that the objects to be related are on the same scale. This usually happens in a multi-step problem, and the plans may involve other schemas.

Execution knowledge. Some of the knowledge here, as in other schemas, has to do with finding unknowns, identifying relevant parts of the situation, and applying the operations of arithmetic. All four operations are relevant to the Restate situation. Other pertinent knowledge involves using rational numbers and determining percentages and proportions.

The Vary schema

Identification knowledge. Once again, time plays a key role in the recognition of a situation. In the Vary situation, the primary constraint is that a relationship is expressed that will remain pertinent over time. The relationship binds two very different things: either two distinct categories (e.g., "for every dog there are three bones. . . .") or one thing and a numerable property (e.g., "each apple costs 35 cents. . . ."). The important aspect is that the relationship holds for more than a single instance and is almost infinitely extensible. That is, it is true for every dog, for example, not just a specific one, and it holds not just for one apple but for as many apples as one cares to purchase. Thus, the relationship expressed has a different nature than that of the Restate situation, which demands specificity. Often, the Vary situation has a conditional form, either explicitly stated as "If X, then Y" or implicitly expressed.

An important aspect of many Vary situations is the expression of a per unit value. The notion of a fixed value per unit may be explicitly stated (e.g., 35 miles per gallon) or may be merely implied (travels 180 miles in 3 hours).

A second common characteristic of the Vary situation is the assertion of property values. That is, some object, which may be considered only one of many possible identical objects, is defined as having a particular property, such as cost, weight, length, or height. The key here is recognizing that the object under discussion is prototypic and that characteristics attributed to it apply equally well to other members of its class. Thus, in a problem such as

> I want to buy 10 apples. Each apple costs 35 cents. How much must I spend for the apples?

no single apple is identified. They all have the same property (i.e., cost).

A second formulation of the Vary situation does not rely on properties at all. Rather, it allows a relationship between two quite different things.[6] A combination of unlike objects is, indeed, a hint of the possible presence of the Vary situation. Common to these problems are statements such as "For every 3 girls who played softball there were 4 boys. . . ."

Elaboration knowledge. Three problem elements can be distinguished: the main subject, an object with which it is associated, and the nature of that association. The mental model constructed by the problem solver will have four slots into which this information is placed. Essentially, two pairs of associations compose this mental model. First, there is the basic statement about the subject, the object, and the association holding the two together. Second, there is a similar statement in which the quantity of either the subject or the object has been varied. Unknown is the variation in the other entity that accompanies it.

To employ this mental model, the solver should determine that the problem satisfies three conditions: The subjects of both expressions must be of the same type, the objects of both expressions must be of the same type, and the associations must be the same. Failure of any of these conditions renders the problem unsolvable under the Vary situation. The following examples demonstrate these failures.

The cost of one apple is 35 cents. How much will 5 bananas cost?
The cost of one apple is 35 cents. How much will 15 apples
     weigh?
The cost of one apple is 35 cents. How much will 5 bananas
     weigh?

The first two of these demonstrate the failure to meet one of the conditions; the last one demonstrates multiple failures. The more failures, the more illogical the problem appears to an individual. Note that each part of the last problem is by itself a reasonable statement. It is the conjunction of the two as a single problem, with the unstated implication that the second is a logical extension of the first, that is fallacious.

The problem solver must also bring to this situation some knowledge about per unit value. He or she will realize that every hypothetical instance of the subject as presented in the problem will have an identical object value associated with it. Thus, we have "an apple costs 35 cents" or "the car travels 30 miles on a gallon of gas" as examples. Knowledgeable solvers will understand without being told directly that a second apple will also cost 35 cents and that another gallon of gasoline will enable the car to travel an additional 30 miles. Within a problem, the per unit value remains stable.

Planning knowledge. The planning knowledge for the Vary situation is similar to that for Restate. If the fixed relationship is already known, expressed as the object value associated with a single instance of the subject of the problem, then the plans involve making the necessary computation for different quantities of the subject. If this relationship is not known, it generally must be found, and the plan is to find the value of the object that corresponds to a single instance of the subject. In this case, the solver must determine the per unit value for himself or herself.

Execution knowledge. The execution knowledge most closely associated with the Vary schema is knowledge about multiplication and division, about ratios and proportions, and about rates. As before, it also entails searching for the unknowns.

The practicality check

All of the aforementioned steps are an exercise in futility if the situations hypothesized are not usable by problem solvers. At this point in the analysis, it is infeasible to consider systematic observation of individuals as they develop full schemas, because such development takes an extended period of time and probably requires an entirely new curriculum of study. It is premature to invest time and resources in this new curriculum until the fundamental premise about situation recognition is tested. Such a study of schema development will certainly be necessary at a later time, but the initial question concerns only whether the basic identifications can be made. Thus, at this juncture we ask only whether individuals can acquire and use basic situation knowledge. That is to say, are the situations discriminable by the problem solvers? Can the problem solvers quickly and easily learn to incorporate their own prior knowledge about things such as change or class inclusion into the framework of the five situations? In short, this is the step in which we see whether it is practical to make the situations the core of our desired problem-solving schemas.

Four learning experiments were carried out to determine if individuals could learn to recognize the situations of arithmetic story problems. In each experiment, subjects were first instructed about the characteristics of the five situations and then were asked to perform a classification task similar to the one described previously. The conditions for each experiment were somewhat different and are described separately below. In three of the experiments, the subjects were the same individuals as those who participated in the sorting tasks described earlier. The exception is the group of community college students, who did not participate in a learning experiment. The fourth learning group consisted instead of first-year college students.

Experiment 1: Accelerated sixth-graders

Twenty-five students participated in this study (the 21 original students plus 4 students who were absent from school when the earlier task was carried out). The children's regular classroom teacher provided instruction about the situations. Instruction consisted of five 30-min segments, presented over a period of 2 1/2 weeks. During instruction, the teacher demonstrated the situations by example problems, by illustrated drawings of situations, and by general definition. Students were given the opportunity to create their own problems. Following the fifth and final instructional segment, students were once again asked to sort the original 20 problems (as described previously) into five categories. For this task they were explicitly instructed to sort the problems into groups corresponding to Change, Group, Compare, Vary, and Restate. If they encountered problems they could not classify, they were asked to create a new category called "Other."

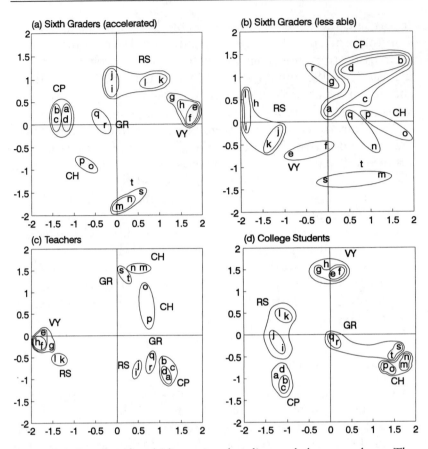

Figure 3.3. Results of multidimensional scaling and cluster analyses: The situational sorting task

Figure 3.3a contains a summary of the results of their categorization. The five categories consistent with the situations are labeled in the figure by **CH** (Change), **GR** (Group), **CP** (Compare), **VY** (Vary), and **RS** (Restate). As can be seen in the figure, the children successfully identified most of the situations, especially those of Compare, Restate, and Vary. Students classified an average of 62% of the problems correctly ($M = 12.36$, $SD = 2.68$). The range of correct classification was 8 to 17. The primary confusions were between some of the Change and Group items.

Experiment 2: Less-able sixth-graders

Participating in this study were the same 21 students described previously plus 1 student who was absent from school for the first task. The teacher of the accelerated class of sixth graders provided instruction for this group of students as well as for her own class. The students received 2 1/2 hours of instruction, spread over a two-week period. Students had the opportunity to study examples and to create their own problems. On the last day of instruction, students were asked to sort the same 20 problems they had sorted earlier. They were requested to sort the problems into the five categories of Change, Group, Compare, Restate, and Vary. They were permitted to put items they could not classify into a separate category called "Other."

Figure 3.3b contains the results of their classification. These students were able to identify rather completely two of the categories, Compare and Restate, and they were partially successful with two others, Change and Vary. They appeared to be confused by the Group situation.[7]

As might be expected, this group of students performed less well than the accelerated group. Their reading skills were not at comparable levels, and their math skills were considerably weaker. Nonetheless, they classified an average of 35% of the items correctly ($M = 7.09$, $SD = 3.383$). The range of correct responses was 3 to 14.

Experiment 3: Elementary and secondary mathematics teachers

The same 30 teachers who participated in the classification task described earlier participated in this study as well. One teacher did not complete the task, so the analyses are based on data from 29 teachers. The sixth-grade instructor who provided instruction in both the experiments for the sixth graders also provided instruction to the teachers. In this case, however, the instruction was given in a single 2-hour session rather than being spaced over a period of several days or weeks. Insofar as was possible, she used the same teaching techniques and the same materials with the teachers that she used with the two sixth-grade classes. The sorting task immediately followed instruction. The teachers were asked to sort the original 20 items into five categories, one for each situation, and to place those they could not identify in a category labeled "Other."

Figure 3.3c displays the results of the teachers' sorts. In general, the groupings are all consistent with the five situations. The items most often misclassified were Restate situations. The teachers grouped correctly an average of 47% of the items ($M = 9.45$, $SD = 4.924$). The range was 0 to 17 correct responses.

The amount of difficulty encountered by the teachers in carrying out this task was somewhat surprising. Indeed, two of them had scores of 0 on the task. This contrasts with the sixth graders' performance. The lowest score in the accelerated class was 8, and the lowest in the slower class was 3. One reason for the lack of cohesion in the teachers' classifications may be the time constraint. They received information about all five situations at one time. It is possible that some of them simply did not understand but would do so if they had more instruction. Another reason may be that they have much more prior knowledge about story problems than did the students. Perhaps they experienced some conflict between certain parts of this prior knowledge and their newly acquired knowledge.

Experiment 4: College students

For this study, 123 college students participated as partial credit fulfillment for an introductory psychology course. As part of a larger experiment, these students individually studied a short workbook that described and provided practice with the five situations. They spent about 30–45 min using the workbook and then classified the 20 problems into five categories corresponding to the situations (plus the category "Other" for those not recognized).

Figure 3.3d illustrates the results of the college students' classification. Notice that all items were clustered in the five categories and that the items are appropriately located according to their defining situation, unlike the other solutions in Figures 3.3a–3.3c, which have some misclassifications, isolates, or unconnected sub-clusters. The average percent of correct identification by the college students was 71% ($M = 14.24$, $SD = 3.25$), and the range of correct responses was 5 to 20.

Summary

These four studies provide evidence that students and teachers can acquire knowledge about situations in a rather short time. All four groups seemed to gain some understanding of the situations. Some methods of instruction were clearly superior to others. In particular, the instruction for the college students was developed after the completion of the other experiments and contained modifications made in response to some of the difficulties that emerged from the three other experiments. It resulted in higher success rates of classification.

Significant in these results is the fact that at least 25% of the members of each experimental group were able to sort items according to situation after a very small amount of instruction, ranging from 1/2 to 2 1/2 hours. One expects the percentage to be even higher with increased instructional time. Thus, although the earlier studies indicated that students did not initially have much knowledge about the five situations, these studies suggest that such knowledge is relatively easy to acquire.

Discussion

Situational knowledge seems far superior to key words as the basis for schema knowledge. Many problems, especially those that arise in the nonschool world, do not have key words. It is typically only the poorly developed textbook exercise that contains problem after problem with identical wording. Moreover, in the English language, words frequently have more than a single meaning. What may be a key word in one problem can have an entirely different meaning in another. Thus, a key-word schema is inherently unreliable. One prefers to encourage students to develop and use their own knowledge about the world.[8] This knowledge resides in schemas.

The complete schema analysis described here yielded three main findings. First, situational knowledge is sufficient to characterize story problems. Only a small set of situations is required to make the distinctions. This is a key point, because it renders feasible the quest for a basis set of schemas. Second, although situational knowledge may seem so obvious to the experienced researcher and educator as to be almost blatant, in fact, almost no students or teachers appear to be using it in problem solving. Virtually none of the more than 100 individuals in the studies here showed any awareness of situational detail. Third, as one would hope, situational knowledge is relatively easy for students to acquire. Even the mathematically naive students were able to understand and learn about the situations.

The fundamental question, of course, is why should they? Of what use is situational knowledge? Its importance lies in the development of strong schemas for problem solving. Situational knowledge has the potential to serve as the anchor for the creation of a basis set of coherent, cohesive schemas that link all of a student's knowledge about story problems. Situational knowledge is the means by which semantic and syntactic information may be compiled in an individual's knowledge network about such problems.

The five situations described here offer a sound underpinning for schema development. The number of distinct situations is sufficiently small even for young children to consider simultaneously. The major characteristics of the situations are distinct so there is little ambiguity. The situations are simple ones that exist in everyday experience, so children and adults have no difficulty understanding them. In short, they are accessible and usable.

Appendix: Other classifications of story problems

There are a number of related classifications of arithmetic story problems, generally conditional to the type of arithmetic operation contained in the problem. The most prominent of these is found in the research on semantic relations. Much of this work has focused on three themes: the conceptual development of children's thinking about addition and subtraction, children's strategies for solving addition and subtraction story problems, and the nature of addition and subtraction problems.

The study of semantic relations had its origins in research on young children's first problem-solving experiences in elementary school, and much of it grew out of studies about how children learn to add and subtract (e.g., Riley et al., 1983; Carpenter & Moser, 1982, 1984). Consequently, the first semantic relations – Change, Combine, and Compare – were derived for problems reflecting only two arithmetic operations, addition and subtraction. They were initially described by Heller and Greeno (1978) and later expanded by Riley et al. (1983) and Riley and Greeno (1988). They correspond roughly to the Change, Group, and Restate situations presented in this chapter.

A similar set of categories was developed by Carpenter and Moser (1982, 1984) in their studies of how children add and subtract. They examined the strategies that children develop for counting and how these strategies are used to solve different kinds of story problems. They defined six categories of problems: Joining, Separating, Part-part-whole, Comparison, Equalizing-add on, and Equalizing-take away (Carpenter & Moser, 1982, pp. 12–13). These categories are to a great extent a function of the arithmetic operation used to solve them and reflect the action that is to be taken. Carpenter and his colleagues are now involved in using the categories of Join, Separate, Combine, and Compare in classroom-based research called CGI, Cognitively Guided Instruction (Carpenter, Fennema, Peterson, Chiang, & Loef, 1988). In this research they contrast the teaching of first-grade teachers who have received instruction about the semantic structure of problems with teachers who have not. Initial results indicate that teachers who received the special training are more aware of their children's problem solving strategies and spend more time in class on problem-solving activities than do other teachers.

Other researchers have focused on additional semantic features of story problems. For example, De Corte and Verschaffel carried out several studies of students' problem representation and solution strategies (De Corte & Verschaffel, 1985, 1987; De Corte et al., 1985). Their work relates directly to that of Riley et al. and Carpenter et al. They began with addition and subtraction problems and showed, for instance, that a strong connection exists between the semantic structure of problems and children's solution strategies for them. They also demonstrated that rewording problems to make the semantic relations more explicit results in more successful problem solving by children.

Nesher and her colleagues have likewise made substantial contributions to research in this area, looking at important semantic characteristics of story problems and tracing children's conceptual development of semantic categories for addition and subtraction problems (Nesher & Katriel, 1977; Nesher, Greeno, & Riley, 1982). More recently she has turned her attention to how children understand multiplication and has focused on children's ability to recognize different kinds of multiplication story problems (Peled & Nesher, 1988).

Most of these studies begin with the assumption that students have a body of knowledge about arithmetic operations that they can then use to understand a story problem. My point, in contrast, is that this is not the memory organization that we desire and that it will not lead to competent problem solvers. The difficulty is that the operational approach assumes that the student already knows which operation to use and then determines whether the current problem matches any of the stored categories that "fit" the selected operation. How does the student know which operation applies? Typically, it is the one most recently under discussion, or it is the one specified by the teacher or text (e.g., "Use addition to solve the following problems."). This approach misses an important point, namely, that the operation itself is frequently difficult for students to identify and must usually be determined from elements in the story situation.

II

Schemas and instruction

It is difficult to say where schema theory should have its greatest instructional impact. Certainly the organization and delivery of instruction are prime candidates. Under schema theory, the student is given the dynamic role of active learner rather than passive recipient. It is up to him or her to take incoming new information and attach it meaningfully to previously stored knowledge. The teacher in this scenario becomes the facilitator, making sure the new information is pertinent, pointing out explicitly its links to other, known information, and providing understandable examples to help the student make the appropriate connections. I have elsewhere likened the teacher in schema-based instruction to a tour guide whose responsibility is to help the student learn to appreciate a new environment by pointing out the major landmarks and telling interesting stories about it (Marshall 1993a). On a tour of a new city, the guide is not bound to a fixed route but may explore any number of different aspects of the environment, stopping longer than usual when the tourists want extra time to experience some feature. The teacher as tour guide should be flexible and sensitive to ways of highlighting specific connections that draw on students' own interests and prior experience.

Adopting schema theory as the basis of instruction almost certainly necessitates a complete restructuring of the curriculum. It also raises questions about the nature of learning. In this part and the next, I address these two issues.

First, I present the theoretical linkages between schema theory and instruction. Chapter 4 contains an extension of schema theory to instructional concerns. Among other things, it addresses how schema theory accommodates some of the major problem-solving approaches prevalent in instructional theory today.

Chapter 5 shows how schema theory can be practically implemented. It gives a detailed description of one example of schema-based instruction, the *Story Problem Solver (SPS)*. SPS is a computer-based system of instruction constructed around schema theory, using the basis set of schemas developed in chapter 3. It provides fundamental instruction enabling students to build schemas. A second computer program, the *Problem Solving Environment (PSE)*, is also described in chapter 5. PSE provides an exploratory environment in which students can practice and utilize their schema knowledge about story problems.

4

Theoretical issues for instruction

Two characteristics of the schema have far-reaching effects on instruction. One is the componential nature of knowledge associated with it, and the other is its network structure. The impact of the four components of schema knowledge is that we may create sequences of instructional material to focus on each of them. The influence of the network structure is that we will tend to make many more explicit connections between topics of instruction than we might otherwise. Schema-based instruction looks very different from instruction based on other principles.

A point to be highlighted is that students will develop schemas about the subject matter whether instruction takes a schema-based approach or not. Learners will search for structure and relationships. Thus, the questions to be asked about schema-based instruction do not center on whether or not students create schemas. They do. The questions focus instead on the nature of the schemas that are developed. We ask whether the instruction itself can promote more cohesive and better structured schemas than would instruction having another foundation. It is here that the basis set of schemas becomes important, because these lay the groundwork for the instructional design.

A key aspect of schema theory, insofar as instruction is concerned, is that schemas organize knowledge stored in memory. Thus, they provide the necessary scaffolding for a domain, and, as such, they will serve as supports for future instruction and learning. It is useful to consider a simplified overview of instruction to see how this works. Essentially, in an instructional situation, students with varying amounts of knowledge of a subject are attempting to expand that knowledge. They may be building on little or much previous knowledge. All will have different prior experiences, and they will be attempting to add new information to their knowledge store. How the students integrate the new knowledge with the old is the critical issue. If it is done well, they will achieve meaningful learning. If it is done badly, they will develop misconceptions or simply not learn at all. It is here that schema-based instruction will have its impact, because it can provide appropriate clues about fundamental connections that must be developed. Students cannot know in advance how best to organize the incoming information of instruction because they cannot yet know all its ramifications. They need help in creating a strong memory organization, preferably an organization that facilitates both the encoding and the retrieval processes.

An objective of this chapter, and indeed of much of this book, is to illustrate the importance of linking instructional practice and assessment to a theoretical approach. Schema theory provides a new conceptual foundation for the organization of instruction and the subsequent assessment of students' learning from it. In this chapter, I discuss some of the theoretical and practical issues involved in using schema-based instruction. In Chapter 5, I describe a functioning instructional system that is schema driven.

Current instructional organization

Learning hierarchies

Much of today's instruction, either explicitly or implicitly, has its organizational roots in learning hierarchies, as put forth many years ago by Robert Gagné (1970). Learning hierarchies have been extraordinarily valuable to us as researchers and teachers because they help us to understand at a very detailed level the many subordinate skills and prerequisites of a task. However, they have less value as models of learning, and they often fail when used as guides for instructional development.

The premise behind the learning hierarchy is that one can analyze a task into its many constituent parts, building a hierarchy of skills and establishing prerequisites for each one. The general form of a learning hierarchy contains several levels, ordered from top to bottom in terms of their prerequisites. To achieve the skill at the topmost level, one must be able to do all the subordinate skills at the level immediately below it. To achieve the skills at the next level down, one must first master its necessary subordinate skills. And so on. One ends up with a tree structure that has the desired skill at the top and as many branches as needed to represent subordinate skills. At the bottom of the hierarchy are those elements for which there are no prerequisites. Instruction aimed at the target skill (the task at the highest level) commences with the elements at the lowest level of the hierarchy, and the skills at each level are addressed in order such that instruction about the prerequisites always precedes instruction about any skill. Eventually, all necessary prerequisites will be satisfied.

It is attractive to imagine that all we have to do to ensure learning in students is to analyze the task we wish to teach, which is a top-down process, and then teach the various pieces of the hierarchy, which is a bottom-up process. Under this model of instruction, we start with the elements in the lowest boxes at the bottom of the hierarchy, provide instruction on all elements at this level, move up a level and do the same thing, and continue until we reach the top of the tree.

Many teachers and textbooks overtly or covertly take this approach. The difficulty with it is that only the creators of the hierarchy have the benefit of seeing the whole structure. For them, it is evident why a specific subskill is needed and where it fits in the general scheme of things. For students introduced to a new subskill without knowing why it is important or how it contributes to a larger pattern of knowledge, the new subskill is just one more unconnected thing to be memorized.

One of the features of the learning hierarchy is that by definition the elements at the bottom of the hierarchy are independent. That is, each may stand alone and does not depend upon the others. If this were not the case, one or more would serve as a prerequisite for another. This independence is a potential problem for learners. Unless great care is taken during instruction to construct the necessary scaffolding of a schema and to highlight necessary connections among these elements, learners may not perceive that these elements will ultimately work together in the full task.

Students who are introduced only to the individual, independent elements at the bottom may not see any relationship at all and cannot build a coherent knowledge structure from these disparate pieces. Bottom-up learning is very difficult, mostly because the learners never know where they are headed. They lack the unifying vision provided by seeing the whole hierarchy. If the target task is a complex skill made up of lesser skills just like it but having fewer components, students may progress with little difficulty. Typically, however, the many different parts of the learning hierarchy do not reflect application of the same procedure, and it becomes difficult for students to perceive a relationship between the prerequisite skills at the bottom of the tree and the target task at the top.

An additional problem with the learning hierarchy approach is that it may emphasize the learning of algorithms at the expense of conceptual knowledge. All too often, the hierarchy consists of things that the learner must "do" rather than things the learner ought to "know." *Knowing* and *doing* are not synonymous in learning, and one does not necessarily imply the other. A learner may develop algorithmic skills without ever understanding the conceptual structures behind them. This lack of understanding usually causes real problems in future learning.

Finally, the structure of the hierarchy itself is at odds with schema theory. The schema is a network of related knowledge, not a branching tree with distinct levels. A great deal more connectivity exists in the schema than in the learning hierarchy, and instruction based on schemas focuses directly on these connections.

Other approaches to instruction

Developing learning hierarchies is but one of several ways that instruction may be carried out. Consider for a moment how one might structure a college course, or, for that matter, a semester of any subject in elementary or high school. Some approaches that I have encountered are as follows:

1. Pick the key topics and work through them, one by one. This approach seems to be very popular with textbook authors, probably because it is the easiest. College texts often have this outline. Unfortunately, one often finds two concepts that have little relation to each other presented back to back. Continuity is lacking.

2. Lay out everything according to some measure of difficulty, then start with the easiest and move to the most difficult. This strategy builds directly on the principles of task analysis that underlie learning hierarchies. The approach has some advantages, but the danger is that the most difficult topics will never get covered because earlier topics take more time than expected. Moreover, it obscures the fact that difficulty is not a unidimensional characteristic. What is difficult for one student may not be difficult for another. This approach is seen quite often in elementary school textbooks.

3. Take one theme and examine all the aspects of the domain with respect to that theme. The thematic approach is an elegant one, but texts having this structure are hard to find. It is used most often in graduate seminars having no text but focused instead on a collection of articles on the same topic.

4. Pick a few topics and let students discover for themselves the important characteristics. This approach, which is a variant of discovery learning, has recently become popular, especially at the elementary school level. The guiding principle behind it is constructivism: Students must construct their own knowledge, and they will do so best if they can explore a domain at their own speed and in directions they prefer. This approach works in some cases but has severe limitations.

Discovery learning or guided exploration is not particularly appropriate for all learning. In particular, it has drawbacks for the acquisition of procedures and rules. Lately, some cognitive scientists and mathematics and science educators – adopting a constructivist viewpoint – have tended to support discovery learning in the classroom to the exclusion of all else. I believe this to be a mistake. It is certainly true that students' understanding seems to be greatest when they have the chance to develop it through their own exploration, experimentation, and action. However, we can help students learn some things by demonstration, and it is to their advantage to be told that there are specific rules that people follow when certain specific outcomes are desired.

The advantage of discovery learning, it seems to me, is the construction and strengthening of connections between different knowledge components. Exploration of a new domain should be more productive if the explorer has sufficient prior knowledge with which to work and from which meaningful new understandings can be derived. Thus, discovery learning seems best suited for strengthening and expanding schemas, not for initial creation of them.

5. Insist that students memorize some pre-selected collection of material. Here, the focus is on having students memorize some explicit set of material. Understanding is not the central objective. An underlying belief seems to be that, if students do memorize a set of facts and skills of a domain, they will automatically connect these pieces of information in a meaningful way. Drill-and-practice instruction in elementary arithmetic is frequently cited as an example of this approach.

Contrary to popular belief, rote memorization may have a role in meaningful learning. Sometimes it is quite useful to use rote memory techniques to learn facts and formulas. Let me give an example: the variance formula from statistics. For many years while teaching statistics, I observed that students were trying to memorize a number of equations that might be used to calculate this statistic, but they were not learning much about what variance means or why it is a useful concept. I mistakenly thought that if students focused on what the formula was trying to do, rather than on memorizing a set of symbols, they would achieve a level of understanding that would allow them to derive the formula for themselves. Thus, they would not need to memorize it. I no longer believe this to be true. The difficulty seems to be that, without having the formula already memorized and operating in memory as a single chunk, the students are overloaded by what they perceive as unrelated elements when they attempt to understand the concept of variance. Rather than replace the memorization, we need to build on it. I now advocate that the students memorize the formula immediately upon its introduction, and I think they probably need to overlearn it, so that its expression comes automatically to them. The formula is an important piece of the elaboration knowledge associated with the conceptual understanding of variance, and it has the advantage of providing a stable visual aid. Alone, it has little value (like any other single piece of elaboration knowledge). Combined with the additional identification, elaboration, planning, and execution knowledge that make up a schema, it provides easy access to a wealth of interrelated knowledge.

The point here is that the memorization is useful as a starting point, not a final objective, of instruction and learning. The danger is that instruction could stop at the point that students demonstrate that they remember the formula. In fact, this point is the real beginning of instruction. The prior memorization allows a deeper discussion to take place because all students will have the common anchor upon which to build a comprehensive schema. Students are cheated if this discussion does not occur. Unless the memorized knowledge is meaningfully related to other knowledge that the student has, it will soon be lost from memory. Both direct instruction and rote memorization have their necessary place in learning and instruction. We must ultimately go beyond them, however, and provide the necessary links that allow meaning to be the basis of memory. This means, of course, that we need to facilitate the development of schemas, and we can best do so with schema-based instruction.

Schema-based instruction

The goal of schema-based instruction is the creation and expansion of students' schemas for the domain in which instruction occurs. To implement this approach, one must first identify the major ideas of a field and the circumstances in which these ideas are manifested, and then one can construct a curriculum that concentrates on learning to recognize these ideas (situations), on developing sound mental models about how they function, on formulating ways to use the ideas creatively, and on developing the skills and procedures that are requisite to the field. Notice that many of the other approaches mentioned in the last section do some of these but stop short of achieving all of them.

It is useful to consider how schema-based instruction differs from other approaches. One important difference is that schema-based instruction de-emphasizes the quantity of factual bits of information that the student acquires. More is not always better. Factual detail is important, but it is incidental in the development of schema knowledge. It will accrue steadily as part of identification and elaboration knowledge, but it is never the central focus of instruction and learning. The focus is on integrating those facts that are essential rather than on acquiring more and more facts.

A second distinction that sets schema-based instruction apart from other approaches is that schema-based instruction emphasizes doing something with the domain knowledge. The objective is to cultivate learners who will be active problem solvers in the field – not to produce students who have a large store of passive or "inert" knowledge. Successful learning from instruction will not be measured by recalling a wealth of knowledge but rather by demonstrating the ability to integrate and apply it.

A third difference between schema-based instruction and many other approaches is that in schema-based instruction, one wants to introduce the domain to students in a top-down rather than a bottom-up way. It is essential to give them the big picture of the domain so that they can begin to organize their knowledge about it in meaningful chunks.

Finally, schema-based instruction differs from other instruction in that it targets explicitly the development of links that are central to the basis set of schemas. This aspect of instruction is frequently taken for granted. Schema-based instruction will stress repeatedly how and why different elements of the domain are related.

Imagine what instruction looks like under schema theory. First, it is crucial that students get some overall notion of what is in the domain so that they can develop an ability to distinguish the main situations that occur within it. This requires the teacher to introduce the fundamental situations, ideas, and events and their distinguishing characteristics, not one at a time, as in the usual sequence of concepts, but more or less simultaneously. There should not be a great many, and students can understand from the start what is important in the domain. The teacher will not give too many details at this point; he or she will explain only how the central issues can be distinguished from one another. The teacher needs to ascertain that the students understand these basic distinctions before going into any elaborations. The goal here is to familiarize the students with the core units of the discipline (i.e., the basic situations), get them comfortable with the descriptors and identifying characteristics, and allow them to feel confident that they can make the basic discriminations. This part of instruction, of course, allows students to acquire the necessary identification knowledge for creating a set of schemas about the situations. It is relatively brief and should take very little time.

The next part of instruction focuses on elaboration knowledge. Probably at this point it will be necessary to work on one situation at a time, exploring it in depth. It is crucial to have good examples that will serve as the foundation of elaboration knowledge. My research suggests that students first acquire knowledge from examples and then from abstract definitions, and the initial examples selected for introducing a situation may be the most salient and the most remembered by the students.[1] The message here is: Choose examples wisely or they may return to haunt you.

It is probably most efficacious to begin instruction about planning as soon as possible. This usually means overlapping to some extent with the elaboration knowledge instruction. Initially, students will be able to develop only the simplest plans, but they need to understand the importance of planning and to have some model of how to do it. We, as instructors, often fail to show our students how to construct plans.

The two best examples I know that illustrate planning are from mathematics and chemistry. A colleague who is a mathematician once mentioned to me that for his theorem-proving class, he does not look *at all* at the theorems to be proved before going to class. In fact, he goes out of his way to avoid doing so. The purpose is to model for students as best he can the way that mathematicians go about proving a theorem, and that includes showing the goofs, the wrong turns, the starting overs. Had he worked out the proofs ahead of time, the students would indeed have seen more elegant proofs but would have missed the important planning and executing steps that he demonstrates for them.

The second example involves a course in chemistry. The professor in this case invites her students to challenge her by finding problems outside class. The students bring the problems to class, and she solves them with no advance preparation. Sometimes she is wrong, sometimes she makes mistakes and has to backtrack, and sometimes she solves the problems easily. The point is that her students learn that problem solving is not a 10-sec affair, that one utilizes all of one's schema knowledge, that one makes plans about how to solve the problem, and that one carries out the plan.

A word of warning should be interjected here. An instructor has to be careful in using the approach taken by the mathematician and the chemist. It demands a great deal of self-confidence and very good communication with the class. When this approach goes wrong, the consequences are disastrous both for teacher and for students. If students are uneasy about the course and have not developed a positive rapport with the instructor, they may well decide that this instructor is just as lost as they are and lose interest altogether. Students are conditioned to expect that instructors are experts who make no mistakes. Sometimes the realization that there are problems the instructors cannot solve causes the students to turn away from the field. Nevertheless, it is well worth developing the skills needed to carry out this approach to teaching because the method is so powerful in helping students develop effective planning knowledge.

Planning knowledge leads naturally to execution knowledge. One does not end problem solving with a plan for solution; one carries out the plan. Presumably, students already have acquired at least some of the procedures that will be used with the schemas under instruction. It is probable that new ones will need to be developed as well or old ones modified for application in the new domain. These rules or procedures will be created in the context of the schemas, so that their execution becomes an integral part of schema knowledge.

The outcome of schema-based instruction is that students will have the opportunity to develop all the knowledge components for the core schemas, because the components have all been explicitly addressed. The components will be linked together as cohesive bodies of organized knowledge, allowing the students easy access to and retrieval from their store of knowledge. Moreover, the knowledge structures that result from schema-based learning will remain accessible and useful as students continue to learn.

Other approaches to problem solving

Although the application of schema theory to instructional design and practice pertains to almost all learning situations, the one that is of most interest here is that of problem solving, because it is in this arena that the current evaluation of schema-based instruction takes place. There have been several well-received efforts to teach methods of problem solving; most notable are those of George Polya and Alan Schoenfeld, two mathematicians concerned with improving students' abilities to solve problems. Although neither Polya nor Schoenfeld explicitly embraced schema theory (and indeed neither gave much attention to the issues prevailing in psychological studies of cognition such as memory organization) nevertheless both intuitively advocated an approach to problem solving that is extraordinarily consistent with schema-based problem solving.[2]

Polya's view of instruction

In 1945, the eminent mathematician George Polya expressed his ideas about teaching problem solving in a very readable book entitled *How to Solve It*. Polya approached the teaching and learning of problem solving from the perspective of a mathematician. It is interesting that a number of his suggestions directly correspond to the underlying principles of schema theory. Interspersed in *How to Solve It* are a number of pithy statements that could easily have been written with schema-based instruction in mind. For example (Polya 1945/1957):

"Too many or too minute particulars are a burden on the mind .
. . . Therefore, let us first of all understand the problem as a
whole" (p. 76). (identification knowledge)
"Seek contacts with your formerly acquired knowledge" (p. 34).
(elaboration knowledge)
"To conceive a plan and to carry it through are two different
things" (p. 68). (planning versus execution knowledge)

Problem solving for Polya extends well beyond mere formulations of mathematical problems. In his view, much of human cognition is concerned with solving problems, and he goes so far as to assert that "solving problems is a fundamental human activity" (p. 221). He recognizes that there will be great variability in individuals' abilities to solve problems, and he talks about differences between expert and novice problem solvers. One important difference is that the expert may not have more information available than does the novice, the expert simply uses it better. From the schema perspective, we interpret this as saying that novice and expert may both have the same number of pieces of information stored in memory but the expert's knowledge is more efficiently organized. Hence, the expert may have a well-developed schema, whereas the novice may have only a collection of loosely related bits of knowledge.

As most mathematics educators know, Polya advocates four basic steps: understand the problem, devise a plan, carry out the plan, and reflect on the solution (pp. 5–6). Much of what Polya terms "understanding the problem" comes from the problem solver's use of identification and elaboration knowledge. For instance, he recommends that to begin the problem solving, the solver should be concerned with a broad image of the entire problem and not with particular details. The advantage of this is that it will "stimulate your memory and prepare for the recollection of relevant points" (p. 33). Clearly, part of problem understanding is recognition of what's going on, and this recognition depends on using prior knowledge stored in memory. Part of that prior knowledge will be derived from similar problems already encountered. Polya stresses the importance of analogical reasoning, asking repeatedly for the solver to search for related or analogous problems in his or her attempt to understand the problem.

The technique that Polya advocates is to teach the problem solver to ask a series of questions as he or she goes about solving a problem. Many, if not all, of these questions have to do with accessing relevant parts of schema knowledge. For example, questions focusing on understanding the problem as a whole point to identification knowledge, questions dealing with how all the information in the problem is to be used tap elaboration knowledge, questions about decomposition of a problem concern planning knowledge, and questions about how to implement strategies that worked on similar problems involve execution knowledge. The goal of this question-based instruction is to aid the student in developing what Polya calls mental habits and what I call schemas.

Polya argues that prior knowledge, which he calls knowledge of the subject matter, is essential for understanding the problem. He also stresses that this is initially dormant or inert knowledge and must be mobilized.[3] For *mobilization*, we can read *activation*. Further, he goes on to point out that collecting isolated pieces of information will not suffice; the solver must have a well-connected set of knowledge. This he terms organization. For *organization*, we can read *connected network of knowledge*. And thus, we are back at the basic structure of a schema: developed from prior knowledge, linked through a network structure, capable of receiving and transmitting activation so that the network as a whole is available for processing.

Polya illustrates his theory of problem solving with numerous examples. His approach borders on example-based learning; he clearly believes that individuals learn from examples and use examples to make sense of new problems. He presents many hypothetical dialogues between teacher and student, using these conversations to highlight the important features of his approach. These exchanges provide information about specific patterns, mental models, and plans. Thus, to a great extent, he is practicing schema-based instruction.

Schoenfeld's instruction on heuristics

Building explicitly on Polya's theory, Schoenfeld (1985) outlined his own attempts to implement it in the college classroom. He points out three major obstacles to success: the need for more detail about the heuristic strategies to be used, the students' lack of rigorous training in how to use the strategies, and the students' lack of sufficient prior knowledge (1985, p. 47). All of these are equally critical under the schema theoretic approach.

As one would expect, problem-solving heuristics are most evident in the planning component of schema knowledge. Schoenfeld describes a number of different heuristics that he has used with varying degrees of success in his research and in his classroom. For example, one strategy (which is also advocated by Polya) is: If you cannot solve the given problem, establish subgoals. Having attained them, build upon them to solve the original problem (Schoenfeld, 1985, p. 81). The heart of his instructional method is to demonstrate to students how a strategy such as this can be applied to a number of different problems. He stresses understanding of the problem and selection of appropriate heuristics based on that understanding. Thus, he assists students in making the explicit linkages between planning, elaboration, and identification knowledge.

An important aspect of Schoenfeld's approach is his demand that strategies be well articulated. If students are to acquire them, the instructor must present them in sufficient detail to allow discrimination and characterization. Again, I would argue that schema theory is being invoked. What Schoenfeld calls for is the creation of schemas based on the situations or events of using each heuristic.

One of the most interesting aspects of Schoenfeld's research is his focus on mathematical beliefs and their role in problem solving. He argues that students have beliefs that lie between the purely affective and the purely cognitive domains of human behavior. Included in a student's belief system are misconceptions, preconceptions, and intuitions about events in the world. These may be at odds with new, incoming instruction and may create dissonance for the student. One can easily imagine that such beliefs are part of a student's prior knowledge and may become, for better or worse, part of his or her schema knowledge. Schoenfeld advocates, and I agree, that we need to better understand these beliefs and to take them into account in our instruction.

Three principles emerge from Schoenfeld's research about teaching heuristics: focus on a small number of strategies, explicate them fully, and provide extended practice in applying them. These are equally important principles under the schema theoretic approach.

Summary

One of the most appealing aspects of schema-based instruction is that it has its roots in longstanding psychological and philosophical theory. It offers us the opportunity to base instruction on the same cognitive framework within which we view the phenomena of learning and remembering. It provides theoretical justification for the abundant use of examples and analogies, of visual representations, of illustrations, and of explicit plans. Under schema theory, we become concerned not just with the content of learning that results from instruction but also with the structure of that learning.

5

The Story Problem Solver and The Problem Solving Environment
Two examples of schema-based instruction

The Story Problem Solver (SPS) is a computer-implemented program of instruction about arithmetic story problems.[1] My research group and I developed SPS as an explicit instructional test of schema theory.[2] Its companion, the Problem Solving Environment (PSE), is also a computer-based system, one that provides no additional instruction but that serves instead as a practice arena in which we can evaluate students' acquisition of schema knowledge. Both SPS and PSE are written in Lisp and run on Xerox 1186 computer workstations equipped with 19-inch display monitors and three-button optical mice. In this chapter, I first describe SPS and its instructional objectives and then explain the contributions of PSE.

The primary instructional objective for SPS is to assist students in creating schemas that are based on the five situations described in detail in chapter 3: Change, Group, Compare, Restate, and Vary. My purpose in developing SPS was to construct a series of lessons that reflected the basic knowledge components of a set of schemas, that allowed direct assessment of those components, and that resulted in students' creation of the specified schemas.

SPS consists of a set of 28 distinct lessons, with one or more specific exercises following each lesson. The lessons are designed to last from a few minutes to a full half hour, with the actual length of interaction dependent to some extent on the individual student's level of skill and attention. The system is fully operational and has been used by almost 150 students. Approximately

50 individuals have completed the entire 8-hour course of instruction, either as part of a remedial mathematics course or while participating in the baseline experiment, and the remaining 95–100 students have used abridged versions during other experimental studies (all to be described in part III).

Instructional objectives

SPS is an experimental system designed to provide instruction through a series of diverse lessons. At the end of instruction, the learner should be able to

- recognize the five situations when they occur in simple or complex problems;
- understand the relationships expressed in story problems;
- connect the stories in the problems to his or her own knowledge;
- use situational knowledge to identify the essential parts of any story, specifying correctly those that are known or unknown;
- formulate a reasonable strategy for solving the problem;
- use his or her understanding of the situation to select appropriate arithmetic operations.

The schema theory behind the instruction is invisible to the student interacting with SPS. At no time does SPS cite schema formation or use; in fact, the word *schema* never occurs at all. Instead, the instruction focuses on situations as vignettes of daily life and emphasizes the need for the solver to use his or her own understanding of them to solve problems.

The intended user

SPS was designed for use by young adults under the assumption that this population shares a body of common knowledge and interests. The subject matter of examples and problems reflects this assumption. Much of the instruction about the situations is direct. Because the targeted population is adult, it is possible to present extended verbal instruction that might tax the attention and working memory constraints of other populations, such as young children.

Users of SPS are presumed to have had a great deal of previous experience with arithmetic story problems and the computations required for their solution. Consequently, almost no attention is given by SPS to explanation of the arithmetic operations themselves. Extensive pretests with members of this population confirmed that most college students have mastered the basic skills of adding, subtracting, multiplying, and dividing and that problem-solving difficulties in this population cannot be attributed to students' inability to perform these operations.

For the most part, SPS users have been community college or university students with poor problem-solving skills, as evidenced by tests containing routine story problems. SPS has served as the basis for a remedial course taken for credit (in one community college) and has been the focal point of several learning experiments in the research laboratory.

System summary

SPS instruction begins with simple stories and problems containing a single situation and moves to complex problems having multiple situations. Along the way, students gain experience in learning to recognize the situations, to identify their principal components, to locate the unknown(s), and to plan the order in which multiple unknowns will be addressed. A description of the lessons in SPS follows, focusing on the schema knowledge they address.

Identification knowledge

Schema knowledge. The first lesson in SPS focuses almost exclusively on identification knowledge. Its purpose is to establish the boundaries of the domain. The student is expected to learn that there are five basic situations, and he or she should acquire some knowledge about the essential nature of each one. At this point, the student is not expected to develop sufficient knowledge to understand all the subtleties associated with each of them.

Instruction. The first lesson introduces the five situations within a common context. We have developed two story lines: One is a vacation in Hawaii and the other is a carnival. Both contexts have worked well with our student population. The purpose in showing all five situations under a common theme is to discourage students from relying on surface features of the stories and to encourage them to concentrate instead on the relationships expressed in each situation.

Each of the five situations is shown within the overall story context. They are introduced as quickly as possible, and salient features are highlighted. For each one, SPS presents a very small vignette and a simple description. A single screenful of material is given for each situation. The screen display contains a bitmap drawing to illustrate the story and two or three paragraphs of text. The first paragraph is the story itself and the remaining ones describe the situation generally.

The situations are not yet presented as problems. Instead, SPS uses complete stories to illustrate the situations. We discovered early in the development of the system that, in the presence of an unknown, students were simply unable to refrain from doing what they have always been asked to do, namely, to compute a value. We were not able to capture their attention fully, because they believed they already understood the task. To force them to concentrate on the situational information, we merely removed the unknowns from the problems and presented complete stories. This was quite effective.

After all the situations have been introduced, SPS proceeds to give more detail to each one. Once again, it displays each of the original vignettes, this time expanding its discussion of the example and giving a more detailed general description. The emphasis here is on understanding the story. Students are shown how they can look for clues to a situation by studying the relationships among the things in the story.

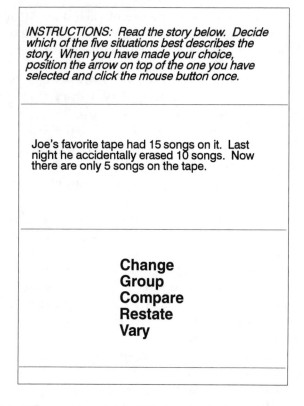

INSTRUCTIONS: *Read the story below. Decide which of the five situations best describes the story. When you have made your choice, position the arrow on top of the one you have selected and click the mouse button once.*

Joe's favorite tape had 15 songs on it. Last night he accidentally erased 10 songs. Now there are only 5 songs on the tape.

Change
Group
Compare
Restate
Vary

Figure 5.1. The initial task of SPS, in which the student is asked to choose the relevant situation name from the menu of names

Exercises. The initial lesson concludes with two exercises. The first one presents a series of simple stories and requests the student to identify the situation expressed in each one by selecting one of the situation names from a menu (see Figure 5.1). The basic form of this exercise is used often in SPS. It consists of a three-part window. The top portion is reserved for SPS instructions or comments to the student. For instance, feedback about the student's response appears here. The middle portion contains the current item to which the student will respond, and the lowermost portion is the area in which the student's response will occur. In this case, the bottom part of the window contains a menu, and the student response is a menu selection.

The items used in this exercise may be randomly selected by SPS from a large pool of stories or they may be a fixed selection, chosen by the instructor or experimenter.[3] We have used both approaches. The number of items presented to students in this exercise has varied in our experiments from 10 to 20.

A second exercise follows a different format (see Figure 5.2). This exercise serves both as an introductory exercise at the end of the first lesson and also as an end-of-session quiz for subsequent instructional sessions. In it, the student is shown five stories and the five situation names. The object is to match the name to the story. For the initial lesson, SPS provides immediate feedback. No feedback is given when this exercise occurs as an end-of-session quiz. Notice that all of the stories in this exercise share a common context. Once again, the common theme reinforces the point that it is the relationships, not the surface features of a story, that should be heeded.

Elaboration knowledge

Schema knowledge. Most of the second phase of instruction focuses on elaboration knowledge and attempts to tie it to the newly learned identification knowledge. There are important verbal and visual details to be learned, and it is imperative at this point that students acquire both of these aspects of elaboration knowledge.

Instruction. Beginning with the second lesson, SPS launches into systematic instruction about the required elements for each situation. One of the most important features of SPS is its use of special diagrams to illustrate the situations. The five diagrams are illustrated in Figure 5.3. Each part of each diagram represents an important and identifiable part of its situation.

Two lessons are devoted to each situation. The first demonstrates how a complete story can be mapped into the appropriate

INSTRUCTIONS: *Read each of the following stories and decide which situation is described. For each one, move the arrow over the name of the selected situation and click the mouse button. Then move the arrow into the box next to the story. Click the button again to drop the situation name in the box. If you make a mistake and want to change your answers, just go back and select another name and place it in the box.*

	Change	Group	Compare	Restate	Vary

Jeannie paid $35.00 for a business law text and a management text. If the management text costs $12.00, the business law text is more expensive. It costs $23.00.

Jim spent $35.00 on text books this semester. Gary had to spend twice as much as Jim did. Gary spent $70.00 on text books this semester.

Tom had to buy twelve books for his classes this semester, but he dropped one of the classes, so he returned three of the books. Now he only has nine books for his classes.

Sam bought one notebook for every three text books that he purchased. If he bought four notebooks, Sam must have purchased twelve text books.

Stephanie bought three English books, two biology books, two history books, and one political science book. Stephanie bought eight text books.

OKAY

Figure 5.2. The second task of SPS, also used subsequently as a quiz for students, in which students are asked to match one situation with one story

diagram, and the second shows how the diagram is used when an unknown has been introduced into the story.

SPS begins its discussion of elaboration knowledge with the Change situation. Instruction first centers on the three necessary components of a change (i.e., the starting amount, the amount of change, and the result). The lesson begins with two new example stories. For each example, an analogy is drawn between the three

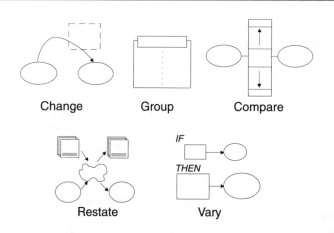

Figure 5.3. The situation diagrams used in SPS

principal elements of the Change situation and the corresponding details of the example. The Change diagram is introduced (see Figure 5.3) as a vehicle for understanding and representing the analogy.

SPS provides a broad description for each part of the diagram, so that the student will perceive that (1) the oval on the left indicates the starting amount, (2) the arrow from the leftmost oval to the box suggests the passage of time, (3) the box contains the amount by which the original amount will be altered, (4) the arrow coming out of the box and pointing to the rightmost oval again suggests the passage of time, and (5) the oval on the right contains the result of the change. SPS demonstrates for the students first how complete stories can be mapped onto the diagram and subsequently how problems can be.

Instruction about problems focuses on how one's understanding of a story shifts according to which part of it is unknown. SPS begins with an incomplete story in which the end result of the change is unknown. It describes how this problem is mapped and talks briefly about how it can be solved. SPS then takes the underlying story of the problem and changes the location of the unknown, so that the end result is given but the amount of change is unknown. This new problem is also mapped, and SPS discusses the difference between the two problems. Finally, the story is presented with the starting amount unknown. This problem is mapped, and the differences among the three Change problems are discussed.

The remaining four situations – Group, Compare, Restate, and Vary – are treated similarly in SPS, with each of them being the focus of two lessons. At appropriate times, two comparison lessons are interjected in the sequence of instruction. They serve to emphasize differences between pairs of situations. The first comparison lesson follows immediately upon completion of the Group situation, and it contrasts the Change situation with the Group situation. The second comparison lesson follows the lessons about Compare and Restate, and it contrasts these two situations.

Exercises. A mapping exercise follows every lesson in this set. In each exercise, the student is asked to map two items into the appropriate diagram (see Figure 5.4).

Notice that these exercises have the three-part window design described earlier, with the top portion reserved for instructions or feedback, the middle containing the current story or problem, and the lowermost reserved for student response. For the mapping exercises, the lower portion of the window contains a diagram. To make a response, the student selects a part of the story or problem text and places it in the diagram. (Exact technical details of response and feedback are described later in this chapter.)

For the special lessons in which two situations are contrasted, the accompanying exercises have two parts. The student first selects the appropriate visual representation, choosing one of two reduced versions of the relevant diagrams from an icon menu, and then attempts to map the story or problem into a larger and expanded version of the selected diagram, as before.[4] These exercises combine elements of both types of exercises used in SPS. First, there is a menu selection similar to that described in the first lesson, except that in this instance the menu options are figures instead of situation names. Second, there is a mapping task requiring the student to copy relevant parts of the text into the appropri-

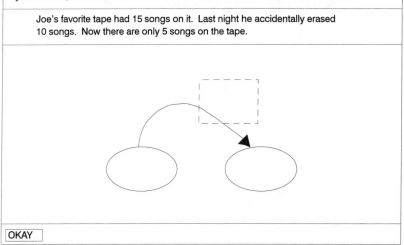

INSTRUCTIONS: Read the problem below. Identify the parts of the problem that belong in the diagram. Move the arrow over each part. Click and release the mouse button. Drag the dotted rectangle into the diagram and click the mouse button again when you have positioned the rectangle correctly in the diagram. If you make a mistake, return to the problem and repeat the process. When you are satisfied with your answer, move the arrow into the OKAY box below and click the mouse button.

Joe's favorite tape had 15 songs on it. Last night he accidentally erased 10 songs. Now there are only 5 songs on the tape.

OKAY

Figure 5.4. The mapping task of SPS, in which the student is asked to map elements of the problem into the diagram

ate parts of the diagram. A fuller version of this exercise, which concludes all mapping instruction, allows students to select from all five diagrams, as in Figure 5.5.

The final exercise in this block of instruction presents 10 items in random order: 5 stories and 5 problems. The appropriate diagram accompanies each item, and the student is requested to map the item components onto the diagram.

Planning knowledge

Schema knowledge. The instruction in this set of lessons assists the student in developing essential planning knowledge. Given the presence of more than one situation in a single problem, the student must acquire the necessary knowledge for selecting which one

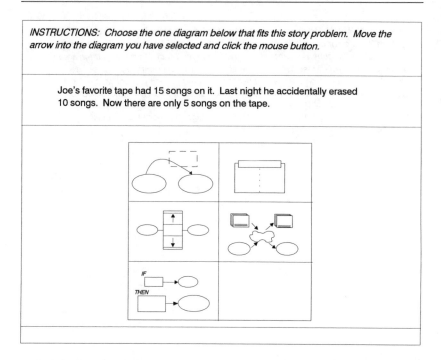

INSTRUCTIONS: *Choose the one diagram below that fits this story problem. Move the arrow into the diagram you have selected and click the mouse button.*

Joe's favorite tape had 15 songs on it. Last night he accidentally erased 10 songs. Now there are only 5 songs on the tape.

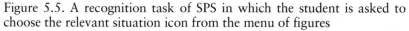

Figure 5.5. A recognition task of SPS in which the student is asked to choose the relevant situation icon from the menu of figures

to examine first and for understanding how two or more situations are related within the story.

If the student is ever to be successful in solving complex problems, he or she must acquire the skills needed to formulate a plan of action. SPS's objectives in the planning lessons are to aid the student in identifying the situations and determining their order of importance for solution and to assist in formulating the goals that will drive the application of arithmetic operations. An ultimate goal is for the student to establish the habit of taking a broad view of problems, of making plans that will reach from the initial conceptual steps through to the final computational procedures.

Instruction. After the elaboration knowledge instruction is complete, SPS instruction begins to focus on complex problems, that is, those composed of two or more distinct situations. These are introduced to the student as *combination problems,* and very specific instruction is given about the need to identify the multiple situations that compose them. Much of the instruction centers on showing students how the situations fit together, and SPS especially stresses how one value in the problem, whether known or unknown, will have a role in two different situations. It illustrates this point by first presenting a combination story that contains both a Change situation and a Group situation and then illustrating four other combinations of situations.

SPS points out that there is a main situation expressed in any problem or story and one or more secondary ones. Figure 5.6 illustrates the instruction for one of the combination stories. This particular display has been preceded first by a display screen containing only the story and the way part of it maps into the Vary diagram and second by a screen displaying the story and its mapping into the Restate diagram. The two diagrams are then shown together, as in Figure 5.6, and SPS emphasizes that one of the values from the first (or primary) situation will of necessity be part of the second situation. This is demonstrated graphically by drawing both diagrams and linking the parts that contain the same value with a large boldface arrow.

SPS spends quite a bit of time on the introduction of combination stories and problems. The initial example alone fills six screenfuls of display. Students are unfamiliar with looking at problems as combinations of multiple simple situations, and this explicit instruction is needed if they are to acquire appropriate schema knowledge.

Part of the instruction about combination problems has to do with the way multiple situations fit together in stories, and part of it describes multiple situations when there is an unknown in a problem. After the students have become familiar with the idea that problems are composed of different situations, SPS moves on to instruction that deals directly with making plans for solving the combination problems.

Instruction at this point continues with an explicit discussion about top-down planning and bottom-up execution. SPS bases its

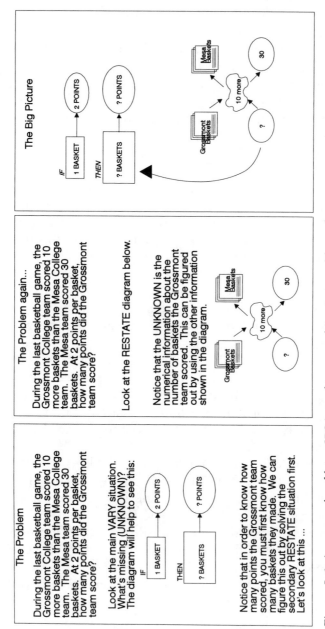

Figure 5.6. An example of how SPS introduces combination problems

discussion on a real-world example, in this case admission to medical school, and then displays a flow diagram that works backward from the goal to the specific subgoals that must be achieved. This diagram represents the plan, and everything flows downward from the ultimate goal. Once the plan is formed, one executes it by starting at the lowermost stages and working back upward. SPS shows a second figure, quite similar to the first, in which the arrows now point up from the lower subgoals to the topmost goal. The point of this instruction is to get the students accustomed to thinking of a visual representation of a complex event. SPS moves immediately to a combination problem to show how the student can develop a visual plan.

Figure 5.7 shows the screen display of a problem and its plan. The instruction at this point focuses on how to identify the major goal of the problem in terms of the situations and shows the student how the situations can be ordered so that the ones that are immediately solvable can be used to find some of the unknowns in other situations. Combination problems almost always have at least two unknowns, and typically they both occur in the primary situation expressed in the problem. It is up to the student to recognize additional situations that are present and that will contribute to the solution of one or more of the primary situation unknowns, as shown in Figure 5.7. SPS walks the student through the plan presented in this figure and goes through the problem-solving steps needed to reach a solution. It then does the same thing with a much more complex problem involving four distinct situations, one Group, one Restate, and two Varys.

Exercises. The planning exercises are of three types. The first gives the student the opportunity to practice recognizing which situations are primary and which are secondary in combination problems. The format of this exercise is similar to that shown in Figure 5.1. The problem is presented and the student makes a menu selection for the primary situation. Next, the student makes a second menu selection for the secondary problem. Thus, the student makes two responses to each item.

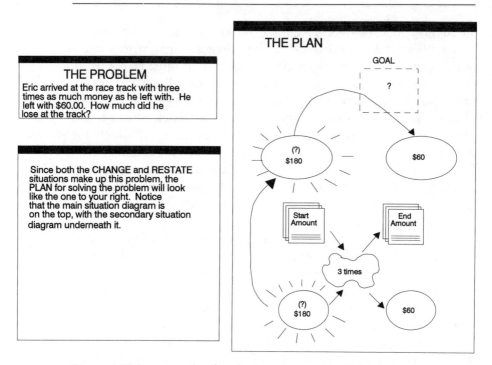

Figure 5.7. An example of a plan as presented in SPS instruction

A second planning exercise involves use of the diagrams. SPS presents a combination problem with the appropriate diagram for the primary situation. The student is asked to identify which parts of the diagram can be filled from the problem information. An example of this exercise is given in Figure 5.8. This exercise resembles the usual mapping ones but has an additional window containing a horizontal menu of three items: *Given, Partial Answer,* and *Final Answer.* The student places *Given* in any part of the diagram whose value is stated directly in the problem. The student places *Partial Answer* in any part of the diagram whose value is at present unknown but is immediately findable from another situation. And the student places *Final Answer* in that one part of the diagram corresponding to the final and as yet unknown solution to the entire problem. In any problem, there may be more than

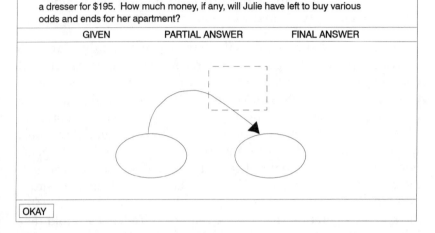

Instructions: *Read the problem below and study the diagram. For each part of the diagram, decide whether the necessary information is already GIVEN in the problem, whether you can find it by first getting a PARTIAL ANSWER, or whether you can find it as the FINAL answer to the problem. Fill each part of the diagram with one of the three choices. Click in the OKAY box when you have filled the diagram.*

Julie had a budget of $1200 to furnish her new apartment. She found a five-piece living room set on sale for $625. She also found a queen-sized bed for $350 and a dresser for $195. How much money, if any, will Julie have left to buy various odds and ends for her apartment?

GIVEN   PARTIAL ANSWER   FINAL ANSWER

OKAY

Figure 5.8. One of the planning tasks of SPS in which students are asked to identify which parts of the situation are already known and which correspond to overall and secondary unknowns

one *Given* or *Partial Answer* in a diagram, but there will always be a single *Final Answer* response.

The third planning exercise is a variation of the second one. Here the student is asked to identify only the location of the final and overall unknown by placing the word *Unknown* in the appropriate part of the given diagram.

Both of these last two exercises represent an attempt to have the student step back from the immediate details of the problem and reflect on the more general framework of their problem solving. The objective here is to encourage the students to include some techniques for analyzing complex problems in their repertoire of planning knowledge.

Execution knowledge

Schema knowledge. As I have elsewhere noted, we were not very concerned with students' acquisition of execution knowledge with respect to computational skills, chiefly because students already have very well developed algorithms for the arithmetic operations. We opted instead to focus our attention on developing students' understanding of when and why to select the different operations.

Instruction. SPS suggests directly to the student that there are two critical steps in solving problems: recognizing the situation and choosing the appropriate operation to solve the problem. In its final five lessons, SPS focuses on the latter step. Using a simple problem, SPS illustrates how important it is to determine correctly both which situation is present and where the unknown falls within it. It demonstrates for the student how the choice of operation is influenced by both of these factors. SPS first goes through the three Change problems that may be created from one situation, and it points out that the location of the unknown dictates the specific operation that will be required. Students are told that it is not sufficient to understand only that the change results in an increase (which to them may suggest addition) because the solution may require subtraction, depending on the location of the unknown.[5]

SPS discusses each of the five situations in turn. The set of lessons concludes with a summary of the key points about each one, an example story, and the set of permissible problems that can be derived from the story.

Exercises. Following the entire set of lessons, the student completes an exercise in which he or she identifies an appropriate arithmetic expression or procedure for solving a problem. Ten problems are presented, and the student has the opportunity of selecting from a menu the appropriate arithmetic operation, expression, or equation.

Final exercise. The final task that follows all SPS instruction presents a series of complex problems. This exercise, once again, is a combination menu and mapping task. The student first selects an appropriate icon for the overall situation described in the problem from a menu of icons. No feedback is given about the correctness of the selection. The corresponding enlarged diagram immediately replaces the menu of icons on the screen. At this point the student uses the mouse to position the word *UNKNOWN* in the appropriate part of the diagram. The student is allowed to change his or her response if so desired, by returning to the menu of icons and making another selection.

An extension to SPS: The Problem-Solving Environment

One limitation of the SPS system is that it does not provide students with the experience of creating their own elaborate problem-solving plans. Consequently, as an adjunct to the instructional system of SPS, we created an additional practice and evaluation system called the Problem Solving Environment (PSE). In PSE, students have the opportunity to use all of their schema knowledge, and the system is designed so that we can evaluate that schema knowledge by looking at the sequence of steps the students go through and the decisions they make as they solve problems.

PSE is especially useful for examining students' development and exercise of planning knowledge. Of all the components of the schema, planning knowledge tends to be the most difficult to evaluate. The difficulty stems from several sources. Planning tasks are the hardest for instructors and developers to construct, and they are the most time-consuming for students to perform. Planning knowledge is often difficult to separate cleanly from other types of knowledge. Planning knowledge is not always outwardly manifested; often one can only assume that it was used. And yet, planning knowledge is perhaps the most critical part of schema knowledge, because it governs so completely the way that the schema is used.

As already described, SPS focuses a part of its instruction on planning knowledge, just as it focuses on identification and elaboration knowledge. In its exercises, SPS requires the student to do one of three things: indicate the relative importance of situations that occur in a problem, locate the unknown with respect to the overall situation that governs the problem, and discriminate among information that is already known and information that can be determined from other features of the problem. Although these exercises are adequate as practice tasks for students as they first develop their planning knowledge, they are insufficient to provide us with much insight into the plans a student might generate on his or her own while solving a problem.

To gain such insight, we use the PSE. It serves two important functions: It provides a complete practice ground for students, one in which they can exercise all their schema knowledge; and it yields detailed step-by-step information about how a student develops and executes a plan to solve a particular problem. Moreover, it makes visible some of the usually invisible intermediate steps and decisions of problem solving without creating an intrusion or interrupting the student's line of reasoning.

The Problem-Solving Environment in which students operate is shown in Figures 5.9–5.12. Unlike SPS, PSE consists of a fixed configuration of windows, arranged so five windows are on the left half of the display (Information Window, Icon Menu Window, Problem Window, Student Work Area Window, and Final Answer Window) and two windows are on the right half (Mapping Area Window and Correct Plan Window). Upon a student's request, a Calculator Window pops up and overlays the Correct Plan Window, as in Figure 5.12. Additionally, a pop-up response menu appears in the center of the screen whenever the student has completed one of the possible mouse-controlled options and is ready for another selection, as shown in Figure 5.10. Most of the student's activity takes place in the two largest windows, identified in the figures as the Student Work Area and the Mapping Area.

Initially, the Information Window, located at the top left-hand part of the display, holds instructions telling the student how to select one of the icons from the window immediately below it (as in Figure 5.9). This is an invariant first step in initializing the PSE session. Later, whenever the student positions the mouse cursor over one of the response menu selections, a brief description of the

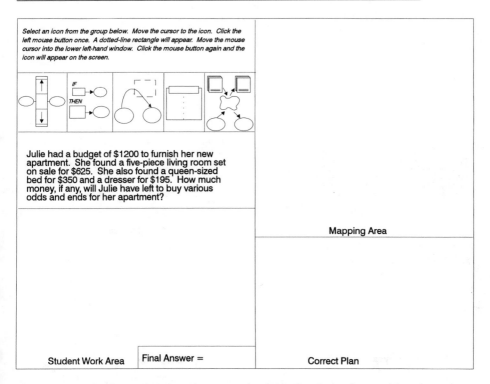

Figure 5.9. The basic layout of PSE at the initialization of a problem-solving session

consequences of making that choice appears in the Information Window.

The window underneath the Information Window is the Icon Menu Window. It contains a menu of the five situation icons. Each of these may be individually selected and copied to the Student Work Area using mouse routines with which the student is already familiar. Selection of four of the icons – Change, Compare, Restate, and Vary – is straightforward: The student selects the icon and points to a location in the Student Work Area for placement. For the Group icon, however, the student must make an additional decision, namely, how many partitions to include in the figure. When the Group icon is selected in the Icon Menu, another menu

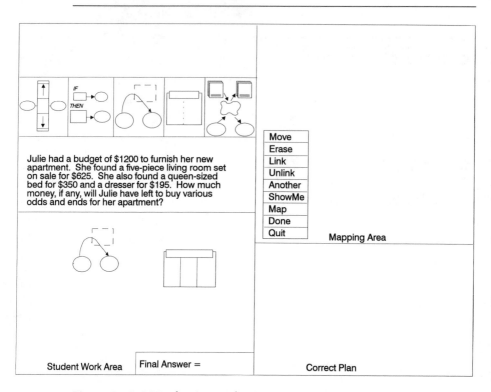

Figure 5.10. PSE after icon selection

pops up, containing three additional icons: one has two subgroups, one has three subgroups, and the third one has four subgroups. Only one of these will be appropriate for a given problem.[6] The student selects one of these three icons for placement in the Student Work Area.

The Problem Window contains the current problem. As in the mapping tasks of SPS, the text of the problem is computationally active rather than inert, so that parts of it may be copied as before into diagrams in the Mapping Area. As long as the student is working on a particular problem, its text remains continually on display in the Problem Window. Both Figure 5.11 and 5.12 show the results of mapping.

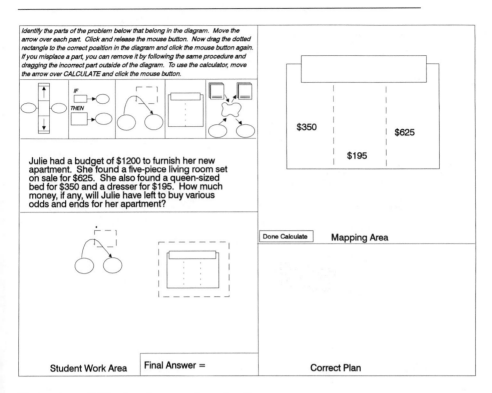

Figure 5.11. PSE after the mapping of a diagram

The Student Work Area occupies the lower left quadrant of the display. Here, the student works with the icons: positioning them, moving them, and linking them together. Much of the information garnered by PSE about the student's plan comes from activity in this window. Once the student has selected and positioned the first icon in the Student Work Area, the pop-up response menu appears in the middle of the display. It contains the basic response options available at any time to the student. The options are as follows.

- *Move* allows the student to move an icon from one location in the Student Work Area to another location.
- *Erase* deletes an unwanted icon from the Student Work Area.

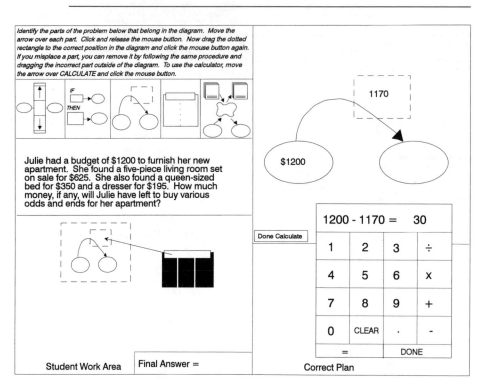

Figure 5.12. PSE following linkages and a request for the calculator

- *Link* allows the student to link two icons together. The student must specify which parts of the icons are to be connected. The link is directed, so that it originates in a specified part of one icon and points to a specified part of the second icon. This signifies that whatever is contained in the originating component is to be transferred to the terminating component. As a reminder to the student, the link is displayed as an arrow, with an arrowhead pointing to the terminating component. (See Figure 5.12 for an example.)
- *UnLink* reverses the action of *Link* and removes an unwanted link.
- *Another* allows the student to make another selection from the Icon Menu.

- *ShowMe* displays a correct plan of the solution.[7] It first presents all the needed icons and all links that connect them. It subsequently focuses on each icon, one at a time, displaying its diagram in the Mapping Area Window with the correct elements already mapped. The student controls the speed with which the plan is shown by pressing the mouse button.
- *Map* allows the student to select one of the icons already in the Student Work Area for display as an enlarged diagram in the Mapping Area. At this time the student may copy parts of the problem from the text display into the diagram. When the student elects to leave the Mapping Area (by selecting Done from a small pop-up menu that appears whenever a diagram is placed in the Mapping Area), PSE provides a continual reminder of which components contain mapped information by blackening them in the corresponding icon located in the Student Work Area, as illustrated in Figure 5.12. Thus, the student can see at a glance which parts of which icons he or she has already filled with information from the problem text. Moreover, whenever the student has linked two icons, elects to map one of the diagrams corresponding to these icons, and places information in the part of the diagram from which the link emanates, PSE automatically transfers that information to the termination of the link as well (in the second diagram). Thus, when the second diagram is examined, the transferred information will automatically be displayed.
- *Done* is the student's signal to PSE that an answer has been placed in the Final Answer Window. At this point, and only at this point, PSE checks to see if the student has obtained the correct answer. The only feedback to the student is whether the solution is correct or incorrect.
- *Quit* allows the student to terminate the session.

The two windows on the right half of the screen contain visual displays solely upon student request. The top one is the Mapping Area Window. It can be entered by the student only when he or she has already placed at least one icon in the Student Work Area and has requested the *Map* option. Immediately below the Mapping Area Window is the window in which a correct plan is displayed for the student upon his or her request. To see the display, the student must select *ShowMe* from the pop-up response menu. The student can make this selection at any time the menu is displayed.

While in the process of mapping a problem into a diagram, the student may wish to make a calculation. To do so, he or she selects *Calculate* from the pop-up menu that appears whenever a diagram is displayed in the Mapping Area. A simple four-function calculator appears, overlaying the Correct Plan Window, as shown in Figure 5.12. The student uses the mouse to make a calculation and has the option of moving the result of the calculation either into the diagram, as if it were part of the problem text, or into the Final Answer Window, if it is the student's final answer to the problem. Closing the Mapping Window (by selecting *Done* from the pop-up menu) closes the Calculator Window as well.

To use PSE, the student logs on and initiates the program. The display at this point shows only the icons at the upper left, a complex problem (containing at least two situations) in the Problem Window, and the message in the Information Window that the student must select an icon and move it into the workspace below the problem (see Figure 5.9). As soon as the response is made, the pop-up menu appears, giving the student the full range of choices for his or her next move.

One of its unique features is that PSE allows the student to make a visual model of the problem using the icons. It is a non-directive system, and it provides no feedback (except to check for the correctness of the final solution when the student desires). The student is free to explore the domain in any way that he or she chooses. While solving a problem, the student makes several decisions, such as opting to select other icons, to examine an already-selected icon more closely, or to ask for help. The student works at his or her own pace, moving back and forth between the Student Work Area and the Mapping Area to modify and confirm the situational elements found in the problem.

Thus, the solver moves around in the environment, looking at the various situations represented by the icons and developing a plan for solving the problem. A fully developed plan would have a set of completely filled icons with correct linkages. Computations would have been made at different points of the plan, with a final computation yielding the answer to the problem. Most students stop short of achieving a fully developed plan, but they do develop plans that can be studied and differentiated. Importantly, the plans reveal what the students have learned or not learned from their instruction by SPS. Results of experimental studies using PSE and examples of student plans constructed in PSE are presented in chapter 8.

Issues of instructional design

In any system of instruction – particularly if it is computer-based – the critical issues are often the decisions that must be made prior to or in the early stages of development. In the following description of SPS's instruction, I focus on two types of decisions that influenced the shape of the instructional system: those having to do with the mechanics of presenting information or recording responses and those having to do with the way that schema theory is incorporated. Whenever possible, both types of decisions were made on the basis of experimental investigations, either research done in my laboratory or published studies by other researchers.

Interface and presentation issues

Mouse response versus typed response. An early decision about the design of SPS was that all student interaction would take place via the mouse. Given the purpose of the system – to examine schema-based instruction – my research group and I chose to avoid the problem of natural language understanding by computers. Observations of our target population indicated that (1) students could easily learn to use the mouse, even if they had no prior experience using computers; and (2) most of them were not expert or even moderately good typists, so open-ended responses were difficult and time-consuming for them. Moreover, typing skill may become an *unintended* variable of influence with open-ended responses because students with good skills are more likely to provide longer and more elaborate answers than those with marginal skills, regardless of how well the instructional content is understood. An additional concern was that the open-ended verbal response is not necessarily a natural part of the problem-solving process and thus would be an intrusion or interruption of the student's cognition.

Opting for mouse communication does not mean that interactions are restricted to simple menu choice. Students make many sophisticated responses using only the mouse, and they have ample opportunity to demonstrate what they know and do not know about problem solving.

The impact of the decision to use the mouse is that the flow of control in the system resides with the user, because no action can be taken by SPS or PSE unless it is preceded by a mouse event. Thus, each user regulates the speed with which the instruction (and subsequent evaluation) occurs.

A special tutorial instructs students in the use of the mouse prior to the onset of SPS instruction about story problems. Students move into the SPS instruction only when they have demonstrated competent use of the mouse. The mouse tutorial takes only about 5 min. It explains to the student how to move the cursor on the screen by moving the mouse, and it gives the student practice in making menu selections and in moving items around on the screen. At the end of the tutorial, the student completes a short exercise using the skills just learned. If the student appears to have trouble manipulating objects on the screen, the tutorial provides additional practice.

It has been our experience that all students very quickly become capable mouse users. In fact, the mouse is probably an unintended enhancement of the system, because the students were, on the whole, quite pleased with themselves for learning how to use it. During the interviews following the daily sessions with SPS, a number of students volunteered how much they liked various features of the computer system, especially the mouse.

In SPS, students use the mouse in two ways. The first way allows students to make an ordinary menu selection, as in the exercise of the first lesson (see Figure 5.1). Typically, a menu contains two to five items, and the student need only move the cursor to the item selected in the menu and press the left or middle mouse button.[8] The second response mode involves copying or repositioning items on the screen, as in the mapping exercises (as shown in Figure 5.4). To make a response, the student aligns the cursor with the item to be copied (usually text) and presses the left button. When the button releases, the selected item changes to inverse print on the screen and a dotted rectangle having the approximate size of the selected item appears. When the cursor is moved, the dotted rectangle moves with it. The student positions the dotted rectangle in the desired new location and again presses the mouse button. On release of the button, the inverted text returns to normal print, the dotted rectangle disappears, and the selected item is copied onto the new location. If the student is not satisfied with the chosen location, he or she can again "pick up" the text and "drop" it at another location or discard it altogether and retrieve another piece of text instead.

Other mouse activities are introduced by PSE, including operating the calculator and manipulating the icons. The most difficult one involves linking two icons together. This procedure requires the student to identify the two icons to be joined, the specific part of the figure from which the link emanates, and the specific part of the figure at which it terminates. Students usually need no more than one or two attempts to master this activity. As with all mouse options, PSE displays instructions to remind the student how to make the connection when the *Link* option has been selected.

Traditional versus novel presentation.   A second design issue hinges on the visual form of the instruction. Because students are accustomed to having instruction presented in textbooks, one page at a time, we elected to use the "page" as the unit of information in SPS. The impact is that the instruction looks very traditional. This was an important decision. Recall that the central issue here is whether the organization of the information contained in the instruction results in a particular knowledge organization in students' memories. Although it was tempting to create a completely new visual form of instruction, we had no means to assess a priori its efficacy against the more traditional form or to separate the impact of form from content. Moreover, both the content of the material and the form of evaluation were already novel to the students, as was the computer implementation. We hypothesized that students would be more comfortable and less distracted with a familiar instructional format.

The SPS page is a 6 1/2 by 9 inch window displayed in the middle of the 19 inch monitor. Attached to the bottom of this window is a menu box containing the options *Next Page* and *Last Page*. Students may take as long as desired to study each screenful of material, moving to the next page when ready or returning to previously displayed instruction if desired.

Additional windows, up to three at a time, appear at various times during instruction, as illustrated in Figure 5.7. These windows are of differing sizes and locations. They allow simultaneous presentation of an example problem, a description of its structure, and a graphical illustration. The additional windows also function as concentration markers, capturing the student's attention by their opening and closing.

Traditional versus nontraditional exercises. Although the instructional presentation is traditional, the assessment of it is not. Virtually all existing classroom and textbook instruction about arithmetic story problems requires only that students come up with a numerical response. SPS very rarely requests the student to do so. Instead, SPS has the student identify the type of situation(s) present in a problem, demonstrate an understanding of how the various pieces of the problem fit the situation, recognize which of several situations is the primary one in a multisituation problem, and show the order of steps one would take to solve a complex problem.

SPS exercises emphasize the particular features of problem solving covered by SPS instruction. Many of these concepts are evident only in intermediate problem-solving steps, which may be difficult to observe under traditional evaluation. Hence, the decision to use nontraditional assessment was an easy one: It was the only means by which we could observe the impact of specific instruction about specific schema knowledge components.

SPS contains 30 different exercises, one for each of the 28 lessons and two end-of-lesson quizzes. The individual user may encounter all of them or only a subset, depending on the time limitations for instruction. Typically, whenever a new concept is introduced through instruction, it is followed by a simple exercise that further illustrates the concept and allows the student to use it directly. The exercise also provides us with an initial evaluation of how well the student understands the material.

The exercises are designed to allow explicit evaluation of the four components of schema knowledge as described earlier. Some of them require only a single choice from one menu, some contain multiple menus and hence multiple selections, and still others necessitate moving elements around on the screen.

When the response is a simple menu selection, as in the first exercise, shown in Figure 5.1, SPS evaluates the student's response as soon as it is made and makes appropriate feedback (as described below). Evaluation is delayed in tasks requiring the student to position screen items. Such tasks generally have more than one item to be moved. SPS gives the student several opportunities to respond and delays evaluation of the response until the student signals completion by buttoning *OKAY* in a control menu window. SPS assesses the accuracy of each item that has been positioned and allows the student a second attempt if any of them is incorrectly located (or missing). The student first buttons on the *FIX* option in the control menu window, clearing the screen of his or her previous response. Next, the student repositions the items as desired. Once the student is satisfied with the new alignment, he or she buttons on the *OKAY* option. At this point, SPS evaluates the response and gives feedback. The problem, the student's solution, and the correct solution remain on the screen for the student's scrutiny until the student selects *GO ON* in the control menu window.

The exercises of PSE are similarly nontraditional, although they do culminate in a numerical solution. Along the way, however, the student engages in several activities that would not necessarily be evident were we to watch the student in a typical problem-solving setting. What we gain from this nontraditional approach is information about decisions the student makes during the problem solving (such as which icons to look at first and the order in which to carry out different steps) and the degree to which the student monitors and corrects his or her performance.

Instructional organization issues

Sequential versus parallel introduction of concepts. In addition to the presentation issues, several important instructional ones had to be considered. A key design issue was how to introduce the situations. We had two basic options: (1) introduce each situation, describe its components fully, and allow the student to master it before encountering another; and (2) introduce all five situations more or less at one time, giving brief descriptions and simple examples only, and let the student get a rough idea of how the situations differ. We took the second approach: presentation of all the important situations as quickly as possible. This was an important choice, because it guided much of the future construction of SPS.

We made our decision on the basis of results of a brief experimental study using members of the intended user population: 125 undergraduate students. Each student worked through a short workbook containing one of two forms of instruction and a set of recognition exercises. Students were randomly assigned to two instructional conditions. Half of them were given *sequential* instruction, and half were given *parallel* instruction. In the sequential instruction, each situation was developed fully, and practice exercises for it were given before the presentation of another one. In the parallel instruction, all situations were presented at once and were discussed together. Exercises followed the full presentation. After completing the workbook, all students were asked to solve a set of complex problems and to perform a sorting task in which 20 story problems were to be classified according to situation type. This task was described in detail in chapter 3.

The results of this study were very interesting. To be sure, the groups did not differ in their postexperiment problem solving, but we had no expectation that they would. After all, the students' problem-solving skills had evolved over at least 12 years of schooling. It would be naive to expect a 1-hour experiment to alter strategies that took 12 years to develop. When we examined the sorting task results, however, we found striking differences. The group receiving parallel instruction formed stronger and more cohesive categories than did the group with sequential instruction. Because the sorting task depended only on the experimental setting and not on previous learning, it was a good indicator of whether and how the two instructional conditions differed.

Numerical versus nonnumerical responses. Students' reliance on previous learning is both a help and a hindrance, depending on the circumstances and the previous learning. It is a negative influence when we are trying to get the students to focus on the nature of the situations. Most of their previous instruction has centered exclusively on finding the correct numerical value as quickly as possible, and students have generally developed strategies for doing so. These strategies have been habituated to such an extent that we have frequently been unable to stop students from using them. Students want to make computations, even though few of our exercises ask for them. The interference coming from previously learned problem-solving strategies was enormous. We eliminated the interference to a great extent by eliminating the computations. That is, we developed the instruction and initial exercises using nonproblem situations to force students to concentrate on other features of the problem-solving experience and to create a second cognitive route into the problem-solving domain. Most of the exercises in SPS and PSE are non-numerical, and calculations are allowed only in PSE.

Explicit versus implicit analogical reasoning. SPS deliberately makes use of analogies. Typically, these have the form of nonproblem examples that are first introduced and then related directly to story problems. For instance, in the initial lesson, SPS talks about how most people have been taught that there are distinct basic groups of food. One may eat a variety of different foods, but they will all fit these categories. SPS then develops the analogy of food groups for problem situations. It is not a very long discussion, but it is intended to tap into a means of categorization already well understood by the students.

We made the decision to use analogies to help the students access their prior knowledge. The analogies are usually very simple and were selected to be widely recognizable to most of our population. Given that one of SPS's instructional goals is to have students recognize similarities and dissimilarities in situations, it was desirable to have them begin to consider how seemingly unlike things can have common features. By using analogies in the instruction and by describing exactly how to recognize common features, SPS gradually leads the students into making the analogies for themselves.

Individually sequenced lessons versus a common path.   An early decision with multiple later consequences was to maintain a common sequence of lessons for all students. This choice was predominantly driven by the experimental nature of the system. That is, we intended to use SPS as the basis of research study, and we desired to control as many variables as possible, including order of instruction. Nonetheless, we developed SPS with an eye to promoting individualized instruction. The modular construction of SPS allows great variation in the presentation of individual lessons or blocks of lessons, and the student model that allows the tailoring of instruction to the individual is already in place.

Feedback versus no feedback. SPS provides feedback on all but the end-of-session exercises. The nature of the feedback depends on the particular exercise. In the recognition tasks, SPS's responses to the student are conditional on how the student is doing on the particular exercise. If the student makes two errors in identifying a particular situation, SPS gives a supplemental review of that situation. If the student has erred on three consecutive items, SPS provides a general review of all situations. For both cases, a review window opens on the left side of the display, containing either a brief summary of the key features associated with the five situations or a review of the single situation that is causing difficulty. The window remains on the screen for 20 sec or until the student clicks the mouse button. If the student is generally doing well but makes an occasional error, SPS gives only a short message indicating why the student's answer is incorrect. This feedback is displayed in the uppermost part of the task window itself.

Feedback on the mapping tasks is even briefer. Others' research (e.g., J. R. Anderson 1988) as well as our own pilot studies suggested that it was sufficient to tell the student only whether his or her answer was correct. More than this tends to elicit frustration and resentment. When a student first errs on an item, SPS signals the student that the response is incorrect and asks the student to try again. After a second error on the item, SPS simply shows the student the correct mapping. SPS's mapping is displayed in italics just outside the various parts of the diagrams. The student's own attempt remains on the screen together with the correct answer so that the student can see how his or her answer differs from the correct assignment. As on all other tasks, the display remains until the student opts to continue.

The planning exercises demand a different type of feedback. When the student selects an incorrect primary or secondary situation, SPS gives problem-specific feedback, indicating why the student's selection is in error and identifying specific characteristics of the problem to which the student should attend. As in the other, simpler, recognition tasks, feedback here is presented in the top portion of the task window.

Each instructional session ends with a task for which no feedback is given. Sessions are typically 50 min in duration (similar to a class period in high school or college). SPS monitors the time, estimates how far the student will progress through the lessons before the session will end, and terminates the instructional session at an appropriate juncture, usually at the conclusion of a paired set of an instructional lesson and its related exercises. Before the student leaves the workstation, he or she is asked to respond to an end-of-session task that functions as a daily quiz. In the early sessions, the task involves matching the five situation names with examples of the situations. In later sessions, the student identifies the location of the unknown in a problem. On both of these tasks, the student makes his or her responses to a small number of items and exits the program.

PSE offers even less feedback than SPS, and it is clear from student responses to the system that they do not desire more feedback than PSE provides. Most students using PSE eventually correct their own mistakes. Sometimes this correction is immediate, but it often is delayed. Were the system to point out errors at the time of commission, the students would be denied the rewards of correctly monitoring their own problem solving.

Other instructional issues. At many points in instructional design, one must make decisions first and confirm them experimentally a posteriori. We made two (at least) such decisions: our choice to rely heavily on visual representations and our choice to incorporate both example and abstract description equally in the initial instruction. Both of these issues have been the focus of rigorous experimental study with SPS, and the outcomes of the research are presented in chapters 7 and 9.

Additional features of SPS

The necessary mechanics that allow SPS to run are outlined briefly in what follows.

Item banks. SPS utilizes three item banks: situations, one-step problems, and multistep problems. PSE shares the multistep problem bank. Each problem bank contains a large number of items, and each item has a set of properties associated with it. SPS uses these properties to assess correct responses to the various exercises and to provide relevant feedback to students. Each item may be used in a variety of exercises, and there is no single correct answer associated with each one. Depending on the exercise, the appropriate answer might be the identification of the underlying situation, the correct mapping of the specific elements of the item into a graphical representation of the situation, a more abstract mapping, or an arithmetic expression.

SPS uses problems and situations that were created for it and that conform to the following criteria. Traditional key words and phrases are avoided whenever possible. The story lines are appropriate for young adults. Items are worded for clear mapping into the schema diagrams, and numbers used in the problems are simple. The items are purposely rather bland. To make the desired assessments it was necessary to ensure that content unfamiliarity did not play a role in determining problem difficulty.

Record keeping. SPS keeps a continuous log of each student's activity. It records the date, the amount of time required for each exercise, the specific problems used in the exercises, the student's responses to each problem, and SPS's rejoinder. During each exercise SPS refers to the log and to the student's current responses to develop a model of how the student is performing. At various points in the exercises, SPS will stop the student and will provide additional instruction if the student appears to need it. This supplement may take the form of a quick review or may be an extensive remediation.

SPS also uses the log information to avoid duplicate presentation of any of the problems or stories. It keeps an updated list of all problems previously seen by a student and eliminates them from consideration by any of the random problem generators used by the exercises.

Both SPS and PSE maintain a record of mouse events. Each event corresponds to some action taken by the student, and the student record is a history of all events in the order in which they occurred. Interspersed with the mouse events are the system selections, such as the identification of the current problem and the type of feedback given. The primary mouse events that occur in SPS are menu choices or selections of elements of a problem text for mapping purposes.

There are many more mouse events in PSE than in SPS, because the student has a wider range of activities. The following are key events recorded by PSE:

- *IconSelected*. This event indicates that the student selected one of the five icons and placed it in the Student Work Area. The name of the corresponding situation and its position in the window are recorded, as well as its rank order in the set of selected icons.
- *Map*. Whenever the student requests that an icon be displayed in the Mapping Area, this event is recorded, together with the name of the icon and its original ranking. The ranking is an important piece of data because it is possible for a problem to have two instances of the same situation (e.g., two Vary situations such as 2 pounds of cheese for $3.50 per pound and 3 quarts of milk for 99 cents each). PSE must keep track of which of these is mapped, modified, and/or linked to other situations.
- *LiftWord*. This event is recorded whenever the student selects a part of the problem or a result of a calculation for placement in a diagram or in the Final Answer Window. The record contains the activity, the words or numbers that have been lifted, and where they are placed. Only one map is available at any time, so there is no confusion about which diagram is designated. The integer values following the *LiftWord* event in the record indicate the part of the diagram used. Each component of each diagram has its own identification number. When *NIL* appears at the end of the event instead of a number, it signifies that the student has removed the selected text from the diagram and disposed of it. Thus, *(LiftWord . . . NIL)* indicates an erasure.
- *CalculatorSolve*. This event indicates that the student requested a calculation. The expression to be calculated and its result are recorded.
- *Link*. The link event has four parts: the rank order of the icon from which the link emanates, the numbered part of that icon from which it originates, the rank order of the icon to which the link extends, and the numbered part of the second icon, in which the link terminates.

- *ShowMe.* Every time the student requests *ShowMe* from the response menu, the event is recorded. The student may make this request more than once.
- *WrongAnswer* and *RightAnswer.* If the student has placed an incorrect response in the Final Answer Window and selected *Done* from the response menu, PSE records *WrongAnswer* plus the incorrect response. If the student has given the correct response, PSE notes it with the event *RightAnswer* together with the correct value.

General conclusions

This section might well be entitled "Things We Have Learned So Far." We have made several observations from watching and listening to students as they interacted with SPS and PSE, and they have bearing for other instructional systems, not just SPS and PSE.

Daily review

One of the things that showed up quite early in our pilot studies was the need for an initial review or memory refresher at the start of each session. Having a general review of the situations and/or the diagrams allowed the students to move rapidly into new areas of instruction. When we omitted the review, students took much longer with each lesson and made more errors on the exercises. The final form of the reviews used in the first half of SPS instruction is quite simple, consisting of a single screen of text on which is displayed the five situations in simple stories and a brief general description of each situation. The review for the latter part of instruction, and also for PSE exploration, consists of providing the students with the icons, printed on paper and displayed for easy reference next to the keyboard.

Feedback

Students do not want much feedback unless they are really stuck. Usually at that point, they request some help. Generally, we found that the desire for feedback is a function of how far along the student is in using the system. Initially, students needed a relatively great deal of help, and they did not resent receiving it. In the later lessons, they needed less and less. As noted earlier, we eventually developed PSE without any feedback at all except to tell the student if his or her answer is correct. Lack of specific help in PSE has not bothered any of our students. None has requested additional help in this environment.

Positive impact of the mouse

Our students greatly enjoyed using the mouse to make their responses. Consequently, they had a positive attitude while interacting with SPS. This was especially important for our older students (many of those enrolled at the community college) and for those students having little or no prior computer experience.

Avoiding problem-solving intrusions

Mouse events are non-intrusive. Students did not seem to mind making a number of mouse responses during their problem solving. All adjusted quickly to using the mouse, and we saw no indication that their thinking was disrupted or altered by mouse communications.

Affective responses

Students like visual representations. We received many spontaneous reactions to the figures used in SPS and PSE. Students liked the idea of having "pictures" that represented types of problems. Often in interviews the students indicated that they felt their understanding was enhanced because of the figures.

The instructional medium

One of our biggest disappointments was the extent to which students' learning and problem-solving strategies were linked to the medium in which they received the instruction. Our students had no difficulty performing the tasks SPS and PSE set for them, and they solved complex problems on-line relatively easily by the end of the instruction. We rarely saw intrusions of earlier learning. When asked to do the same tasks using paper and pencil rather than the computer, however, they frequently reverted to their old problem-solving behaviors. Our observations suggest strongly that instruction should be made using multiple media, so that students do not develop behavioral patterns that are media dependent.

An overall conclusion

The bottom line is that it is possible to develop instruction around a specific set of schemas. SPS and PSE are working examples of systems that focus on particular aspects of schema knowledge and that allow detailed evaluation of how that knowledge develops. One of my earliest questions as I began this research was whether such instruction was possible. The answer is clearly yes. The questions that remain to be answered have to do with the nature of the learning that follows schema-based instruction. Some interesting answers have emerged in response to these questions, as will be seen in the following chapters.

III

Learning from instruction

Part III describes the ways in which students learn. In particular, the chapters in this part focus on learning that occurs under the instructional conditions presented in part II.

Part III begins with an overview of some of the important issues in learning, especially with respect to schema theory. Three areas of study are most relevant: the type of information that individuals acquire from learning, the way in which the information is retained, and the strength and reliability with which it is used again. Chapter 6 focuses on recent developments in these three areas.

The remaining chapters of part III describe experimental outcomes from studies of learning. They contain descriptions of different experiments, each designed to look at learning from a different perspective.

In chapter 7, I describe two experiments that examine the learning that occurs in the initial stages of schema development, especially students' ability to recognize the situations and their different elements. The focus here is on students' acquisition of identification and elaboration knowledge.

In chapter 8, the nature of students' planning is examined. The research reported here centers on problem solving as it is manifested in the extended problem-solving environment of PSE.

And, finally, in chapter 9, I describe two experiments that focus on the importance of visual representations, contrasting learning with diagrams and learning without them. Both studies have interesting results about long-term retention of visual information.

These experiments provide evidence of students' acquisition of identification knowledge, elaboration knowledge, and planning knowledge. They yield a great deal of information about how schemas for problem solving develop.

6

Learning and schema theory

As one might expect, cognitive science has had a significant impact on research about learning, and learning today is usually studied in one of two ways: by detailed studies of individuals (rather than groups) and by computer simulation. The most informative studies employ both approaches, drawing on the human studies for observable responses and using the computer simulations to evaluate nonobservable ones.

Cognitive science also deserves some of the credit for shifting the content of learning research from artificial and/or superficial stimuli to meaningful topics. Much of what we think of as traditional learning theory was derived from the behavior of subjects in laboratory settings. The learning to be studied usually took place in a very short period of time, perhaps 15 minutes to 1 hour. Its content was often nonsensical or irrelevant, because the research paradigm called for the use of material of which subjects had no prior knowledge. Hence, much of the learning that learning theories explained was not functional learning as we see it in the world, and predictions from these theories often were in conflict with observations made in other settings such as the classroom. Many of the aspects of learning that we now find worthy of study were deliberately and systematically eliminated from these studies.

With the emergence of new methods of investigation and a strong emphasis on meaningful topics, the study of learning has advanced in several fresh directions. Three general questions, frequently asked in cognitive research, are especially relevant when we think about the roles that schemas play in learning: What is it that individuals learn? How do they remember it? Can they use it again? These may be recast as issues of contexture, long-term memory storage, and competency.

The contexture of learning

Of the many foci of psychological learning studies, two have particular relevance for schema development: the acquisition of cognitive skills and the development of pattern recognition.

Cognitive skills

Various types of information can be acquired during learning, and studies of them take many different paths. One avenue is the investigation of how individuals acquire cognitive skills. The study of skill acquisition has yielded valuable new methods for studying learning, and researchers have developed computational models of learning to explain how individuals develop and use their skills. It is possible – and almost essential – to construct a model to depict one's view of learning. These models differ enormously from earlier models of learning, which were essentially mathematical predictions dependent on group parameters. The newer computational models are computer programs that require highly specific detail about the learning process and the structure of the material to be learned. They typically depict the cognitive processing of a single individual meticulously and in very small steps.

Considerable attention has been paid to how individuals develop cognitive skills, most often in real settings requiring complex knowledge. The skills that are studied are often procedures used in technical fields, particularly in science and mathematics. One thinks here of the impressive work done by cognitive researchers such as John Anderson (1982) and Kurt VanLehn (1990).

As individuals acquire skills, they develop rules that govern these skills. Recall the learning hierarchy described in chapter 4, and consider that the acquisition of the hierarchy corresponds roughly to the formation of the appropriate sets of rules for carrying out the various procedures. Each branch of the tree has its own set of rules. These, in turn, become part of a larger set at the next level as several subskills become linked under one larger skill.

The acquisition of procedural skills is vital to schema development, because they are key constituents of planning and execution knowledge. They ultimately generate an individual's response to a problem, based on the schema knowledge held by the individual. They are not, however, sufficient by themselves because they do not account for the identification and elaboration of the problem conditions. Furthermore, it is possible to develop procedures that are not tied to understanding. An example is the procedure many individuals use for dividing one fraction by another. Many people cannot explain why they invert the second fraction and then multiply the two together, although a great many can voice an "invert and multiply" rule learned in school, and they can carry out the procedure effortlessly.

Pattern recognition

A second line of study having to do with the nature of information to be learned focuses on pattern recognition and classification. An example is the investigation of how individuals recognize the letters of the alphabet or recognize words.

Much of the cognitive research on pattern recognition looks at human performance in recognizing known or slightly modified patterns rather than at learning to recognize patterns in the first place. Recently, however, the emphasis in studies has shifted subtly from human learning to machine learning, as the goal has become a plausible explanation of how pattern recognition takes place given the conditions and constraints of a particular model. The models used in these studies "learn" to recognize patterns (see, e.g., McClelland, 1986).[1]

Studies involving pattern recognition, like studies of skill acquisition, also depend heavily on computer models, but the models are of a different type. The models of skill acquisition are generally composed of a set of rules that operate one by one as needed. They are often referred to as production systems or production models.

The models of pattern recognition, commonly called connectionist models or neural nets, are networks of small, highly related pieces of information that are processed simultaneously. That is, the collection of features that identify an object, such as a letter or a word, are processed at the same time by the model rather than one by one, and it is the presence or absence of the set of features – together with the ways in which they are linked – that determines recognition. An interesting characteristic of these models is that each learner can develop a unique recognition system that depends on different subsets of features of a pattern.

Patterns are as important to the development of strong schemas as skills are. It is through pattern recognition that a schema is initially activated, and the information stored as identification knowledge is essential. Just as skills alone do not constitute a schema, patterns alone also do not suffice. In the absence of the other necessary schema components – elaboration, planning, and execution knowledge – one has only a concept, not a schema.

Long-term memory storage

A second broad question of interest in learning research is how new information becomes intertwined with existing knowledge. Again, a number of research areas have emerged. The one most relevant to schema theory has to do with the organization of long-term memory.

In several ways, one can investigate organization. As Baddeley (1990, p. 175) points out, there are at least three levels at which it is important: (1) the way that long-term memory itself is organized, (2) the way that the new material to be learned is organized, and (3) the way that these two are merged so that the new material can be easily retrieved. I am interested in these three levels with respect to learning from instruction.

The predominant view of long-term memory holds that knowledge stored there is associated with other knowledge. There seems to be little disagreement about the general associative nature of memory; the disagreement comes in the attempts to define the nature of the association. These disagreements have fueled many of the major arguments about learning theory. One can point to at least three, each of which in its turn has concerned the field for a number of years: (1) whether human associative learning can best be explained by behaviorist or cognitive theory, (2) whether the acquisition of associations is a gradual, continuous process or a sudden leap, and (3) whether the appropriate model to represent human memory is a neural network or a production system. None of these disagreements can be resolved definitively by research in favor of one alternative or the other. One can only conclude that memory is much more diverse than most researchers have hypothesized, and it is likely that all of the alternatives are valid under appropriate circumstances. We are not much concerned with the first two any more, and the third is slowly being resolved as it becomes evident that the integration of the two representations is probably superior to either one alone.[2]

The second level of organization that is important to memory has to do with the ways that the instructional materials themselves are organized. One example of this approach is example-based learning (e.g., Sweller & Cooper, 1985; Kieras, 1991). In this paradigm, one presents elaborate examples to individuals and examines the learning that occurs as a result of studying the examples. Typically, the effectiveness of this approach is evaluated by measuring the extent to which individuals can apply what they have learned from the examples to new problems. This area of study is particularly important to researchers in machine learning (see, e.g., Reinke & Michalski, 1988).

It seems obvious that the structure of the example will have a substantial influence. John Sweller and his students have carried out a number of studies in which the structure of an example was varied (e.g., Sweller & Cooper, 1985; Sweller, Chandler, Tierney, & Cooper, 1990; Ward & Sweller, 1991). Their studies are based on Sweller's theory of cognitive load, and they pay particular attention to the way that cognitive resources are managed during learning. One of Sweller et al.'s key findings is that all the information presented in an example needs to be fully integrated, and learning is facilitated if the learner does not have to perform the integration. That is, different representations, such as graphics and text, need to be presented so that the learner does not have to use valuable and limited cognitive resources to integrate the instruction; these resources should be saved for learning. Sweller's solution is to superimpose text on diagrams so that learners do not have to shift attention from text in one location to graphics in another.

A somewhat different type of study about learning focuses on the link between instruction and learning as a way of understanding the content that is learned. Studies of this type ask which aspects of instruction lead to learning and whether the linkages of information are those that were intended. When these questions are asked from a cognitive science perspective, they go beyond the educational implications of whether the student learned a specific fact, skill, or concept. Instead, they stress the cognitive mechanisms that are at work. Included here are analogical reasoning studies, such as the well-known work done by Dedre Gentner and her colleagues (see Gentner, 1983). Gentner argues that analogy is the cognitive mechanism that allows individuals to map systematic relational structures from one domain to another. A fundamental concept in her theory is systematicity, and she has carried out a number of detailed experiments to investigate the importance of systematicity. Among other things, she has found that analogical mapping is facilitated when the initial story that comprises the instruction has systematic structure (Clement & Gentner, 1989).

Gentner's work demonstrates very clearly that in order to examine the learning that takes place, it is essential to look carefully at the specific features of the content that is acquired and applied. One may learn much about how individuals develop analogical reasoning if one pays attention to the specific characteristics of the stories given in the analogies. This conclusion underscores the need for studies in schema research to begin with a well-formulated description of the schema's content.

A number of studies have examined the interaction between the organization of instruction and the resulting organization of information in memory. Most typical are studies in which individuals are asked to memorize lists of items. When subjects are given suggestions about how to organize the material in meaningful ways, such as to group similar items or to make up sentences using the words, they are usually much better able to remember the items. Sometimes subjects are given specific mnemonic rules to apply, and sometimes the organizational advice consists solely of a general suggestion that organization might be helpful. A useful review of experimental studies of this type is given by Baddeley (1990, chap. 8).

Competency

The only way we have of knowing that an individual has learned something is if he or she can somehow demonstrate it for us.[3] Not every individual demonstrates the same degree of success; some are clearly more competent than others. A relatively recent line of research, frequently referred to as the study of expertise, addresses this issue of competency. Studies in this area compare the performance of individuals having different degrees of competence, usually experts and novices.

These comparisons of competence reflect an underlying theory of learning, although it may not be explicitly stated. Virtually all of the studies make the implicit assumption that experts *learn* their expertise over time under conditions of multiple exposures to the subject matter. Most of them also assume that experts eventually have a more cohesive knowledge representation of the domain than do novices. Hence, one would expect to observe schema differences.

There is an ongoing effort to develop a theory of expertise (see, e.g., Ericsson & J. Smith, 1991). By examining a number of different fields, researchers are attempting to determine the general characteristics of expertise. They have been forced to develop research procedures that differ dramatically from those used in earlier learning experiments. Thus, new methodology has emerged from the novice-expert studies. For the most part, this new methodology shifts attention away from the end product of reasoning and focuses instead on early and intermediate steps, which are usually unobservable. To tap into these unobserved processes, re-

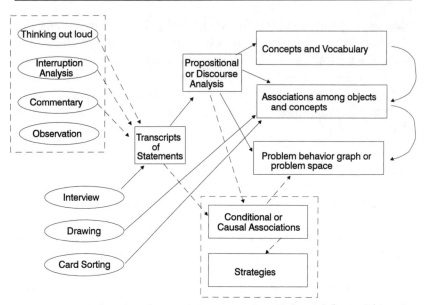

Figure 6.1. Techniques for studying expertise (Adapted from Olson &
Biolsi, 1991, with permission from Cambridge University Press)

searchers ask their subjects to describe in detail their mental reasoning as they solve problems.

Asking individuals to think aloud while solving problems is just
one method used in novice-expert studies. Figure 6.1 shows some
of the other direct techniques used for representing expert knowledge. Most of them require obtaining some verbal account from
experts and novices. The ways in which these verbal accounts are
analyzed vary, but most researchers make an analysis that will
allow them to condense the verbal transcripts to manageable units
that can then be further evaluated. One of the greatest difficulties
with think-aloud protocols is their enormous size. It is not unusual
to have several hundred pages of transcript from a novice-expert
study. This information is typically unusable in its raw form and
must be condensed.

Think-aloud protocols lead to many types of analyses, such as
comparisons of the kinds of errors made, of the perceptual cues
detected, or of the differing strategies employed. Such analyses are

time-consuming and often fraught with difficulty, as pointed out by Ericsson and Simon (1984), but they are well worth the effort. The level of detail demanded by production and connectionist models can only be obtained through systematic analysis of individuals' performance. Whenever possible, researchers tend to use overt measures of performance, such as videotapes, paper and pencil responses, or computer keyboard records. However, these measures are not always sufficient to capture the phenomenon of interest. With increasing frequency, it is becoming necessary to rely on subjects' own introspection because the mechanisms under study are not typically displayed as overt actions.

The methods and techniques of expertise studies have direct value for schema research. Much of what we want to study shows up in intermediate, rather than final, stages of problem solving, and we need procedures that will allow us to gather a wide variety of data. The techniques of Figure 6.1 can be easily adapted for schema study, as will be seen in subsequent chapters.

The role of schemas in learning

The scope of schema theory embraces all three of the areas just described. Schemas have a natural place in each of them: contexture, memory, and competency. Moreover, schema theory provides the relationships that tie all three together. The research in the following chapters illustrates this point.

Schemas and contextural issues

Given the schema theory developed in part I, specific questions about how schemas develop may be constructively addressed. One critical issue about schema formation is the determination of specific knowledge that individuals acquire from schema-based instruction. Typically, instruction will offer several different kinds of information, including visual aids, examples, formulas, general principles, and definitions. To study schema creation and development, we will need to know which pieces of information are encoded by students and in what relation. It is particularly important to determine the first pieces of knowledge that students retain, because these will be the building blocks to which other knowledge is later attached. As will be demonstrated in the following chapters, such determinations are possible, and they yield both interesting and informative clues about individual differences in information processing.

Of special interest also are the types of knowledge that become incorporated into different schema components. Three salient types that are abundant in most instructional materials are examples, abstract characterizations, and graphic representations. It is worthwhile ascertaining when these are acquired as a result of instruction and how they fit together as part of schema knowledge.

Schemas and memory issues

The network view of memory is eminently consistent with schema theory, with nodes representing individual pieces of knowledge and links between them denoting a relationship. Schemas depend on connections; schemas with few connections will not serve an individual as well as schemas with many connections.

There are two ways to study connections that individuals develop as part of their schema knowledge. First, we can evaluate these linkages by examining students' own statements. Second, we can make predictions about an individual's performance in the presence or absence of specific connections and then compare our predictions with observed performance. Both methods yield valuable information, as I will show.

Schemas and competency issues

In several different ways, we can look at competency. On the one hand, we might try to evaluate the competency with which an individual applies any one of the four schema knowledge components. Thus, we might focus on rapid and accurate recognition, efficient use of mental models, and suitable goal setting. On the other hand, we might aim to evaluate competency over an entire domain, in which case our attention would be on application of the entire schema rather than individual parts. The latter corresponds more closely with novice-expert studies.

Declarative and procedural knowledge

There has been a recent tendency to divide memory (and the knowledge stored therein) into two parts, procedural and declarative. Consequently, any discussion of learning – as the acquisition of knowledge – needs to address this distinction.

The declarative/procedural dichotomy shows up both in cognitive psychology (e.g., J. R. Anderson, 1983) and in cognitive neuroscience (Squire, 1987), although the characterizations are not identically drawn. Anderson makes a fundamental distinction between declarative and production knowledge in his theory of cognition, and these give rise to a distinction between declarative and production memory. Declarative knowledge contains all that individuals know about their environment. Production memory contains procedures that allow them to act in the world. These two memories have different mechanisms for the encoding and retrieval of information.

Squire makes a somewhat different distinction between declarative and procedural knowledge, based in part on his research with amnesia patients. According to Squire, declarative knowledge can be accessed uniquely and directly by conscious recollection, whereas procedural knowledge cannot. Not only are the two types of knowledge different, but they are acquired through different brain mechanisms. A central distinction is that declarative knowledge is presumed to be acquired directly, usually with one trial learning. On the other hand, procedural knowledge is considered to be anything that improves with experience or practice.

What appears to be missing in both Squire's and Anderson's memory dichotomy is an explanation of how the two types of memories work together. I suggest that both declarative and procedural knowledge are required in any activation of a schema.

Moreover, I hypothesize that they are closely tied together, so that the retrieval of one probably facilitates the retrieval of the other. As a simple case in point, consider the decision to eat in a favorite restaurant. Both declarative and procedural knowledge are immediately active. The declarative knowledge, according to Anderson and Squire, would refer to specific memories of eating in that particular restaurant. The procedural knowledge would involve typical skills such as making a reservation, ordering from the menu, using the eating utensils, and paying the bill.

Schema theory as it is defined here places declarative and procedural knowledge within a broader framework. The schema is not itself a different type of knowledge, in the sense in which Anderson and Squire define knowledge types, but rather it is an interweaving or union of the two already recognized types. Not all declarative knowledge will be incorporated into a schema, nor will all procedural knowledge necessarily have ties to schemas. We can easily imagine facts and skills that are isolated in memory. In contrast, a schema always has associated with it some declarative knowledge (which is the basis of the general identification and elaboration knowledge) and some procedural knowledge (which will be used to make plans and execute them). Not only does schema theory allow these connections, it demands them.

Schemas can be instantly modified (e.g., by the incorporation of a new piece of declarative knowledge), and they can be gradually tuned over time, as the result of repeated application. Experimental evidence suggests that schemas can be triggered unintentionally and retrieved deliberately. For instance, in problem solving studies, subjects sometimes recognize some feature in the problem that brings an entire schema into working memory immediately. On the other hand, a subject may be at a loss as to how to proceed and may deliberately and consciously attempt to recall any schemas that he can remember ever using to see if one suffices.

As has been mentioned a number of times already, schemas have a network structure. In schema-based learning, we are mostly concerned with two issues having to do with networks, and they may be characterized simply as input and output. The input issue reflects how new information comes into a network, and the output issue looks at how the information is retrieved from it. The remaining chapters of part III describe studies whose purpose was to provide some answers to these two questions.

7

Learning from schema-based instruction

An important consideration in an investigation of schema development is the nature of the first pieces of information relevant to the schema that an individual acquires. Judging from the structure of many textbooks and the outlines of many class lessons, we should pay special attention to two kinds of information available in instruction, namely, examples and definitions. It is these types of information that are typically used in instruction, and it is from them that students will begin to develop their schema knowledge.

Consider for a moment the familiar instructional situation in which an instructor introduces a new concept to students. Remember that our interest here centers on the initial introduction of the concept, not a long-term elaboration of it. Several options are available to the instructor. For instance, she could begin with a prototypic example of the concept. The example contains specific details and is couched in a setting that is presumably well understood by the students. Students are expected to figure out for themselves the general properties of the concept from the example. An alternative approach would be for the instructor to give a general definition. This information is abstract and contains basic characteristics that should apply to all possible instances of the concept. In this case, students are left to generate their own example to illustrate the concept. In practice, the instructor will typically do both, first giving a representative case in which the con-

Part of this chapter is a revised description of the research first reported in Marshall (1993b) and reproduced here with permission of Kluwer Academic Publishers.

cept clearly occurs and then immediately defining it. By using both types of information, the instructor is helping the students create a bridge between the specific and the abstract. Thus, the instructor presents two distinct types of information, and students have the freedom of learning from either or both of them.

We frequently encounter instructional situations such as this one, and given our interest in the way students learn, we ought to ask immediately about the extent to which schema development is influenced by the type of information used in the instruction. That is, is an individual more likely to create a strong schema when the instruction begins with an example, when it opens with a definition, or when both types of information are presented simultaneously? This central question gives rise to several related ones:

- Given access to typical instruction in which specific information (i.e., examples) and abstract information (i.e., definitions) are both available, which will a student remember?
- How important is it that both types of knowledge be part of the instruction?
- Are there noticeable individual differences in what students' learn?
- If individual differences are found in the types of information encoded, will they have an effect on performance?

Initial answers to these questions can be found in the two studies described in the following pages of this chapter. Both experiments were designed to investigate how learning comes about when the focus of the learning is on the situations found in story problems. The study of how individuals acquire situational knowledge is the first step in understanding schema development.

Experiment I: Abstraction, coding, and performance

The overall objective of this study was to follow a group of students as they moved through the full instructional sequence provided by SPS. The study is noteworthy for two reasons. First, it provides some empirical evidence of what students are learning from the initial instruction, and some interesting and valuable conclusions can be drawn about abstract and specific information in instruction. Second, and equally important, the study introduces a methodology that can be used to test elements of the basic models of story-problem schemas. The methodology involves using schema theory to create hypothetical networks of knowledge for each student and comparing students' performance on outcome measures with measures of network structure.

Subjects

Subjects were 27 college students recruited from introductory psychology classes. These students had relatively weak problem-solving skills: On a pretest of 10 multistep word problems, they averaged four wrong answers.

These subjects were members of the targeted population for which SPS was created, that is, adults with limited problem-solving skills. Having them as subjects allowed us to disentangle schema development from skill acquisition, something that might be difficult with children just beginning to master arithmetic operations. The older students could be expected to have mastery of basic computational skills. (This was, in fact, confirmed by analyses of our subjects' pretest performance; their errors were not usually arithmetic in nature.) Moreover, these college students could be expected to have good reading skills and broad vocabularies, so we avoided confounding reading ability with schema development.

Experimental procedure

Students worked independently on SPS, the computer-based instructional system described in chapter 5. Each student completed a 5-hour instructional program during a 2-week period. The full course of study consisted of five sessions, each spanning about 1 hour. The sessions took place approximately every 2–3 days. In each session, students spent 45–50 min working with the computer and 5–10 min talking with the experimenter in the interview.

All instruction and exercises were displayed on the monitor, and the student responded using a three-button optical mouse. Only the first session – the introduction to the five situations – is described here. Details from other sessions are described later in this volume. As I pointed out in chapter 5, this first session is critical because it is the point at which students develop their initial identification knowledge and acquire the ability to recognize the situations. Hence, this initial session is very important for schema formation.

Data collection

The data consisted of students' answers to the first exercise presented by the computer and their responses to the interview questions. Each is described below.

Identification task. The first source of data was the computer exercise that followed the initial instructional session. (The format of this exercise was shown in Figure 5.1.) The items in this task were selected randomly for each student from a pool of 100 items, and they are similar to those of Table 7.1. During the exercise, one item at a time was displayed, and the student responded to it by selecting the name of the situation depicted in the item from a menu containing all five names: Change, Group, Compare, Restate, and Vary. The student received immediate feedback about the accuracy of the answer, and if the student responded incorrectly, the correct situation was identified by SPS.

The order of item presentation was uniquely determined for every student, and each one responded to 10–20 items, depending on his or her success in identifying the situations. SPS continued to present items until the student had made two correct responses to each situation or until the student had seen a maximum of 4 items for any situation still eligible for presentation.[1] Thus, every student responded to at least 2 items of each type and to no more than 4. The minimum number of items displayed in the exercise for any student was 10, which occurred only if the student answered all of them correctly. The maximum number that could be presented

Table 7.1. *The five situations*

Change	To print his computer job, Jeffrey needed special paper. He loaded 300 sheets of paper into the paper bin of the laser printer and ran his job. When he was done, there were 35 sheets of paper left.
Group	The Psychology Department has a large faculty: 17 Professors, 9 Associate Professors, and 16 Assistant Professors.
Compare	The best typist in the pool can type 65 words per minute on the typewriter and 80 words per minute on the word processor.
Restate	In our office, the new copier produces copies 2.5 times faster than the old copier. The old copier produced 50 pages every minute.
Vary	An editor of a prestigious journal noticed that, for a particularly wordy author, there were five reference citations for every page of text. There were 35 text pages in the manuscript.

Source: From Marshall 1993b, with permission of Kluwer Academic Publishers.

was 20 items, which could happen only if a student erred in identifying the first two items representing each of the five situations. The number of items actually presented to students in this study ranged from 10 to 18.

Interview responses. The second source of data was information given by each student in the interview that immediately followed the identification task. Students did not know in advance that they were to be interviewed. After a student had finished the computer task, the experimenter asked him or her to spend a few minutes discussing the instruction. During the interview, each student was asked to talk about the situations, first giving the names for all the situations he or she could recall and then describing each one as fully as possible. After each of the student's comments, the experimenter prompted the student to provide additional information if possible. The probes continued until the student indicated that he or she could not remember anything else or did not want to add anything more to the response. Most of their responses were very brief. All interviews were audiotaped and transcribed.

The interview data reveal which pieces of information from the instruction were encoded and subsequently retrieved by each student. It is to be expected that students have more knowledge than they can access (as pointed out by Nisbett & Wilson, 1977), and we would not expect *all* of their new knowledge to be revealed in an interview. Nevertheless, the interview data are indicative of how the student has organized his or her knowledge of the newly acquired concepts, and they do suggest which pieces of knowledge are most salient for the individual. From well-known studies such as Collins and Loftus 1975 or Reder and J. R. Anderson 1980, we can assume that an individual will tend to retrieve the most closely associated features as well as those with highest salience for the individual.

Cognitive maps and knowledge networks

Data from the student interviews were used to construct cognitive maps, one for each student. Each map is a simple, undirected graph consisting of a set of *nodes,* representing the distinct pieces of information given by the student, and *links* between nodes, representing associations among the pieces of information. The construction of the cognitive maps was relatively straightforward and unambiguous. Two research assistants and I coded each interview independently with complete agreement.

The interviews were coded in the following way. First, irrelevant comments were eliminated. These were things such as "Um, let me think" or "I'm trying to remember." Next, distinct components or elements of description were identified. They were usually phrases but could also be single words. These elements became the nodes of the cognitive maps, with one node created for each distinct component. A direct link between two nodes was added to the graph if the student linked their associated pieces of information in his or her interview response by mentioning them together.

Several types of new information are revealed by a student's cognitive map. First, of course, it serves as a general indication of how much the student remembered. The number of nodes in a cognitive map provides an estimate of this information. Second, the cognitive map shows which pieces of information are related to each other. A measure of association or connectivity can be made by counting the number of links in the map. Node count and degree of connectivity are standard graph measures, and I have discussed elsewhere how they may be used to estimate a student's knowledge of a subject area. I will not repeat the discussion because the primary issue here is the nature of the information contained in the nodes, not the estimation of the size of the cognitive maps. The interested reader is referred to Marshall 1990b and Frank 1971 for details about making such estimates.

To explore the nature of the nodes in more detail, I examined two additional types of information that could be derived from the cognitive maps: (1) *specificity,* which is the student's tendency to recall specific, as opposed to abstract, features in describing the situations and (2) *confusions,* which show the extent to which the student confused different aspects of the five situations. One can examine nodes to estimate the former and links to estimate the latter.

Specificity. Three measures of specificity were developed: the number of specific responses, the number of abstract responses, and the ratio of abstract to specific responses. To derive these measures, each node in a student's cognitive map was first coded as representing one of two types of detail: specific or abstract. *Specific knowledge* refers to elements of information having to do with the examples presented in instruction, and it reflects the particular details of the example. *Abstract knowledge* refers to the general features or definition of the situation. Every distinct piece of information (i.e., each node) recalled by a student was categorized as being specific or abstract. Illustrations of both kinds of responses are given in Table 7.2, which shows actual responses made by students during the interviews. The italicized phrases in the specific response are illustrations of specific detail deriving from the initial example in SPS instruction. Those in the abstract response indicate the abstract detail. The final example in Table 7.2 shows the unfortunate, but realistic, case in which neither abstract nor specific detail can be recalled.

Table 7.2. *Examples of student responses*

Abstract	Q:	What do you remember about Group?
	A:	Group is when you have different items, *different groups of items, that can be categorized into one general group.*
Specific:	Q:	What about Group?
	A:	That was when you bought *7 shirts and 4 pairs of shorts and they grouped it into clothing. So you had 11 separate things of clothing.*
None:	Q:	Tell me about Change.
	A:	I pressed that review button so many times and I can't remember anything right now. Um, change was, um my mind is blank right now. I did okay on the computer. I've forgotten just about everything. I'm trying to think of an example. I know they change something and make something else.

Source: From Marshall 1993b, with permission of Kluwer Academic Publishers.

The choice of a coding scheme for developing the cognitive maps is a critical one. One might be tempted to use a simple coding scheme in which each word can be represented by a node. The drawback is that students typically use many more words when they give specific responses than when they give abstract ones, because students tended to embellish the example stories. Consequently, equating the number of nodes with the number of words could result in a potentially large bias in favor of the specific responses. Therefore, keeping in mind that our objective was to capture the main ideas or components of a response, we devised a coding scheme to reduce this bias. The scheme defines the contents of a node in broad terms, and each node represents a chunk of information. To give an example, we coded the (non-empty) responses of Table 7.2 as each having two nodes representing the Group situation. For the specific case, the nodes are the name of the combination of items (i.e., clothing) and the individual items (i.e., shorts and shirts). For the abstract case, the nodes are the supercategory (i.e., the larger group) and the smaller categories (i.e., subgroups that make up the larger group).

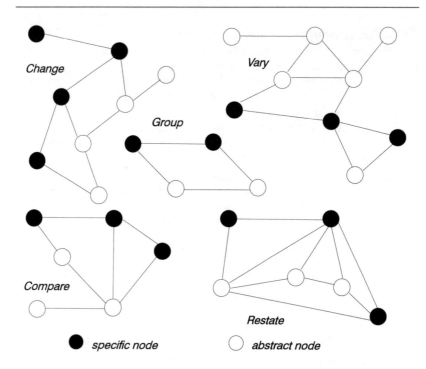

Figure 7.1. The plenary cognitive map corresponding to SPS instruction. (Reprinted from Marshall, 1993b, with permission from Kluwer Academic Publishers)

Figure 7.1 shows as a cognitive map the basic information that could be derived from the SPS instruction, coded in the same way that the student interviews were coded. Thus, it contains both abstract and specific nodes. The abstract nodes are indicated by hollow circles, and the specific nodes are represented by filled circles. To understand Figure 7.1, consider that eight different pieces of information were part of the instruction about the Change situation: four abstract characterizations and four example details. Hence, there are eight nodes in the Change graph. A link between two nodes indicates that their two corresponding pieces of information were presented together in SPS.

Figure 7.1 depicts the case in which all relevant information provided in instruction is included in the cognitive map. This cognitive map can be interpreted as the ideal cognitive map that might ever be constructed for any student, because it contains all of the essential information found in the instruction. The measures of specificity for the full graph of Figure 7.1 have roughly equal numbers of specific and abstract nodes (Specific = 15; Abstract = 18), with a ratio of abstract to specific somewhat greater than 1 (Ratio = 1.2).[2]

Normally, students do not retain all the details of instruction, and the cognitive maps that represent their knowledge are generally much sparser than is the map shown in Figure 7.1. Nevertheless, their cognitive maps also are combinations of specific and abstract nodes. Whether the student maps have a predominance of one type of node is one of the questions addressed in the analyses below.

Confusions. The confusions that arose for students were usually errors in linking features (i.e., the nodes shown in Figure 7.1) to situation names. Students sometimes linked one feature to several situations, and they sometimes linked features only to the wrong situation. Confusions are more easily seen when we represent the cognitive map as a two-layer knowledge network, the upper layer representing the five different situation names and the lower one representing the feature nodes. Figure 7.2 shows a two-layer network for the cognitive map of Figure 7.1. All 33 nodes represented in Figure 7.1 are present in this figure as nodes at the lower level. Each of them connects to one and only one node at the upper level.

Connections among the nodes at the lower layer represent situational links. Generally, the more connections an individual makes at this level, the greater the understanding on the part of that individual. Such links are usually judged to be valuable. If two nodes are connected to each other, then the retrieval of one of the nodes ought to facilitate the retrieval of the other. This facilitation accords with the principle of spreading activation. Moreover, if both nodes are also associated with the same situation, then recognition of that situation ought to be facilitated as well. In general, the more knowledge the individual has about a concept and the

Change Group Compare Restate Vary

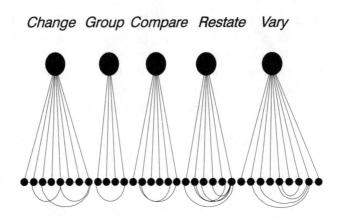

Figure 7.2. A two-layer knowledge network. (Reprinted from Marshall, 1993b, with permission from Kluwer Academic Publishers)

greater the number of associations connecting that knowledge, the better the individual is able to recognize the concept.

In contrast, multiple links between a node at the lower level and several nodes at the upper level may or may not be of value to the individual's learning, because they are a potential source of confusion. Such links will not always reflect confusions; situations could in principle share one or more features. In the present case, however, the instruction was carefully designed to eliminate common features among situations. This is reflected in Figure 7.2 by the fact that each node at the lower level connects to one and only one node at the upper level. Given the design of instruction, no node at the lower level should connect to more than a single upper level node. Such linkages would be confusion links and reflect a misunderstanding about the two situations linked to the common feature node.

An example of how confusions are manifested in students' responses is given in Figure 7.3. Two student networks are presented in this figure. Both students encoded a relatively large amount of information from the instruction compared with other students in the experiment, but it is clear from the figure that they recalled different elements of information. The remembered ele-

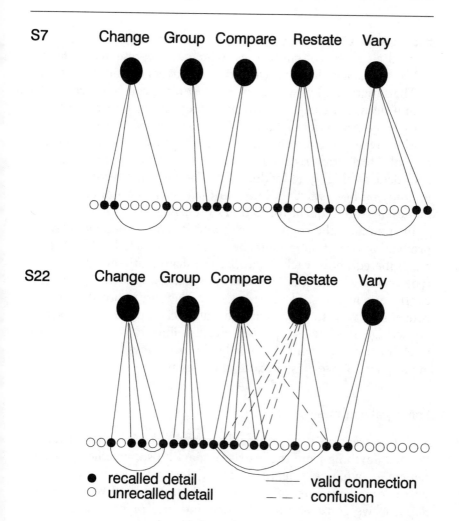

Figure 7.3. Examples of knowledge networks for two students. (Adapted from Marshall, 1993b, with permission from Kluwer Academic Publishers)

ments are presented here as filled circles and those that were not recalled by the student are hollow circles. As can be seen in the figure, Student S7 remembered distinct pieces of information about each situation and showed no confusions (i.e., each feature node connects to a single situation node). S22, on the other hand, expressed a number of confusions, which are represented in Figure 7.3 by the dashed links between the two layers of nodes.

The situational knowledge of every student can be described by such a network, using the student's interview responses. The two knowledge networks of Figure 7.3 illustrate the wealth of information available from the networks. Obviously, the amount and type of information recalled as well as the particular confusions of a student are highly individualized. The networks provide a way of studying how students differ in their initial encoding of information and subsequent formation of schemas.

In summary, the cognitive map and its corresponding network provide information about the number of details the student remembered about each situation, the degree of connectivity, the type of knowledge (i.e., abstract or specific), and the number of confusions in the student's response. They are more than just a convenient way to represent the data. The cognitive maps and knowledge networks supply new insights into the data. The ability to characterize students' knowledge in these ways has many exciting implications for instruction and assessment.

Statistical analyses

The two central issues, broadly stated, are whether students learned anything from the instruction and, if so, whether they can remember what they learned. Thus, the first question to ask is whether students learned to distinguish among the five situations. Suppose we consider only the first instance of presentation for each situation to each student. Remember that students saw varying numbers of items for the identification task, depending on how successful they were in responding. Looking only at the first five responses for each student gives us a common ground for comparison and provides an excellent opportunity to determine if they responded systematically or simply guessed. Under a guessing strategy, each of the five menu options is equally likely to have been chosen, but only one is correct. Thus, the student has a 20% chance of guessing the correct answer and should on the average

Table 7.3. *Summary statistics for Experiment I*

Situation	Mean number of nodes recalled	Mean number of potential nodes	Mean proportion recalled
Change	3.7	8	.46
Group	2.3	4	.59
Compare	3.4	6	.57
Restate	2.2	6	.32
Vary	2.7	9	.30

respond correctly to one of the five items by chance. In actuality, the mean number of correct responses was 3.0, and the difference between the two is statistically significant: $t(26) = 10.39$, $p < .01$. This difference corresponds to a proportion of successful responses that is 3 times greater than the guessing strategy would predict.

Next, we ask whether the students remembered anything of the instruction. It is evident from the interview data that students varied greatly in the amount of information they were able to recall about the five situations. The number of different details retrieved by students extended from a low of 3 to a high of 20. The mean number of details was 13.5, with a standard deviation of 4.02. We can state with confidence that students recalled a great deal of information.

They did not recall uniform amounts of information about the five situations, however, and there were distinct differences in how much they remembered. Table 7.3 provides some summary statistics about students' recollections. A multivariate test of repeated measures shows that the mean numbers of nodes recalled for the five situations differed significantly, $F(4, 22) = 7.96$, $p < .01$. That this difference is not attributable just to the differing numbers of potential nodes that could be learned can be seen in Table 7.3, where the number of nodes found in instruction is given as well as the proportion of these nodes that were recalled on average by the students. If students had some fixed propensity to remember each detail they encountered in instruction, they should be more likely to recall information having to do with situations with more details than with situations having only a few. Under this argument, their average for Vary should be the highest, not the lowest.

There was great variability in the students' memories for each situation. Some students could not recall any details at all about one or more of the situations, but these students were few in number. Other students remembered a great deal about some situations but relatively little about others. In terms of the nodes presented in instruction, one student recalled seven of the eight details about Change, three students recalled all four details about Group, and four students remembered all six details of Compare. These three situations were well understood and were described with relative ease by most of the students. No students remembered entirely the details of either Restate or Vary. These situations were clearly more difficult for the students to understand, and students varied greatly in their recall of them.

Students differed in the type of information they recalled as well as in the amount. Evaluation of the cognitive maps shows that some students were more likely to encode mostly specific details, some were more likely to encode mostly abstract information, some encoded both in about equal proportions, and some encoded almost nothing. The number of abstract and specific details recalled varied widely, and the observed ratio of abstract to specific detail ranged from a high of 14 to 3, for a ratio of 4.67, to a low of 6 to 14, for a ratio of 0.43.

A closer look at the nature of the specific information recalled in the interviews showed that students very frequently gave details about the *very first* example of a situation encountered in SPS. Of the total 175 specific nodes recalled by this group of students, 63% were taken directly from the initial SPS examples. Another 14% referred to other examples presented in SPS or to items on the identification task. Thus, students constructed their own examples relatively infrequently, accounting for only 23% of the details. Moreover, they usually did not formulate complete examples, and often part or all of a self-generated example was incorrect and did not match the situation being described.

In the interviews, we discovered that students often developed misconceptions about the situations. They were not shy about expressing confusions that existed in their understandings of the five situations and often confided to the interviewer that they had great difficulty in distinguishing one specific situation from another. Altogether, 12 of the 26 students expressed a confusion of some sort. The most prevalent misunderstanding arose between restate and compare, with 6 students developing the same confusion.

Given that students did learn something and were able to recall it, we can now ask the more critical question of whether a student's performance on the identification task can be explained in terms of what we know of his or her responses in the interview. In other words, can we predict a student's overall performance level knowing the information contained in the cognitive maps and knowledge networks? One way to look at this issue is with a linear model of multiple regression based on the different pieces of information available from the interview data. Taking the number of correct responses given by a student as the dependent variable RESPONSE, the model has four predictor variables:

NODES	The total number of nodes present in the cognitive map
RATIO	The ratio of abstract to specific nodes in the cognitive map
CONFUSION	The number of confusions expressed by the student during the interview
NODES^2	A quadratic term based on NODES

The full model has the following form:

$$\text{RESPONSE} = 4.478 + 0.628 \text{ NODES} + 0.097 \text{ RATIO} - 0.210 \text{ CONFUSION} - 0.021 \text{ NODES}^2$$

with coefficients on all but the RATIO variable reaching the conventional level of significance at a = .05. The model accounts for a significant proportion of the variance of the RESPONSE variable,

$F(4, 21) = 4.23$, $p < .025$; with a multiple correlation of .66 and adjusted $R^2 = .33$.

There are a couple of interesting points to be made about the regression model. First, the quadratic term should be noted. The inclusion of this factor, and its significant contribution to the model, suggest that, initially, the more details recalled, the better the performance, but that, eventually, adding more details does not improve performance, although there is certainly room for improvement.

Both CONFUSION and $NODES^2$ have negative coefficients, serving to pull down the performance level. In contrast, NODES and RATIO both exert positive influence. NODES, of course, is a general measure of the size of the cognitive map. In general, more is better, but as shown by the presence of $NODES^2$, one can have too much of a good thing. RATIO shows the importance of the abstract nodes compared with the specific ones. In general, students with higher ratios of abstract to specific detail performed with greater success on the identification task than students with smaller ratios.

Discussion

One of the most striking findings of this study was the way that students tended to encode and use specific details from the initial examples used in instruction. Almost all of the example nodes had to do with the five introductory examples, despite the fact that several other examples appeared later in the instruction and in the task. This finding suggests that the very first example of a concept is highly salient and should, therefore, be developed with special care. For many students, the initial examples provided the scaffolding for the development of knowledge networks. Some of the details of those examples led to erroneous connections. As a case in point, the example for one of the situations was based on money, leading a few students to expect (incorrectly) this situation to be present whenever money was in the problem. These faulty connections showed up quite explicitly in the interview responses and knowledge networks.

A general pattern of encoding was apparent from the students' responses. If students had abstract knowledge, they always seemed to use it in preference to giving example details. That is, their initial responses were generalizations, but when prompted for more information, they were usually able to provide example details to support their abstract descriptions. In contrast, several students described the situations only in terms of the examples. When prompted, they were unable to embellish their descriptions by using abstract characterizations. We recorded a number of instances in which the abstract information was followed by an example but *never* observed the opposite case of an example followed by abstract information.

The statistical analyses suggest that the degree to which a student is able to use his or her abstract information is positively related to the student's success on the identification task. Those able to express mainly abstract knowledge apparently had the best understanding of the five concepts and were most easily able to identify them. Those for whom the abstract characterizations were somewhat incomplete (e.g., those who were able to give abstract description for some concepts but needed example details to describe others) performed less well but still were more successful than those who predominantly relied on example details.

The primary instructional implication of these findings is that instruction should be developed to facilitate the linkage of abstract knowledge to easily understood example knowledge. The examples used in SPS were salient and easily encoded by almost all students. For some students, the abstract characterizations were equally easy to encode, but this was not true for everyone.

What do these findings suggest about schema development? There are at least two competing arguments, and at this point they are only offered as suggestions; a great deal more research is needed before we can draw firm conclusions. One argument holds that example knowledge is retained first. Under this argument, students first encode the example information and then build an abstract network around it. Thus, in Experiment I, we observed varying levels of this development. Some students had only the initial example portion of knowledge, and others had more expanded knowledge containing both example and abstract information. Following the argument to its conclusion, we can hypothesize that once the abstract portion of the network is formed, it becomes dominant, presumably because it becomes stronger upon exposure to each additional example, as parts of these examples are related to specific pieces of the abstract knowledge. In contrast, example knowledge should not be strengthened when new examples are presented, because the specific details of old examples are not reinforced by the new ones. If the abstract information is not yet encoded by an individual, the details of the original example – which received high strength initially – remain the most salient elements of the network and hence are the only pieces of information available to the student in the interview responses.

An alternative argument takes the reverse position, namely, that the abstract information is encoded first and then is used subsequently to encode the example information. The possibility that this argument holds cannot be ruled out without additional experimentation. For this case, we would have to explain why students could readily provide details about the examples but were unable to articulate abstract knowledge, which they must have already encoded under this argument. Experiment II sheds additional light on this issue.

Experiment II: Abstract versus specific information

Experiment I demonstrated clearly the importance of abstract and specific information for instruction. Experiment II studied the impact of introducing the situations *wholly* through examples or *wholly* through abstract characterizations and looked not only at the initial impact but also at the long-term effects. Some of the results are surprising.

Subjects

Subjects for this study were 40 students recruited from introductory psychology courses, the same population as before. They were randomly assigned to the two experimental conditions.

Experimental procedure

All students participated in three 1-hour sessions with a modified version of SPS. During their first lesson, one-half of them received SPS instruction that introduced the five situations using only examples. The remainder received instruction that contained only definitions. At the end of the first lesson, they responded to the identification task described in Experiment I and were briefly interviewed. The second session occurred 1 week later, and all students had identical instruction about using the diagrams and mapping problems into the diagrams. This second day of instruction contained both abstract and example information. Again, students were interviewed at the conclusion of the session. The third session took place 1 week later. One third of the students proceeded through the usual multistep instruction and exercises, and the remainder used PSE, the Problem Solving Environment. The first two sessions are the focus of the analyses presented here.

Instructional modifications

Because the original form of SPS was not intended to have only examples or only abstract characterizations about the situations, it required modification. Thus, although very similar, Experiment II is not an exact replication of Experiment I in terms of instruction.

Data collection

The data were again from two sources: the SPS exercises and the interviews following the first two sessions.

SPS exercises. The same exercise described above for Experiment I was used in Experiment II. For this study, a set of 10 items was selected a priori for presentation in the identification task, and all students responded to the set. The order of item presentation within the set was randomly determined for each student. This exercise was undertaken by each student at the end of initial instruction – either specific instruction using only examples or abstract instruction using only general descriptions.

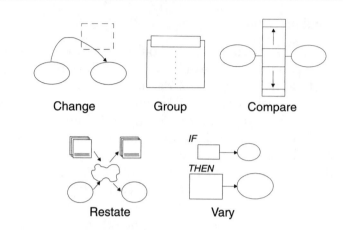

Figure 7.4. The diagrams used in SPS instruction

Mapping tasks were interspersed throughout the instruction of the second session. These tasks were described in detail in chapter 5 (see the section describing the exercises for elaboration knowledge), and an example of the format used in these tasks was presented in Figure 5.3. Upon the presentation of an item, which was either a complete story or a problem, students were asked to position the appropriate parts of the text in the diagram shown on the monitor. The five diagrams used in these tasks are reproduced in Figure 7.4. Students responded to a total of 20 mapping items, four for each situation.

Students also gave answers to a final task at the conclusion of the second session. They made two responses to each of five problems, first selecting the appropriate miniature diagram from a menu (similar to the configuration of Figure 7.4) and then mapping the parts of the problem into the corresponding enlarged diagram. All students saw the same five items, presented in random order.

Interviews. Following each instructional session, students were interviewed individually for about 5–10 minutes about what they had learned. In the first interview, the format for Experiment I was followed. The student was asked to recall the names of the situations and to describe them as fully as possible. In the second interview, students were asked to draw the diagrams and describe them. All interviews were audiotaped and transcribed.

Results

The purpose of this experiment was to compare the impact of learning from abstract or specific instruction. The two groups of students learning under these different conditions were compared on a variety of different measures.[3]

The identification task. There was no statistically significant difference in the mean number of items recognized by the two groups on the first computer task. Students who saw only the specific instruction (i.e., concrete examples) performed slightly better than those who saw only the abstract instruction (i.e., the general descriptions of the situations), with both groups identifying correctly about one half of the items ($M_{SI} = 5.7$ and $M_{AI} = 5.2$, $t < 1$).

Cognitive maps. As in Experiment I, the interview responses at the end of the first day were coded and transformed into cognitive maps and knowledge networks. The most striking result of these data is the large discrepancy between the number of things recalled by the specific-instruction group (a total of 168, with $M_{SI} = 8.8$) and the number recalled by the abstract-instruction group (a total of 128, with $M_{AI} = 6.7$). The difference in means is statistically significant, $F(1,36) = 5.15$, $p < .05$. The abstract-instruction group had great difficulty verbalizing what they knew. Many of them struggled but could only iterate that they knew what the situations were without being able to describe them in any way.[4] The specific-instruction group, like the students of Experiment I, tended to recall the exact details of the initial examples. Of the 114 specific details they reported, 68% were about the initial examples of instruction. An additional 3% came from the task items.

It is useful to examine whether the specific-instruction group recalled only example details or whether they developed their own abstract characterizations. Likewise, it is informative to investigate the extent to which the abstract-instruction group recalled only the abstract information or constructed their own examples. For the specific-instruction group, 51 of 168 nodes, about 30%, were abstractions they developed by themselves and used to describe the situations. Likewise, for the abstract-instruction group, 37 of the 128 nodes identified from the interviews, or approximately 29%, were specific information. That is, the individuals in this group came up with their own examples to describe the situations, and about one-third of the time they used this example information to define the situations. Thus, in the absence of the second type of information, whether it be specific detail or abstract definition, students provided evidence that they could nonetheless construct it by themselves.

One can ask what kind of examples did the abstract-instruction group construct for themselves? It turns out that about half the time, they did not so much construct their own examples as encode as examples the first situation they encountered of each type, which turned out to be the items on the identification task. Thus, of the 37 specific-example nodes identified for the abstract-instruction group, 18 of them referred explicitly to details from items from the identification task. Moreover, all 18 were drawn from the *first* instance the students saw, never the second. Once again, we see the importance of the first example that students encounter.

We can also look at the number of confusions in the networks developed from the interviews. For the specific-instruction group, 12 of the 168 nodes were linked erroneously by the students to one of the five situations. That is, a student could retrieve a particular piece of information but believed it referred to some situation other than its appropriate one. The confusions accounted for about 7% of their total nodes. The figures for the abstract-instruction group were 20 of 128 nodes, which was about 16% of their responses. Thus, the abstract-instruction group developed over twice as many confusions as did the specific-instruction group. This difference in proportions is statistically significant, $z = 2.337$, $p < .05$.

Mapping tasks. Responses to the five mapping tasks – each task consisting of four items – were combined for every student, and the numbers of correct responses made by the two groups were compared. The group receiving abstract instruction made marginally more correct mappings than the group receiving specific instruction, with means $M_{AI} = 13.8$ and $M_{SI} = 11.9$ ($t = 1.79$, $.10 < p < .05$, $df = 36$). Similar but slightly stronger results were obtained for the mapping component of the end-of-session task. The abstract-instruction group again performed better than the specific-instruction group on the mapping part of the task, with means $M_{AI} = 3.1$ and $M_{SI} = 2.1$ ($t = 2.07$, $p < .05$, $df = 35$).

One striking difference between the responses of the two groups was the nature of the errors they made in mapping. For the specific-instruction group, 16% of their errors (i.e., 25 of 153) were blank responses. That is, they did not attempt any mapping at all. The corresponding percentage for the abstract-instruction group was 4% (i.e., 5 of 113). This difference in proportions is statistically significant, $z = 3.04$, $p < .01$.

Interestingly, there was no difference in the two groups' ability to recognize the situations (i.e., the first part of the end-of-session task). Both groups performed well, and on average, members of both groups were able to recognize four of the five items. The respective means for this task were $M_{AI} = 4.10$ and $M_{SI} = 4.11$. This similarity in recognition performance was also noted on the first identification task, but the overall performance of both groups was substantially improved by the end-of-session task of the second week. It seems clear that the two groups consistently performed at about the same level in recognizing the situations. A difference emerged only on the second part of the end-of-session task, which involved mapping the situations to the diagrams.

Diagram recall. At the conclusion of the second day, students were asked to draw from memory the five diagrams used in SPS instruction. No statistical difference was observed in the performance of the two groups. Both groups were able to draw more than half of the figures correctly, with means of $M_{SI} = 3.3$ and $M_{AI} = 3.8$, and $t(35) = 1.17$, $p > .05$.

Discussion

Let me try to summarize what I think these results tell us. First, there did not initially seem to be any clear-cut differences in identification ability between the two groups. Both groups recognized about half of the test items. They obviously had acquired enough information to make some of the needed discriminations among the situations, although the nature of that information was, by design, quite different for the two groups. The specific-instruction group appeared to have distinctly more information available to them, but this advantage in amount did not lead to better performance. Thus, we may conclude that either specific or abstract instruction can lead productively to the acquisition of useful identification knowledge.

A second point to be made is that there seems to be a delayed advantage for the abstract-instruction group with respect to the acquisition and use of elaboration knowledge. The abstract-instruction group performed consistently better than the specific-instruction group on the mapping tasks. The interesting thing about this finding is that the only difference in instruction was the way the situations were introduced on the first day of the experiment (i.e., abstract versus specific details). On the second and third days, both groups had identical instruction about mapping.

These results are very suggestive. On the one hand, there is some evidence that providing instruction through specific examples aids in students' development of identification skills. Certainly, the data from the interviews support this point: The students in the specific-instruction group were able to recall more details than those in the abstract-instruction group. Had we stopped the experiment at this point, we might have been tempted to conclude – erroneously, as it turns out – that the specific-instruction condition was at least as successful as the abstract-instruction condition. And, if we were only interested in the quantity of information recalled (as given in the interview), we might even prefer the specific-instruction condition, because students in it articulated a great deal more than students in the other condition.

The results from the second week of the experiment dispute the claim that the effects are equal under the two instructional conditions. Although it is apparent that both groups appeared to be developing sufficient identification knowledge from the first session, it is equally apparent that the abstract-instruction group had an advantage in developing the accompanying elaboration knowledge. This conclusion is based on the fact that the students in the abstract-instruction group performed better than those in the specific-instruction group on the mapping tasks, that is, those tasks for which elaboration knowledge is required. Further, they had many fewer "no response" errors; the students who received abstract instruction were almost always able to make some attempt to map the items.

How can we explain the difference in performance between the two instruction groups? At this point, and without further experimentation to verify it, we can only speculate about why the learning of the students in the specific-instruction group was constrained. Having used the examples successfully in the first lesson, the students may have relied too heavily on them in the second. Or they may have attempted to compare a memorized example with the current mapping items and found that they had insufficient knowledge to make a fruitful comparison. Or the example-only instruction may have fostered a rigid knowledge structure that lacked the flexibility to expand as the additional abstract details became available. Or, finally, it may be that the students felt sufficiently comfortable with their understanding of the situations after the first lesson and that they simply paid less attention to the abstract explanations of the second.

An interesting by-product: Diagram use. In this second study a hint emerges about the importance of the diagrams used during the instruction. They may serve two very different uses. One use is as a recognition device, as in the first part of the end-of-session task, with the diagrams operating in much the same way as the verbal labels (e.g., *Change*). The individual parts of the diagram may not be important for this function, and just the overall configuration and shape may suffice. As can be readily seen in Figure

7.4, the visual representations of the five situations are very distinct, and it is unnecessary to focus on each nuance of each figure to distinguish among them.

The second use of diagrams is that they may also serve as templates against which students compare individual parts of specific problems. For this use, students must have knowledge of the different components and what characterizes them. Thus, the student must understand the way that the figures are constructed and the meaning assigned to their different parts. The overall shape is less important.

These two functions are no doubt related, but they are not redundant. Some students in the experiment were clearly adept in using diagrams for recognition but were unable to use them as templates. That is, they could make the situation recognition based on the diagram but could not map items correctly into it. We see this most clearly in the end-of-session exercise that requires the student to recognize and map a set of items. Altogether, the 39 students recognized a total of 159 situations (out of a possible 195) but were able to map only 58% of those that were recognized.[5] Others apparently developed the template knowledge (i.e., could map successfully) but lacked the recognition knowledge. This relatively rare event can be seen by looking at each student's overall rate of success in the mapping exercises versus their rate of success in the identification part of the final two-part mapping exercise. It is interesting to note that two students were quite successful in mapping the items when given the correct map (answering 75–80% of them correctly) but unsuccessful in recognizing the situations by their appropriate diagrams (identifying only two of the five situations). The most successful students manifested both skills.

Further research about the impact of diagrams is warranted if we are to understand their function in instruction and learning as well as their role in schema formation. It is curious that some students develop one of the uses and not the other. The role of visual representations in schema-based learning is examined in the next two chapters.

Table 7.4. *Summary statistics from Experiments I and II*

		Experiment I	Experiment II
Identification task	M	6.27	5.45
	SD	1.46	3.08
Nodes recalled	M	13.50	7.70
	SD	4.02	3.08

Comparisons from the two experiments

From the advantage provided by hindsight, we can look at the results of these two experiments side by side and make comparisons between them. Table 7.4 contains several relevant statistics from both studies. To construct Table 7.4, only the first 2 items of each situation were considered for the students of Experiment I, making this task equivalent to the 10-item one of Experiment II.

Consider first whether the results of the second experiment are statistically different from those of the first. A simple t test confirms that the value 5.45, the mean of the identification task in Experiment II, would not arise by chance if the true mean value were actually the 6.27 previously observed in Experiment I ($t = -3.36$, $df = 41$, $p < .05$). Similarly, one must reject the hypothesis that the observed value of 7.7 for the number of nodes recalled does not differ significantly from 13.5 ($t = -11.69$, $df = 37$, $p < .01$). It is important to point out here that these tests are not as rigorous as they would be for a true comparison in which we randomly assigned students to either experiment. We must take into account the possibility that the students in the two experiments differed on some factors other than the experimental conditions. However, it is not easy to discern any systematic differences. Both groups of students were drawn from the same population under identical conditions, and both groups participated in the same room with the same equipment. They did meet with different interviewers, but that difference should influence only the recall of information, not the computer tasks, and students responded to the same interview questions in both experiments.

We can conclude that the differences between the two experiments are quite large and consistent. The students having both types of instruction did much better on the identification task and recalled more information than those students having only one type of instruction.

Earlier in this chapter, I brought up two possibilities about how students might be encoding abstract and specific knowledge, with one or the other being acquired first before the second could be successfully encoded. The results of the second experiment generate another alternative, namely that for either type of information to be encoded fully, the other type also needs to be available for cognitive processing – although it will not necessarily be encoded as part of long-term memory. Under this explanation, both types of knowledge would need to be present in instruction for the most efficient encoding of either type of knowledge, but only one might be encoded and retrievable at a later time. Thus, it may have been easier for the students in the first experiment to encode the abstract knowledge having read – but not remembered – the specific example of a situation. This additional information was not available to students in the abstract-instruction group of the second experiment and thus limited their encoding. Or, vice versa, it may have been easier for students in the first experiment to encode the example knowledge in the presence of the abstract knowledge. Overall, the students in the second experiment encoded less information and performed less well than the students in the first experiment.

General conclusions

What conclusions can we draw from these two experiments? First, they provide compelling evidence that students' initial learning from instruction varies tremendously. It is not just a matter of degree, although they do retain differing amounts. It is a matter of substance: Some students learn mostly examples, some learn mostly abstract generalizations, and others learn a mix of the two.

At this point, we can only speculate about why some students acquire more of one type than another when both are equally available. Further study is needed to ascertain whether these differences are due to habit, preference, or some specific aspect of prior learning or instruction.

We can draw a number of conclusions about the importance of both types of knowledge. First, although many students show a preference for one or the other type of knowledge, it seems evident that students learn more in the presence of both types of information than when only one or the other is employed. This seems to be the case even if the students cannot explicitly recall the additional information. One inference we can make is that it is important to introduce the abstract information very early in instruction so that it enhances what the students understand of the examples. A second inference is that the first example encountered by the student is very important and is likely to be remembered for a long time. Recall that in the first experiment, most of the example information that students related came from the initial example of the instruction. And in the second experiment in the absence of example instruction, many students nevertheless relied on the first example they encountered – which turned out to be the items of the identification task. Careful selection of the initial examples may turn out to be a critical factor in any instruction.

A very intriguing finding emerged in the second experiment and concerned performance over time. Initially, the two forms of instruction appeared to be approximately equivalent in their impact, although in terms of students' ability to articulate what they understood, the specific instruction was superior to the abstract. However, after further instruction, the students in the abstract-instruction group performed substantially better than the students in the specific-instruction group. If we look at their performance in terms of schema development, we can hypothesize that the students in the abstract-instruction group had the rudiments of the targeted schemas in place, because they were using both types of knowledge – identification and elaboration – quite easily. The same can also be said for the specific-instruction group, but their schema development seemed to lag behind that of the abstract-instruction group in the incorporation of elaboration knowledge. Both groups of students were beginning to develop and use schema knowledge acquired from the SPS instruction, and the evidence of their learning supports the hypothesis that schemas take time to develop. One can speculate that the inability of some students to articulate what they knew in the first interview was a temporary state that improved dramatically, given more time and further instruction.

When both types of information were available in instruction, students acquired more knowledge and performed better than when only one type of information was present. With only a single type of information in instruction, regardless of whether it was specific or abstract, students demonstrated more confusions and were less able to articulate what they knew. In the absence of one or the other type of information, many students generated the missing type by themselves, either by creating their own knowledge or by adopting an early test item to serve as the base example for a situation. The self-generated examples were not always well thought-out, and they were not always correct. It was evident in the interviews that students were grappling with the problem of developing useful information with which to evaluate the situations. Their frustration was often evident as they lamented that they knew what the situations were but just could not describe them. Having both abstract and specific information as part of instruction makes a very great difference in their ability to pull their knowledge together, to make correct identifications, and to describe what they know.

8

The acquisition of planning knowledge

Two studies have incorporated the use of the Problem Solving Environment (PSE) in their design. One was the second experiment of chapter 7, which contrasted learning from abstract and specific instruction. As the final part of that study, one group of students worked for one session with PSE while another group completed the original SPS instruction. The essential conclusion we drew from the study was that 1 hour was simply too brief a time for the students to become comfortable in the interactive environment. They were able to use PSE but not as freely as we had hoped, and we suspected that their freedom to develop their own plans for problem solving was hampered by a lack of familiarity with the computer system itself.

We did gain some information about how valuable PSE could be with pairs of students, because some of the students using PSE worked together as part of the experimental design and their conversations were audiotaped. PSE seems to be an ideal setting for the interaction of pairs or small groups. They can describe their plans to each other in terms of the diagrams and icons, which are always visible on the screen, and they can try out their ideas with no ill consequences. The computer display is large enough to accommodate several students easily, so all of them have clear visual access. Moreover, PSE does not try to force students to follow one solution plan, so students working together can formulate multiple plans and evaluate all of them, thus discovering for themselves that no single plan is necessarily the only correct one.

The abstract/specific instruction study was promising but yielded inconclusive results about how students formulate plans. Consequently, a second planning study was undertaken, whose central objective was the investigation of plans. In this study, we monitored the progress of students who worked through the initial lessons of SPS, including the introduction to multiple situations and plans, and who then spent two 1-hour sessions using PSE. The first PSE session was used only to familiarize the students with the options and to let them explore the environment as they wished. The second session was an evaluation session in which all students were asked to solve a set of common problems. The planning data analyzed here come from this second session.

The analysis of plans requires some cunning. Planning knowledge is rarely displayed in overt measurable settings; more often it is completely hidden, detectable only by inference. To make things worse, it may also appear as an all-or-none process or as one giant leap. PSE was purposely designed to tap into this hidden aspect of problem solving, at least insofar as the acquisition and use of planning knowledge for schemas is concerned. Often in traditional problem-solving exercises, we can do no more than evaluate the written computational steps a student has recorded, looking at the order in which these steps were taken as an indication of the student's overall plan. The design of PSE allows us to go much further; we can now look at a number of other aspects of problem solving, including important organizational decisions the student has made.

The study to be described here is not an experiment in the usual sense. For the most part, it is a qualitative, rather than a quantitative, study. There are no statistical hypotheses to be tested and no parameters to be estimated. Instead, the focus is on delineating individual behavior. Some aggregation of data has been done, but the primary intent is to describe in detail individual performances in PSE.

Experimental details

Subjects

Subjects were 17 students drawn from the same population as those who participated in the studies described in chapter 7 (i.e., college students who demonstrated poor problem-solving skills).

Procedure

Each student took part in three instructional sessions. In the first session, they were presented with a condensed version of the original SPS instruction. The session lasted a full hour (in contrast to the 45–50 min of the studies described in chapter 7), and students worked through the introductory lesson and task, completed the mapping instruction and tasks, and began the instruction about multistep problems and planning all in one session. Some of the students completed the planning instruction on the first day. Those who did not finish the entire sequence in one session completed it in 5–10 min at the start of the second session.

The second and third sessions were devoted to use of the PSE. In the second session, each student was given an introduction to the system by the experimenter and allowed to explore and investigate the various options available. Most of the students worked on one to three problems, but many did not make any systematic efforts to solve them.

During the third session, each student was asked to give complete solutions for the five multistep problems shown in Table 8.1. They were scheduled to spend 50 min, if needed, to solve the five problems. All students completed the task within the allotted time.

Data collection

The key to the analysis of plans in PSE is its simple, yet comprehensive, record keeping. PSE maintains a full history of every action taken by the student. This is not as cumbersome as it sounds, because the actions are mouse events and they can be

Table 8.1. *Multistep problems in PSE*

1. Joe won $100 in the state lottery. He spent some of it on toys for his two children. He bought a doll for Sue that cost $25 and he bought a stuffed bear for Ellen that cost $28. How much of his lottery winnings remained after he bought the toys?
2. Maria gave correct answers to 80 percent of the test questions on the Chemistry final examination. There were 240 questions on the test. How many items did she miss?
3. Mr. Solin used a coupon to save 40 cents on a bottle of 100 aspirin. The aspirin was originally priced at $2.40. How much did each aspirin cost Mr. Solin?
4. Alice was a sales clerk at a local department store. The store was having a sale on sweaters, and every sweater was selling for a discount of 20 percent off the original price. It was Alice's job to mark the new price on the price tag of each sweater. If a sweater originally cost $45, what price should Alice write down as the sales price?
5. At half-time during the last football game, the Chargers had a score of 6 points. During the second half, they scored twice as many points as the Raiders. The Raiders scored 7 points. What was the Chargers' final score?

briefly noted in a form that is easily read, interpreted, and aggregated.

An annotated example of one student record for one problem is presented in Table 8.2. The material of Table 8.2 in the left-hand column is an unedited output for one of the students participating in the study. The only modification is the insertion of blank lines to accommodate the output explanation of the right-hand column.

A brief description of what the student is doing physically as this record evolves may be informative. Initially, the screen was mostly empty, with the two major work spaces in the upper and lower quadrants blank (see Figure 5.9). Upon reading the problem, the student elected to drag the icon for Change into the Student Work Area and then the icon for Group. Notice that the system output for the Group icon is "GR3," indicating that the student made the decision to use the icon having three partitions for subgroups. Having positioned the icons, the student next elected to map the Group situation. Now the activity transferred to the Mapping Area. His first action, picking up the value $1,200, was a mistake, which he self-corrected (indicated by the NIL). He then proceeded to pick up and insert correctly the three values that form the subgroups of the Group situation. Opening the calculator, he computed the value of the total group and placed the result into the diagram. Having concluded with the mapping, his next move was back to the Student Work Area, where he linked the two previously selected icons by drawing an arrow from the newly computed value of the Group icon to the appropriate part of the Change icon. At this point, he returned again to the mapping window, having made the decision to map the Change situation. When this diagram appeared, the result of his linkage was automatically positioned. His first action was to complete the mapping with the available information from the problem, namely, the $1,200 (which he had first picked up and discarded in mapping the Group situation). The remaining component of the situation was unknown, and he resorted to the calculator once again for its value. To complete his problem solving, he moved the calculator result first to the appropriate part of the diagram and then into the Final Answer Window at the bottom of the screen. Closing the Mapping Area, he informed PSE that he had reached a solution by selecting "Done" from the pop-up response menu. PSE concluded that the response was correct and so informed the student.

As can be seen in Table 8.2, it is very easy to read through the history of the student's response and to gain a thorough understanding of how the student went about solving the problem. Anyone can do it with a bare minimum of training (needing only to learn, for instance, how to interpret the numbers associated with the link command). The amount of detail displayed is enormous. The record contains information on how the student perceived the problem generally, on any misunderstandings the student had about the problem (including whether these were self-corrected and the point at which they were modified), and on how the student went about finding a solution.

Table 8.2. *Example of one student's problem solving*

System output	Explanation of output
(Problem M16)	System randomly selects Problem 16 for presentation.
(IconSelected CHsmall 1 (78 . 285)) (IconSelected GR3small 2 (252 . 248))	Student selects the Change icon first (1), which is the overall situation of the problem. (The numbers in parentheses indicate the location on the screen at which the student positioned the icon.) Student then selects the Group icon (2), which is an embedded subproblem.
(Map GR3small 2) (LiftWord $1200 NIL) (LiftWord $625 4) (LiftWord $350 3) (LiftWord $195 2) (CalculatorCalled) (CalculatorSolve (625+350+195) 1170) (LiftWord (Calculation 1170) 1)	Student opts to map the parts of the Group icon. (At this point the enlarged diagram appears in the upper right-hand window on the screen.) Student first erroneously picks up the number $1,200 and then releases it – presumably realizing that it was not needed. Student then maps as subgroups the values $625, $350, and $195. Student calculates their sum and places it in the supergroup position of the diagram. Student closes the enlarged diagram and returns to the Student Work Area.

General findings

It will be recalled that PSE was developed with two purposes in mind: First, it was to be an environment in which students could practice using their newly acquired knowledge of problem solving, and second, it was to provide the setting in which to examine planning knowledge. Both objectives were realized. All students used the flexible computer environment easily and seemingly with enjoyment. Many volunteered how much they liked certain features of it. Thus, at least anecdotally, the first function of PSE was

Table 8.2. (*cont.*)

System output	Explanation of output
(Link 2 1 1 2)	Student apparently realizes that the supergroup value calculated for the Group diagram is also a value needed in the Change diagram. Student uses the link command to connect the "supergroup box" of the Group icon with the "amount of change" box of the Change icon.
(Map CHsmall 1) (LiftWord $1200 1) (CalculatorCalled) (CalculatorClear (1170 - 12)) (CalculatorSolve (12) 12) (CalculatorClear NIL) (CalculatorSolve (1200 - 1170) 30) (LiftWord (Calculation 30) 3) (LiftWord (Calculation 30) NIL) (LiftWord (Calculation 30) AnswerWindow) (Done)	Student then maps the Change icon, placing the previously rejected value of $1,200 into the initial position of the enlarged diagram. (The value $1,170 already appears in the map because of the explicit link made by the student.) Student opens the calculator but makes an incorrect calculation. Clearing the calculator, student then correctly calculates the value $30 and places it first in the diagram and then in the Final Answer Window.
(RightAnswer 30)	System records that student has answered the problem correctly.

Note: This is an actual output from one of the students in the study. The problem was solved during the first session with PSE. The output appears here exactly as it is recorded by the system. Blank lines have been inserted to highlight the different segments of the problem solving.

fulfilled: Students did, indeed, use it as a practice ground, and it allowed them to demonstrate their problem-solving skills – even some skills not included in SPS, such as how to use the calculator efficiently.

As to the second function of PSE, namely, to provide a means of examining the development of problem-solving plans, we have more concrete evidence. The intent was to find out whether a system such as PSE yields useful information about an *individual's* problem solving. To that end, each student's performance was examined separately. At the same time, important observations were made that pertain to the problem solving of many, if not all, of the students, and these deserve to be mentioned as well. Thus, the analyses look initially to the individual and then to the aggregate to make full use of the available information.

What conclusions could be drawn from students' problem solving? First, reaching the correct solution was not by itself a sufficient indicator that a student really knew what he or she was doing. Almost all the students eventually reached the correct solution for the five problems, but they took very different paths, they required differing amounts of time to reach solutions, and we had little difficulty identifying those whose schema knowledge was weak. These students demonstrated very little structure in their approach, using essentially a trial-and-error strategy for selecting icons and making calculations. If we had looked only at the final outcome of the problem solving (i.e., whether the answer was correct), these students would be indistinguishable from those who had an excellent grasp of problem structure. Thus, focusing our attention on schema knowledge leads to a deeper and richer evaluation of student understanding and allows us to make a better diagnosis of problem-solving capabilities.

Individual responses

A number of different phenomena emerged from our analyses of students' use of PSE. Six of these are documented in Table 8.3.

Poor understanding and weak schema knowledge are demonstrated in the first episode of Table 8.3. This student evidently felt it necessary to carry out some computation using two values available from the problem, but he obviously did not know *which* calculation to make – so he tried several variations, presumably hoping to recognize a sensible solution if it appeared. Failing that, he finally opted for help (i.e., the call to *ShowMe*).

Table 8.3. *Some examples of students' responses in PSE*

1. Weak schema knowledge:
    The student made multiple trial and error computations while trying to
    find 80% of 240. The following attempts were consecutive steps in his
    solution. After the last attempt, the student closed the calculator and asked
    for help with *ShowMe.*
    (CalculatorSolve (240/80) 3)
    (CalculatorClear)
    (CalculatorSolve (8/240) .03)
    (CalculatorClear)
    (CalculatorSolve (240/.80) 300)
    (CalculatorClear)
    (CalculatorSolve (20 + 0) 20)

2. Uncertainty:
    The student moved back and forth between two diagrams. The correct
    icons are CHand VY.

(IconSelected CHsmall)	
(Map CHsmall)	
(LiftWord . . .)	To starting amount of CH diagram
(LiftWord . . .)	To amount of change in CH diagram
(CalculatorSolve (2.4 - .4) 2)	
(LiftWord (Calculation 2) . . .)	To end result in CH diagram
(LiftWord (Calculation 2) AnswerWindow)	Erroneously thought this was final step
(WrongAnswer 2)	
(Map CHsmall)	Opens but closes again, doing nothing
(IconSelected VYsmall)	Selects another icon
(Map VYsmall)	
(LiftWord . . .)	Maps one part of the VY diagram
(LiftWord . . .)	Maps a second part of VY diagram and closes map
(Link . . .)	Links the two icons
(Map VYsmall)	Opens diagram for VY but closes, doing nothing
(Map CHsmall)	Opens diagram for CH
(CalculatorSolve (2.4 - .4) 2)	Redoes same calculation as before and closes diagram
(Map VYsmall)	Opens diagram again; still does nothing

Table 8.3. (*cont.*)

(Map CHsmall)	Opens diagram and closes without doing anything
(Unlink . . .)	Erases the link between the two icons

. . .

3. Self-monitoring:
   The student first selected RS erroneously, then switched to CH, which was correct.

(IconSelected RSsmall 1 . . .)	
(Map RSsmall)	
(LiftWord . . .)	
(IconSelected CHsmall)	
(Map CHsmall)	
(LiftWord . . .)	
(LiftWord . . .)	Mapped the same part of the problem as before in RS
(CalculatorSolve . . .)	

. . .

4. Confident problem solving:
   The student presumably is relying on some internal problem representation. The following is the record in its entirety.

(IconSelected CHsmall)	This is the overall situation; there is an embedded RS
(Map CHsmall)	
(LiftWord . . .)	A phrase representing second situation
(LiftWord . . .)	The original amount
(CalculatorSolve (45 * .2) 9)	The student does not map but merely remembers it
(CalculatorClear)	
(CalculatorSolve (45 - 9) 36)	Uses the previous calculation result
(LiftWord . . .)	Copies the calculation result into the final result of the CH diagram
(LiftWord . . .)	Copies the result of the calculation into the Final Answer Window
(Done)	
(RightAnswer 36)	

Table 8.3. (*cont.*)

5. Efficient use of *ShowMe:*	
...	Several previous steps in which student attempted to use CP icon and diagram
(ShowMe) (IconSelected RSsmall) (Map RSsmall) (LiftWord . . .)	Three separate calls to map three parts of RS
(LiftWord . . .) (LiftWord . . .) (CalculatorSolve (45 * .20) 9) (LiftWord (Calculation 9) . . .)	Places result of calculation in diagram
(LiftWord . . .)	Fills in the final part of RS diagram and closes diagram
(Map RSsmall)	Opens diagram again and immediately closes it, doing nothing with it
(Map CHsmall)	Student had already selected it prior to calling *ShowMe*
(LiftWord . . .) (CalculatorSolve (45 * .20) 9)	Repeats calculation made previously
(LiftWord (Calculation 9) . . .) (CalculatorSolve (45 - 9) 36)	Places calculation in CH diagram
(LiftWord (Calculation 36) . . .) (LiftWord (Calculation 36) AnswerWindow) (Done)	Places calculation in CH diagram Places calculation in Final Answer Window
(RightAnswer 36)	Tells PSE he has completed the problem
6. Multiple calls to *ShowMe:* (IconSelected RSsmall) (Map RSsmall) (LiftWord . . .)	Student calls this six times, four to place numbers and twice to remove them
(ShowMe) (Map RSsmall)	First call Returns to RS diagram

Table 8.3. (*cont.*)

(LiftWord . . .)	Two calls to remove erroneous placements from before
(LiftWord . . .)	Two calls to place new information
(Link 1 4 1 4)	Attempts to link icon with itself
(ShowMe)	Second call
(IconSelected CHsmall)	
(Map CHsmall)	
(LiftWord . . .)	Maps one part of CH diagram
(Link . . .)	Two aborted attempts at linkages
(MoveIcon RSsmall . . .)	Repositions RS icon
(Link 1 4 1 4)	Same error as before in linkage; attempts to link icon with itself
(ShowMe)	Third call
(Link . . .)	Another aborted call to link
(Link 1 4 2 2)	
(Map RSsmall)	
(CalculatorSolve (12 + 7) 19)	Note: The number 12 is not contained in the problem
(CalculatorClear)	
(CalculatorSolve (14 + 7) 21)	
(LiftWord (Calculation 21) . . .)	Places calculation result in diagram
(LiftWord (Calculation 21) AnswerWindow)	Places result in AnswerWindow
(ShowMe)	Fourth call
. . .	Student continues for another 27 events before reaching correct answer

We frequently are interested in how confident or uncertain a student is of his or her problem-solving decisions. Uncertainty shows up in the second episode of Table 8.3. Here, the student vacillates back and forth, opening and closing the two diagrams of interest. This student eventually solved the problem without help, but she took a total of 68 mouse events to do so. This episode shows how the problem-solving records are useful for locating the points at which students were unsure of their solutions, demonstrated by shuttling repeatedly between two maps.

A striking phenomenon was the degree to which students engaged in self-monitoring and self-correction as they selected and used the icons, as illustrated in the third episode of Table 8.3. Here, the student initially selected the Restate icon and tried to map a Change situation into it. After mapping one element, the student closed the diagram for Restate and never again accessed it.[1] Instead, the student (correctly) opted to select the Change icon and to map it. He then continued to solve the problem.

Many students exhibited this characteristic of self-correction. Almost without exception, their behavior consisted of two contiguous events, icon selection and diagram display. Sometimes the student went so far as to map some part(s) of the problem into the diagram. Sometimes the student made no explicit mapping and simply closed the Mapping Window as soon as it opened. Very rarely did students select an icon and then discard it (or simply never use it) without opening the Mapping Window to see the enlarged version of the diagram.

Other self-corrections came about as students picked up a part of a problem and subsequently realized that there was no suitable place for it in the current diagram. Such action can be seen in the initial *LiftWord* command of Table 8.2, described previously.

We observed surprisingly little guessing in our students. To be sure, there was some. A few students appeared to select icons at random and then proceeded immediately to use the calculator, combining all or some of the numbers in a hit or miss fashion, as already demonstrated in the first episode of Table 8.3. These students were, needless to say, among the least successful of the group. Most of the time, when an incorrect icon was accessed, the student eventually discovered this for himself or herself and moved on to the appropriate one.

The degree of difficulty of the problem clearly influenced the level of detail needed in students' plans, as indicated by the number of mouse events required to reach final solution. For example, if a student immediately understood the problem, he or she often did only a small amount of mapping for one situation, performed the relevant calculation(s), and completed the mapping without ever accessing the diagram of the second situation. Most of the time, the situation that was initially mapped corresponded to the primary, or overall, situation of the problem. The fourth episode in Table 8.3 shows an example of this. The example contains the entire record for this student as he solved this problem. Only 10 mouse events occurred.

The manner in which students utilized the help mechanism also revealed something of their understanding and overall schema development. In general, students watched the display of a correct plan using the *ShowMe* option and then proceeded to carry out that same plan themselves. There was striking variation in their ability to do so. On the one hand, some students had a very good grasp of the situations and their constituents. These students were able to work steadily and accurately in mimicking the plan. They successfully selected the appropriate icons, mapped their elements, linked the icons, and carried out the needed calculations. Such performance required that they be able to maintain some representation of the plan in working memory, because it was no longer displayed on the computer monitor. Given the many different steps to be carried out and the large number of problem components to be dealt with in different ways, it seems highly unlikely that these students simply memorized the plan without understanding it when it was displayed to them by *ShowMe*. Moreover, the way in which *ShowMe* displays its solution does not facilitate such memorization, because various windows open and close as the solution is presented, and the fully connected solution is never displayed at one time. Certainly, the students' behavior as traced through the problem-solving events does not suggest rote memorization. Rather, it points to sophisticated understanding of the icons and the underlying situations. The fifth episode in Table 8.3 delineates one student's activities following a call to *ShowMe*. Note that there is little confusion or hesitation evident in the student's solving of the problem.

One may contrast the behavior of the student who apparently understands the situations with that of one who does not. The sixth episode of Table 8.3 provides an example of the latter. This students makes four calls to *ShowMe*, and her subsequent behavior suggests that she has focused each time on some small part of the problem, without forming an overall representation of the problem. Consequently, she is forced to return repeatedly to the plan of *ShowMe* because she cannot create the sequence of problem-solving steps by herself. The failure to understand how the two icons are linked is particularly striking because it pinpoints an important gap in the student's understanding. Unless a student comprehends that a component of one situation may equally well be a component of a second situation, he or she will not fully understand complex problems. It is precisely this overlap or intertwining of components that holds the problem together and gives it a coherent meaning.

As an aside, it is interesting to note that one student frequently created a full and accurate plan for a problem and then confirmed his plan using *ShowMe* before checking his answer using *Done*. He did this on three of the five problems. This cautious behavior suggests that the student may have been uneasy with his understanding, thus utilizing *ShowMe* as an extended form of self-monitoring.

The nature of plans

Although the plans developed by each student were unique, they nevertheless exhibited many similarities in their general or overall structure. In particular, the following types of plans emerged frequently. The analysis and description of the different plans are based on the 85 problem-solving episodes of the 17 students during the second PSE session.

Select all relevant icons

Before doing anything else, the student selects and positions all of the icons he or she wishes to use to create the plan. When this is the initial behavior, we can assume with some confidence that the student is using his or her schema knowledge. A set of sub-problems has been identified – otherwise, the student could not have selected the different icons. Moreover, the student must have at least a vague idea of how the different situations are related.

Useful information can be found in the order in which the student selects the icons. The student may begin by selecting the first situation that arises in the problem, moving steadily through all necessary ones, and culminating with the selection of the overall situation that governs the problem. Such a strategy represents a sequential processing of information and tends to cause a student some difficulty if the problem contains unusual structure or phrasing.

A second approach is for the student to select first the primary situation that describes the problem (i.e., the situation containing the ultimate unknown of the problem), followed by the secondary situation(s). In this case, the student displays a real understanding of the overall structure of the problem and is not bound by the order in which information is presented in the problem.

It is my belief that the second approach reflects stronger schema knowledge structures and a more integrated set of schemas in memory, but I have insufficient data to confirm or deny it. My argument is as follows: If the student first selects the primary situation and then the necessary secondary one(s), he or she must possess the capability of abstracting and manipulating the basic information found in the problem. This action requires extended access to elaboration knowledge. Selecting the situations in the order in which they appear in the problem does not necessarily require this capability.

Focus on one icon at a time

Students who were well on their way to having coherent schemas and using them as a related set tended to exhibit similar plans. First, they made a selection of one icon and attempted to map it. If the mapping was unsuccessful, they closed the diagram and selected another icon, attempting to map the same problem elements they had previously used in the first diagram. Thus, they demonstrated the self-monitoring behavior mentioned previously. Very rarely did any student incorrectly map part of a problem and then continue as if the mapping were correct.

If successful in the initial (or revised) mapping, the student returned to the icon menu and selected another icon with which to work. At this point, two different strategies appeared. Some students immediately linked the two icons. Others performed a second mapping before attempting the linkage.

To make the immediate linkage, the student had to know already which part of the second icon contained an unknown quantity that corresponded to a part of the first icon. This demands a strong schema foundation, especially elaboration knowledge, and a good understanding of how schemas may overlap. This approach was relatively rare. We would expect to see it only after students had grown very confident about their knowledge and after more extensive experience using the PSE environment than was available in this study.

More often, students displayed some uncertainty. In a few cases, this showed up in the PSE record as an aborted call to *Link*, with the student making the menu selection but failing to specify how to connect the two icons. Instead of trying anew to make the connection, the student opted to map the second icon, returning to link the icons after the mapping was completed.

The majority of students made no attempt at linkages until problem elements had been mapped into both diagrams. Occasionally, a student went so far as to place the correct answer in the Final Answer Window. However, the student did not select *Done*, the signal for PSE to check the correctness of the answer, until he or she had made the explicit link between icons.

We can speculate that this linking after the answer was known is the student's way of self-reinforcement and satisfied a need to demonstrate how the icons fit together. For these students, it was necessary for them to verify that two icons held identical quantities by making the actual computations first. In many instances, as can be seen in some of the episodes of Table 8.3, they went so far as to carry out precisely the same calculation twice: once for the first diagram and again for the second. Only at this point did the students appear to realize how the situations overlapped. With extended practice, one could expect them to begin to anticipate how the icons are linked before they carry out the calculations. Again, extended experience using PSE would be required.

The plan that depended on mapping one icon at a time was by far the most prevalent of all plans created by the students. At one time or another, every student but one participating in the study used this approach.[2] They carefully went through every step and every linkage. After solving several problems in this way, they frequently switched to the strategy described below in which only the first diagram was completely filled. This switch suggests that students' use of their schema knowledge was becoming more routinized and that they were able to formulate and make use of expectations about connected situations.

Focus on the overall situation

The basic plan for many students focused on the overall situation in the problem. They began by selecting only the icon for the primary situation and then turned immediately to the mapping of the problem into the expanded diagram. They mapped the appropriate quantities from the problem to the diagram and also mapped the full verbal description of the subproblem, as stated in the text, directly into the diagram. Thus, their mapped representation contained two unknowns, one usually completely blank component, representing the overall unknown, and one containing some verbal manifestation of the subproblem that needed to be solved first. They then made the necessary calculation(s) for the subproblem and substituted it directly into the diagram, replacing the verbal description. The important feature of this plan is that the students did not need to utilize a second diagram to take this last step. Students displaying this strategy usually had a good grasp of the overall and subproblem icons and had performed very well on the earlier SPS computer exercises. They selected the correct quantities for the calculations and showed a high level of confidence in what they were doing. Their performance and their attitude suggest that they had developed the ability to make mental representations of the problems without having to have explicit visual displays at every step. This interpretation was bolstered by a reexamination of the transcripts following PSE use from the earlier abstract/specific study described in chapter 7. A few students in that study confirmed in interviews that they were indeed using mental models of the unshown icons and diagrams.

Focus on the calculation

A strategy that was generally unsuccessful, and that revealed the lack of a structured approach to solving the problem, was to focus only on the calculations to be made. The basic plan here seemed to be to select any icon at random and to choose the mapping option solely for the objective of reaching the calculator (which could be accessed only through the Mapping Window). Icon selection for these students appeared purposeless and without meaning. One or two student always selected the same icon. Others' choices appeared to be random. In no instance did these students attempt to map any part of the problem. They all turned immediately to the calculator.

Usually, students using this plan displayed many problem-solving weaknesses. They often made mistakes in the calculations, either reversing the position of the quantities in the calculations or selecting inappropriate quantities to include in the calculation. They also tended to overlook one (or more) of the subproblems required for solution. Thus, they turned a complex problem into a simple one-step one.

These students displayed little or no tendency to use the five schemas targeted by SPS instruction. Although they had developed the facility of identifying the icons and mapping the problems into the diagrams in previous instructional sessions, they elected not to use their knowledge of the icons and/or diagrams and relied instead upon previously learned (and frequently incorrect) problem-solving strategies.[3]

Conclusions

PSE allows us to do what any good teacher with sufficient time does, that is, look at the solutions created by a student in order to understand more about what the student knows. PSE is substantially different, however, from an ordinary problem-solving setting in that it provides an access to knowledge that is not usually directly available. When teachers look at the problem-solving steps taken by a student, they typically observe a series of calculations. They must infer the mental processes used by the students to generate the calculations. In fact, they may not even have the series of calculations available. In many of our problem-solving experiments, we observed that a number of students of all ages often erased all but their final response. Thus, no hint of their problem-solving path remained.

With PSE we also must make inferences but we have available a set of intermediate steps, which are events related to the student's perception of and knowledge about problem-solving situations. To be sure, some of the events are calculations, but most of them are not. Thus, we have not only the same data as the teachers (the calculations) but a great deal more.

What have we learned from PSE? First, it is possible to isolate planning knowledge and to examine individual differences in how students develop plans. We can examine direct linkages between planning knowledge and other critical aspects of a schema, such as identification knowledge and elaboration knowledge. We can follow the student's execution of the plan and observe the order with which he or she carries out the necessary steps.

This study confirms the importance of planning knowledge for a schema. The students who demonstrated the most complete identification and elaboration knowledge also formed the most efficient plans. These students used the icons easily and mapped the problems confidently. The students who used weak strategies, such as focusing only on the calculation, had difficulty solving the problems. One surmises either that they did not have appropriately linked schema knowledge that allowed them to make full use of their identification and elaboration knowledge or that their previous problem-solving instruction had created bonds that were still stronger than their new knowledge gained from SPS.

This study also shows that we may obtain very useful diagnostic and assessment information from programs such as PSE. The data collection is unobtrusive, students are not interrupted as they work on the problems, and a number of useful measures are available for assessing the student's performance. These will be described more fully in chapter 11, which addresses issues of assessment.

9

The diagram: Marker and template

Over the past 25 years, visual representations have received considerable attention under the various designations of graphics, diagrams, visual aids, or simply pictures. No matter which name is used, the issue is whether their inclusion in instruction makes a significant difference in how and what students learn. The question of their importance extends naturally to schema theory. The most interesting issues have to do with how visual representations fit into the knowledge organization of a schema and what role they have in its access and use.

It is reasonable to expect visual information to be a critical component of schema knowledge. As described in some detail in chapter 1, one of the earliest meanings of σχημα had to do with color, shape, and form. Certainly, the figural representation of a triangle entered into Aristotle's and Kant's conception of it and their elaboration of the triangle schema.

All the available evidence suggests that visual representations should play an important role in schema formation and use. Psychological research has produced a number of notable results about their value in memory storage and retrieval. For instance, pictures are remembered more easily than words (e.g., Pavio, 1975), spatial arrangements of shapes are remembered more accurately than linear orderings of words (e.g., Santa, 1977), visual imagery promotes learning of associations (e.g., Bower, 1972), drawings of problems guide inferences (Anzai, 1991), and visual cues facilitate analogical transfer (e.g., Gick, 1985). Recent work documents some of the interconnections between mental imagery and different aspects of cognition, including perception, memory, and problem solving (Cornoldi & McDaniel, 1991; Hampson, Marks, & Richardson, 1990).

Some research about visual representations in instruction has focused specifically on the use of diagrams, such as those in SPS. For example, Willis and Fuson (1988) found that children's performance on word problems improved when diagrams were used to display the problems, but they offered little psychological justification for the finding.

For a likely explanation, we can turn to Larkin and Simon (1987), who viewed results like these in terms of computational efficiency. Larkin and Simon argue that verbal representations and diagrammatic representations may be informationally equivalent but computationally quite different. The use of diagrams to represent problems is preferable to verbal representation, they suggest, because diagrams facilitate the search process and enhance recognition.

Larkin and Simon were not concerned with schema formation and instantiation, but their arguments can be logically extended to these areas. The extension leads from Larkin and Simon's view of the diagram as an external aid for problem solving to consideration of the diagram as an internal knowledge structure stored in the learner's long-term memory. One can hypothesize that if diagrams facilitate the search process, as Larkin and Simon maintain, they may well influence the original encoding process also. That is, the presence of diagrams during initial instruction could result in knowledge acquisition that differs substantially from knowledge acquisition under instruction without diagrams. Therefore, in addition to computational efficiency, encoding efficiency is of interest. The inclusion of diagrams in instruction may result in greater amounts of knowledge being added to the memory store. Alternatively, the diagrams may influence the degree of connectivity of the acquired knowledge rather than the amount itself.

At the heart of this issue is the question of how diagrams are used by the learner. Potentially, any diagram has a dual nature. This duality was briefly discussed at the end of chapter 7. On the one hand, a diagram may function as a marker, serving as the point of access to a large body of knowledge and vital for the recognition of, and discrimination among, various concepts. On the other, it may play the role of template, operating as the scaffold on which to hang specific knowledge components about a particular concept that are central to reasoning about the concept. These are two very different functions, and they represent two distinct aspects of schema knowledge. Both of these functions – marker and template – are critical for schema development, and the time has come to consider how they influence schema formation and use.

Markers are highly salient figures whose components carry additional knowledge beyond their spatial arrangement. Markers have several characteristics: They are usually small; they are relatively simple figures; they are easily recognized; they convey a large amount of information through the spatial display; and they are linked to additional procedural and/or declarative knowledge in memory. As an example, consider the marker function of the familiar trash can icon found in popular computer software. It is a simple figure, users easily recognize it, it conveys a great deal of information about discarding unwanted objects, and it is linked in memory to the steps the user takes to discard a computer file. Its specific parts are not particularly important; we work with the whole image.

In SPS, markers are used to trigger students' recognition of situations. Markers are always miniature versions of the diagrams (like the trash can icon), and they appear in two places. First, they serve as menu items when students are asked to recognize situations in problems, as in Figure 5.4. Second, they serve as small models of parts of complex problems in the problem solving environment, as in Figure 5.9. Students manipulate the markers in PSE to develop a full visual representation of a complex problem.

In contrast, templates have a different function in SPS. Diagrams as templates serve as visual maps of situations against which individual problems are to be compared, and the specific components of the templates have great import. Each part of a template represents a describable part of the situation and corresponds to some particular aspect of a given problem.

It is fair to say that markers convey their information as a whole, whereas templates require a parsing of the elements that make up the whole. The two functions are clearly related to each other but they are not identical. Students are content to deal with markers as a whole and make no attempt to work with their different parts, as they do with templates. Moreover, it is possible to acquire the identification knowledge associated with the marker while still lacking the elaboration knowledge required for detailed mapping of problems to templates (as shown in chapter 7). And, the converse may also happen, that is, acquisition of the elaboration knowledge without the identification knowledge.

The issues most germane to the present chapter are whether and how diagrams enhance schema development when they are used as a primary vehicle of instruction but are not the object of it. In presenting my case, I rely on two experimental studies. One is a follow-up to Experiment I of chapter 7, designed to look at long-term retention, and the other is a graduate student's study carried out in my laboratory using SPS (M. A. Brewer, 1988). The former provides insight into how diagrams influence students' learning and recollection. The latter examines specifically the impact of instruction using diagrams by contrasting it with instruction lacking diagrams.

The diagrams

Each of the five situations is associated in SPS instruction with a diagram. It occurs in two forms, a full-screen version and a miniature version. The diagrams are presented in Figure 9.1. For the most part, these are graphic representations with no text. Each one has a distinct overall form, and each can be decomposed into several components.

In the Change figure, the left oval represents the initial or starting point, the rectangle indicates the change that occurs, the right oval corresponds to the ending or final point, and the arrow directs the action.

The Group figure consists of several small rectangles and a long, thin rectangle spanning their tops. The spanning rectangle

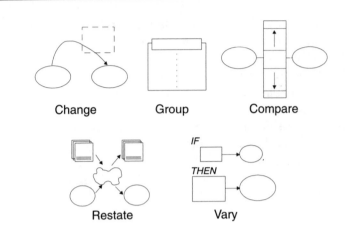

Figure 9.1. The diagrams used in SPS instruction

corresponds to the superordinate group formed by combining two or more sets of objects, and the small rectangles represent the sets in the problem that are to be grouped. This figure has three versions in SPS; it contains either two, three, or four small rectangles below the spanning rectangle, depending upon the number of distinct sets in a given problem that are to be grouped.

The Compare figure reflects two statements about values that are to be judged (the left and right ovals). One will correspond to "more" (i.e., the up arrow) and the other to "less" (i.e., the down arrow).[1]

The Restate figure has five components, two representing the verbal statement of association, two representing the numerical statement, and one representing the relationship expressed in the problem. The boxes at the top are "text boxes" and correspond to verbal descriptions of the two objects that are related. The "squiggle" in the middle of the figure holds the function or rule that relates the two objects. The ovals at the bottom represent the numerical values, which correspond numerically to the verbal descriptions in the text boxes. The arrows indicate the direction of the relationship. Thus, the left box bears an association to the right box in exactly the same way that the left oval bears that association to the right oval.

The Vary figure has four main components, broken into two distinct groups of two arranged so that one group is directly above the other. Each grouping reflects a relationship, depicted by the arrow running from left to right. Two shapes are used to show that the relationship is between two different things. The two sizes – smaller figures on top and larger ones on the bottom – represent the proportionality between the top relationship and the bottom one, illustrating the systematic variation that occurs in a Vary situation.[2]

When the full-screen version of a diagram is used, only one diagram appears on the screen, and the task utilizes the template function of the diagram. When the miniature version is used by a task, all five diagrams appear together on the screen and the marker function is employed.

Experiment I: Follow-up

As described in chapter 7, Experiment I involved a group of 27 students who worked through the entire system, each one taking approximately 5 hours spread over a 2-week period. At the end of the fifth session, the students were dismissed from the experiment. At that point, they (and we) believed their participation was ended. However, 3 months later, I decided to contact this group of students again and ask them to return to the lab for one final session. Students were under no obligation to come back, but 17 of them agreed to do so.

The original purpose of the follow-up study was to ascertain whether any long-term effects could be observed from the schema-based instruction. Three months had passed, a relatively long period of time in a student's life and ample time for students to forget completely the details of the material studied in Experiment I. After all, the students had little reason to retain the material. It was not part of their formal coursework, they (presumably) had virtually no opportunity to use their situational knowledge in the intervening time period and thus had engaged in little or no retrieval and rehearsal, and, of course, their initial motivation for learning about the situations was not outstandingly strong. All in all, one would expect that very little would be retained. My question was: What, if anything, was sufficiently salient to become part of their retrievable long-term memory? The importance of the visual information emerged as the students demonstrated for us what they did remember.

Procedure

In the follow-up study, the students were first given a set of 20 story problems and asked to sort them into similar groups of items. This was essentially the same experimental task described in chapter 3. Each problem was printed on a 3 × 5 inch card, and students made groupings of the cards according to their own notions of problem similarity. No limit was placed on the number of categories they might form. Students were next asked to provide the names of the situations they had studied in the earlier experiment and to draw any of the figures that they could recall. With prompting from the interviewer, they were encouraged to describe each situation as fully as possible.

At this point, each student was then given an abbreviated refresher lesson in SPS. This lesson lasted for about 5 min and merely described the situations again, using the original examples from the first SPS session. No computer exercises were presented. Finally, students were given a second set of 20 problems to sort, with explicit instructions to use their situational knowledge to form the groups. The entire session lasted about 1 hour.

Results

First sorting task. The students, of course, remembered that the subject of the earlier experiment was arithmetic problem solving, and most of them attempted to use situational knowledge to carry out the sorting task. A few resorted to using arithmetic operation as the basis of the sort (reminiscent of the sixth graders in the initial validation study described in chapter 3). Most of the sorts were rather messy. The typical student was able to recognize the Compare situation, which does not call for any computation. These items were easily grouped together. Usually, some part of the Change and Group situations formed the basis for categories, although students rarely classified all of these situations correctly. There was a great deal of confusion about Vary and Restate situations, consistent with the observations made during the first experiment. These two situations are the most difficult for students to recognize.

What we want to look at here is the extent to which students were successful in grouping similar items. Once again, cluster analysis is a useful tool for making the evaluation. Figure 9.2 contains summaries of both sorting tasks for the follow-up study. The figure provides a visual summary of the strength of the clusters formed in each task. In each part of Figure 9.2, the solid black corresponds to the clusters formed by the students in the classification. Each cluster is depicted as the actual cluster obtained from the students' sorting (in black) and as the hypothetical cluster that could be obtained if all students had grouped all items of a situation together (the cross-hatched area). Erroneous clusters – those combining items that represent different situations – are shown in areas having diagonal lines. The items that form each cluster are identified along the horizontal axis. Thus, the best solution – in terms of the students' categorizing all items perfectly according to situation – would show five black rectangles with no cross-hatch or diagonal lines at all. The greater the area that is non-black, the weaker the cluster.

The clusters of Figure 9.2A show the initial sorting that students made with no prompting or reminders about the situations. These clusters are noticeably weak and sparse. Only a few items were consistently grouped together by the students. Nonetheless, from the students' verbal statements about why they grouped items together, it was clear that fragments of situational knowledge were available in memory that they could access easily and were attempting to use in making their grouping decisions.

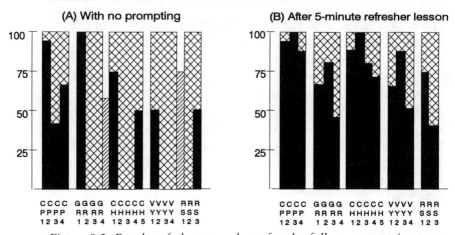

Figure 9.2. Results of cluster analyses for the follow-up experiment on the sorting task

Recall information. Students recalled a surprising amount of information about the situations, and that knowledge seemed to be well organized. More than half of the students recalled three or more names. Others recalled associated cues but could not retrieve the name (e.g., "I know it starts with a *v* . . ."). The average number of situation names recalled was 2.5. Only 2 of the 17 students failed to recall anything.

Surprisingly, students' diagram retrieval was almost as good as their name recollection. I consider this surprising because the diagrams were not the focus of instruction. Students were able to draw correctly an average of 2.3 figures, most often Change, Group, and Compare. Again, they remembered bits and pieces of other diagrams but could not sketch the complete figures correctly.

One of the more interesting results was that fully one-third of the students had accurate memory for a diagram but could not retrieve the name associated with it. The correlation between the number of names recalled and the number of figures recalled was a mere .18. The most extreme cases were the two students who could not remember any names but could draw some of the diagrams and the three students who remembered the names but could draw no diagrams.

Second sorting task. Students were remarkably adept in their second sorting of problems into the five situational categories. Their performance is summarized in Figure 9.2B. A full 41% of them sorted all of the items perfectly, and the others also achieved a high degree of success. The mean number of items assigned correctly to the situational categories was 17.2 of a possible 20.

Summary

Students recalled a great deal of information about the situations long after the instruction had ended. Moreover, they apparently had even more additional knowledge that could be easily primed by a short refresher session in SPS. This is evident in the differences between the two sorting tasks as shown in Figures 9.2A and 9.2B. Five minutes of instruction produced an immense gain, one that can only be explained by accepting that students already had most of the knowledge encoded in long-term memory. The instruction moved the knowledge from an inert to an active status, presumably by reactivating existing paths for retrieval from memory.

The knowledge that students retained from the initial experiment was composed of visual and verbal details. These were apparently not redundant encodings of the same knowledge if we judge by the fact that some students could do one and not the other and other students had the reversed pattern of response. Moreover, we found a low correlation over all students between the number of names recalled and the number of diagrams recalled. Hence, one can surmise that there is some additional information encoded with the diagrams above and beyond the verbal description.

To investigate just what that additional information might be was the purpose of the next study. Brewer's investigation of diagrams sheds considerable light on this topic.

Brewer's experiment

M. A. Brewer's original study (1988) was a well-designed and thoughtfully executed experiment in which she contrasted the normal mode of SPS instruction, complete with its diagrams, with a specially constructed alternative version of SPS lacking the diagrams. Her purpose was to document which aspects, if any, of students' learning from SPS instruction were dependent on diagrams. She did not address the question of how diagrams contribute to schemas, and the application of schema theory to her findings as presented here is new. Because her study is not available elsewhere in print, I describe it in some detail and use it to illustrate the importance of visual representations for schema development.

As always, the goal of SPS instruction is for students to learn about the situations of problem solving, not for students to memorize the diagrams. In Brewer's experiment, students are not merely learning to associate figures with verbal labels, as is the case in many other studies of visual representations. Rather, they are learning to use the diagrams as markers to represent a larger body of knowledge, and they are also learning to use them as templates for exploring that larger body of knowledge.

Students

A total of 44 undergraduate students participated in the study. Students were randomly assigned to two treatment groups, the Diagram group and the No-Diagram group.

Materials

Each student worked independently in SPS. All instruction was delivered by computer, and all student responses were made with the mouse. Additional experimental materials included a paper-and-pencil questionnaire administered 2 weeks after the instructional sessions and two sets of 20 story problems. Table 9.1 contains one of the problem sets. The second was an analogous set that used matching but slightly different stories. These problems were used in the three classification tasks described below.

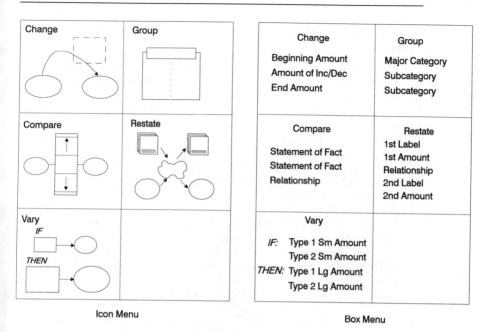

Figure 9.3. The alternative menus for the Diagram and No-Diagram conditions of M. A. Brewer's (1988) experiment

Experimental conditions

For Brewer's study, two experimental conditions were developed. The first consisted of instruction using the diagrams under the ordinary circumstances of SPS, as described in chapter 5. This is the Diagram condition. For her second experimental condition, she and I developed a No-Diagram condition to parallel the normal instruction as closely as possible without using the figures. For this condition, an alternative verbal representation was created, as shown in Figure 9.3. In this representation, each situation was depicted as a set of labeled parts, with each label corresponding to one of the components of the SPS diagrams. Figure 9.3 shows both the original icon menu for the Diagram condition and the box menu for the No-Diagram condition.

Table 9.1. *Problems used in the classification tasks of Brewer's experiment*

1. The Psychology Club has 49 members. 31 are women. How many are men? *[GR]*
2. At the beginning of summer vacation Dan was 5'5" tall. He grew 4" over the summer. How tall was Dan at the end of summer? *[CH]*
3. If you can buy 3 cookies for 25 cents, how much will a dozen cost? *[VY]*
4. Joe's Burger Joint fires 2 cooks a month. Patty's Pizza Palace fires 4 chefs a month. Which restaurant has the highest turnover rate? *[CP]*
5. When Mary became pregnant she weighed 120 pounds. By the end of her ninth month, she weighed 155 pounds. How much weight did Mary gain during her pregnancy? *[CH]*
6. 10 men attended the Bridal Fashion Show. Three times as many women attended. How many women attended? *[RS]*
7. A case of 24 generic colas costs $8.00. How much is each cola? *[VY]*
8. Molly has 70 free passes to the zoo. She gave 56 of them away. How many passes does Molly have left? *[CH]*
9. Jane is 7" shorter than her boyfriend Tom. Tom is 6'2" tall. How tall is Jane? *[RS]*
10. Joan wants to become fluent in Spanish. It would cost her $3,480 to spend the summer studying in Spain. It would cost her $1,200 to study in Mexico for the summer. Which is the less expensive alternative? *[CP]*
11. Bruce works 8 hours a day at the bank. He spends 3 hours processing bad checks, 4 hours with customers, and the rest of the time balancing his money drawer. How long does it take him to do this? *[GR]*

Because the mapping exercises are a central feature of SPS instruction, it was essential, even in the No-Diagram condition, to have a representation into which problem parts could be mapped. Thus, it was impossible to eliminate all visual representations from the instruction and still maintain fidelity with the system. Our compromise solution was to make the box mapping figures as similar to each other as possible for the No-Diagram condition. All box mapping figures are essentially alike, differing only in the number of boxes and in the words used in the labels. For each case the labels were listed in a single column, and each had a small box adjacent to it. Individuals placed parts of the problem into the boxes with the appropriate labels. Figure 9.4 shows an example of the mapping task in the No-Diagram condition, using the same Change situation shown previously in Figure 5.4.

Table 9.1. (*cont.*)

12. The Wafer Thin Diet helped Sally lose 15 lbs. Karen lost 40 lbs. on the Stick Figure Diet. Which diet worked the best? [CP]
13. As soon as Jim received his paycheck he went shopping and spent $150 for new clothes. He has $400 left to pay his bills. How much was Jim's paycheck? [CH]
14. The chapel seats 150 people. If there are 15 pews in the chapel, how many people can sit in each pew? [VY]
15. For her birthday Margaret received a bottle of perfume, 2 necklaces, and 5 tickets for next season's Padre games. How many gifts did she receive in all? [GR]
16. For every dollar that Kim puts in her savings account, her father puts in $2.00. Kim saved $45.00 last month. How much did her father put in her savings account? [VY]
17. Houses in Fresno cost about a third of what they cost in San Diego. If a house sold for $450,000 in San Diego, how much would you expect to buy it for in Fresno? [RS]
18. A weekend ski package at Marshmallow Mountain includes $50 for lodging, $75 for skiing, and $30 for food. How much does the entire package cost? [GR]
19. After buying books for the Spring semester, Ken had $210 less than before he bought books. After he bought books he had $15. How much money did he have before he bought his books? [CH]
20. Dean and Jim had a competition to see who was the strongest. Dean lifted 210 lbs. Jim lifted 280 lbs. Who was stronger? [CP]

Wherever the diagrams were used in instruction for the Diagram condition, the labeled boxes of Figure 9.3 were used for the No-Diagram condition. All other instructions and exercises were identical in the two conditions.

Procedure

Computer tasks. Every student participated in three 1-hour sessions. The first two sessions were scheduled between 2 and 5 days apart, with the second session following the first by an average of 3 days. Sessions were arranged so that two students could be working at the same time on separate computers. Students were randomly assigned to experimental conditions under the con-

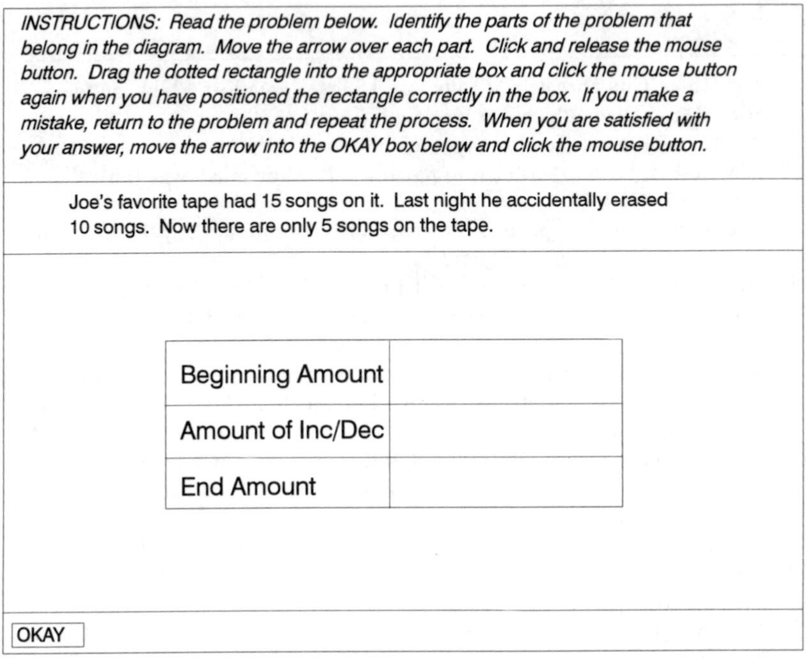

INSTRUCTIONS: *Read the problem below. Identify the parts of the problem that belong in the diagram. Move the arrow over each part. Click and release the mouse button. Drag the dotted rectangle into the appropriate box and click the mouse button again when you have positioned the rectangle correctly in the box. If you make a mistake, return to the problem and repeat the process. When you are satisfied with your answer, move the arrow into the OKAY box below and click the mouse button.*

Joe's favorite tape had 15 songs on it. Last night he accidentally erased 10 songs. Now there are only 5 songs on the tape.

Beginning Amount	
Amount of Inc/Dec	
End Amount	

OKAY

Figure 9.4. An example of the mapping task in the No-Diagram Condition

straint that any students working in the room at the same time were assigned to the same condition. At the conclusion of the second session, the students were told that the third session was not yet available. They were asked to return in 2 weeks to complete the experiment. The third session provided a glimpse into students' long-term retention.

The first session included the mouse tutorial, initial instruction and exercises about the five situations, and some (or all) of the instruction and exercises involving the mapping of simple one-step problems onto the figures, i.e., the diagrams for the Diagram group or the boxes for the No-Diagram group. Students varied in the amount of time they spent in SPS. Some finished all the simple mapping exercises in the first session. Others required more time and completed some of these exercises at the start of the second session. In each exercise, students responded to a common set of problems that varied only in the random order of presentation. For all students the second session concluded with instruction and exercises about multistep story problems.

Data were collected on five variables from SPS tasks:

- ID1 is the number of correct responses given by a student to the recognition task that follows the first instructional session.[3] Ten items were selected a priori for this task and were presented in random order to each student, yielding an ID1 score of 0–10.
- MAP1 is the sum of a student's correct responses to the mapping exercises (as described in chapter 5). A standard set of 10 problems were presented, 2 for each situation, resulting in a possible MAP1 score of 0–10.
- ID2 is the number of correct responses made by a student to a second identification task, which required selection of a spatial display rather than the situation name. The tasks that generate ID1 and ID2 are identical. In the former, students respond with the situation names. For ID2, students respond by selecting either the situation icons or the labeled boxes shown in Figure 9.3. A set of 10 standard problems, none of which had been seen previously, were presented in random order to each student, for a possible ID2 score of 0–10.
- MAP2 is the sum of correctly mapped elements for a set of five complex problems. The exercise generating it builds on the multiple-situations instruction. The appropriate figure – either diagram or box representation – for each of the five problems is presented, and the student is asked to determine which components are already known from information given in the problem (GIVEN), which can be found immediately by solving an embedded, or secondary problem (PARTIAL ANSWER), and which corresponds to the overall unknown of the problem (FINAL ANSWER). The student places the words GIVEN, PARTIAL, and FINAL in the appropriate parts of the diagrams. This is the task illustrated by Figure 5.8. Each situation appears once in this exercise, and a total of 18 components can be identified (i.e., the sum of the parts of the five figures), yielding possible scores of 0–18.

- P/S is the number of correctly identified primary and secondary situations expressed in a set of nine multistep problems. Students make two responses to each problem by first selecting one situation from a menu of five names as the primary situation and then selecting another situation as the secondary one. Possible scores are 0–18.

Other tasks. At the conclusion of the second session (and following all SPS instruction) each student completed a classification task, SORT1, which consisted of categorizing 20 simple story problems according to the five situations.[4] The student was asked to form five groups, placing all problems reflecting the same situation into one group. Five label cards were provided, each containing the name of one situation. If unable to categorize any problem, the student was allowed to create a sixth group called "Other" (a sixth card carried the label "Other" for unrecognized problems). The variable SORT1 reflects the number of problems the student categorized correctly.

Delayed recall. All students returned for the third and final session 2 weeks after their second session. Data on two additional variables were obtained by questionnaire at this time:

- NAME is the number of situation names the student could recall in the interview, ranging from 0 to 5.
- DRAW/DESC is the number of complete visual or verbal descriptions given by a student. Students were given the options of drawing the visual representations (either the diagrams or the labeled boxes) or of making a verbal description of the situations. To receive credit, the student needed to reproduce the diagram or box figure exactly or needed to specify accurately each component composing a situation. The value of DRAW/DESC ranges from 0 to 5.

The final two experimental tasks were classification tasks. The student was given a set of cards with problems analogous to those used in the classification task described above. Again, the task was to classify the problems according to the five situations. The procedure was identical to that of the earlier task. Immediately following completion of this task, the category name cards were removed, the problems were randomly ordered, and the student was asked to reclassify the problems, this time with respect to the set of figures that had been used in instruction. Diagram students were given five cards, each containing one diagram. No-Diagram students were given five cards, each containing one box figure and its respective labels. In neither case were the names of the situations attached to the figures. The variable SORT2 reflects the number of items students correctly classified in the presence of the name cards. The variable SORT3 refers to the number of items correctly classified when the prompts were the figures. As for SORT1, the variables SORT2 and SORT3 could take values from 0 to 20, reflecting the number of problems correctly categorized by a student.

Results

For convenience, Brewer's results for all variables are reproduced in Table 9.2. A quick summary of her findings is that the groups were significantly different on the recall measures and on the sorting tasks but did not differ very much on the SPS tasks. The greatest discrepancy in the recall measures was the recall of visual representations or details about them (DRAW/DESC), with the Diagram group recalling significantly more than the No-Diagram group. All three sorting tasks showed group differences beyond the usual level of statistical significance ($\alpha = .05$). Consistently, the Diagram group performed better than the No-Diagram group.

A second analysis of the sorting tasks yielded additional information about how accurately students perceived similarities and differences among the problems they classified. Notice that these are not tests per se about whether students learned to associate names with figures. Rather, they assessed aspects of the students' learning about the situations.

Once again, cluster analysis was used to investigate the patterns of classification. The results of all the cluster analyses are given in

Figure 9.5. In forming these clusters, a target diameter of 0.50 was set for each cluster in the final solution. The diameter reflects the strength of association within the cluster. Because the similarity data are frequencies of co-occurrence, a diameter of 0.50 means that each item in a cluster was associated with every other item in the cluster at least 50% of the time (i.e., by 50% of the students). This percentage reflects much better than chance performance in grouping the items and provides a strong test of how well students learned the necessary characteristics defining the situations. It also provides evidence that the characteristics were learned by a substantial number of students in relatively uniform ways.

Figure 9.5A shows that Diagram students performed very well immediately after instruction, incorporating 18 of 20 items into well-formed groups. Their performance two weeks later on the second task was still quite good (Figure 9.5C), although a new incorrect cluster emerged here, combining two items from different situations (shown as the area containing the diagonal lines). The third task for this group shows better performance in identify-

Table 9.2. *Means (and standard deviations) for all variables in Brewer's experiment*

Variable	Diagram group	No-Diagram group
*SPS variables:**		
ID1	7.18 (1.500)	6.45 (1.371)
MAP1	7.19 (0.981)	6.73 (1.077)
ID2	7.50 (1.504)	6.55 (1.765)
MAP2	11.68 (3.092)	10.59 (2.153)
P/S**	9.05 (3.109)	6.68 (2.056)
*Recall variables:***		
NAME	3.64 (1.217)	3.05 (1.527)
DRAW/DESC**	3.37 (1.329)	1.46 (1.262)
*Classification variables:***		
SORT1 **	15.59 (2.754)	13.18 (2.130)
SORT2 **	13.00 (2.777)	10.14 (3.212)
SORT3 **	14.05 (2.699)	9.86 (2.336)

*Multivariate analysis of this set of variables not significant.
**Univariate analysis significant, $p < .05$.
***Multivariate analysis of this set of variables significant, $p < .05$.

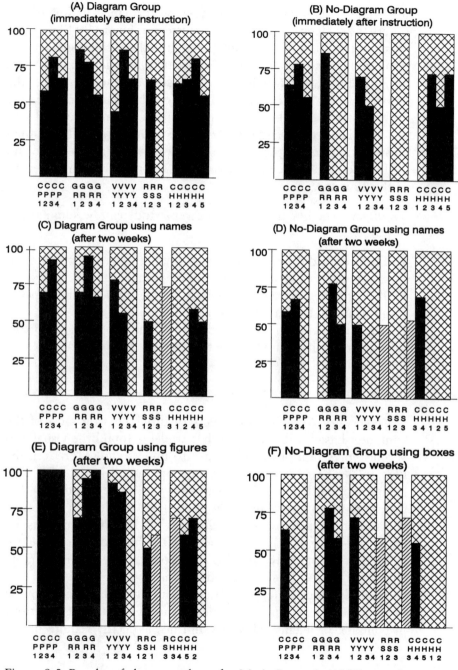

Figure 9.5. Results of cluster analyses for M. A. Brewer's (1988) experiment

ing some situations and weakening performance in identifying others (as evidenced by the mixed clusters in Figure 9.5E).

In contrast, the No-Diagram group initially formed smaller and weaker clusters immediately after instruction (Figure 9.5B). There are, in general, fewer items in each cluster and the strength of the association for the clusters is lower (i.e., the total black area for each cluster is small). Only 13 of 20 items are incorporated into clusters. The second and third sorts are weaker still, with the final cluster solution dropping to only 12 items (Figures 9.5D and 9.5F). In contrast, the third task of the Diagram group involved 18 of the 20 items.

Summary. The key findings of Brewer's study can be summarized as follows:

- The groups did not differ in performance during instruction on simple tasks of identification and mapping.
- The groups differed significantly in the amount and type of information they recalled over time.
- After instruction the groups differed significantly on all sorting tasks, regardless of when the task occurred or how the task was structured.

In all cases, the Diagram group surpassed the No-Diagram group.

Differences on SPS tasks. The lack of differences on most of the computer-based tasks suggests that students found the visual and verbal representations equally easy to understand. Moreover, the high rates of success for the two groups on all but the P/S task means that both representations were well understood and that their components were properly recognized. In addition, since students in both groups could equally well identify situations by name and by visual form (ID1 versus ID2), both visual representations were apparently encoded in association with the defining characteristics of the situations they represented.

The only group difference observed during the instruction phase of the experiment was on the identification of multiple situations in complex problems. This task did not explicitly require use of the diagrams, although it followed instruction in which they were used to demonstrate the structure of problems with several nested situations. The two groups received identical verbal instruction, differing only in the visual representation used to depict the situations. However, group performance on the task was different, as can be seen from the means in Table 9.2.

Classification differences. The groups also differed significantly on all three classification tasks, with the Diagram group more successful in every case. As demonstrated by the cluster analyses of Figure 9.5, the Diagram group formed stronger and more accurate clusters of greater size than did the No-Diagram group. Additional evidence about the importance of visual representations in instruction comes from the comparison of the second and third classification tasks. In the second, students classified problems in the presence of the names of the situations. In the third, they classified problems in the presence of either the diagrams (Diagram group) or the boxes (No-Diagram group). A secondary analysis of the data shows that the Diagram group classified significantly more problems correctly when allowed to use the figures than when they used only the names in the classification (t (21) = 2.21, $p <$ .05). This difference is also reflected in the clusters shown in Figures 9.5C and 9.5E. The clusters formed earlier and were larger when the diagrams were used as the basis of classification. In contrast, there was no difference in the mean numbers of correct classifications for the No-Diagram group on these two tasks ($t < 1$). Additionally, a comparison of the cluster analyses for these two classifications shows that the third classification is structurally weaker than the second. The clusters contained fewer problems and formed at lower levels.

Recall differences. The final difference observed between the groups was in the nature and amount of information retained over time. The Diagram group recalled significantly more information about the situations than did the No-Diagram group. Both groups remembered equally well that there were five situations, but the Diagram group had somewhat greater success in naming them. The largest difference in recall derived from the students' attempts to draw or describe the situations. This is particularly evident in the extreme cases of remembering all five situations versus remembering none of them. In the Diagram group, 7 students (32%) drew all five diagrams correctly. No student in this group failed to recall at least one of them. The situation is reversed for the No-Diagram group: No student recalled details about all five situations, and 7 students failed to recall any of them. In the Diagram condition, 6 of the 22 students chose to draw the figures and write descriptions of the situations; all the rest chose draw the figures. In the No-Diagram condition, only 3 of 22 students attempted to reproduce the lists of labels. The remainder wrote short phrases to describe the situations.

Interpretation

The importance of diagrams is better understood when examined with respect to several general issues of memory research, namely, differences in encoding, differences in retrieval and activation, differences in interference, and differences in usage. Each of these issues offers some explanation about the findings of Brewer's experiment.

Encoding. One benefit of using diagrams may be their marker function: They serve as rapid points of access to a great deal of related knowledge. The ability to perceive differences and make relevant discriminations calls upon knowledge stored in long-term memory. Using figures to depict the situations and to unify the various components of the situations may make it easier for individuals to encode and recognize salient features. Thus, even though the memory of the diagram is not explicitly called for by a task, the figure may nevertheless be retrieved from memory and used to structure the recall of related information, as in the P/S or SORT1 tasks.

Why would diagrams be superior to the label representation? One difference between the two representations is that each diagram is a distinct figure as well as the logical composite of its constituent pieces. The label representation uses the same general form for each situation, that is, each is a list of components. I hypothesize that the uniqueness in shape and configuration of the diagrams aids in their effectiveness. Again, this is a marker function: The diagrams can be readily distinguished at a glance. The encoding of their general shapes would be sufficient to distinguish them. The same cannot be said of the label representations. The shape or form of the list alone carries little distinguishing information. One needs instead the verbal information contained in the labels, which requires the more specific componential knowledge. Thus, some important spatial or visual cues may be present for the diagrams and absent for the label representations.

Retrieval. An alternative interpretation would be that the two representations are encoded in much the same way but differ in their retrieval, principally through the levels of activation and strength of association. If the diagrams are particularly salient pieces of information about the situations, they should form strong associations with the identification knowledge of their respective situations. Research on semantic memory suggests that closely related associations are more quickly retrieved than elements less closely tied. Extending this theory to figures suggests that they will be retrieved more easily than the label representations because the diagrams have become more strongly associated with the situations than have the sets of labels.

Retrieval may also be aided by the spatial configuration of the diagrams. Individuals' use of spatial information to search memory is well documented and we all have many personal anecdotes (e.g., not remembering a route but remembering what the corner looked like at which a critical turn must be made; not remembering a citation, but remembering what the page looked like on which it was printed or remembering that a quotation of interest was at the top right-hand portion of the page). The diagrams may provide this same access. For example, in trying to classify a particular problem, an individual might remember mapping part of a similar problem into an oval connected to a rectangle. This might be sufficient information to retrieve the diagram for Change. Retrieval of the diagram would then activate pertinent features associated with the Change situation, and the individual could determine whether the current problem indeed fit the situation. Here the template and marker functions merge. Again, it is the uniqueness of the diagrams that allows this type of retrieval. Memory of mapping part of a similar problem into a box with a label would not be sufficient to identify one of the label representations and hence to begin activation.

Interference. One possible explanation of why students in the Diagram group recalled more information than those in the No-Diagram group is that the latter may have experienced more retroactive interference than the former when they attempted to retrieve knowledge about the situations. Consider that both groups apparently learned to distinguish among the situations in the initial instruction tasks. At the conclusion of the initial instruction, and prior to the instruction incorporating the two alternative representations, there were no differences in mean group performance. Students in both groups identified about 70% of the situations correctly. Those in the No-Diagram group maintained roughly this same percentage correct on the first classification task at the conclusion of instruction, whereas students in the Diagram group improved to 77% correct.

Both groups experienced some forgetting over the interval between the second and third experimental sessions, with performance dropping by about 15%. However, in the presence of the figures, the Diagram group moved back to 70% correct on the third sorting task. They were clearly aided by seeing the diagrams. One concludes that recognition of the figures led to retrieval of additional information that was useful in categorizing the problems.

In contrast, seeing the labels did not aid the recall of the No-Diagram students. Their success in categorizing the problems actually declined slightly from the second to the third sorting task (from a mean of 10.14 to 9.86). Items that had been correctly classified when only the names were available to the students were *mis*classified in the presence of the labels. The interference explanation suggests that the similarities among these verbal representations in some way caused retroactive interference for the students, making it more difficult for them to recognize the situations.

Usage. A final consideration is that students' use of the two forms of visual representation may have differed. The label representation may lead to a linear or sequential processing in which individuals do not necessarily link the various parts. Students may "see" the problem as the set of its parts as defined by the situation, but they do not necessarily comprehend all the ways that those parts are connected to each other. This is probably a function of the linear ordering of the labels in this representation.

In contrast, the diagrams were constructed so that the connections among their constituent parts are emphasized. An individual does not necessarily map these figures in a linear or sequential way. Moreover, the individual using the diagram would have a continual reminder of the way particular components are linked. This linking feature is absent in the label representation.

These four explanations are not independent. If students use the information differently, they have probably encoded it differently. Similarly, the activation and retrieval differences are necessarily related to the encoding and organization of knowledge as it is initially learned. All four are generally consistent with well-accepted theories of cognitive processing, including dual encoding of visual and verbal knowledge and interference and decay theories of forgetting.

Visual representations in schemas

The evidence suggests that visual representations have several ways of influencing schema development. In a sense, the visual form can anchor the schema, with some of its aspects clearly necessary for identification knowledge and other aspects needed as elaboration knowledge. One of the central features of a schema, as pointed out in chapter 2, is the integration and connectivity that exist among its constituents. The visual representation enhances that integration and connectivity. It appears to be much more powerful than a verbal anchor, although the power can probably be manipulated by changing various features of the visual representation. It seems likely that the visual representation provides an initial key path of connectivity among the different parts of a schema as it develops.

Visual representations enhance learning, but some are more effective than others. For situations such as the one described here, the visual representations are highly useful in promoting the development of concept discriminations. A set of visual figures is needed, one for each concept or idea, and each of these should be distinct.

What makes a good visual representation? I suggest the following criteria. First, the representation should reflect the essential components of its target. These components need to be meaningfully connected both in the representation and in the target. Second, the representation should be as simple as possible while meeting the first criterion. Only the essential components need to be represented visually. Extraneous detail only adds clutter. Finally, each representation should have spatial uniqueness. Each figure should be distinct from any other.

The important finding in the present research is that the superior strength of the diagrammatic representation asserts itself in the retention tasks. Diagrams and labels both looked good in instruction, and in short-term retention tasks both were apparently effective in promoting successful performance. However, the diagram representation had a positive and lasting influence, affecting the recall and performance of students a considerable time after the conclusion of instruction. The label representation did not have an enduring positive effect, and in fact it apparently hindered performance. This finding implies that we should use caution in interpreting the immediate impact of visual aids in learning, especially when follow-up performance is not evaluated.

In their discussion about verbal and visual representations, Larkin and Simon (1987) suggested that the two representations may carry the same information load in problem solving. Does this translate into a similar amount of encoding of knowledge in learning? Or does the visual representation produce a larger (or smaller) store of retrievable information?

In light of the differences in performance observed in the present studies, these are pertinent research questions to be followed up. The Diagram group clearly remembered more. Either they had encoded more information or had better access to it than did the No-Diagram group. This may not be a case of better computational efficiency but simply of having more knowledge with which to compute. We may hypothesize that a larger amount of encoded information yields more linkages that can be easily traversed than does a small amount of information, assuming that the information is encoded efficiently. Thus, as the search takes place through the encoded material, the nature of the encoding should influence the efficiency of the search. When given appropriate prompts (i.e., either names or figures), the Diagram students performed very well. In contrast, the prompts did not help the No-Diagram group. One surmises that we are observing the results of differential storage, either different in arrangement or different in total quantity.

It seems clear from the findings presented here that any schema-based instruction ought to contain good visual representations of the schema situations. Learning is enhanced by their inclusion: Immediate recognition is good, and long-term retention seems to be greatly facilitated by them. It is important, however, to ensure that both functions of visual representations are maintained: Markers are necessary parts of identification knowledge and templates are essential for the mental models of elaboration knowledge. Strong schemas will have both.

IV

Schemas and assessment

The purpose of part IV is to describe some of the important issues involved in assessing schema knowledge. The primary focus is on assessing learning that accrues from schema-based instruction. In its simplest form, the argument presented here states that there should be a common theory governing instruction, the learning that occurs as a result of the instruction, and the assessment of the learning. I propose that schema theory uniquely provides the needed framework for all three.

Instruction and learning from instruction have been the topics of the previous two parts. Now, the focus shifts to issues of assessment. To some degree, the ideas offered here have already been introduced, because it has been impossible to discuss the evaluation of learning from schema-based assessment without delving into some of the assessment questions and techniques. These issues are elaborated more fully here.

The two chapters of part IV describe the theory and practice of schema-based assessment. Chapter 10 looks at the theoretical issues that accompany schema-based assessment. Chapter 11 describes assessment as it is performed in SPS and PSE, pointing out how the theory can be put into practice and examining some of the unique features of the evaluation in these systems.

10

Schema-based assessment

Schema-based assessment has the same focus as schema-based instruction but a different goal. The goal of the instruction is to facilitate the creation of schemas by students who experience the instruction. The goal of the assessment is to examine the extent to which learners have developed and can use the schemas that guided instruction. Schema-based assessment requires us to specify a priori the structure of the schemas to be assessed so that items evaluating those schemas can be constructed. In assessment, to a much greater extent than in instruction, the structure of the schema itself becomes a crucial factor because it influences the way that the test items are developed and interpreted.

Schema assessment presents some difficulties that do not arise in other types of assessment. A central one stems from the fact that schemas are highly individualized. Schemas are created and tailored by individuals to reflect their own experiences and understandings of the world. No two individuals will form identical schemas because no two individuals can experience the world identically, but both of them may have well-formed and useful schemas. The assessment question is: How can we obtain a true snapshot of schema development for these different individuals?

Consider for a moment a case in which individualization is not a factor, namely, the acquisition of a particular fact by several individuals as a result of some instruction. There is no ambiguity whatsoever in what these individuals know: They either have memorized the fact or they have not. Suppose the fact of interest is the date of the first Battle of Bull Run. A test item aimed specifically at this fact – "What was the date of the first Battle of Bull Run?" – will reflect identical learning of it by each individual who makes the correct response. That is not to say that individuals will not differ in the amount of other knowledge they may have linked to the fact. They almost certainly will. However, our particular item was not designed to test that knowledge. We test only knowledge of the fact. Either the student responds with the year 1861 or he does not.

Now consider the assessment of schema knowledge. No single item can possibly assess schema knowledge commensurably for a group of individuals in the same way that one item can assess a solitary fact. It is likely that all individuals have identical knowledge of the latter, but it is unlikely that they do so for the former. To be sure, some common ground should exist in the schema knowledge acquired by a group of individuals. Through schema-based instruction, individuals are provided with common experiences that facilitate the development of targeted schemas, and consequently, some of the elements of any schema will undoubtedly come from this common background of instruction. Thus, individuals' schemas may contain some of the same features, but other features will be unique to each learner, because each one will bring his or her own prior experiences to the instruction. Our objective as assessors is to develop a means of examining the common schema knowledge and the way the student has incorporated it into his or her knowledge base, without rewarding or penalizing the student for his or her other knowledge that is unique. Plainly stated, we want to focus the assessment only on the results of our instruction, and we must guard against assessing the experiences the student brings to the instruction.

The impact of individualization is change in the scope of assessment, making it much broader. Whereas an individual may not have a specific piece of information stored in memory as part of a schema, that individual may nonetheless have sufficient schema knowledge to use the schema well. A test of a specific piece of information will not be a fair test of schema development, unless the assessor believes that the specific piece being tested is, in fact, quintessential for schema development in *every* individual. In this case, one might want to determine first that the individual has indeed acquired this piece of information and second that he associates it with the correct schema and in correct relation to other requisite schema knowledge.

A second difficulty generated in the testing arena by schema-based assessment is that it does not conform to the same underlying view of learning that governs many other tests. This mismatch is both bad and good. The chief drawback is that the lack of conformity forces us to look for new psychometric models. The advantage, which seems to far outweigh the disadvantage, lies in its agreement with new theories of learning. Traditional test development is frequently at odds with modern cognitive theory. Until recently, many tests have been based, explicitly or implicitly, on several premises that are now considered by many cognitive scientists to be in error. The first has to do with the nature of intelligence and the way we assess it. There has been a widespread (and sometimes unstated) belief that intelligence is general and broad and that it is the accumulation of lots and lots of knowledge. Under this view, more is definitely better. From this belief has emerged a tradition of testing a large number of different things in a single test. And we have drifted into a pattern of measuring achievement in the same way. Both teacher-developed tests and externally constructed ones tend to emphasize a broad coverage of many different aspects of a subject area, and each is typically assessed as if it were independent of the others.

Making much the same point, L. Resnick and D. Resnick (1992) argue that some of the problems with today's assessment stem from two faulty assumptions they call decomposability and decontextualization. Decomposability refers to the way in which knowledge is viewed as a composite that can be broken into small isolated pieces, ignoring the interrelations among them. Decontextualization refers to the belief that the use of skills is context free, and it suggests that they will be used in consistent ways, no matter what the assessment task. Together, these two assumptions provide a basis of assessment that is at odds with the nature of human cognition as we view it today.

The consequences of these premises on test development have been enormous. Testing, teaching, and learning have all been influenced by them. The practice of developing a test comprised of many unrelated items has spread to achievement tests, both standardized instruments and classroom evaluations. One unfortunate outcome is that we now have many tests that are composed of a great many small items that assess relatively trivial knowledge. Consider the extreme testing situation in which we have a group of individuals, we have delivered excellent instruction, and we want to know their relative ranking on some topic. In an effort to measure a multitude of independent pieces of information, we must sometimes grasp at trivial and obscure knowledge, because with effective instruction everyone should have learned the obvious and commonplace. Thus, to make a ranking, we extend the test questions, moving progressively from the familiar to the unfamiliar, until we find questions that only some individuals can answer, namely, those individuals who have learned the most facts. One can imagine that the items that are most discriminating may well be the most obscure and the most trivial. Can we really believe that the individuals who can respond to them are the brightest and have the most understanding?

Students know full well that the above-mentioned premises underlie most of the tests that they take. We have only to look at their study habits for confirmation. They memorize dates, figures, isolated facts, lists, and as many trivial details as they can. They expect to be quizzed on these things. They do not expect to be asked to demonstrate their reasoning, their ability to apply their understanding in a meaningful way to a new situation, or to create anything. In fact, they may become aggrieved when asked to do so, because it disrupts their expectations (Marshall, in press). Have we not all heard complaints that some tests were unfair because students were not told in advance that they would be asked a particular type of question? Tests have become routine look-up or recall exercises. Students memorize some material and with any luck can retrieve the needed information when it is called for on the test.

Schema assessment places a different demand on the student. The call to a schema is not a rote process. To be sure, students must access their schema knowledge in long-term memory, and to some extent the access itself is a look-up procedure, but the students must do something with the knowledge that is retrieved. Each schema instantiation will be slightly different, depending upon the student's prior knowledge and the details of the situation that are perceived. All or only a part of the schema knowledge may be activated, varying in accordance with the circumstances of the test situation. Other schemas may be needed, and the student must determine which ones are useful and which are not. From the stored schema knowledge, the student *constructs* his or her response to a well-formed item of schema assessment.

Therefore, as the above paragraphs suggest, schema-based assessment requires a reconsideration of the basic principles behind test construction and use. The issues just mentioned outline some of the differences between schema-based tests and traditional tests. The remainder of this chapter examines some of the major implications of schema theory for test development and test interpretation. Some of the implications are far-reaching and must await new methodologies. Others are candidates for immediate implementation.

Test development

The most obvious consequences of schema-based assessment show up in the content of test items. Innovative items are needed for the simple reason that traditional items will not suffice. Different questions are to be posed; different answers are to be sought. The innovations may derive from a modification in the nature of instruction, or they may result from a shift in test objectives. Both of these reasons are operative when we consider schema-based tests.

The most noticeable difference in test content between a schema-based test and a traditional test is the emphasis in the former on intermediate decisions. A schema-based test will attempt to tease apart the four knowledge components of one or more schemas, and these knowledge components may be utilized at different points in the formulation of a student's test response. It is very difficult to construct a test item in which all four knowledge components for one schema are assessable. Almost certainly some will be invisible. Thus, to evaluate a single schema, one probably will need several items, each devoted to the evaluation of one or perhaps two of the components. The questions that tap into the various knowledge components are unlike those that typically appear on tests because they target the intermediate steps at which these knowledge components are needed. Consider, for example, the nature of the questions asked in the exercises of SPS (see Chapter 5).

Further, the content of the schema-based test may also be quite different from that of the traditional test because of the emphasis in schema theory on connectivity. A well-developed set of schemas will yield a great many connections, both within schemas and between schemas. A good test of schema development will focus on correlated, rather than uncorrelated, knowledge, so that test items having to do with small, unrelated pieces of knowledge will have relatively low value. Notice that this feature of a schema-based test would potentially eliminate a large number of items found on a typical non-schema-based test.

The best schema-based tests will probably be adaptive tests, that is, tests tailored for each individual. Because all students do not have identical schema knowledge, the assessment of their knowledge will almost surely demand different test items. One can imagine that the typical testing experience will begin with a standard question to which all individuals respond. The next question will depend entirely on a student's response to the first one. If the student demonstrates satisfactorily the acquisition and use of the targeted schema knowledge, he or she will move on to another aspect of schema assessment. If the student's reply is ambiguous, a second question will be used to clarify his or her knowledge. If the student is unable to respond to the standard question, a simpler one aimed at the same schema could be utilized. Thus, the best assessments will be adapted to the individuals and will require a different number of items for each one.

A striking feature of schema-based tests is the inclusion of a number of novel situations and problems. One piece of evidence about a student's development of a coherent schema is the ability to use it in a new setting. In mathematics education, for example, one frequently sees requests from educators to test developers for novel items or loosely structured problems because these items are perceived to stretch and extend a student's understanding (Silver 1985). Not surprisingly, such items also demand that the student possess appropriate schemas (and have experienced the appropriate schema-based instruction that facilitates their development). The importance of such items is that they demand that the student generate or create a response, not merely look up a memorized procedure.

It should be apparent that test developers must ensure that some relevant hook into schema knowledge be present in a novel problem so that the student will retrieve a useful schema from memory. Novice problem solvers will not have as many avenues of access to schema knowledge as will experienced solvers, and they may need several overt cues to help them access their schema knowledge. Test items that do not activate schema knowledge have little value for our assessment, because we are left not knowing whether the item itself is at fault for failing to tap the schema or whether the schema is indeed missing or malformed.

An example of how novel items can fail to address key schemas may be informative. This example derives from the California Assessment Program (CAP), which for several years was a national leader in the movement to develop open-ended questions for mathematics assessment. As part of the CAP Mathematics Advisory Committee, I worked with the rest of the committee in reviewing items which had been field-tested to determine their suitability, including those that were used in the first statewide

Problem 1:
James knows that half of the students from his school are accepted at the public university nearby. Also, half are accepted at the local private college. James thinks this adds up to 100 percent, so he will surely be accepted at one or the other institution. Explain why James may be wrong. If possible, use a diagram in your explanation.

Types of Student Responses:[1]
a. Deny validity of problem statement
     e.g. "That's wrong because everyone doesn't go to college."[2]
b. Form an equation
     e.g., carry out some computation using 1/2
c. Use wrong mental model (i.e., visual representation)
     e.g., form 2x2 table, make graph with students on one axis and school on the other
d. Modify the problem
     e.g., "If 175 students apply, and 1/2 are accepted to the public university and 1/2 are
         accepted to the local private college,
         1/2 of 175 is 87,
         87 go to the university,
         87 go to the college,
         leaving one student out, which can be James."[3]

Problem 2:
The square below has sides of length 2 units. Connect the midpoints of the sides of the square, in order, to form an <u>interior</u> square. Repeat the same process to make squares within squares.

(a) **Draw the first five <u>interior</u> squares.**

(b) **Write the sequence of numbers that represent the areas of the first five <u>interior</u> squares.**

(c) **What rule can be used to find the area of the *nth* <u>interior</u> square?**

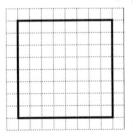

Types of Student Responses:
a. Make no response
     e.g., leave page entirely blank
b. Focus only on some of the terms in the problem, ignore others
     e.g., draw 5 squares anywhere in figure
c. Do only part of the problem
     e.g., draw the 5 embedded squares and compute areas but fail to look for
         functional relationship specified in part (c)
d. Generalize to an inappropriate rule

[1] All responses in this figure are summarized from those reported in the California Assessment Program's *A Question of Thinking* (1989).
[2] *A Question of Thinking*, p. 25.
[3] *A Question of Thinking*, p. 27.

Figure 10.1. Examples of two open-ended items used by the California Assessment Program (Items reprinted from *A Question of Thinking,* with permission from the California State Department of Education, copyright © 1989)

implementation. Some of the items were successful, and some were not.

Two of the items that elicited schema-based failures are shown in Figure 10.1 together with descriptions of some student responses.[1] The item analyses were based on 500 student responses each. As reported by CAP (1989), about 25% of the students answering the first question "digressed from the point of the problem" (p. 28). That is, they wrote short essays about going to college, but they never realized that this was intended to be a mathematical question. They chose to talk about requirements, admissions policies, and similar topics, but they did not access the relevant schema knowledge envisioned by the developers of the item. Instead, the students retrieved schemas that were inappropriate for the testing situation. An even larger number of students made inappropriate mathematical responses. They tried various means of representing the problem as a graph or table, or they tried to carry out computations based on "one-half." One may suppose that the first group of students had primarily errors of schema access (i.e., they used the wrong schemas), whereas the second group of students had errors of schema instantiation (i.e., they mapped problem elements incorrectly to their elaboration knowledge).

On the second problem in Figure 10.1, many students were unable to make any response at all. As reported by CAP (1989), more than 20% of the students turned in blank pages for this problem. One interprets this failure to respond as an inability to tap any schema knowledge at all. Without some initial clue about which schemas to use, students may end up with no access to their knowledge at all. And, if there is no response, we have no means of diagnosing or interpreting their difficulties. We cannot know if these students had never developed appropriate schemas or if they were simply unable to recognize the key features of the situation.

Test construction and item generation under schema theory require new approaches. It is worth considering how test items can be constructed to reflect the linkages expected in students' knowledge of a subject. The nature of the linkages points to two possible representations: a hierarchy and a network.

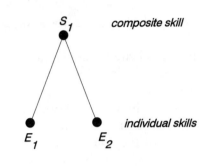

Figure 10.2. An example of a knowledge hierarchy in which one skill is a composite of two others

A hierarchical representation

Knowledge can be represented by a hierarchy if some pieces of it are prerequisites for others. One imagines a tree structure, with various branches, as in Figure 10.2. This representation is reminiscent of Gagné's learning hierarchy described in chapter 4. The elements at the end of each branch are the individual skills required to carry out the composite skill formed at their juncture. A hierarchy would exist, for example, for the case in which one wished to evaluate a composite skill, *S1*, that was composed of two separate elements, *E1* and *E2*, as shown in Figure 10.2.

One can easily imagine quite a large hierarchy with a great many composites and individual elements. The questions we ask ourselves are how many test items are needed to evaluate the hierarchy, do we need to test all composites and all individual elements, and how do we select which parts of the hierarchy to evaluate next? In the simple example of one composite with two constituents, as in Figure 10.2, we have potentially three test items, one for each element and one for the composite. The assessment could involve all three items, or we could make use of only one or two. In some instances, one item would suffice: A successful response on the composite implies success on all constituent elements as well. The converse is not necessarily true. It may be that success on *E1* and *E2* individually does not ensure a successful response to *S1*. This pattern implies an interaction between *E1* and *E2* that appears only in the composite. Further, the one-item assessment would not suffice if the composite were answered incorrectly; we would need to follow up with separate items for the constituent elements. The response to the composite in this case would not provide enough information about the student's knowledge of individual elements that make up the composite. Thus, even in this highly simplified case, there are many options.

The actual construction of test items is relatively easy under the hierarchical representation because it requires only that we be able to identify the individual elements and combine them logically as needed in various test items. With respect to schema assessment, the hierarchical structure is most appropriate for assessing execution and planning knowledge, under the conditions of needing several skills to perform a task. For example, the procedure of adding two fractions requires a number of different skills, including finding a common denominator, adding digits, and so on. If one takes as an objective the determination of whether a student can add fractions, one is faced with the options of testing only the composite, testing the composite and some of its individual elements, testing the individual elements only, or testing everything individually. The last is rarely an acceptable avenue because in any meaningful situation it demands a vast number of small test items.

Tests of hierarchical knowledge are best designed as adaptive tests, so that one has the flexibility to select the most appropriate items based on students' previous responses. It is enormously difficult to determine how many items to use in the assessment of a hierarchy. I have elaborated on this issue elsewhere (see Marshall 1981), where I developed two heuristics for approximating optimal item selection. I will not repeat the details here. The point is that flexibility is required, so that one can go back and forth as needed between items testing composites and items testing individual elements.

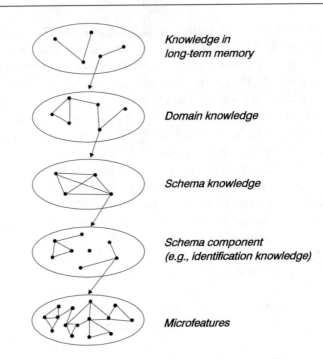

Figure 10.3. Multiple layers of schema knowledge. (Reprinted from S. P. Marshall, "The assessment of schema knowledge for arithmetic story problems: A cognitive science perspective," G. Kulm [Ed.], *Assessing higher order thinking in mathematics* [Washington, DC: American Association for the Advancement of Science, copyright © 1990], p. 168)

A network representation

In schema assessment, we are more often faced with a network, rather than a hierarchy, of related knowledge. The network to be assessed is rarely a simple structure. Most of the time, we have a collection of schemas that are not entirely independent of each other. Parts of one may also be parts of another.

The network assessment can be carried out at many levels, as shown in Figure 10.3. First, a network of schemas constitutes domain knowledge. Next, each of the schemas itself is a network with four parts, that is, the four knowledge components. And finally, each knowledge component is itself a network of the individual knowledge elements relevant to it. Tests can target any of these levels of networks, depending upon their purpose. For example, a comprehensive examination at the conclusion of graduate studies would likely target the entire set of schemas making up a student's domain knowledge. Classroom tests would be more prone to focus on individual schemas and the knowledge components of each one.

To assess schemas, the testing focus must shift to ways of evaluating networks. This is an abrupt shift from the evaluation of independent pieces of knowledge or from assessing levels of hierarchies. There are several useful ways of looking at networks. One comes from the perspective of graph theory and has formed the basis for some of my own research (e.g., Marshall, 1990b). In this view, the network is considered to be a graph containing nodes and links, allowing us to take advantage of several well-known mathematical properties associated with graphs. For explanatory purposes, it is convenient to assume that the graph is simple and undirected; that is, the links are not directional, no node may be connected to itself, and there is at most one link between any two nodes.

From previous work (e.g., Frank, 1971; Marshall, 1990b), it is evident that we can derive some of the statistical properties of a network, particularly estimates of the number of nodes and the number of links in it. This is a relatively simple exercise for a network in which the nodes are all of a kind, as is the case if one wishes to assess only one component of schema knowledge. Elsewhere, I have laid out the methods by which one may sample nodes and links from an idealized network and use the sample to estimate the number of nodes and links in an individual's knowledge network (Marshall, 1990b). These estimates are just a bare beginning. We must develop procedures for making estimations from a full graph, representing an entire schema, that contains the four subgraphs of schema knowledge components. Frank (1971) discusses the evaluation of subgraphs, but more research is needed on this topic.

Two other approaches to assessing networks appear promising. One is Pathfinder, a system of network evaluation that may be described as a structural approach to knowledge assessment (Goldsmith, Johnson, & Acton, 1991; Goldsmith & Davenport 1990; Schvaneveldt, 1990). With Pathfinder, Goldsmith et al. make the attempt to link cognitive representation with psychometric prediction. Pathfinder is a computer program that evaluates an individual's judgments about the degree of relatedness of a set of concepts, and it uses the evaluation to construct a network representing the individual's knowledge. Most interesting in the Pathfinder approach is the possibility of making statistical comparisons about graph similarities, as described by Goldsmith and Davenport (1990). It seems feasible that one could adapt the technique to compare schema graphs of different students.

A second approach to network assessment is through probability-based inference networks. The work by Robert Mislevy and his associates is a good example (see, e.g., Mislevy, Yamamoto, & Anacker, 1991; Beland & Mislevy, 1991). Using techniques developed in medical expert systems research, especially the computer systems HUGIN and MUNIN originating in Denmark (Andersen, Jensen, Olesen, & Jensen, 1989, as cited in Beland & Mislevy, 1991), Mislevy has constructed models that are appropriate for assessing students' understanding. The models are directed acyclic graphs, and they blend cognitive theory and statistical inference. Mislevy and his associates have applied this technique successfully to problems involving a balance and to problems of proportional reasoning. It seems likely that inference networks can be modified for schema assessment as well.

Test interpretation

Perhaps the single most important outcome of schema-based assessment is that it leads to a reexamination of the test's place in the instructional process and subsequently to a new interpretation of test results. At present, it is no secret that many educators feel that tests drive the curriculum and that teachers feel compelled to "teach to the test" (Shepard, 1991; M. L. Smith, 1991). The tests in question are, for the most part, standardized tests created at the state or national level to assess student mastery of fairly large bodies of knowledge. If the educators are correct, and they seem to be, then the key implication of these circumstances is that test developers are determining what students will learn. Moreover, they are also interpreting student responses. It is the interpretation that I call into question.

For purposes of discussion, we can view the educational process as a three-component process consisting of instruction, learning from instruction, and assessment of the learning. The teacher provides the instruction, the student learns from it, and either the teacher or a testing specialist develops the test instrument for measuring the amount of learning that takes place as a result of the instruction. Sometimes the assessment takes place immediately after the instruction or after some subset of it. Usually, this type of evaluation occurs via a teacher-developed test such as a midterm or final examination. Sometimes the assessment culminates several years of specialized study, as exemplified by advanced placement tests in high schools or comprehensive examinations in graduate programs. And sometimes the assessment caps one or more years of general studies, as in the CAT in elementary school, the SAT in high school, or the GRE in college. These latter examples are standardized tests constructed by testing specialists rather than the providers of instruction.

My argument about the interpretation of test results begins with the premise that the purpose of instruction is to promote learning, that is, to enhance students' understanding of a specified subject matter domain. The purpose of assessment is also to promote learning, as well as to determine how much learning results from the instruction. That is, the assessment should measure the current level of understanding about the important issues of the domain. Thus, both instruction and assessment are tightly bound to learning. These connections reflect not just the contents of learning but its form as well. Consequently, the underlying theory of how individuals learn is just as important in test development and interpretation as it is in curriculum development and presentation of instruction.

For meaningful assessment, the goals of assessment ought to reflect as closely as possible both the goals of instruction and the contents of instruction. Otherwise, the assessment capitalizes on incidental learning or on general intelligence or on previous instruction. All of these might be valuable sources of student knowledge, but they do not provide much indication of what the student learned from a specific course of instruction.

It may be difficult to formulate goals that satisfy the conditions for good instruction, meaningful learning, and useful assessment. Consider the interactions among the three components of the educational process (i.e., instruction, learning from instruction, and assessment of learning). Students' actual learning does not directly influence the framework of instruction. Nor does it influence the construction or interpretation of the form of assessment. However, the conception of what we want students to learn from instruction does influence the nature of the instruction, and if we have some idea of how that learning comes about, how it is organized in memory, or how it is facilitated and enhanced by additional information, then we should use that knowledge to build the instruction. This is the form of the argument presented in parts II and III. The same argument applies to assessment.

As I stressed in earlier chapters, schema theory is highly suited to be the organizing rationale behind instruction. It requires that the instructor take a good look at what constitutes understanding in his or her domain and come up with the key schemas. Having those schemas in mind, the instructor embarks upon a course of curriculum development that maximizes the probability that students will develop these schemas as a result of instruction. This process necessitates that the instructor not only decide whether any individual piece of knowledge should be learned but also specify the significance of that knowledge and its relationship to other knowledge.

The case for assessment is more complicated than for instruction. The connection between assessment and learning is indirect and thus depends upon two direct links, the one between instruction and learning and the one between instruction and assessment. The instruction-learning link has already been discussed and presents no conceptual difficulty. The instruction-assessment link poses some problems. On the one hand, the connection between assessment and instruction is obvious when the same individual – the teacher – develops both. We can easily assume that the same theory of learning influences both of the other processes in this case. The connection between assessment and instruction is less evident when different individuals have responsibility for the two components, as is the case with externally developed tests. One cannot make the assumption of a common view of learning when two different people or two groups of people have these separate responsibilities.

Teacher-constructed tests

One can be reasonably sure that a teacher-developed test will reflect, at least to some extent, the curricular philosophy expressed by that teacher in the classroom. Ideally, if teachers have adopted a schema approach to instruction, they will use the same approach in their assessments. This approach may show up in the way they construct their tests and/or in the way in which they interpret them.

However, teachers are not generally trained to develop tests, and it may be unfair to expect them to be responsible for test development as well as teaching. As those of us who teach know all too well, it is difficult to construct tests and few of us do it with great proficiency. An examination of classroom tests shows that, despite good intentions, teachers do not always write tests that match their instructional aims. In part, this outcome results from the fact that teachers usually spend very little time writing tests. In part, it stems from a general "coverage" philosophy: Teachers may feel constrained to make sure that all areas of instruction have been covered equally, and this view generally leads to a sampling of small and independent items. Finally, teachers tend to model the behaviors they have themselves experienced in the classroom. If their experience has been only with traditional tests, they are unlikely to develop schema-based ones on their own.

Although teachers will probably not be able to construct schema-based tests easily, they can and should use schema theory to interpret existing tests. It is true that these tests are not perfect and will not give a full accounting of schema development. However, under a schema theoretic interpretation, it is quite possible to derive useful estimates of schema knowledge from them.

Perhaps an example will clarify how this might be done. Suppose we have a test item that requires the student to write an essay about a historical event. We could adopt several different approaches to the grading and interpretation of the student's response. One looks primarily at the writing style; another looks for a fixed number of accurate historical details; another looks to see if the student reasoned correctly about the importance of the event; another requires the presence of a particular argument. For schema-based assessment, only the interpretations that are consistent with the schema-based instruction should be used. The student's response should be evaluated according to how well he or she demonstrated appropriate identification, elaboration, planning, and execution knowledge. This may include knowledge of specific facts, application of particular analogies, invocation of definitive arguments. It is incumbent on the instructor to understand that these elements are part of schema knowledge and to determine how well integrated they seem to be.

Some instructors compose answers themselves to test items and use these as templates for grading. This approach works reasonably well for simple problem solving exercises, but it does not capture all of the schema structure that may reside in a student's response, because the student may construct a very different answer from the teacher's that nevertheless reflects good schema knowledge. The key here is to move away from the notion that there is a single correct response to any item and to recognize that we should be looking instead for evidence of understanding. This evidence shows up in the way the student perceives the test item, the pieces of knowledge that he or she connects in the response, the plans that lie behind the presented argument, and the skill with which the argument is developed. One way of looking at it is to view the response as a pattern and to evaluate the structure of the pattern rather than viewing it as a collection of specific pieces.

An approach that may be well suited to interpreting schema-based assessment is to use expert knowledge found in expert's responses to test items and to develop a generalized scoring scheme from them. One would have the opportunity here to see how experts use schema knowledge and to look for similar implementations by students. Exact specification of schemas would seem to be critical for this approach.

Externally developed tests

All of the above difficulties in constructing schema-based test items hold for tests developed outside the classroom as well as for those constructed by teachers, and an additional problem is that the developers may be far removed from the actual classroom experience. Thus, there is no guarantee that they hold the same view of learning as do the teachers who guide the instruction.

A frequent criticism made by teachers today of many tests is that the tests do not reflect the teaching and learning occurring in the classroom, which is to say the tests are not based on the same theory that is guiding instruction. There are two ways to resolve this dilemma: Bring the teachers into accord with the test developers or, conversely, bring the test developers into accord with the teachers. At present, many educators fear that the former is the predominant approach – hence the fear that "teachers will teach to the test." This is a problem only if the test does not reflect accurately what we want to have taught and what we want to be learned.

There is currently a movement to embrace the second approach, namely bring test developers into accord with the teachers. This approach has its most obvious manifestation in substantial structural changes in tests, such as performance assessments, portfolios, and other forms of what is called authentic assessment (Linn, Baker, & Dunbar, 1991). It will succeed only if these changes can be shown to be theoretically justifiable. Structural changes in test construction that lack a theoretical basis will not necessarily be improvements. The prevailing hope is that these new forms of assessment are inherently more valid than traditional ones. This will be true only insofar as they can be shown to reflect student knowledge and understanding accurately. The way to reflect them is to make a theoretically sound interpretation.

Schema theory should be very appealing to developers of innovative measures because it provides precisely the theoretical grounding that so many test instruments lack. For example, one problem with performance-based assessment is that only a few situations can be evaluated due to the fact that the assessment is usually very time-consuming. As Shavelson, Gao, and Baxter (1993) point out, we currently need an impossibly large number of performance-based assessments to make accurate estimates of student knowledge. One can argue that some of these assessments will provide more useful information than others because they will be based on more fertile situations. Selecting the situations that will give the most information is a thorny issue. Under schema theory, one could determine which situations would be most likely to elicit the richest schema knowledge, would allow students the greatest flexibility in schema use, and could be the most unambiguously interpreted. Schema theory could aid in generating the assessment items as well as in interpreting the results.

The much-criticized multiple-choice item: How bad is it?

The most common format of achievement test items is the multiple-choice question. This is certainly true of commercially developed tests and is becoming true of more and more classroom tests, especially at the college level. Multiple-choice items certainly have a number of limitations, and there is no doubt that students have more freedom of expression on open-ended questions. It is well understood that items requiring generation and construction of responses by students usually produce richer data than simple recall and recognition items. However, multiple-choice tests can be effective if they are carefully developed, and they may be especially useful in conjunction with other types of items that allow the generation of responses.

In general, the structure itself of the multiple-choice item should not be blamed for a test's deficiencies; rather, the way in which the item content is derived, the manner by which items are aggregated, and the theory under which test results are interpreted cause much of the difficulty. As most testing specialists know, it is possible to construct good multiple-choice items that do require a student to demonstrate an understanding of the subject matter. These items are not easy to develop. Their content is usually complex, and their response options are carefully crafted to glean information about the student's knowledge.

Frequently, multiple-choice items are constructed to be independent entities so that the student's response on one item is not dependent on his or her response on another. The multiple-choice structure itself says nothing about independence: One can perfectly well have several related items that probe in some detail how a student views some topic. Moreover, one can score the items in a number of different ways; the structure does not dictate that each one receive equal weight in our interpretation. In several other places, I have given examples of how we can use existing multiple-choice items to evaluate student understanding and schema development. Examples of arithmetic are given in Marshall 1988 and Marshall 1990a; examples of rational numbers are found in Marshall 1993a.

Currently, there is movement in the testing community away from the use of multiple-choice tests to other innovative and alternative forms, such as portfolio assessments and performance-based tests. The arguments behind this movement tend to be based on the failure of multiple-choice tests to measure students' cognitive abilities in a meaningful context. What is happening in part is that the format of the test item is being blamed for the lack of theory behind the test. The argument is not entirely sensible. It is not the structure of the item so much as the structure of the theory underlying the construction and use of the item that is to blame. If we take the sampling, full-coverage approach to the assessment of learning, it does not matter very much whether we sample with multiple-choice items or with some other type of item. We still will not have a structured way of interpreting the learning that has occurred or the cognitive processing that is manifested.

Basic issues

Three issues of any assessment are *"what," "why,"* and *"how."* *What* is being assessed and *why* it is to be done are the driving forces behind an assessment. The issue of *how* is not the first issue to be addressed, although it is clearly an important one. Until recently, the *how* was often taken for granted, and the tests have been collections of multiple-choice items. At present, several test developers are seeking alternatives to multiple-choice tests. Among the alternatives are techniques such as portfolios, performance assessments, and free-response items. For the most part, these are presented as alternatives to the *how* question, and little attention has been given to any theory of learning or understanding that should underlie them. As demonstrated here, the explicit linkage between instruction, learning, and assessment is crucial, no matter what the form of the test. The common underlying theory provides the basis for interpreting the assessment. Without it, one is left only with a collection of isolated student responses. Thus, the format of the item is much less important than its interpretability. Merely changing the format will not by itself automatically bring about more meaningful assessment.

Schema-based assessment puts the *"what"* and the *"why"* of assessment first, and it does so by supplying an integrated picture of memory, learning, and assessment. The schema comprises multiple knowledge components, each made up potentially of many different pieces of information. Any test item for a schema will call for some subset of one or more of these knowledge components. The task of the test developer is to create items to test various subsets and thereby estimate efficiently the completeness of an individual's schema knowledge.

Summary

The instructional process presented here can be summed up in the following way:

- Schema theory shapes both the nature and the order of information in instruction.
- Schema theory explains both the encoding of knowledge in and the retrieval of knowledge from memory.
- Schema theory guides the construction of tests and their interpretation.

These three facets make up the educational experience, and the student is at the center of each one. It is the student who receives instruction, the student who learns from it, and the student whose knowledge is tested. Ultimately, it is schema theory that coordinates and connects our understanding of these three experiences.

The theme of this chapter is the importance of having a theoretical basis for all aspects of the instructional process, not just for the assessment component. It is not reasonable to look at assessment as if it had no relationship to learning and instruction. The theoretical basis for our tests cannot be a measurement model alone. We require a theory that has a meaningful cognitive interpretation as well as a psychometric one, so that the assessment results are viewed as cognitive consequences of specific instruction and the learning from that instruction. A fundamental goal of educational testing is to determine as accurately and fully as possible the depth and breadth of a student's knowledge, especially knowledge that has been acquired or modified as a result of some companion instruction. If one assumes that objectives of testing are aligned with objectives of instruction, it makes sense to focus the test on determining the extent to which students have developed the schemas that underlie the instruction. A test is considered to be an indication of the effectiveness of instruction. Schema-based tests, as part of the normal educational process, naturally follow schema-based instruction.

11

Assessment in SPS and PSE

The two computer-implemented systems described earlier, SPS and PSE, each offer unique assessment opportunities. SPS provides a way to track schema development for each individual over a common set of exercises, allowing comparisons among individuals as well as determination of which knowledge components are weak or strong. PSE adds diagnostic information about the ways in which an individual structures his or her own problem solving, giving explicit details about how the individual constructs and implements a plan. This chapter asks two questions of assessments derived from the PSE and SPS systems: First, how do they compare with traditional assessments, and second, what do they offer beyond traditional ones? To examine the first question, we compare the results of a problem-solving test with those of an aggregation of SPS questions. To answer the second, we look to performances of individual students as well as to single item analyses. Before doing either, however, I shall review the structure of the SPS exercises and the assessment variables associated with them.

Schema-based measures and SPS exercises

Identification score

Students indicate their acquisition of identification knowledge on two exercises. Both exercises require the student to apply identification knowledge in order to judge whether the conditions necessary for a particular situation have been met. For one exercise, the student's response is the selection of the name of the situation from a menu of all five names. For the second exercise, the student's response is the selection of the appropriate icon from a menu of icons. These exercises are illustrated in Figures 5.1 and 5.5. Each item of each exercise is scored 1 (correct) or 0 (incorrect). The identification score is the combined number of items a student answers correctly on both of the exercises. It is also possible to develop separate identification scores for each of the five situations.

Elaboration score

Two exercises of varying difficulty are used to assess elaboration knowledge. In the first exercise, the student is shown a story problem and asked to place phrases of the problem in the correct positions on the accompanying diagram. This exercise was illustrated in Figure 5.4. In this exercise, instruction for one situation is followed by a congruent set of exercise items involving only that situation. The appropriate diagram is always presented, and it will always correspond to the situation that was the topic of the just-concluded instruction.

The second elaboration exercise differs from the first in that the student does not know in advance which situation will appear. The second exercise is presented at the conclusion of instruction about all five situations, and all of the situations are possible candidates for every item in the exercise. In this exercise, the situations are randomly ordered so that the student cannot anticipate which one will appear next. As in the first elaboration exercise, the student does not select either the icon or the situation. The diagram that is appropriate for the situation depicted in the problem is shown to the student, and the student's job, as in the first exercise, is to fill in the diagram with the correct elements from the problem.

There are two possible elaboration scores. First, the items may be scored 1 (correct) or 0 (incorrect), and the elaboration score is the combined number of items for which all components are mapped correctly in these two exercises. The items may also be scored according to the number of correct problem elements that are mapped, which results in a possible item score of 0–3 for Change and Compare items, 0–4 for Vary items, 0–5 for Restate items, and 0–k for Group items having $k - 1$ subgroups in the problem. In general, I have found the 0/1 scoring system to be useful for aggregations over all situations and the alternative scoring by components to be informative when looking at a single situation.

Planning-identification score

SPS does not assess planning in isolation.[1] Its exercises were designed to look at planning and goal setting with respect to elaboration and identification knowledge. These exercises all use complex problems involving several situations and query the student about how to deal with them.

To evaluate the conjunction of planning and identification knowledge, SPS asks the student to identify first the situation that corresponds to the primary question asked in a problem and then to recognize the (unstated) secondary question and its associated situation. The exercise that assesses their understanding requires two menu choices of the student, one for the overall situation and one for the embedded, or secondary, one. Each item thus contributes 0–2 points, one for the correct primary question and one for the correct secondary question. The planning-identification score is the total number of correct identifications made on all items in this exercise.

Planning-elaboration score

Planning and elaboration knowledge are required on exercises requiring the student to make decisions about how the unknown of the problem fits into the primary situation. For example, the Change situation has three parts: the beginning, the amount of change, and the result. In a story problem, any one of these three parts may be unknown. Choice of arithmetic operation and ultimate solution of a problem depend upon which part of the situation is the ultimate target. SPS focuses on this point by presenting to the student a story problem and its appropriate diagram and asking the student to place the word UNKNOWN in the appropriate part of the figure. The UNKNOWN indicates the final part of the situation that answers the question posed in the problem, and the student must think ahead to the plan of how he or she would solve the problem.

In a related exercise, SPS asks students to recognize which situation governs the problem and which subproblems are to be solved before the top-level situation can be addressed. SPS asks the student to demonstrate his or her understanding by identifying in the diagram for the overall situation which components are given in the problem, which are partially known but immediately solvable, and which are the true unknowns. For this exercise, instead of actual problem components, the student places the terms GIVEN, PARTIAL ANSWER, and FINAL ANSWER in the diagram. Again, the student must think about the overall plan of solution to complete the task successfully. Figure 5.8 contains an example of this exercise.

The planning-elaboration score is the combined number of correct responses to these two exercises. Each item is scored 1 (correct) or 0 (incorrect).

Comparison of schema-based measures with other measures

The most common measure of problem-solving ability on story problems is a paper-and-pencil test in which several problems are presented to students and they are expected to compute correct numerical answers. It stands to reason that any new measure of the same ability should bear a strong relationship to the problem-solving test.

Experiment II

The straightforward way to examine whether schema-based measures account for problem-solving ability is to look at two types of assessment over one group of students. The four schema-based measures introduced above and a traditional test score are the assessments of interest. The students are those who took part in Experiment II of chapter 7, in which the two groups of students received different initial instruction. In this experiment, 14 students completed the SPS exercises necessary to construct the schema-based measures for all situations. They also took a short test at the conclusion of the experiment. The test contained four items, each having either two or three situations. Within these four items, each situation appeared exactly twice, so that the test could be scored by situation as well as by overall item. That is, we can either score the test 0–4, according to whether a student answered entire problems correctly, or we can score it 0–10, according to whether the student correctly solved the part of the problem involving each situation. Using the latter score allows us to look at individual performance on each situation as well as total test score, and it is the measure adopted here. Scoring the items in this way corresponds to allowing partial credit to students who get part of a problem correct, a common practice on classroom tests.

The question of interest now becomes whether the schema-based measures can account for the total test score, and we take the following linear model as the statistical model of interest:

$$\text{TOTAL}_i = \beta_0 + \beta_1 \text{ID}_i + \beta_2 \text{ELAB}_i + \beta_3 \text{PLAN\_ID}_i + \beta_4 \text{PLAN\_ELAB}_i + \varepsilon_i,$$

where TOTAL_i is the test score, ID_i is the identification score, ELAB_i is the elaboration score, PLAN_ID_i is the planning-identification score, PLAN_ELAB_i is the planning-elaboration score, and εi is the residual error for individual i. A multiple regression analysis gives us the following parameter estimates:

$$\text{TOTAL} = 1.61 - .054 \text{ ID} + .488 \text{ ELAB} + .207 \text{ PLAN\_ID}$$
$$- 1.10 \text{ PLAN\_ELAB},$$

with a multiple correlation of .90 and $F(4,9) = 9.88$, $p < .01$. The adjusted R^2 equals .73, suggesting a strong linear relationship in the population. Thus, we draw the tentative conclusion that problem-solving test scores can be predicted from schema-based measures. (It must be tentative because the analysis is based on a small number of subjects.)

Additional support for the conclusion comes from looking at each situation separately. For example, scores from all Change situations on the test were aggregated for each student and regressed on the scores on the schema measures. This is not an especially robust analysis because of the small number of subjects and items, but it provides another clue about the relationship between traditional problem solving and the more detailed schema analysis. Using the situation scores instead of total scores, the multiple regression analyses yield significant results for three situations: Change (adjusted R^2 = .50, $F(4,9)$ = 4.22, $p < .05$); Group (adjusted R^2 = .45, $F(4,9)$ = 3.67, $p < .05$); and Vary (adjusted R^2 = .47, $F(4,9)$ = 3.90, $p < .05$). The model did not satisfactorily explain scores for the other two situations, Compare and Restate, which were the easiest and the most difficult situations for students, respectively. In the case of Compare, most of the students answered the test items correctly, and when there is little variability in the dependent variable, differences in the predictor variables become irrelevant. In the case of Restate, most of the students erred on the mapping exercises. Limiting the regression analysis to only two predictors, identification score and planning-identification score, results in a model that satisfactorily predicts the test score (adjusted R^2 = .38, $F(1,11)$ = 4.98, $p < .05$).

In addition to giving students the test at the end of the experiment, we also gave them a pretest having the same structure (i.e., 4 items containing 10 situations, 2 each of Change, Group, Compare, Restate, and Vary). Students improved a small amount from pretest to posttest, moving from a mean of 2.7 to 3.0 ($t < 1$). The small and nonsignificant gain is to be expected; it is unrealistic to expect large gains from only 3 hours of instruction, given that students have spent large parts of 12 years developing their old problem-solving strategies. Of greater interest is whether a relationship existed between schema knowledge and performance prior to instruction. Such a relationship would suggest either that students already had some situation knowledge but were not actively aware of it or that the schema measures were reflecting influences other than schema knowledge. Taking the general form of the model described above with the same predictor variables, a second analysis was made using the dependent variable PRETEST instead of TOTAL. This model did not account for a significant proportion of variance in the dependent variable, with $F(4,9) = 2.53$, $p > .10$, and adjusted $R^2 = .32$. Pretest performance was not strongly associated with the schema variables. The relationship between paper-and-pencil test and the schema measures arises only after instruction based on schema knowledge. We have no estimate of students' knowledge about the situations prior to instruction.

Experiment I

Students in Experiment I also responded to a paper-and-pencil test at the conclusion of the study, and their performance can similarly be compared to the schema measures. Unfortunately, some student responses to the later exercises – from which the planning variables are derived – were irretrievably lost due to computer malfunction. As a consequence, these data are not as complete as those for Experiment II. Nevertheless, we still find a significant relationship between schema measures and posttest performance, with a best model of

$$\text{TOTAL} = 16.94 + 11.25 \text{ ID} + .74 \text{ PLAN\_ID},$$

where TOTAL is again the number of times the student solved correctly the part of the problem associated with a specific situation, and ID and PLAN_ID are the schema measures defined above. The model accounts for a significant proportion of variance of TOTAL, with $F(2,18) = 3.92$, $p < .05$, and adjusted $R^2 = .23$.

Brewer's experiment

We can also compare the schema-based measures with a different outcome measure, still using the same general approach described above. One candidate for comparison is the first sorting task of M. A. Brewer's experiment (1988), described in chapter 9. The dependent variable in the analysis now is CLASSIFICATION, the number of problems correctly classified according to situation. Only the responses from the students in the DIAGRAM group were analyzed because these students saw the original SPS instruction with diagrams and their learning most resembles that of students in the other experiments.

Once again, we derive the four schema-based measures from the SPS exercises, but this time we evaluate how well they account for classification accuracy. It turns out that only the schema-based measures involving planning are needed in the model, with

CLASSIFICATION = 11.248 + .448 PLAN_ID + .137 PLAN_ELAB.

The model yields a multiple correlation of .55 (adjusted R^2 = .29, $F(2,19) = 11.25$, $p < .05$). Thus, the schema measures bear a significant linear relationship with this outcome measure as well as with the paper-and-pencil tests.

Contributions of schema-based assessment

The above analyses suggest that schema measures account well for typical outcome measures. One characteristic of these analyses is that they all depend upon groups of students and upon aggregates of test items. It seems likely that we will also want to know something of individual students and individual items, and for this information we can turn to other analyses involving the schema measures.

We know by definition that there must be individual differences in schema knowledge. If schemas depend upon experience, then each individual must have some unique knowledge that other individuals will not have. We also know that some of the schema knowledge should be common to many students' schemas, because they have had the same instruction. What we would like to ascertain is how important the various elements of schema knowledge are to each student's performance. Cognitive diagnosis and item analysis are two of the procedures through which we gain the needed information.

Cognitive diagnosis

Cognitive diagnosis[2] is an emerging area of research that represents joint efforts of psychometricians and cognitive scientists.
From my point of view, the importance of cognitive diagnosis is
that it provides the critical union of cognitive theory and assessment: Diagnosis is guided by cognitive theory with the aim of providing information relevant to instruction decisions. It should
come as no surprise that schema theory is the basis of the cognitive
diagnosis described below.

Cognitive diagnosis has two defining characteristics. First, the
focus of the assessment process is on the individual, and second,
the unit of observation is much smaller than is usually seen on
assessment outcomes. We rarely see aggregations of group data,
although frequently the diagnoses for several individuals will be
contrasted. Also, more detail is present in the assessment of the
individual than is usual for other forms of assessment. Thus, not
only do we see a movement away from aggregation of data over
individuals, we also see the same movement away from aggregation of data for the single individual. This is not to say that each
and every response by an individual is to be examined and reported by itself. Some consolidation is essential if we are to interpret the results of the diagnosis.

Under schema theory, we achieve cognitive diagnosis by creating profiles of schema development for each individual. A profile
pertains to a single schema and provides information about how
the individual is developing the different types of knowledge
essential for a strong schema. Thus, the diagnosis focuses on identification knowledge, elaboration knowledge, planning knowledge, and execution knowledge. The profiles described below concern the first three types of schema knowledge. As I have
elsewhere indicated, execution knowledge is omitted from the
analyses because SPS does not emphasize it.

Consider a set of individual profiles created from the responses
of students in Experiment I, described in chapter 7. The four response variables described earlier in this chapter as schema measures are the bases of the profiles: the identification score (ID), the

Table 11.1. *Schema profiles: A comparison of students having comparable overall performance on Change items*

Student	Percentage Correct				
	ID	ELAB	PLAN_ID	PLAN_ELAB	Overall
S1	75	67	50	25	65
S2	83	83	100	0	67
S3	57	83	100	67	68
S4	100	83	0	33	69

Note: ID = identification exercises, ELAB = elaboration exercises, PLAN_ID = exercises requiring both planning and identification knowledge, PLAN_ELAB = exercises requiring both elaboration and planning knowledge.

elaboration score (ELAB), the planning-identification score (PLAN_ID), and the planning-elaboration score (PLAN_ELAB). These measures are derived from the exercises of SPS. The schema of interest is the one that students have begun to develop for the Change situation. Table 11.1 illustrates four profiles, developed for students with comparable performance. The overall performance of the students was quite similar, in terms of both the number of items to which they responded and their total proportion correct. On average, they responded to 19 items and answered 65.25% correctly. In Table 11.1, their performance on the different SPS exercises is categorized according to the schema knowledge components.

What the profiles reveal is that students have different knowledge about Change, despite their similarities on the overall measures of items attempted and percentage correct. On three of the four schema measures there are large differences in how students responded. For instance, S4 identified all Change situations correctly, whereas S3 erred on about half of them. S2 and S3 both answered the planning-identification items correctly, but the other two students had difficulty with the same exercises. Everyone had trouble with the planning-elaboration exercises, as shown by the generally low percentages for all four students.

If we had access to the information in Table 11.1 and were responsible for selecting the next instructional lesson for these students, we would probably opt for individualized lessons. Consider what these might be.

In terms of schema knowledge, S1 is the weakest student, and she would profit by a general review of all parts of Change instruction. It is unlikely that she is ready to move to a more difficult or complex lesson.

In contrast, S3 looks relatively strong. Her initial identification score is low, but she was quite successful on the identifications combined with planning, suggesting that she has overcome by herself any identification difficulties. We might want to keep in mind that S3 was somewhat weak on the planning-elaboration exercises and watch her future development in this area. Most likely, we would suggest that she continue on with new instructional material.

S4 has a different profile of development. He did quite well on the individual exercises of identification and elaboration, but his performance fell on the exercises requiring these types of knowledge combined with planning. Almost certainly the best course of action for him is additional instruction about and practice in integrating planning knowledge with his other knowledge.

Finally, S2 presents a bit of a puzzle. She was very successful on all but the planning-elaboration exercises, and her failure to answer a single item correctly on the planning-elaboration exercises seems to be an anomaly. We probably would want to talk with her about what happened on these exercises, in case some external factors influenced her performance (such as illness or distractions). Our instructional objective for her might include a quick review of how planning and elaboration knowledge can be integrated, followed by a few additional exercises. We would expect her to be ready to join S3 in tackling new instruction in the very near future.

Judging from the differences shown in Table 11.1, these students would not benefit from the same sequence of instruction at this time. For some students, review is essential. For others, it is time to move to new material. The schema profiles help us deter-

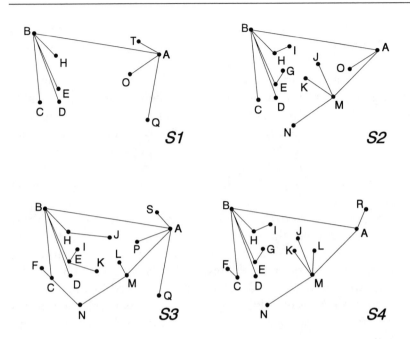

Figure 11.1. Cognitive maps of four students for the Change situation

mine which type of instruction will be appropriate for each student.

A useful supplement to the schema profile is the cognitive map, first introduced in chapter 7. Figure 11.1 contains the maps for the four students whose performance is recorded in Table 11.1. It will be recalled that cognitive maps result from interviews with students. The maps of Figure 11.1 were constructed following the interview of the fourth instructional session, at the conclusion of the planning exercises.

For all four maps of Figure 11.1, the letters A, B, C, ..., T consistently represent the same knowledge nodes. That is, A refers to one specific piece of information that was recalled by each of the students, and it is part of each map. The nodes (and their identifying letters) have fixed spatial positions on the four maps for ease of comparison. As before, location and distances between nodes are unimportant. The critical features are the presence or absence of any node and the links between it and other nodes.

The cognitive maps show important similarities and differences among the four students, just as the schema measures of Table 11.1 do. All four students have 6 nodes in common, and a number of other nodes are shared by two or three of them. Nevertheless, three of the four students have unique pieces of information in the cognitive maps, indicated by nodes that are not present for any other student. Strong and weak students alike have unique schema knowledge.

The cognitive maps support the profiles presented in Table 11.1. For example, the student with the weakest pattern of responses on the schema measures was S1, and it is not surprising that her cognitive map has the fewest nodes and links. Overall, S3 had the strongest schema development, evidenced by good performance on all measures. Her cognitive map has more connections among the nodes, suggesting an integration of knowledge about Change.

Taken together, the profiles of schema development and the cognitive maps provide us with estimates of schema knowledge for each student. The profiles give us an indication of how well developed the schema is, which areas are strong and which are weak, and how the different knowledge types are integrated. The cognitive maps help us understand how large the student's store of schema knowledge is and how well the information is interconnected. Comparisons between students are possible using either the profiles or the cognitive maps. From the comparisons, we begin to understand some of the differences and similarities in students' schema formation.

Item analysis

Just as we gain information about the individual student by examining performance as measured by the schema measures defined above, so too can we find out more about individual test items from the same measures. The reason for doing so is to better understand what determines an item's difficulty. Many factors contribute to item difficulty, such as types of numbers (e.g., fractions, proportions, large numbers), complexity of prose, and number of operations (see, e.g., the factors described by Loftus & Suppes, 1972). I propose that item difficulty is also a function of situation complexity as represented by the schema measures. By including schema measures in our estimates of item difficulty, we can achieve more informative appraisals of which items are difficult for which students.

Consider as an example, two items from the four-item test used to evaluate Experiment II. The first item contained the two situations of Change and Restate, and the second item contained the two situations of Group and Vary. For the first item, we can construct a new model in which success or failure on the item as a whole is a function of schema measures derived only from Change and Restate exercises. The model looks similar to the linear models described previously and has the same predictor variables of ID, ELAB, PLAN_ID, and PLAN_ELAB. The dependent variable is now the dichotomous variable SUCCESS, scored 1 if an individual has answered the item correctly and 0 if he has not.[3] The predictor variables reflect an individual's performance on SPS items about Change and Restate, and all others are excluded. A test of the model reveals that the schema measures predict a significant proportion of the variance of the item, $F_{(4,9)} = 5.65$, $p < .05$, $R = .85$, and adjusted $R^2 = .59$. Thus, the difficulty of this item for any student can be explained to a great extent by the student's own prior knowledge of the situations which are embedded in the item.

That the schema measures are highly situation-specific can be seen in the fact that the same schema measures for the first item, which are based only on the students' responses to Change and Restate exercises, do not account for responses on the second item, which contains a Vary and a Group situation ($F_{(4,9)} < 1.0$). Similarly, a model based on schema measures for Group and Vary satisfactorily accounts for the second item which contains those two situations ($F_{(4,9)} = 7.74$, $p < .01$, $R = .88$, adjusted $R^2 = .67$) but fails to account for the first item containing Change and Restate ($F_{(4,9)} = 1.69$, $p < .25$).

Analyses for items of the paper-and-pencil test of Experiment I yielded similar results. On five items for which full data were available, the adjusted R^2 values were .81, .50, .40, .39, and .18, indicating that performance on the individual items could be predicted from the schema measures for the appropriate situations. As before, these results must be evaluated with caution because of the small number of subjects.

Not all items can be assessed using schema measures, because there may be very little variation in students' responses to the test items (i.e., all students answer some items correctly). For example, in SPS students tended to answer a large percentage of Compare items correctly. In general, however, we gained useful information about most of the items used in the two studies reported here.

These analyses suggest that item difficulty may have a number of parameters. Recent models of item difficulty based on item-response theory (IRT) already incorporate several parameters, with some based on features of the items and some based on characteristics of the individuals responding to the items. It may now prove useful to consider whether we can develop IRT models having schema parameters. To the best of my knowledge, this has not yet been tried. It would seem to offer the opportunity of bringing a theory about underlying cognitive mechanisms to psychometrics as well as bringing the precision of IRT models to cognitive models.

Assessment in PSE

To date, most assessments of schema knowledge have been through interviews or think-aloud protocols (e.g., Chi, Feltovich, & Glaser, 1981). One reason that these procedures have been widely used is that schema assessment requires a great deal of flexibility. Many aspects of schema instantiation, especially those having to do with planning knowledge, cannot be easily assessed through a single question. It simply cannot tap the richness of schema knowledge held by most individuals. More likely, an assessment will begin with a standardized question and then allow a variety of follow-up questions to probe each individual's schema knowledge.

The assessment of PSE is in many ways parallel to a protocol analysis, with the important exception that the individual does not talk aloud about what he or she is doing. One of the strongest criticisms of protocol analysis is that being required to talk steadily about what one is doing potentially breaks an individual's train of thought. Moreover, there is some question about the accuracy of think-aloud protocols. An individual may not be aware of what he is doing and thinking (Nisbett & Wilson, 1977).

What we have implemented with PSE is an on-line protocol composed of the actions the individual takes during problem solving. Thus, the on-line history is itself the assessment. For such a technique to be viable, at least two conditions must be met. First, there must be an underlying theory to guide the interpretation, in essence supplying a meaningful template against which to measure an individual's performance. And, second, the activities that are recorded must be sufficiently detailed to be of use in the interpretation but not so trivial that they interfere with the individual's flow of thought in problem solving.

Consider again the individual protocol originally displayed as Table 8.2 and reproduced here as Table 11.2. One of the advantages of using the on-line record is that we can reproduce exactly the steps the student took in solving the problem. Working in PSE we can view the display at each point of the problem-solving process, knowing that we are looking at exactly the same configuration the student saw. We can determine, for example, the spatial configuration of the two icons after the student placed them in the Student Work Area. This is potentially important information, because it may be an indication that the student already has a full mental model of the problem.

Consider that in the problem the student is solving in Table 11.2, the Change situation is the overall one. The student must use knowledge from his Change schema to represent and solve the problem. He first positions the Change icon and then selects and places the Group icon nearby. We can tell from the coordinates recorded by PSE that the placement of the Group icon is such that

Table 11.2. *Example of one student's problem solving*

System output	Explanation of output
(Problem M16)	System randomly selects Problem 16 for presentation.
(IconSelected CHsmall 1 (78 . 285)) (IconSelected GR3small 2 (252 . 248))	Student selects the Change icon first (1), which is the overall situation of the problem. (The numbers in parentheses indicate the location on the screen at which the student positioned the icon.) Student then selects the Group icon (2), which is an embedded subproblem.
(Map GR3small 2) (LiftWord $1200 NIL) (LiftWord $625 4) (LiftWord $350 3) (LiftWord $195 2) (CalculatorCalled) (CalculatorSolve (625+350+195) 1170) (LiftWord (Calculation 1170) 1)	Student opts to map the parts of the Group icon. (At this point the enlarged diagram appears in the upper right-hand window on the screen.) Student first erroneously picks up the number $1,200 and then releases it – presumably realizing that it was not needed. Student then maps as subgroups the values $625, $350, and $195. Student calculates their sum and places it in the supergroup position of the diagram. Student closes the enlarged diagram and returns to the Student Work Area.

the appropriate parts of the two icons that will be linked are close together. In this instance, the Change icon has been positioned on the left and the Group icon is to the right of it and a bit lower on the screen. These two icons could be arranged spatially in the Student Work Area in many ways, and most arrangements will not allow a clean linkage between the supergroup of the Group icon and the amount-of-change box of the Change icon. It is perfectly true (but statistically unlikely) that the student could have made a lucky placement. In an assessment, we would note the configuration and check this student's placement of icons on other prob-

Table 11.2. (*cont.*)

System output	Explanation of output
(Link 2 1 1 2)	Student apparently realizes that the supergroup value calculated for the Group diagram is also a value needed in the Change diagram. Student uses the link command to connect the "supergroup box" of the Group icon with the "amount of change" box of the Change icon.
(Map CHsmall 1) (LiftWord $1200 1) (CalculatorCalled) (CalculatorClear (1170 - 12)) (CalculatorSolve (12) 12) (CalculatorClear NIL) (CalculatorSolve (1200 - 1170) 30) (LiftWord (Calculation 30) 3) (LiftWord (Calculation 30) NIL) (LiftWord (Calculation 30) AnswerWindow) (Done)	Student then maps the Change icon, placing the previously rejected value of $1,200 into the initial position of the enlarged diagram. (The value $1,170 already appears in the map because of the explicit link made by the student.) Student opens the calculator but makes an incorrect calculation. Clearing the calculator, student then correctly calculates the value $30 and places it first in the diagram and then in the Final Answer Window.
(RightAnswer 30)	System records that student has answered the problem correctly.

Note: This is an actual output from one of the students in the study. The problem was solved during the first session with PSE. The output appears here exactly as it is recorded by the system. Blank lines have been inserted to highlight the different segments of the problem solving.

lems. If he consistently made appropriate placements, we would be justified in concluding that he had a clear mental representation of how the situations overlapped.

An additional piece of data that is potentially available in the PSE record keeping but that we have not elected to use is the length of time a student takes between mouse events. We considered including this information as part of the record but decided not to do so. In the absence of confirming evidence that longer or shorter times were truly indicative of slower or quicker processing – and thus indicated greater understanding in some way – we felt that these data could easily be misinterpreted.

As described in chapter 8, many diagnostic decisions can be aided by observing some of the problem-solving characteristics that emerged from the PSE records, such as students' tendencies to correct their own errors. I will not repeat all of them here, but the episodes described in Table 8.3 about planning are additional evidence of how we may interpret PSE records.

There are several important reasons for employing computer-based assessment as it is presented in PSE. First, it is appropriate for the computer-based instruction it assesses. Students are familiar with the types of required responses and understand the idiosyncrasies of the system. Second, it is unobtrusive. Students may suspect that their responses are being recorded, but they do not seem to think much about it.[4] They are free to pursue their problem solving without interruptions, without being asked to write down a particular step or without being stopped to clarify what they are now doing and why. Third, a system such as this is economical because it serves a dual purpose. On the one hand, it is an instructional aid, providing a practice ground for individuals to hone their understanding of the structure of word problems. On the other, it functions as an assessment tool, allowing us to determine which aspects of schema knowledge are well developed in an individual and which are weak.

A final advantage of this system of assessment is that it can provide both diagnostic information for the individual and summative information for a group of students. Of interest in the individual evaluation are questions such as which strategy is employed or whether the individual has difficulty with one or more of the diagrams. At the group level of assessment we are concerned with questions such as determining whether the group as a whole is successful in solving complex problems or whether most (or all) of them demonstrate a sufficient level of competency in organizing their problem solving. Thus, at the group level, we are much less concerned with the fine-grained details. Both types of assessment are typically needed, and this system easily provides them.

Summary and conclusions

Schema assessment rests on the acknowledgment that situations are characterizations of the major themes and ideas of the subject domain to be assessed. Several points should be kept in mind.

First, it is useful to remember that before an individual can begin to use landmark information for purposes of navigation, he or she needs to be able to recognize and distinguish the landmarks. The parallel for schema development is that if we expect students to use schemas, we must first determine that they recognize the major characteristics of the situations embedded in the schemas. Moreover, they must be able to distinguish among these situations. This understanding uses both elaboration knowledge and identification knowledge; it facilitates the development of strong links among these two components of schema knowledge and is the core of schema knowledge.

One can argue that it is feasible to make an initial assessment only with respect to students' development of identification knowledge, that is, that part of schema knowledge that contains the major features and conditions required for the situation to exist. This is the approach taken in SPS. The assessment may take the form of simple recognition (i.e., What is this?) or of justification (i.e., What makes it a good example?). The situations used in the assessment need to be meaningful to the students and to reflect with emphasis the characteristics developed in instruction. They should not be identical to situations presented in instruction, however, because students need to develop the skills involved in understanding the details of new instances of a known situation.

Conventional types of objective assessment can be used for this evaluation. One might present a sequence of distinct situations embedded in very different stories with a multiple-choice menu of situation names (as done in SPS). An extension to the assessment requires the justification of response choice for each task. Not only does the student identify the situation, but he or she also indicates which features of the situation influenced the choice. This type of assessment should strengthen the bonds between elaboration and identification knowledge. We often use this type of task in interviews.

As part of their schema formation, students develop abstract characterizations of the situations. This development of the general or abstract characterization is facilitated by instruction and assessment requiring the student to identify specific situations and to articulate *why* a situation is applicable. A nontrivial by-product of this assessment is that students develop the facility for communicating important aspects of the domain. This shared communication is a necessary ingredient for successfully dealing with the subject matter.

Second, an important aspect of the assessment of elaboration knowledge is the inclusion of visual representations, and these should be part of assessment if they are part of instruction. Much of the students' knowledge may be linked to specific visual images. The assessment can provide important information about which linkages have been made and which have not. When visual representations are routinely part of assessment, students may rely more frequently on them and may better use the wealth of knowledge that is stored with them in memory.

Third, the assessment of planning knowledge builds directly on the assessment of elaboration and identification knowledge. Typically, the tasks become less structured and more open-ended. Ideal tasks would be those for which a number of different plans could be correctly made, allowing the students some flexibility in creating a solution. Again, it is not necessary to ask the student to reach a final numerical result. One could easily present a task, and ask the student to describe the situations in it and how she would use this information to reach a solution. These intermediate, usually unrecorded, planning steps are the target of the assessment. Does the student make a reasonable plan? Will it work? Would another plan work just as well? Is the student overlooking any vital information? Focusing on planning knowledge provides needed diagnostic information about the student's linkage of this component to the others needed for a well-developed schema.

Fourth, the level and scope of assessment will vary in a number of ways as students mature and create well-developed schemas. For younger children, most of the assessment should be tied to real-world experiences. Real-world experiences are not those gained by using manipulative materials in the classroom such as chips or blocks. These objects may be highly useful in demonstrating algorithms and computations, but they are not necessarily successful as representations of real-world objects.

As students mature and their schema knowledge networks develop further, the assessment should maintain some contact with the real world but should also explore various symbolic representations. Schemas are flexible, dynamic, ever-changing cognitive structures. As students develop deeper understanding, they will build both deeper and broader networks. New nodes and links will be incorporated, and one expects to see extensive linking to other knowledge networks. Assessment tasks can attempt to evaluate this extension by focusing on aspects of relationships with other subject domains, looking for both similarities and differences.

This chapter has described how schema knowledge may be assessed in individuals, and it has outlined an approach for making the assessment. The results obtained thus far using schema theory are encouraging. Test items can be successfully parsed by using the components of schema knowledge. Student profiles of schema knowledge can be developed on the basis of their performance on collections of these items. Validity of the schema approach is demonstrated by comparing test performance with problem solving and interview data.

The schema perspective developed in this chapter differs from a traditional testing approach in several ways. First, schema knowledge has many dimensions, each of which should be measured. Items can measure single or multiple dimensions and are not necessarily parallel in structure or significance. Second, the test is not a sample from a universe of items. The items are well chosen to examine schema development but they do not necessarily reflect the entire domain. Third, fewer items are used in a test of schema knowledge, because in general, responses to these items take more time than responses to conventional items. Fourth, assessment of different individuals may involve different items. Once a particular linkage is demonstrated by the student response to a test item, we may not need to assess the link again. Failure to show the link, however, might lead to a set of probing questions to determine whether it is the link itself that is missing or the nodes that were to be connected. Thus, schema assessment is an example of adaptive testing. Finally, much of what is tested involves intermediate processing. The final numerical answer given by a student to a problem may be less interesting than the steps the individual took to obtain the answer. As a consequence of these differences, new kinds of inferences can be made, based upon the results of the assessment. One forms an estimate of how the individual's knowledge of a domain is organized and how well the individual can use the knowledge acquired.

For wider application of schema assessment it is necessary to extend the concepts of validity and reliability. At present, we lack the alternative tests for measuring schema acquisition that could supply validity estimates. At this point, validation comes from the comparisons of schema measures to interview responses given by the students at the end of each instructional session and to paper-and-pencil tests. Reliability also needs further study. We assume that use of schema knowledge is a reliable gauge of the individual's network. However, the individual may access elements of a schema on one occasion but fail to do so on another. We need to examine what is meant by reliability in schema access and to develop ways to estimate it.

Some of the major points about schema assessment can be summarized as follows:

- Schemas are used to recognize situations in which one's knowledge can be usefully applied. They reflect the active seeking of understanding or the effort to minimize lack of understanding. This schema characteristic is assessed primarily through identification tasks.
- Schemas are not completely fixed structures. Typically, there is a core of knowledge required about the situation, and details about the situation are allowed to vary. Pertinent assessment questions have to do with which variables may vary and what allowable limits they have.

- Schemas contain both procedural and declarative knowledge and extend well beyond the usual formulation of concept knowledge. Full assessment calls for the demonstration of all types of related schema knowledge and their interaction.
- Schemas are interrelated, and one schema may call on another or require the output of another. Typically, the call to another schema reflects planning knowledge. Complex problem solving almost always involves more than one schema, and the evaluation of whether the individual is able to shift easily from one to another as problem solving demands is an important ingredient of assessment.

These characteristics combine to give us a very nontraditional approach to assessment. They force us to focus on qualitatively different features of problem solving and understanding. The assessment of schemas requires not so much the posing of different tasks as the asking of different questions. Especially important is the assessment based on different levels of the networks (as in Figure 10.3). That is, the interpretation of one assessment task might be at the complete schema level, at the point of interaction between schemas, at the level of identification or elaboration knowledge, or at the union of two types of knowledge. One draws different conclusions about the schema development of an individual, depending upon the level of assessment.

V

Schema models

Models of aspects of human learning and performance serve a multitude of different purposes. The purposes for which the models are applied here are twofold. First and foremost, they evaluate specific aspects of schema theory. If associations are developed as suggested in earlier chapters, then models embedding those associations ought to capture a number of characteristics of human performance accurately and efficiently. Second, the models provide evaluations of how accurately a domain is specified. A central premise of schema theory is that the underlying situations are sufficiently distinct to warrant development of separate schemas for them. If models can recognize and distinguish among those situations, they provide strong support for the separability.

Chapter 12 describes three types of models: production systems, neural networks, and hybrid models. The general structure of each is described as well as the most well known examples.

Chapters 13, 14, and 15 describe particular models developed from the schema theory and problem-solving studies discussed in previous chapters. Chapter 13 contains details about a full computer simulation of the first experiment of Chapter 7. Chapter 14 describes a back propagation connectionist model for the same conditions. And, finally, chapter 15 contains the full hybrid model of schema implementation.

12

Production systems, neural networks, and hybrid models

Until quite recently, cognitive scientists have tended to adopt one of two competing views about how to model the various mechanisms of cognition. On the one hand is the production system approach, which builds on condition-action rules. John R. Anderson's (1983) ACT* and Allen Newell's (1992) SOAR are exemplars. Such models are sometimes referred to as symbolic systems. On the other hand is the neural network approach. Models of this type are also called connectionist models or parallel distributed processing models. The PDP models of McClelland, Rumelhart and the PDP Research Group (1986) fall into this category. Now, a third alternative has appeared, one that merges these two approaches. Models illustrating this new approach are called hybrid models of cognition. There are, as yet, few examples. Not surprisingly, the hybrid model approach appears to be the best alternative for modeling schemas.

Relatively few attempts have been made to model schema acquisition and use. To be sure, the interpretation of a number of models depends upon the concept of a schema, but the structure of the schema itself is not part of the model. Consequently, to look at existing models of schemas we must broaden our view so that it encompasses not only explicit schema models but also models that are similar to those presented in the next few chapters but that are not focused on schemas. These latter models are models of learning, performance, and recognition. They tend to be either production system models or connectionist models.

The construction of a cognitive model requires a great deal of reflection about the underlying mechanisms at work. To a large extent, a researcher's beliefs about the cognitive mechanism will dictate the choice of representation. Moreover, because most cognitive models are computer programs intended to simulate human behavior, the nature of the programming language also necessarily plays a role in making the decision. Some programming languages facilitate the construction of one type of model more than another. To illustrate this point, consider that most production systems are written in LISP or LISP-like languages. At the heart of many LISP programs is the conditional expression having the form (COND ((condition action)(condition action))). In the COND statement, whenever a condition is evaluated as being true, its companion action is taken. Thus, each condition-action pair is similar to a production rule. In contrast, neural nets tend to be written primarily in the C language or derivatives of it. Much of the power of these programming languages comes from the efficient array storage and matrix operations, which are essential for defining and maintaining the weights that characterize a neural network.

Lengthy arguments about the merits of their approaches have taken place between advocates of the production system and the neural network (e.g., Smolensky 1988, and the many rejoinders following his presentation). Underlying the arguments is the distinction between symbolic and connectionist representation, and much of the discussion and disagreement centers on which representation is best for characterizing important aspects of cognition. The importance of this issue is that the representation that is chosen by the researcher will dictate the form of the model used. Thus, if the researcher elects to employ a representation in which symbols are sequentially manipulated, the result almost surely will be a production system model. If the researcher opts for a representation that has a network form with many simultaneous activations, a neural net model will most likely emerge.

The issue of form, which is manifested in the symbolic versus connectionist arguments, is nevertheless only one aspect of cognitive modeling. At least two others also deserve attention. One concerns functionality: What is the model to do? The second has to do with content: What is the context in which the model is to operate and what information does the model require? The three issues of form, functionality, and content are obviously interrelated. However, unique to each of the three issues are special concerns that have some bearing on how we develop and interpret models of schemas, and each of them warrants a closer look. In the following pages, I describe how each of the three approaches – symbolic models, connectionist models, and hybrid models – addresses these issues, and I outline a few examples from each perspective.

Production systems

It is worthwhile to review briefly the history of production system models and their impact on models of human memory and performance. Allen Newell made a singularly important contribution to the study of human cognition with his introduction of the production system (Newell, 1973) to psychological modeling. Indeed, the psychological pursuit of understanding human cognition as information processing derives from his landmark work with Herbert Simon on the General Problem Solver (Newell & Simon, 1972).

Prior to the development of GPS, most models of human learning were carried out within the frame of reference of mathematical learning theory. Models were typically Markov chains or processes having transition states that depended on varying numbers of parameters and represented successive stages of learning. Key issues were whether learning was gradual or all-or-none, and whether it involved accumulation or replacement. Most of the modeling attention was focused on estimating parameters, developing curve-fitting techniques, and making statistical comparisons of competing models. These emphases show up clearly in texts about mathematical learning theory, such as those by Restle and Greeno (1970) and G. Levine and Burke (1972).

The shift in focus that accompanied the advent of production system models was enormous. It was no longer sufficient to consider only whether an individual learned or did not learn; one also had to consider the nature of what was learned. Production system models were much more detailed than mathematical models. They posited not only the contents of human memory but the way in which it was used. Production system models also changed the way in which we evaluate the adequacy of our models. With a mathematical learning model, one could talk about measures of curve fitting, about variance accounted for, or other statistical gauges. With production systems, the proof is in the execution. If a model can carry out its appointed task, we tend to say it is a success. Such models are usually very large and time-consuming to construct. Rarely do we observe that an alternative model has been constructed, that would allow comparison between the favored model and the alternative.

Form

In Newell's early work (1973), as well as in his later development of SOAR (1992), he made it explicit that he considered the production system to be a theory of cognitive architecture. Thus, the way that knowledge was stored in human memory is an important part of his system and his theory. The basic storage mechanism, of course, is the production rule. In general, a production system comprises a set of rules, each having the form:

$$\text{IF} \quad (condition_1, condition_2, \dots, condition_j)$$
$$\text{THEN} \quad (action_1, action_2, \dots, action_k).$$

The IF portion of the rule contains the conditions which pertain to the rule, all of which must be true before the THEN portion of the rule can be implemented. The origin of the production rule has been attributed to the logician E. L. Post (1943). Post recognized that such rules could solve a large class of problems.

Typically, a production system evaluates each of the conditions of a rule in order and then carries out each action if all conditions are satisfied. Some production systems have constraints on the numbers of conditions and actions that are allowed. Most often, the rules allow any number of conditions but relatively few actions.

The production system is at the heart of Newell's theory of cognition, which is best exemplified in the system known as SOAR.

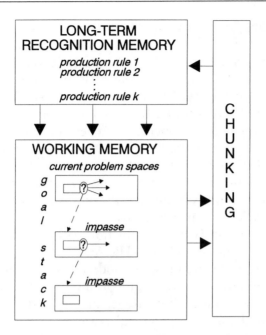

Figure 12.1. The basic components of the SOAR architecture (Adapted from Newell, 1991, with permission from Kluwer Academic Publishers)

The SOAR architecture was created in 1987 by Newell and his colleagues John Laird and Paul Rosenbloom (Laird, Newell, & Rosenbloom, 1987). Figure 12.1 illustrates its basic mechanisms. It is notable in Figure 12.1 that the long-term memory of SOAR contains only production rules. In his early work on production systems, Newell stated that the essence of the production system lies in its function as a control structure (Newell, 1973). This remains an important feature of production system models such as SOAR. Control is maintained in part through a goal structure. Production systems create goals, add goals to a goal stack, satisfy goals, and remove them from the goal stack. Goals are typically kept as a serial list to which new goals are appended as needed. The order in which they are addressed is logically determined; the selection of which goal to pursue is not a random event. Thus, we may conclude that three requirements for using and maintaining a goal stack are seriation, concatenation, and systematicity.

A distinguishing feature of SOAR is that it consists of problem spaces (see Figure 12.1). The system carries out its tasks by searching through problem spaces for appropriate operators to apply. As one would expect, the search depends critically upon the goal hierarchy constructed by SOAR as it performs a task. Within a problem space, SOAR uses production rules to move from one state to another by applying the operators. When the system reaches an impasse, it may search alternative problem spaces or it may utilize a process called chunking to resolve the impasse. Chunking results in the creation of a new production rule, which can then be added to long-term memory. Chunking is the only learning mechanism in SOAR (Newell, 1992, p. 70; see also p. 32).

A rather different type of production system model was developed by John Anderson (1983). His ACT* architecture extended the notion of production system models in two important ways. First, Anderson hypothesized that a distinction exists between procedural and declarative knowledge, and second, he added the important mechanism of spreading activation.

Figure 12.2 shows the main components of Anderson's system. In his conception, declarative memory is a vast network of information chunks that may be connected to each other. All data (i.e., facts, propositions, experiences) are stored in declarative memory. Procedural knowledge is stored in production memory, and it operates on the data of declarative memory. Procedural knowledge consists of production rules. The conditional statements of the rules involve various conjunctions of specific declarative elements that must be true if the production is to "fire," that is, if the action specified in the rule is to be carried out.

As in other production systems, the activity of the model is defined by the firing of production rules. At any single point in time, the model has a vast number of potential pattern matches to consider, one for each condition of each rule. It is essential to have some means by which the universe of possible rules is curtailed to a manageable subset. Anderson uses spreading activation for that purpose. The mechanism of spreading activation ensures that only the most pertinent portions of the declarative network will be available for processing, which in turn means that only a relatively

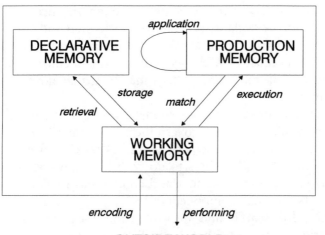

Figure 12.2. The ACT* architecture (Reprinted by permission of the publishers from J. R. Anderson, *The architecture of cognition* [Cambridge, MA: Harvard University Press, copyright © 1983 by the President and Fellows of Harvard College])

small number of production rules need be considered, that is, those whose conditions fall within the activated part of the network.

Spreading activation is useful because it contributes a degree of control: Those elements with the greatest amount of activation are available for processing. Resources are not wasted in evaluating unrelated or irrelevant material. To be currently active, an element must have received some amount of activation that has spread from a source node. Only source nodes generate activation. Source nodes are the result of direct perception or are the consequences of actions taken by production rules. Each source node spreads activation to all other nodes with which it is connected according to a specified rule. (See J. R. Anderson, 1983, pp. 92–96 for exact details.) The rule is based on two parameters, one monitoring the strength of incoming activation to a node and the other monitoring a rate of decay of activation for the node. Hence, a node's activation is constantly changing. The end result of having several source nodes spreading activation through the network is that some portion of declarative memory is activated and consequently becomes part of the system's working memory. This is very important, because only elements of working memory may participate in the all-important pattern matching that governs ACT*'s performance.

In most production system models, search and control are the essential mechanisms that govern the actions taken by the models. Winston (1977) very succinctly describes these two mechanisms. He explains that search has to do with how the system interacts with its external environment and control has to do with how it utilizes its internal components (1977, p. 155). Thus, one has strategies for search and decisions about control. From their descriptions, one sees that Newell's models are primarily concerned with search strategies, because they focus on searching the problem spaces, whereas Anderson's model emphasizes control, because it focuses on decisions of pattern matching.

Function

To call production system models *models of learning* is something of a misnomer. Actually, what is being modeled in most cases is not learning but performance. As Newell and Simon pointed out (1972), researchers cannot do everything at once, and it is necessary to model well the aspects of performance before tackling the mechanisms of learning. Newell and Simon made it perfectly clear that GPS was a performance model and not a learning model (1972, pp. 3–8).

This preference for performance over learning has tended to be the norm in cognitive models rather than the exception. Most models focus more on the manipulation of symbols than on their acquisition. In fact, acquisition was – and still is – a thorny issue. Few production models have specified the means of adding new information to the knowledge store. Thus, we observe that most models focus on acquisition of cognitive skill, transfer, and development of expertise (see e.g., the various models described in

Anderson's edited volume entitled *The Acquisition of Cognitive Skill* or the models contained in Ericsson and J. Smith, 1991).

Most production system models operate as problem solvers rather than as learners. The original GPS was a problem solver, and SOAR is as well. Most of the production system models take as given a body of knowledge upon which they operate. This body of knowledge is taken for granted, and it typically does not change as a consequence of the model's operations. The learning that occurs consists of adding new production rules and fine-tuning existing ones. The creation of new production rules is usually a merging of several small production rules into one larger one. Tuning generally requires the modification of a rule to allow generalization or discrimination.

Content

The issue of content has to do with the type of knowledge utilized in the various models. Mostly, production system models are concerned with procedural knowledge. In terms of the understanding of schemas developed in previous chapters, they are accessing and implementing elements that correspond to planning knowledge and execution knowledge. This is most obvious in their emphases on goal hierarchies.

A primary criticism often leveled against production system models is that they are not easily capable of recognizing patterns. Indeed, John Anderson explicitly acknowledges that pattern matching is a major bottleneck in ACT* (1983, p. 33). Thus, these models rarely capture all that I have described as identification knowledge, in part because they lack the flexibility required for pattern recognition and in part because their authors had other goals. The strength of these models, instead, is in the precision of the sequential processing that comes with applying individual production rules. The formulation of plans and the execution of them demand this step-by-step performance. As I shall describe in the section on hybrid models, production systems are wonderfully suited for the aspects of schema instantiation requiring planning and execution, and production systems are an integral part of the hybrid model of a schema.

Neural networks

The terms *neural networks, connectionist models*, and *PDP models* are essentially synonymous in the research literature. There appears to be a slight preference overall for the use of *neural networks* to describe such models, probably because the term implies some fidelity with neurobiology. This may be a misleading implication, however, because many neural nets are not in the least similar to what is currently understood of the human brain. It may be true that neural networks were originally inspired by the nervous system, but this distinction has been lost as the models have become widely used in many different applications.

Although neural network models have been in existence in one form or another for some time, their current popularity depends in great measure on the work carried out in the 1980s by McClelland, Rumelhart and the PDP Research Group (1986). Their introduction of PDP models, explanation of the basic learning mechanisms used in these models, and descriptions of applications to a wide variety of cognitive phenomena sparked widespread interest and debate. The intensity of the debate between symbolic and neural net modelers was partly due to the strong reactions occasioned by McClelland and Rumelhart's claims about their models.

It is important to recognize that others have made significant contributions to connectionist theory. A very good review of the history of neural nets is given by D. S. Levine (1991). Anyone wishing to learn more about neural networks will profit from reading it. One contribution deserving special mention is the perceptron. Levine calls the perceptron "a conceptual ancestor" of modern connectionist models (1991, p. 33). The perceptron was defined by Rosenblatt (1962) as a mechanism capable of making choices and of learning to distinguish among different patterns of sensory input. His model was a multilayered network, in which input stimuli excited or inhibited some of the units of the network.

Rosenblatt's work has been the foundation of much of the psychological modeling using the connectionist approach.

A second influential researcher in the field is Stephen Grossberg, who has made a number of significant contributions to our understanding of neural networks (see, e.g., Grossberg, 1976, 1987). Much of his research has appeared in the psychophysics literature, and consequently many cognitive psychologists are not as aware of it as they might be. As his research makes clear, a great deal of mathematical sophistication underlies even the simplest neural network model.

Form

There is no single form that a neural network model must take. The most fundamental requirements are the following:

- The model contains a set of nodes.
- These nodes are interconnected in some way.
- The connections between the nodes have weights that indicate varying degrees of strength.
- A well-specified mechanism governs how these weights change over time.

The simplest models have only two layers of nodes, input and output. Others are more complex, with multiple intermediate layers of nodes whose characteristics may or may not be theoretically determined.

Inputs most often are a collection of feature nodes that describe a stimulus to which the model will react. These feature nodes are typically assigned values of 1 if they are present and 0 if absent. In the simplest models, input nodes are connected directly to a set of output nodes. Connections exist between every input node and every output node, and each connection carries a weight that reflects the strength of the connection. Connection weights are positive (i.e., excitatory) or negative (i.e., inhibitory). Given a particular input, the input nodes having positive value (i.e., those that represent features which are present in the input) influence the output nodes by transmitting activation to them via the connections. The total amount of activation transmitted is a function of the level of activation to be transmitted and the weights of the connections by which it is transmitted. Activation is accumulated in the output nodes, and the model generates a response that depends upon the resulting pattern of activation. Most frequently, the output nodes compete with each other on a winner-take-all basis. The single output node with the highest activation determines the model's response.

There are a number of different types of connectionist models. Some address issues of classical conditioning, some focus on visual perception and binocular vision, some focus on neuronal activity, and some are concerned with issues of knowledge representation at a higher level. It is impractical to summarize all of these, and indeed, many of them are not particularly germane to the topic at hand. The connectionist models of greatest interest here are those that focus on classification and categorization. There are two general forms of models of this type, usually identified as models of supervised learning and models of unsupervised learning. Models of the first type learn in the presence of feedback. Thus, a stimulus is presented, the model makes its classification, and then an external feedback is given about the correctness of the response. Models of unsupervised learning have no feedback. They develop internal prototypes about how similar stimulus inputs are to previously encountered ones. Unsupervised models are of less interest here than supervised ones, because we are interested in how schemas develop from instruction. In most supervised models, feedback is the means of instruction. Hence, it is important to retain the feedback function.

Probably the most prevalent model of supervised learning is the back propagation model proposed by Rumelhart, Hinton, and Williams (1986). The back propagation model owes much to Rosenblatt's early work, and in fact, Rosenblatt originally proposed the technique, calling it "the back propagating error correction procedure" (1962, p. 292, as quoted by D. S. Levine, 1991, p. 24). Rumelhart et al. greatly extended and elaborated the idea, producing the generalized delta rule, which governs the way in

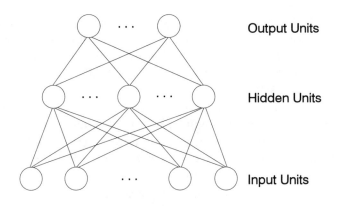

Figure 12.3. A simple connectionist network

which the weights on the connections between nodes are modified.[1]

An important feature of back propagation networks is that they can learn nonlinear as well as linear relationships. Hence, their appeal has been enormous, because they enlarge the number and type of classification problems that can be addressed. The way in which the nonlinear relationships are learned is by the inclusion of one or more layers of hidden units, as shown in Figure 12.3. The hidden units are neither input units nor output units, although they typically are connected to both. As the network learns to make classifications, the hidden units begin to represent the various patterns which are present in the inputs. Rumelhart et al. called them internal representations.

A three-layer network is shown in Figure 12.3. The input units encode the incoming stimuli, and they connect directly to a middle layer of hidden units. The input units pass activation to the hidden units, which, in turn, spread it to the output units. According to the pattern of accumulation of activation at the top layer, the model responds with one of the output units. If the model makes an incorrect response, that is, if the output unit having the greatest activation is not the appropriate one given the input stimulus, the model propagates an error signal backward through the network, causing the weights on the connections to be adjusted. In this way, the entire set of weights for the network becomes fine tuned and eventually settles into a pattern that needs no further adjustment. At this point, we can say that the model has learned to make the appropriate classifications.

The connectionist models of greatest interest here are those that are similar to the one in Figure 12.3, namely, models with at least three layers: an input layer, one or more layers of hidden units, and an output layer. As I will describe in the following two chapters, this middle layer is extremely important for modeling schemas because it is here that schema knowledge resides.

Function

Connectionist models are suitable for modeling both learning and performance. The adjustment of weights by means of back propagation corresponds to a particular kind of learning. Once the network has "settled" (i.e., the values of the weights are no longer changing), it becomes a performance model. No further learning occurs.

When we consider the function of most supervised models of learning, it is evident that their common objective is to recognize patterns. They do so by processing in parallel the many different features that are available as input. Unlike production system models, connectionist models are influenced by the entire collection of features, not the presence or absence of a particular one.

Content

Connectionist models are attractive for modeling schemas for a number of reasons. First, the underlying structure of a schema is hypothesized to be a network, and it seems only appropriate to use a network model to simulate it. More specifically, identification knowledge in a schema involves pattern recognition, and the main attraction of neural nets lies in their ability to recognize patterns. Additionally, aspects of elaboration knowledge also involve parallel processing and are well modeled by connectionist models.

Several discussions of schemas have appeared in the connectionist literature, and it is useful to take a closer look at the way that schemas are viewed within the connectionist framework. Given their influence, Rumelhart and McClelland's perspective is an appropriate starting point. Rumelhart, Smolensky, McClelland, and Hinton (1986) have written at length about schemas in PDP models. The most salient feature of their position is that schemas are not explicit entities but are collections of features that may co-occur. They make it clear that they do not view schemas as important organizational features of memory because nothing is stored that resembles a schema. Thus, there is no representation of a schema because they do not model schemas as such. Rather, they consider schemas to be high-level constructs that themselves consist of distributed representations.

Rumelhart et al. posit that the appropriate level of PDP modeling is lower than the level of schemas. Thus, they focus on the microlevel and examine features much smaller than the schema. They define schemas as "generalized concepts" and stress that schemas must have great flexibility. They argue that a dilemma exists between the need for schemas to be structures of the mind and the need for them to be malleable (Rumelhart, Smolensky, et al., 1986, p. 20). In their view these two needs are nearly irreconcilable.

Rumelhart et al. offer a much narrower view of a schema than the one taken here. Indeed, what they call a schema hardly differs from a concept. For example, they developed a room model to illustrate schemas in a PDP representation. The model learns to recognize five rooms based on forty descriptors such as toaster, bathtub, television, and so on. The model learns to associate particular features with particular rooms, and in fact it develops concepts for the five rooms. Nevertheless, the knowledge structure built by the model lacks many of the critical features of a schema as outlined in chapters 2 and 3.

A more compatible model of schemas comes from harmony theory (Smolensky, 1986a, 1986b). Harmony theory is based on the premise that inferences are made through the activation of schemas. Figure 12.4 depicts the main components of the theory. One

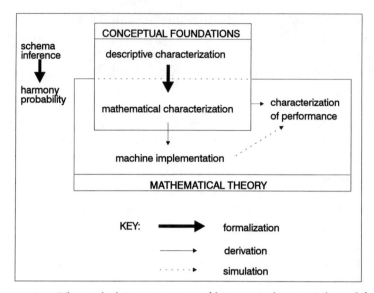

Figure 12.4. The underlying structure of harmony theory (Adapted from Smokensky, 1986b, with permission of the MIT Press)

of the essential points to be recognized from Figure 12.4 is that harmony theory is a new form of a mathematical theory of information processing. However, its conceptual underpinnings come from schema theory. Smolensky focuses on making inferences, and he uses schemas as the bases from which these inferences are drawn. In his representation, schemas are clusters of "knowledge atoms." His basic harmony principle states that the cognitive system functions by activating coherent clusters of knowledge atoms and by drawing appropriate inferences from these activated clusters (Smolensky, 1986a, p. 210). The knowledge atoms themselves are bits of knowledge that are acquired through experience.

Smolensky is more concerned with the mathematical development of harmony theory than with an elaboration of schema structure, although schemas play an essential role in harmony theory. He gives little attention to the nature of a schema, and his examples range from having a schema for a word to having a schema for a birthday party. By the definitions outlined here, only the latter qualifies as a schema. Thus, like Rumelhart et al.,

Smolensky equates schemas with concepts, at least in some instances.

Harmony theory depends largely on probability theory, and one of its innovations is that it uses a probability distribution to represent the environment. Moreover, slots of a schema are filled by elements that have high probabilities. One interesting aspect of schemas in this theory is that they correspond to joint probability distributions and as such yield useful statistical measures.

It is too early to determine the impact of harmony theory. It appears to provide a nice linkage between statistical or probabilistic aspects of modeling and more conventional representations. To date, it has not been widely used or validated empirically.

Hybrid models

Only a few production system models have attained the status of complete models of cognition, for example, ACT* and SOAR. No commensurate connectionist models of cognition have yet been developed, although Rumelhart and McClelland clearly have such aspirations in their PDP work. Most connectionist models are still relatively narrow in scope. For the most part, they lag behind the production system models. The lag can be explained in terms of time. Production systems have been a major part of artificial intelligence research for many years and have been the focus of much research in cognitive science. Connectionist models are just now becoming accepted.

Hybrid models, of course, are even rarer than connectionist ones, despite numerous demands for them. A number of prominent researchers (from both sides of the symbolic/connectionist argument) have suggested that some union of the two representations is in order. For example, in *The Computer and the Mind* (1988), Philip Johnson-Laird hypothesized that one way to get around some of the dilemmas posed by existing models of cognition was to "postulate different levels of representation: high-level explicit symbols and low-level distributed symbolic patterns" (p. 192). The opinion of a long-time connectionist is reflected in the title of a recent article: "Hybrid Computation in Cognitive Science: Neural Networks and Symbols" (J. A. Anderson, 1990). Marvin Minsky echoes the sentiment in his 1991 article "Logical Versus Analogical or Symbolic Versus Connectionist or Neat Versus Scruffy," where he states explicitly that we "need integrated systems that can exploit the advantages of both" (p. 37). And Keith Holyoak (1991) advocates symbolic connectionism as the basis for third-generation theories of expertise.

The need to combine the two representations derives from the fact that neither alone has been entirely satisfactory in modeling complex cognition. Symbolic production systems, as the older and more widely used of the two, have been very successful in describing some important aspects of rule-based problem solving. They have been widely used in artificial intelligence and have greatly influenced the development of intelligent tutoring systems (Wenger, 1987).

At the same time, such systems are noted for their inflexibility on some relatively simple tasks, such as object recognition and classification. Bereiter (1991) provides a good discussion of some of the central problems with rule-based cognitive models. As he (and others) point out, humans are not particularly good at working out extended logical sequences. They make mistakes. A production system does not make mistakes, and one difficulty in working with production models is getting them to produce human-like errors. Many models consistently perform better than the humans they are intended to mimic.

A second difficulty lies in the way that production systems work, namely, systematically, orderly, and efficiently. People do not seem to have those characteristics. We see this difficulty when we try to model complex problem solving using protocols generated by experts or by novices. Very few individuals start at the beginning of a problem and proceed carefully through a top-down process to reach the solution. To model their performance, we are forced all too often to disregard some of what they tell us in the protocols. Moreover, many individuals, including experts, simply cannot articulate why one part of a problem triggers a particular response from them. Actual problem solving is not an entirely neat and orderly process.

Nonetheless, there are clearly many instances in which individuals do engage in rule-based reasoning, and production systems have to date provided our best means of modeling them. This is particularly apparent in well-specified domains from mathematics such as arithmetic, algebra, or probability, and in areas of physics such as electricity and magnetics. What is common in these domains is that highly specific rules need to be acquired and applied by individuals in order to operate successfully in the domain. As a simple example, consider arithmetic operations. It would be the rare person who performed multiplication or long division without resorting to the use of a standard algorithm. Modeling the acquisition and use of such algorithms illustrates precisely the areas in which production models excel.

On the other hand, connectionist models are weak in just these areas. Connectionist models excel in pattern recognition rather than in logical sequences of actions. Unlike production systems, connectionist models do not depend upon the firing of independent units such as rules. Rather, a collection of units (nodes) spreads activation through their connections to other units. One does not trace the history of a cognitive process very easily in a connectionist model because of this feature. Subtle differences in the connection weights can yield large differences in model response. At any point in the process, it is the pattern of weights that matters, not the presence or absence of individual units.

A particular strength of connectionist models is the flexibility allowed for inputs. Because the models depend on the pattern of weights over a great many units, the presence or absence of any single unit is usually not by itself the deciding factor. Any input typically is characterized by a great many units.

Given the unique and complementary nature of the two approaches – the strength of the production system for modeling sequences of actions and the strength of the connectionist approach for modeling pattern recognition – it is reasonable to anticipate hybrid models that will capitalize on their individual strengths. Surprisingly, few true hybrid models have yet emerged, although one suspects that the number under development is somewhat greater. Two that have been proposed are those of

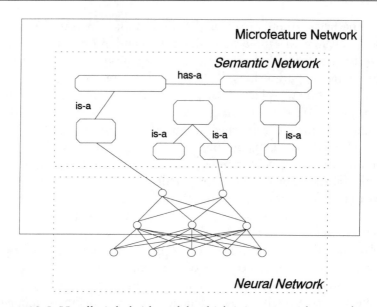

Figure 12.5. Hendler's hybrid model, which joins a neural network and a semantic network (Adapted from Hendler, 1991, with permission from Ablex Publishing Corporation)

Hendler (1988, 1991) and Schneider and Oliver (1991). Each approaches the issues of hybrid modeling in a different way.

Hendler's hybrid model

Hendler's work is an effort to unite symbolic processing and connectionist modeling through the common mechanism of spreading activation (Hendler, 1991). Spreading activation is an important feature of both kinds of models, although it operates in different ways. Hendler suggests that symbolic marker passing is the common framework allowing the formation of hybrid models. Marker passing is a mechanism for spreading activation by means of markers that are passed to elements within an associative semantic network. Marker-passing models differ from connectionist models in that in the former, activation spreads in a network in which both the nodes and the links have specific meaning. In most connectionist models, this is not the case, as demonstrated, for example, by the hidden units of the Rumelhart et al. models described earlier. These units are not typically interpretable.

Hendler's (1991) hybrid model combines a semantic network with a neural network, as shown in Figure 12.5. In essence, this model depends upon the neural net to learn the internal representations (i.e., the essential microfeatures) that are associated with a set of input stimuli. Thus, the model develops the hidden unit layer of the network as well as the weights connecting the hidden units to the output units. After the network has settled (i.e., has learned to classify the inputs appropriately), the top two layers of units are accessed by the semantic network model by means of spreading activation. Thus, the nodes of the neural net communicate with the nodes of the semantic net.

Hendler postulates two kinds of activation: symbolic activation, which spreads through the semantic network, and numeric activation, which spreads through the neural network. In symbolic activation, symbolic information (rather than a strength value) is passed along a connection from one node to the next. This is the essence of marker passing. Hendler's hybrid model converts the activation energy of the symbolic information into a form usable by the neural network. The critical importance of linking the two networks is that paths through the entire augmented network can be examined. Hendler hypothesizes that this model will be valuable for similarity-based reasoning, which goes beyond mere recognition.

Schneider and Oliver's connectionist/control architecture

Quite a different solution to the hybrid problem is offered by Schneider and Oliver (1991). Hendler joined the two representations, allowing communication between them. In contrast, Schneider and Oliver modify a connectionist network so that it can learn and generate rules.

The principle behind the Schneider and Oliver approach is that it is efficient to decompose a task into a number of smaller subtasks. Each subtask can then be addressed by a separate connectionist network, while the overall sequencing of the tasks is maintained by a rule-based controller. An important feature of the Schneider and Oliver model is that it allows direct learning from instruction, something that is not possible in ordinary connectionist networks.

The Schneider and Oliver model contains two networks: a modular data network and a control network. The data network is actually a network of networks. It contains a number of modules, and each module is itself a typical three-layer connectionist network that utilizes back propagation for learning. The controller network, although having three layers, is not a typical connectionist network. It is in the controller network that the hybrid innovations of the model reside.

Schneider and Oliver's controller network takes three types of inputs, a coded representation of the task to be carried out, a coded representation of the results of the data networks, and a copy of the activation values of the hidden units from the previous cycle. The model generates two types of output, the control operation that is to be performed and the arguments required for the operation. These operations govern the model's responses to the data networks and allow the data networks to be modified on command.

Schneider and Oliver's approach exhibits several innovations. One is the decomposition of complex tasks, which facilitates sequential controlled processing. The end result is performance in a reasonable time frame. Most connectionist models take unreasonably long to learn simple patterns. The Schneider and Oliver model works very quickly. A second innovation is the generation and use of rules to operate on the data networks. Thus, learning occurs in two ways in this model, by back propagation following multiple presentations of stimuli and by direct instruction from the controller network.

Conclusions

The purpose of this chapter has been to review available techniques that might be appropriate for modeling schemas. It is evident that no current models suffice to capture the coherence and flexibility of schema knowledge. Both production system models and connectionist models have special strengths and are appropriate for modeling specific parts of schemas, as I show in the following chapters. However, neither one alone will do.

The hybrid models described here offer the greatest promise, but neither of the existing models fits the representation required for schemas. In chapter 15, I introduce a new hybrid model with which I have modeled schema instantiation. It has features in common with the models described here and builds on their strengths and innovations.

13

The performance model

In chapter 7, cognitive maps were introduced as representations of data. A cognitive map is a graph structure constructed from an individual's oral or written response. The map represents the main details of the response as nodes that are linked in a network, and it preserves the relationships among ideas – revealed in the responses – as links between nodes. An important feature of the cognitive map is the way in which linkages are determined: Two nodes are connected by a link only if the verbal details represented by those nodes occur together in the verbal response.

The cognitive maps and networks provide the means by which an individual's knowledge base can be represented, and they provide immediate information about the size of the individual's knowledge store (i.e., by the number of nodes) and about the coherence and integration of that knowledge store (i.e., by the number and pattern of links). Figure 13.1 shows again the basic network derived for the full instructional session of SPS, and Figure 13.2 reproduces the networks obtained from two student interviews.[1]

As demonstrated previously, cognitive maps are useful as a basis for the examination of group responses. Thus, as I described earlier, we can study similarities and differences among different groups by aggregating general characteristics of students' maps. For example, cognitive maps can yield information about broad

Part of this chapter is a revised description of the research first reported in Marshall 1993b and reproduced here with permission of Kluwer Academic Publishers.

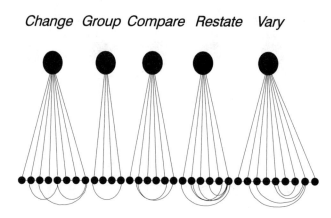

Figure 13.1. A two-layer knowledge network (Reprinted from Marshall, 1993b, with permission from Kluwer Academic Publishers)

categories of responses, such as the impact of abstract and specific details (see chapter 7). They can also facilitate comparisons among individuals, as shown by the two networks of Figure 13.2 and the four cognitive maps of Figure 11.1. One can also summarize a set of cognitive maps using network statistics such as average number of nodes, average number of links, or the length of various paths that can be traveled through the networks.

There is great value in inspecting a single cognitive map as well as in studying a group of them. Several approaches are available. One can look for distinctive nodes or links to determine whether they are present or absent for an individual. One can examine clusters of nodes to determine whether the nodes appear to be used by the individual one by one or as a group. One can begin to formalize the relationship of the cognitive map to an individual's understanding by considering in detail his or her performance on a task requiring the knowledge represented in the cognitive map. This third procedure subsumes many aspects of the first two, and it is more difficult to carry out. It is the third procedure that is advanced here.

The purpose of this chapter is to describe in detail a simulation of the performance of the students who participated in the initial

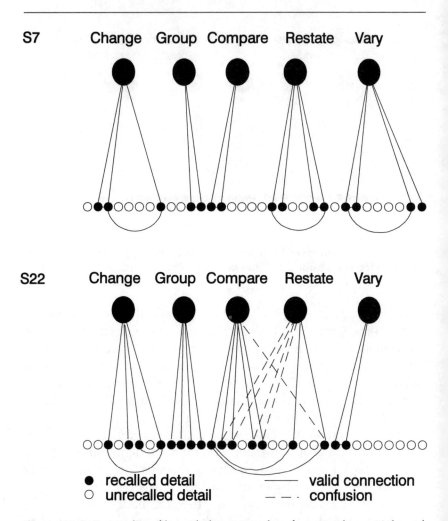

Figure 13.2. Examples of knowledge networks of two students. (Adapted from Marshall, 1993b, with permission from Kluwer Academic Publishers)

learning experiment described in chapter 7. The simulation has several important features. First and foremost, it is an effort to model in depth the cognitive processing of individuals. It explicitly ties their knowledge as represented in the cognitive maps to their responses on the multiple-choice computer task. Moreover, not only does it predict when the students will be successful but also, it forecasts what their failures will be.

The simulated data

The data that were simulated are the responses of the 27 students to the first task presented by SPS following their initial introduction to the five story problem situations. The task was described in chapter 5 (see Figure 5.1), and the experiment from which these data are drawn was detailed in chapter 7. In the task, students responded to a set of items by selecting the name of the appropriate situation for each item from a menu of situation names. For each student, the simulation requires information about the specific items encountered in the task as well as the student's response to them. Because we know how each student performed on the task, we can directly compare the results of the simulation with student performance.

The conceptual structure of the simulation

The conceptual structure underlying the simulation is presented in Figure 13.3. It consists of three parts: an input, a student knowledge network, and an output. Inputs to the model are coded repre-

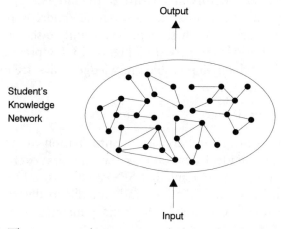

Figure 13.3. The conceptual structure underlying the simulation model

sentations of the problems, and outputs are the names of the situations. Student knowledge networks are derived from the cognitive maps. Each input item is presumed to activate some part of the student knowledge network, which in turn activates one or more possible outputs. The model response is the output with the highest degree of activation.

The performance model

The simulation is implemented as a feedforward connectionist model having four layers of units: an input layer, two layers representing student knowledge, and an output layer. Figure 13.4 illustrates the model.

In a feedforward model, signals that will determine the eventual output are passed only in a forward direction from one layer of nodes to the next. Model activity initiates at the input level, and each input unit sends its signal forward to the layer immediately above it. Because activation can spread only forward and not laterally, two layers of units are needed to represent student knowledge. The first layer receives the activation signals from the input units. The second layer permits the student knowledge nodes to spread activation to each other. By having two layers of nodes, we circumvent the problem of mixing forward and lateral connections and preserve the feedforward nature of the model.

To carry out the simulation, a separate model is required for each student because each student has a unique set of nodes and links in the knowledge network. Figure 13.4 represents the plenary model in which all possible knowledge nodes are present.

The input layer of units

The inputs to the model consist of information about the items that make up the identification task (i.e., the first exercise in SPS). There are 100 possible items that SPS can access, 20 for each situation. Each item was examined individually to determine which general features it contained. Of primary interest were the differ-

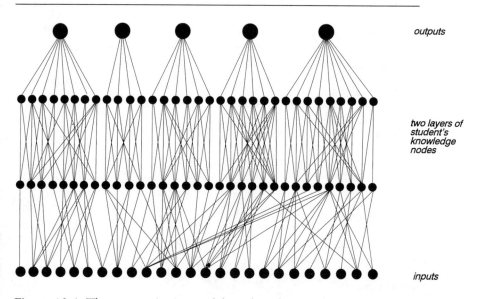

outputs

*two layers of
student's
knowledge
nodes*

inputs

Figure 13.4. The connectionist model used in the simulation (Reprinted from Marshall, 1993b, with permission from Kluwer Academic Publishers)

ent ways that relationships were expressed in the items. The item features were then coded in sufficient detail to capture the main relational aspects. A total of 25 item characteristics were identified. These characteristics reflect general properties and are not necessarily tied to specific situations. The set of characteristics is given in Table 13.1.

Each item was coded according to its characteristics as a 25-element vector containing 0's and 1's, with 1 indicating the presence of a characteristic and 0 its absence. Not all characteristics will be present in any single item; usually a simple situation requires only a few of them. The mean number of characteristics for the 100 items used in the identification task was 4.33. All 100 items were encoded by three raters with complete agreement.

The elements of the input vector are considered to be independent units. The presence or absence of any one of them does not influence the occurrence of another.

Table 13.1. *Item characteristics used to encode story situations*

General Characteristics:
  Set modification
  Permanent alteration
  Class inclusion (explicit or implicit)
  Relation between two objects
  Relation between an object and a property of that object
  Fixed relation (implied)
  Relative size
  Size differential
  Percentage
  Causality
  Multiple agents
  Multiple objects
  Unit measurement
  Two identical relations

Key Phrases:
  Each/every/per
  As many as
  Have left
  Altogether/a total of
  More/less
  Cost
  Same
  If . . . , then
  Money

Time Features:
  Specific time elements (minutes, days, weeks)
  Before/after

Source: From Marshall 1993b, with permission of Kluwer Academic Publishers.

The middle layers of units

The model of Figure 13.4 shows two layers at the middle level, and these layers contain identical sets of nodes. The nodes for the student models were identified from the student interviews conducted at the end of the first SPS session, and they are the bases for the students' cognitive maps. Three trained individuals read the transcript of each student's interview and determined which nodes were present and the extent to which they were linked. The three coders of the interviews were in complete agreement in their identification of nodes and links from the interviews.

The output layer of units

Each of the outputs for the model corresponds to one of the five situation names: Change, Group, Compare, Restate, and Vary. Only one output is produced for a given input vector. The five possible outputs compete, and the one with the highest accumulated activation wins.

Connections between the input and middle layers

An input unit may connect directly to one or more nodes contained in the student's network, which is represented by the two layers of nodes shown in Figure 13.4. Only the lower of the two layers connects with the input layer, and activation spreads from each of the input units having positive value (i.e., those that are present in the problem) to the nodes in the lowermost middle layer with which they are linked.

The connections between input units and nodes are theoretically determined and are not student dependent. In this recognition model, the linkages between input units and nodes are a function of the instruction provided by SPS. Only those linkages consistent with the examples and general descriptions of SPS are present. Each input unit links to a specified subset of nodes, and the subset does not vary across students.

The strength of the connection between the input units and the nodes depends upon the saliency and importance of the characteristic represented by the unit. Some of the characteristics are present in a very large number of items, and some appear rarely. In general, the strength values associated with the input units are approximately 1.0, but some have been adjusted to carry more weight and some to carry less. Altogether, they have an average value of 0.9275.[2]

Although the nature of the linkages between input units and the bottom layer of nodes is invariant across students, their impact for a particular student depends entirely on the individual student's own knowledge structure. Whether or not a specific link is present in a student model is contingent on whether or not the student's cognitive map contains the relevant node at which the link terminates. If the node exists in the cognitive map, the link is present. If it does not, the link is necessarily absent. Depending upon the nature of the student's cognitive map, some input units may activate many nodes in the network, some may activate only a few, and some may fail to make a connection, which will happen if the student lacks all of the critical nodes.

Recall that the input characteristics are general features (see Table 13.1). Most of them activate multiple nodes, as shown in Figure 13.4, and these nodes are frequently associated with different situations. Thus, it is usual for one input characteristic to point to more than a single situation. The full pattern of possible activation is shown in Figure 13.4. Note that this figure illustrates all characteristics as they link to all nodes and is thus a theoretical pattern. The model would never be presented with a problem containing all possible features, nor did any student have all possible nodes at the middle layers.

Connections between the middle layers

As I pointed out earlier, the model contains two layers of nodes at the middle level. The uppermost of these is necessary to show how the nodes spread activation to each other. Every node at the lower middle level transfers its own activation upward to its counterpart in the next layer and also spreads additional activation to any other nodes to which it is connected. If a student has only isolated nodes that do not connect to each other, the activations associated with the nodes at both layers will be identical. Typically, there are connections among nodes, resulting in higher patterns of activation at the upper layer.

The cumulative activation for any node contains the activation received directly from the input layer as well as the intra-set activation that comes from other nodes at the node's own level. The connections between the middle layers of nodes are determined directly from the cognitive maps of the student interviews. Thus, the connections *within* the middle layer are student specific and reflect the relatedness of each student's knowledge as inferred from interview responses.

The amount of activation transferred from one node to another depends upon the input unit that initiated the activation. Each input unit has associated with it a rate of decline. This rate influences the strength of the activation that spreads from one node to another. Like the strength values, the rates of decline vary among the units. We have found that rates of approximately 50% are satisfactory for most units.

Connections between the middle layers and the output layer

Activation spreads from the input units to the nodes, spreads among the nodes to other related nodes, and finally spreads to the output units. The amount of activation for each output unit is determined directly as the accumulation of activation transmitted from the lower layer of nodes on the links leading to it. Given a specific input vector, the five situations compete with each other for the highest level of activation, and the one with the highest value becomes the output of the model, given the specific input vector.

Each node at the upper middle layer of the model will be connected to at least one output unit because all student responses in an interview were focused on one or more of the five situations. Many students had more than one output unit associated with some nodes. These connections reflect the confusions described in chapter 7.

The model of Figure 13.4 is a representation of the entire process, which includes the input of an item, the activation of the student's network, the competition among situations, and the final output as a result of total activation that has spread throughout the model. The simulation of a specific student's performance by the model depends upon the set of nodes for that student, the pat-

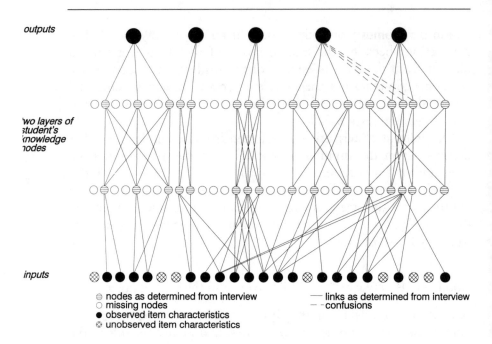

outputs

'wo layers of
student's
knowledge
nodes

inputs

⊖ nodes as determined from interview   — links as determined from interview
○ missing nodes   − − confusions
● observed item characteristics
⊗ unobserved item characteristics

Figure 13.5. The performance model for one student

tern of linkages among them, the overall association of subsets of
nodes with the situation labels, and the input characteristics of the
items. All except the last are derived from the student's cognitive
map. A model for one of the 27 students is shown in Figure 13.5.
It will be observed that the student model contains many fewer
nodes and links than the plenary model.

Model adequacy

As a test of the model's adequacy, a simulation was carried out in
which the plenary cognitive map of Figure 13.1 was used as the
student model. All 100 items available in the SPS identification
task were presented sequentially to the model, and its responses
were compared with the correct answers. The model performed
with 100% accuracy, successfully identifying the situations of all
items.

This is an important result, because it verifies both the veracity of the classification and the adequacy of the instruction about the situations. Recall that the instruction was developed to capture explicitly the hypothesized schema structure for the five situations. The success of the model in recognizing correctly all possible input items indicates that schema-based instruction as developed in SPS is entirely consistent with appropriate schema implementation.

Simulation results

The simulation required that the model attempt to duplicate each student's performance on the identification task. For each student, the response to the first item encountered by that student in the exercise was simulated first, using that item's vector of characteristics and the student's network information. The second item followed, and then all subsequent items. Thus, the simulation covered all items presented to the student in the order in which the student saw them.

As described earlier, the number of items answered by students varied from 10 to 18; altogether the students made a total of 360 item responses. A comparison of the results of the simulation of these 360 responses with the actual student responses is given in Table 13.2.

Table 13.2 presents the observed classification of the students' responses as well as an adjusted classification against which the model was compared. The observed classification comprises all 360 items. In the adjusted classification, some items have been omitted from consideration because the model was constrained by a lack of information from the student interview. This occurred under the following condition: If a student was unable to remember the name of a situation or anything that described it in the interview, the situation remained unmentioned in the interview. The interviewer did not follow up on situations that were not specifically mentioned by the student. The model for that student would have no basis for connecting any nodes at the middle layer to the situation name. Thus, the model would be constrained to ignore that situation and would never generate a response pointing

Table 13.2. *Simulation results: Experiment I of chapter 7*

Outcome	Frequency of observed outcomes	Frequency of adjusted outcomes[a]
CSM	192	192
C_SM	64	64
C_S_M	19	13
CS_M	30	13
CM_S	55	51
Total	360	333

Note: C = correct response; S = student response; M = model response.
CSM = Both model and student answered correctly.
C_SM = Model and student made the same error.
C_S_M = Model and student made different errors.
CS_M = Student answered correctly; model erred.
CM_S = Model answered correctly; student erred.
[a] Impossible matches excluded.
Source: From Marshall 1993b, with permission of Kluwer Academic Publishers.

to it. Therefore, unlike the student, the model could never make a response using that situation, and matches in this case were perforce impossible. Accordingly, if a student entirely omitted a situation in the interview, all items for which the student gave that situation as a response were likewise eliminated from the simulation. There were 27 of these impossible matches. As shown in Table 13.2, 17 of these were items that the student answered correctly, and 10 were items on which the student erred. It should be noted that these are failures of the interview, not failures of the model.

Each application of the model to a single item, represented by a vector of item characteristics, resulted in one of five outcomes, as shown in Table 13.2. In Table 13.2, the letter C stands for the correct response, S is the student's response, and M is the model's response. The result of each input item may be represented by a configuration of these three letters, with the placement of the letters C, S, and M indicating whether the three responses were identical or different. If the letters appear side by side with no intervening underscore *(CSM)*, all three responses were identical. When two letters are separated from the third by an underscore (e.g., C_SM), the responses indicated by the two contiguous responses were identical and different from the third. If all three are separated, none of the responses were the same.

Outcomes CSM and C_SM are exact, successful simulations by the model. In both cases, the model generated a response that was identical to the one produced by the student. In the first, the response was correct; all three responses coincided. In the second case, both the model and the student made the identical error.

The outcome C_S_M is considered to be a partial success of the model. Both the student response and the model response were in error, but they were different errors. In these cases, the model accurately predicted that the student lacked critical knowledge and would err.

The remaining two outcomes, CS_M and CM_S, represent simulation failures. The most serious of these is CS_M, reflecting cases in which the student answered correctly but the model failed to do so. They are serious failures because they suggest that the model did not capture sufficiently the student's knowledge about the situations. It should be noted that more than half of the observed instances of CS_M were impossible matches, as described previously. That is, the student omitted any discussion of the situation in the interview, and the model was subsequently constrained to ignore it. As mentioned above, these instances are considered to be interview failures rather than model failures. Only the remaining 13 instances are true model failures, representing just 3.9% of all responses.

The final outcome category, CM_S, also represents model failure but is less critical than the failures of CS_M. In this category, the model made a correct response when the student did not. Many of the CM_S simulation failures can be explained by considering the students' experience as they respond to the identification task. During the actual task, many students made errors on one or more situations and then apparently learned to classify these same situations correctly. This is evidenced by their patterns of responses, typically an incorrect response to a situation followed by two correct responses to the same situation, with no additional errors. In such cases the student's knowledge network presumably changed during the course of the task. The knowledge base that generated the early incorrect responses is not necessarily the same one that generated the later successful ones. And it is only the latter that is reflected in the student's interview. In such instances, the model would correctly match the two correct responses, but it would also give the correct response to the first item that the student missed. The model does not learn. It simulates the state of the student at the end of the exercise, as reflected in the interview. If the student learned during the course of the exercise, we have no way of knowing what node configuration corresponded to the earlier, incorrect responses. Under the most conservative criterion of learning – an error followed by two correct responses – 25% of the mismatches can be accounted for by student learning. In each case the model gave the correct response to all three items.[3]

Another 25% of the mismatches occurred when both the model and the student selected different wrong situations as the response option. In these cases, the model correctly determined that the student would not give the correct response. The model's answers may differ from the student's for a number of reasons, including guessing. These were, after all, multiple choice exercises in which students were asked to select the correct situation from the menu of five possible ones. Students probably guessed at some of the answers, but the model does not guess.

There are other plausible explanations for the responses that seem to be model failures. For instance, some students may have been prone to "slip" as they made their selections using the mouse, resulting in the unintentional selection of the option residing either above or below the desired one. It is not an uncommon phenomenon, as those who frequently use a mouse can attest. Accidental errors of this sort are undetectable. Alternatively, students may have used a test-taking strategy, such as avoiding the selection of one response if they used it to respond to the item that immediately preceded the current one. These errors are also undetectable. The model does not simulate test-taking strategies.

If we consider the "probable learning" mismatches (i.e., errors that were followed by two correct matches on the same situation) and the "different error" mismatches (i.e., those in which the model and student both erred but selected different errors) as *understandable or explainable* discrepancies, the total number of mismatches between students and the model is reduced from 77 to 51, leaving only 13 CS_M and 38 CM_S as mismatches. Thus, the model satisfactorily accounts for 85% of all student responses.

A final evaluation of the model's performance comes from examining how well individual student performance was simulated by the model. The results for each student simulation are given in Table 13.3. Two measures of success are given in the table. The first is the number of exact matches, excluding the "impossible" ones. The second is the overall percentage of satisfactory matches for each individual and is given in the extreme right-hand column of the table. This percentage is based on the number of satisfactory matches, including the "probable learning" and "different error" mismatches described above but eliminating from consideration the "impossible" matches. As can be seen in Table 13.3, the performance of 6 of the 25 students was fit exactly by the model with 100% agreement. The model simulated the performance of an additional 12 students with an accuracy rate between 80% and 99%. The model's success rate fell below 70% for only 3 students, to a low of 64%.

Verification of the model

Two issues of verification must be addressed. First, would similar results be obtained by chance? And second, would the model fit other data with reasonable accuracy? We can answer both questions.

With respect to the first question, we can look to a model that makes its selections randomly, with each of the five response options having equal probability of selection. We would expect such a model to match the students' responses 20% of the time, simply by chance. The issue is whether the performance model does better than this random model in accounting for the students' responses. We can see from Table 13.2 that the performance model exactly matched the students' responses on 71% of the

Table 13.3. *Simulation of individual performance: A comparison of model responses with observed student responses*

Student (Exp. I)	No. of items	No. of "impossible" matches	% exact matches	% "explainable" matches	Total % matches
1	13	3	100	0	100
2	15	0	80	7	87
3	13	3	90	10	100
4	13	3	80	10	90
5	16	0	75	6	81
6	11	0	100	0	100
7	14	0	86	7	93
8	13	0	92	0	92
9	14	5	100	0	100
10	15	2	85	7	92
11	15	3	67	8	73
12	16	0	63	31	94
13	14	0	71	0	71
14	13	0	69	8	77
15	14	3	100	0	100
16	13	3	90	10	100
17	15	0	73	14	87
18	14	0	79	7	86
19	14	0	79	7	86
20	18	0	67	7	72
21	13	0	69	0	69
22	16	0	69	12	81
23	16	0	56	13	69
24	16	2	57	7	64
25	16	0	69	12	81

Source: From Marshall 1993b, with permission of Kluwer Academic Publishers.

items, those coded *CSM* and *C_SM*. A test of proportions indicates that the difference in proportions of .20 and .71 is statistically significant, with $z = 24.79$, $p < .01$. The performance model matches the students' responses with much greater success than the random model.

One limitation of the above model of random responses is that it does not take into account the number of times that students made correct responses versus incorrect ones. Suppose we take a second random model that has only two options of response, correct or incorrect, and that has a probability of making as many correct responses as did the students. From Table 13.2, we know that students answered correctly on the responses coded *CSM* as well as on those coded *CS_M*, yielding overall proportions of .62 correct responses and .38 incorrect ones. The test of interest is whether the random model sufficiently accounts for similar proportions if we allow the random model to obtain .62 correct responses. We would expect the model responses to match 38.4% of the correct responses and 14.4% of the incorrect ones under these circumstances, for a total of 53%. Comparable values for the performance model come from Table 13.2. The model and student were both correct on 53% of the items (designated *CSM*) and both incorrect on 23% of the items (designated *C_SM* and *C_S_M*), resulting in matched performance on 76% of all items. A test of proportions shows that .76 is significantly different from .53, with $z = 8.74$, $p < .01$. Once again, the performance model was considerably better at predicting student response than a random model.

Turning to the second verification question, namely, whether the model could predict well for another sample of students, we can answer it by taking the model parameters as given above for students from Experiment I and simulating the performance of the students of Experiment II using those parameters.[4] As before, cognitive maps for the 38 students in the experiment were constructed, and the items to which they responded on the computer exercise were coded according to the characteristics listed in Table 13.1. The weights on the connections in the model remain at the same values calibrated for the students participating in Experiment I.

For each student, the model simulated the student's performance on the set of items presented to the student in the computer exercise. The items appeared in the same order that the student saw them. These items were new to the model; they were not ones that had been presented in Experiment I. As before, the model made one response to each item.

Table 13.4. *Simulation results: Experiment II of chapter 7 (using connection weights determined from Experiment I)*

Outcome	Frequency of observed outcomes	Frequency of adjusted outcomes [a]
CSM	139	135
C_SM	35	37
C_S_M	76	74
CS_M	66	52
CM_S	64	64
Total	380	362

Note: For explanation of codes see note to Table 13.2
[a] Impossible matches excluded

A total of 380 items were presented to the model, 10 for each student. The results of the simulation are shown in Table 13.4. Observed frequencies are presented in the left-hand column and adjusted frequencies are given in the right-hand column. The adjustments are the same ones described for Table 13.2 involving impossible matches.

It can be seen from Table 13.4 that the performance model was in general agreement with the students for 66% of the total unadjusted responses, with the model and student both responding correctly on 37% of the items and both erring on 29%. The model matched the student responses exactly on 48% of the items. Given the conditions and results of the two experiments, this seems to be a satisfactory fit. Because the students of Experiment II in general performed more poorly than those of Experiment I, we might expect to find more variation in their responses, and we do. Moreover, because they saw only two instances of each item – instead of a possible four as in the first experiment – we cannot make an estimate of whether they learned during the task as we did for students of Experiment I. It is important to point out that no adjustments were made to the parameters of the model for this simulation. The weights that worked best for the students of Experiment I were applied directly for the students of Experiment II.

We can repeat the two tests involving random models using the results of this second simulation. For the model in which all five options are equally likely, we would again expect to match the student responses with a proportion of .20. From the data presented in Table 13.4, we find instead a proportion of .48, which is significantly higher than .20 ($z = 13.08$, $p < .01$). For the model based on correct and incorrect responses, we again allow the model to make the same number of correct responses as actually observed in the data, which was 205. Thus, 54% of the model's guesses are correct. Under these conditions, we would expect to match 29% of the students' correct responses and 21% of their incorrect responses, for a total of 50%. In fact, the observed proportion of total matches is .68, which is significantly different from .50 ($z = 6.63$, $p < .01$). Once again, we find that the performance model makes significantly better predictions of the data than either of the random models.

Thus, we conclude that we would not arrive at similar results by chance. The performance model predicts student responses much better than either random model. Moreover, it can also be successfully extended beyond the original data from which its parameters were derived. Using the connection weights from the first experiment, the model gave satisfactory predictions for the second experiment as well. The structure of the model holds for additional students responding to additional test items.

Discussion

The connectionist model is a useful way to examine individual performance of students on recognition. The simulation of individual performance was extremely successful. The high level of agreement between model performance and student performance suggests that the model captures most of the salient and discriminating information actually used by the students. More importantly, the model demonstrates the impact of missing nodes and erroneously linked pairs of nodes. In many cases, knowledge of which nodes were missing led to accurate predictions of subjects' erroneous responses. In others, knowledge of incorrect linkages between nodes led to accurate predictions of errors. The model and its simulation provide strong support for the use of cognitive networks to represent the learning and identification of concepts.

One of the most important results here has to do with how successful the model is in predicting student responses based on their cognitive maps derived from the interviews. If we look back at the two student maps of Figure 13.2, it is obvious that the students have quite different sets of nodes. This holds for the other students as well. Each one has his or her own unique set of nodes. Among the 27 students, no two individuals had the same cognitive map. Similarly, each item has its own set of characteristics. It is not the case, for example, that all Change items are identical in their coded representations. Thus, varying sets of item representations interact with varying sets of knowledge nodes in such a way that useful patterns emerge. The model detects these patterns with roughly the same accuracy as the students do. Moreover, the patterns lead to identifiable errors in many cases, which further strengthens the argument that students are using their situational knowledge in ways similar to the model.

The simulation is an affirmation of the basic premise underlying schema theory, namely, that the nature of the connections among situational knowledge elements is critical. The statistical analyses of chapter 7 provide additional support. On the one hand, the simulation allows us to look closely at individual differences by modeling each student's performance. On the other hand, the statistical analyses point to several group characteristics with respect to learning new concepts. Both analyses are based on the cognitive maps.

The performance model is extraordinarily simple. It qualifies as a connectionist model because it depends critically on the ways in which activation is passed from the input units through the knowledge nodes and on to the output units. No learning occurs in this model; its function is to mimic the performance of students. It corresponds to the final form of a connectionist model that has stabilized its learning and is no longer modifying its connections. The effect of learning in a connectionist model that has much the same form as the performance model is the topic of the next chapter. There is much to be gained by comparing the two models.

14

The learning model

As part of the initial stages of developing appropriate schemas, individuals must learn to recognize the situations to which the schemas pertain. This recognition requires identification knowledge. The performance model of the previous chapter focused on how individuals use their identification knowledge to effect the recognition. The cognitive maps and the performance model both target this necessary early step in schema formation.

Identification knowledge can be modeled very well using relatively simple connectionist models, and the performance model of chapter 13 provides one example. A second example is described here. It is a competitive learning model that learns to recognize the problem-solving situations when given appropriate feedback. Both of these models were developed and evaluated as a first stage in building the complete schema model, which is described in chapter 15.

The task to be modeled

This model was developed to learn the appropriate classifications for 100 story problems, using the situations depicted in them as the basis of the classification. Each problem is represented by a set of characteristics that the model uses in making its decisions. Five

Much of this chapter was originally produced as a technical report (Marshall & Marshall, 1991). I have rewritten and elaborated on the material in that report.

output responses are possible, and the model selects the one that appears to be most in accord with the input characteristics.

During learning, the model responds many times to all 100 story problems. In general, there are two options for problem presentation: Either the entire set is presented again and again in some fixed sequence, making an orderly cycle through the entire stimulus list and ensuring that each problem is presented an equal number of times; or each problem is randomly picked at the time of presentation, so that every problem in the set has an equal chance of being selected on every trial. I have implemented the latter, primarily to avoid any possible order effects but also to examine the variability of solutions that result from differing input orders.

The inputs to the model are a set of 100 binary vectors nearly identical to the ones described in chapter 13 for the performance model. Each vector represents one arithmetic story problem, and the problem is coded according to the presence or absence of the general characteristics presented in Table 13.1. The difference between the input vectors of the learning model and those of the performance model is the inclusion here of coded information about the form of the question stated in the problem. In the performance model and in the empirical studies simulated by it, the items were complete stories and contained no questions. Both the learning model and the hybrid model of chapter 15 require problem statements as well as story information if we are to model the full problem-solving process. The two additional characteristics reflect whether the question focuses on "what" or "how much."

The outputs from the model correspond to the identifications of situations given in the story problems. For each problem presented, the model can make one of five responses, one for each possible situation.

The learning model

The performance model supplied guidelines for the learning model.[1] The input units for the learning model are essentially the same ones required by the performance model, as are the output units. A layer of hidden units replaces the knowledge nodes that were derived from the student interviews in the performance model. In the performance model, it was possible to estimate which knowledge nodes were retained in a student's memory by using his or her responses from the interview. For the learning model, we are not trying to mimic the learning of one individual and can no longer use our knowledge about nodes. Indeed, a primary goal of the learning model is that it create its own node set. Thus, the middle layer in the model is made up of hidden units, which are hypothesized to exist but whose character is unknown. Like the knowledge nodes of the performance model, the hidden units of the learning model are linked to the input units below them and to the output units above them. However, the strength of the connections between the hidden units and the input and output units is unknown. The question of interest is whether a connectionist model of this form can develop a set of appropriate weights for the connections such that it can perform in the same way as the performance model, that is, recognize the five situations.

The optimum number of hidden units for the model is undetermined. Theoretically, it depends upon the optimum number of knowledge nodes that a student should acquire, and this number also is not known. From the instructional experiment of chapter 7 we do know that the maximum number would be 33, the number of possible knowledge nodes derived from the instruction. However, no student ever acquired all possible nodes, and it is not clear that having all of them is a prerequisite for maximum performance. Some students made correct responses more than 90% of the time with many fewer nodes. Others had poor performance in recognizing the situations despite a large number of nodes. In the SPS experiments described in chapter 7, we observed that students typically acquired an average of 14 nodes. The range was 6–17. In general, having more nodes did not necessarily mean that students performed more successfully on the task.

Using the instructional experiments as guideposts, we included 14 hidden units in the learning model. The model is constrained to have 3 layers, eliminating the feed-lateral feature of the performance model (which was captured in the two identical middle layers). The additional layer in the performance model was a direct consequence of knowing how the knowledge nodes for each student were interrelated. In the absence of this information, we elected to use the more parsimonious learning model having only three layers. The three layers are the input layer, containing information about the problem to be classified; the hidden layer, containing units that correspond roughly to the knowledge nodes of the performance model; and the output layer, containing the names of the five possible situations.[2]

The model requires specification of a learning rate, η. This rate defines how strongly the model reacts to incorrect answers at each trial. The learning rate must be chosen carefully so that the system will converge to the correct solution in a reasonable amount of time. A learning rate that is too large may cause the system to converge to an incorrect solution, and a learning rate that is too small may prevent convergence in a practical amount of time (and perhaps at all). In general, for the network to stabilize (i.e., for learning to occur), the larger the number of hidden units, the lower the learning rate. For the model described here, learning rates between 0.05 and 0.10 were most satisfactory.[3]

The model also includes a momentum factor, μ, following the arguments put forth by McClelland and Rumelhart (1989). The momentum factor allows the system to carry over learning from previous problems as new problems are presented. As McClelland and Rumelhart point out, without the inclusion of a momentum factor, the system may converge to a "local" solution and stabilize there, even though there is a better "global" solution (1989, p. 132). A suitably large μ prevents the model from getting stuck in such local solutions. In addition, a momentum term tends to speed up the model, because it allows the specification of a higher learning rate than would otherwise be possible.

Testing the model corresponds to running it over enough trials for it to reach some predetermined criterion. Each trial consists of the following steps:

- presentation of a randomly selected input vector
- forward propagation of activation from input units to hidden units and from hidden units to output units
- calculation of the errors associated with each output unit
- backward propagation of errors from output units to hidden units
- modification of the weights of the connections between all layers of units based on the errors

The full cycle during which the model completes a large number of trials to reach criterion performance is called a *learning episode*. For each episode, the model begins with a new set of connection weights and a new ordering of the input vectors. Each of the main components of the model are described briefly below.

Input units

In a single trial the layer of input units comprises one input vector. Each element of the input vector takes a value of 1 if the characteristic it represents is present in the current story problem or 0 if it is absent. The input vector to the learning model contains the original 25 elements used in the performance model plus an additional 2 elements, as noted earlier, to code the question, resulting in a 27-element vector.

Hidden units

The middle layer of the model contains hidden units. Each of these is connected to every input unit in the layer below it, receiving some activation from each one, and every hidden unit in turn contributes to the activation of all output units above it. As mentioned previously, there are 14 hidden units.

Output units

Each situation is represented by one output unit. On any trial, following activation from the hidden unit layer directly below, each output unit has some level of activation. The one with the highest level is the model response for that trial.

Bias

Each hidden unit and output unit has a bias associated with it. The bias is added to the incident activation upon the units and functions like a threshold for the unit (cf. McClelland and Rumelhart, 1989). If insufficient activation is received at the unit to overcome the effect of the bias, then the output of the unit will be insignificant.

Input-to-hidden weights

As in most connectionist models, each of the input units connects to each of the units in the layer immediately above it (i.e., the hidden unit layer), and each connection has its own unique weight. When an input vector is presented to the model, activation spreads from the input units to the hidden units. The amount of activation spread is determined in part by the strength (i.e., weight) of the connection. The initial values of the input-to-hidden weights are randomly determined.

Hidden-to-output weights

Likewise, each hidden unit is connected to every output unit, and each of these connections has its strength, or weight. The values of these weights are also randomly generated for the initial trial, using the same constraints as for the input-to-hidden weights.

Model parameters and initialization values

The model requires that two parameters be set: the learning rate η and the momentum μ. For the results described in this chapter, the parameter settings were $\eta = 0.10$ and $\mu = 0.80$.

Additionally, the model requires that each unit i have a bias term β_i and that each connection between a pair of units i and j have a starting weight ω_{ij}. The bias terms and the weights are generated initially from a uniform distribution ranging from –0.005 to +0.005.

Finally, the learning criterion must be set. This requires choosing a tolerance value that indicates how many – if any – errors will be allowed and specifying how large the output value must be in order to be considered correct. We use a 90% tolerance standard; that is, the model must correctly identify at least 90 of the 100 test items. Moreover, to be considered a correct response, the appropriate output unit must have a value that is at least .25 larger than the next largest output unit.

Under the parameter selections and initialization values described here, the model converges at approximately 5,200 trials.

Technical details of the learning model [4]

The model consists of the three-layer network shown in Figure 14.1, with each layer comprising a set of units. Typically, one thinks of the input units as being at the bottom level of the model and the output units at the top, as in Figure 14.1. The hidden units make up the middle layer. Each layer is fully connected to the layers immediately above and/or below it, as shown in Figure 14.1.

The model contains the following elements: η is the learning rate; μ is the momentum factor; α_i is the activation that accumulates in each hidden or output unit i; λ_i is the activation that spreads from unit i to units above it; ω_{ij} is the weight associated with the connection between units i and j; β_i is the bias associated with unit i ; τ_i is the target level of output activation, externally set as 1 if the output unit i represents the correct situation or 0 if it does not; and ε_i is the error associated with unit i.

The model learns by processing an input vector and forward propagating activation from the lowest level to the highest, by calculating the error at this highest level and then backward propagating the error down through all levels, and by adjusting all weights connecting pairs of activated units accordingly.

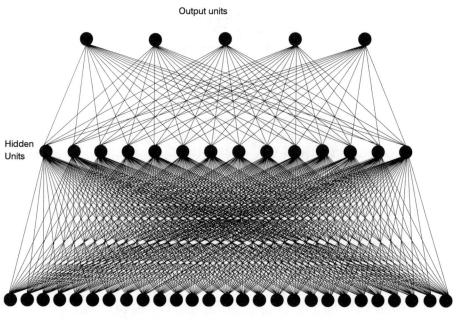

Figure 14.1. The learning model (Reprinted from Marshall, 1993b, with permission from Kluwer Academic Publishers)

The activation spreading out from a unit is defined as:

$$\lambda = \begin{cases} (1 \; or \; 0) & \text{if } i \text{ is an input unit} \\ \dfrac{1}{1+e^{-\alpha_i+\beta_i}} & \text{if } i \text{ is a hidden or output unit} \end{cases}$$

The accumulated activation is determined by:

$$\alpha_i = \sum_{j=1}^{J} \omega_{ij}\lambda_j \; .$$

If i is a hidden unit, j refers to input units, and the summation occurs over all weights between a hidden unit and the input units at the level below and the λ_j's of the input units. If i is an output unit, j refers to hidden units. Each of the units j at the level below unit i will have an associated λ_j that influences unit i. Note that α_i is defined only for hidden and output units.

The spread of activation begins with the input units. Those with values of 1 activate their associated hidden units which in turn pass some of the activation to the output units (by means of their λ_j's) . When the forward dissemination of activation is completed, for every output unit i the difference between τ_i and λ_i is used to compute the error ε_i:

$$\varepsilon_i = (\tau_i - \lambda_i)\,\frac{\partial \lambda_i}{\partial \alpha_i}\,,$$

where the derivative can be expressed as

$$\frac{\partial \lambda_i}{\partial \alpha_i} = \lambda_i(1 - \lambda_i)\,,$$

thus yielding a final form for the unit's error of

$$\varepsilon_i = (\tau_i - \lambda_i)\lambda_i(1 - \lambda_i)\,,$$

with all terms as defined above. The error signal is then passed to the hidden units by:

$$\varepsilon_i = \sum_{j=1}^{J} \varepsilon_j \omega_{ij}\,\frac{\partial \lambda_i}{\partial \alpha_i} = \sum_{j=1}^{J} \varepsilon_i \omega_{ij}\lambda_i(1 - \lambda_i)$$

for each hidden unit i. The summation occurs over all output units j. Input units do not accumulate error.

After the error signal has propagated backward through the network, the weights are adjusted by

$$\omega_{ij}(t) = \omega_{ij}(t - 1) + \Delta\omega_{ij}(t)$$

where t indicates the current trial and $(t - 1)$ is the previous trial. The amount of change is determined by

$$\Delta\omega_{ij}(t) = \eta\varepsilon_i\lambda_j + \mu(\Delta\omega_{ij}(t - 1))\,.$$

Note that ω_{ij} emanating from input units with initial values of 0 will receive no adjustment.

A similar adjustment is made for the bias terms, with

$$\beta_i(t) = \beta_i(t-1) + \Delta\beta_i(t)$$

and the amount of change is computed by

$$\Delta\beta_i(t) = \eta\varepsilon_i\lambda_i + \mu(\Delta\beta_i(t-1)) \, .$$

After the weights and biases have been adjusted, the activation and error terms are reset to zero for the next trial. The only carryover from trial to trial is contained in the weights, the biases, and their delta values (ω_{ij}, β_i, $\Delta\omega_{ij}$, and $\Delta\beta_i$).

The model runs with alternating learning and testing phases. The learning phase runs in blocks of 100 trials. At the conclusion of every block of trials, the model suspends the backward propagation of error and runs a performance test over all input vectors to determine whether it has yet reached the specified criterion for successful learning. During a testing phase, the model maintains an unchanging set of weights, which is the set reached on the last trial of the previous learning phase.

The criterion for learning is the correct response to at least 90 of the 100 input items, with "correctness" established as the activation of the appropriate output unit *i and* with λ_i at least .25 larger than the next largest activation value for any output unit. In practice, the system typically converges with 94–97 items correct in the testing phase. Given the fact that λ_i ranges only from 0 to 1, a difference between two values of .25 is quite large.

During the testing phase, each of the 100 input vectors is presented in a fixed order to the model, and a response is generated following the spread of activation as before. The response is scored as correct or incorrect, and the next vector is presented. If the model fails to reach the defined criterion (i.e., errs on more than 10 of the items), the learning phase resumes with another block of trials. When the model reaches the defined criterion, the weights are stored for later use.[5]

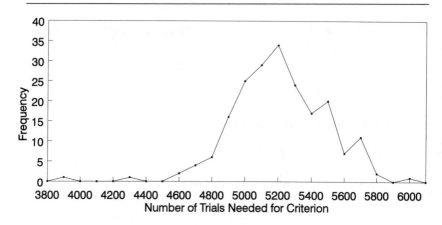

Figure 14.2. The distribution of convergence trials that resulted from 200 implementations of the learning model

Model analyses

The first analysis evaluated whether the learning model works as intended. Results indicate that it does indeed learn to make the appropriate classifications. However, as with many models having multiple hidden units, it takes a long time. Figure 14.2 shows the distribution of convergence trials that resulted from 200 instantiations of the model. The distribution is remarkably normal, and there are relatively few outliers. The mean of the distribution of Figure 14.2 is 5,208 trials and the standard deviation is 282.

One of the more striking results of the distribution analysis is the large difference between the highest and lowest numbers of trials needed to reach criterion. The most efficient learning episode concluded in 3,900 trials whereas the slowest learning episode required 6,000 trials. This is a large difference; it represents an increase of more than 50%.

We can surmise that the variability in number of trials needed for criterion derives from one of two things. Either the order of presentation of items causes it, or the differences in the initial random weights cause it. To determine the influence of each of these factors, two experiments were carried out, each using a restricted model instantiation. In the first experiment, an identical presentation of items was used in 10 different learning episodes. As usual, the weights to initialize each episode were randomly determined. Consequently, any differences in weight patterns for the final solutions in these episodes could result only from the random settings of the initial weights and could not be the result of differential item presentation.

In the second experiment, the conditions were reversed. The weights were held constant and item presentation was allowed to vary. One set of weights was generated randomly in the usual way and was then used to initialize 10 new learning episodes. The order in which the input items were presented to the model was randomly determined for each episode, as in the original model. Thus, for these 10 episodes, the model always began with the same pattern of weights. Only the order of input presentation varied.

Figure 14.3 summarizes the results of these two experiments. Each row in the figure represents a configuration of weights between hidden and output units for one learning episode. Under each possible outcome (i.e., CHANGE, GROUP, COMPARE, RESTATE, and VARY), there are 14 slots representing the 14 hidden units in the model. Each slot contains "." if the activation leading to the output unit from the hidden unit is relatively small; it contains a "+" if the activation is relatively large and positive; and it contains a "−" if the activation is relatively large and negative. For each learning episode, the relatively large values are the 25% having the greatest absolute value. Thus, the figure allows comparison of the strongest associations (both negative and positive) between hidden units and output units over several learning episodes.

The top part of Figure 14.3 contains details about the experiment in which the order of input presentation was fixed. It is evident from this figure that a variety of patterns results from varying the initial configuration of weights. This may be seen by comparing the numbers of hidden unit slots filled by "+" or "−" for each output unit over the set of episodes. No consistent pattern characterizes the resulting connections between the hidden units and each of the output units.

(A). Fixed problems on every episode:

Episode	CHANGE	GROUP	COMPARE	RESTATE	VARY
1					
2					
3					
4					
5					
6					
7					
8					
9					
10					

(B). Fixed Weights on every episode

Episode	CHANGE	GROUP	COMPARE	RESTATE	VARY
1					
2					
3					
4					
5					
6					
7					
8					
9					
10					

Figure 14.3 A comparison of learning episodes under varying initial orders and varying input weights

In contrast, consider the lower part of Figure 14.3, which summarizes the 10 learning episodes for which the initial weights were held constant and for which the input order was allowed to vary. No matter the order of input, the resulting configurations were very similar. The rows are virtually identical. Look, for example, at the patterns of connections shown under the VARY output unit. Almost all of the 10 episodes resulted in the same configuration.

It is interesting to note that although the condition in which the initial weights were fixed resulted in a common pattern of criterion weights, this condition yielded the greatest variability in number of trials needed to reach criterion. That is to say, the effect of varying the order of input changes the length of time it takes the model to reach criterion, but it eventually reaches the same configuration that it reaches on other episodes that start at the same place. The 10 episodes reflected in Figure 14.3B ranged from 5,000 to 5,700 trials. In contrast, the 10 episodes of Figure 14.3A varied only from 5,500 to 5,700, and 6 of these required the full 5,700 trials. However, as shown in the figure, the resulting configurations are not necessarily similar.

Conclusions

The first conclusion to be drawn is that the model learns to make the classifications. It takes many trials, but it does successfully classify the situations. A second conclusion is that it achieves a form that is very similar to that of the performance model. Recall that the performance model does not account for learning. Rather, it begins with a stable state for each student and carries out a set of decisions given that state. The learning model provides a plausible, but by no means unique, explanation of how the stable state of the performance model could be achieved.

A third conclusion, demonstrated clearly in Figure 14.3, is that the model may reach a number of different configurations of linkages between hidden units and output units. This finding is reassuring. If we are to use a connectionist network of this type as the basic structure of a learning model, it must be capable of showing the variety of configurations that we observe in individuals.

It should be mentioned again that the story problems that served as inputs to the learning and the simulation models were developed to be useful in SPS without consideration of how they might influence the models. They do not represent a carefully tailored set of inputs that would produce optimal performance or learning by these models. The results above suggest that the order of presentation influences the rate of learning. We also surmise that prototypicality exerts a similar influence. Thus, it is reasonable to predict that a different set of items, ones that perhaps are more typical of the situations, would elicit faster learning from the model.

In conclusion, I want to repeat that this is not an optimal model with optimal parameters. Its function was to verify that the classification was possible and that learning could result in something that resembles the performance model. I am not arguing that individuals reach the performance model point via this route. They almost certainly do not. We do not present individuals with thousands of problems and expect them to learn the important features. Most individuals learn primarily about such things from direct instruction. However, they also learn by repeated observation, just as the model does, and the learning model is a first step in examining knowledge acquired in this way.

15

The full schema model

This chapter describes the full model of schema implementation in arithmetic problem solving. In current terminology, the model is a hybrid model of cognition, utilizing both production systems and connectionist networks to represent schema knowledge.

As was pointed out in chapter 12, an ongoing controversy in the cognitive science community centers on the nature of the models used to represent cognitive phenomena. The two primary contenders are production system models (such as ACT* and SOAR) and connectionist models (such as those produced by McClelland and Rumelhart or Grossberg and his associates). Critics on both sides argue that the other cannot suffice to capture human behavior. Both appear to be right. Perhaps what is needed is a model that combines the best features – and mitigates the worst features – of both kinds of model. Given the unique and complementary nature of the two approaches – the strength of the production system for modeling sequences of actions and the strength of the connectionist approach for modeling pattern recognition – it is reasonable to anticipate hybrid models that will capitalize on their individual strengths.

A hybrid model of schemas is the focus of this chapter. The defining characteristic of the model is that it incorporates all four components of schema knowledge and models each of them distinctly. In my view, schema knowledge for solving word problems consists of identification knowledge, elaboration knowledge, planning knowledge, and execution knowledge. Key issues are involved in accessing each type of knowledge, and each type of knowledge demands its own distinct representation in the full model of a schema.

Identification knowledge has to do with recognizing patterns. The question of interest is whether the stimulus problem contains a pattern of elements sufficient to activate an existing schema. The pattern recognition is accomplished by a connectionist component of the model.

Elaboration knowledge, on the other hand, has to do with deciding whether the necessary elements are provided in the problem, *after the pattern has been recognized as characteristic of a schema,* so that the full schema can be accessed and used. This is a question best answered by a production system, but there is also a connectionist part to elaboration knowledge. In a single problem, several potential patterns may match the recognized schema, and the most reasonable or most likely one for solution needs to be selected. This is a special case for competitive performance by all candidate patterns to determine which pattern most strongly reflects the identified schema.

Planning knowledge is for the most part sequential, for it consists of setting goals and selecting operations for obtaining them. Again, a production system is appropriate. Planning knowledge guides the entire problem-solving process, and it calls on elaboration knowledge and identification knowledge when it needs more detail or more elaboration about the problem.

Finally, execution knowledge involves the step-by-step execution of already-learned algorithms, which again calls for a production system. Execution knowledge comes into play only when the plans call for it.

As described in part II, both SPS and PSE were designed around schema theory. In particular, they were developed so that each of the four components of knowledge could be isolated and evaluated as students acquired their schema knowledge. The results of the experiments using these systems were given in part III. The importance of the experiments for the present chapter is that they remain the best source of empirical evidence against which the computer implementation of the hybrid model can be evaluated.

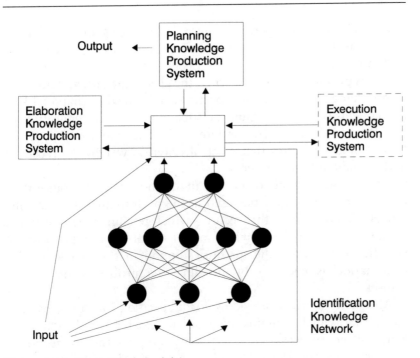

Figure 15.1. The hybrid model

The hybrid model developed to solve story problems has the form shown in Figure 15.1.[1] It has four main components: three production systems of elaboration knowledge, planning knowledge, and execution knowledge, and a connectionist network of identification knowledge. The last is represented in the figure as a set of nodes and links. All of these interact with each other, indicated in the figure by the arrows leading into and out of the rectangle in the middle of the figure. This rectangle functions as a blackboard on which any component of the model may write. Thus, the various components of the model can share inputs and outputs and can send queries to each other.

The connectionist model of Figure 15.1 is the model described as the learning model in chapter 14. It is a three-layer feedforward network with 27 input nodes, 14 hidden units, and 5 output nodes. The network performs here in its testing mode. That is, activation spreads through the network, but no feedback is given and no backward propagation takes place. At this point, the model is presumed to have learned the classifications, and no additional changes in weights will occur. As described in chapter 14, at the conclusion of a learning episode, the final configuration of weights could be stored for later use. The initialization of the hybrid model requires that a set of criterion weights be retrieved and implanted in the network.

The problem input to the full model now includes more than the vector of characteristics used in the performance and learning models. In addition to this vector – which remains the input to the connectionist part of the hybrid model – problem input consists of specific detail about the quantities found in the problem. This information is encoded by dividing the problem into several clauses.

An example of clause coding for a specific problem is given in Table 15.1, which contains the problem text for a multistep problem, the binary vector that serves as input for the connectionist network, and the clause encodings used by the production systems. Each clause contains three types of information: owner, object, and time. Owner contains two fields: name and type. Object contains four fields: name, type, value, and action. The action contains information necessary to determine which arithmetic operation to use. For example, an action might be increase, decrease, more, or less. The final type of clause information is time, which contains just one field that indicates a relative time of occurrence within the problem. A clause can contain multiple owners and multiple objects, and it can omit time.

When a problem is presented to the model, the connectionist network makes the appropriate recognition of the situation using the binary input vector as before, and it passes its output into a common area accessed by all parts of the model (represented by the rectangle in the middle of Figure 15.1). From here the information is available to the production system on the left side of the figure, which models the use of elaboration knowledge. The production system for elaboration knowledge has as its goal the

Table 15.1. *An example of problem encoding*

Problem Text
Joe won $100 in the state lottery. He spent some of it on toys for his two children. He bought a doll for Sue that cost $25 and he bought a stuffed bear for Ellen that cost $28. How much of his lottery winnings did he have after he bought the toys?

Coded Vector
1 1 1 0 1 0 0 0 0 0 1 0 1 0 0 0 0 1 0 0 1 0 0 0 1 0 0

Problem Clauses

clause 1:	owner	Joe person
	object	dollars dollars 100.000000 none
	time	0

clause 2:	owner	Joe person
	object	dollars dollars UNKNOWN decrease;
		toys toys UNKNOWN none
	time	1

clause 3:	owner	Joe person
	object	amount dollars 25.000000 decrease;
		doll toys 1.000000 increase
	time	1

clause 4:	owner	Joe person
	object	amount dollars 28.000000 decrease;
		stuffed_bear toys 1.000000 increase
	time	1

clause 5:	owner	Joe person
	object	dollars dollars UNKNOWN none
	time	2

recognition of relevant elements of the problem once the situation is known. It uses the output from the connectionist network, and it in turn passes its results back into the common area to be used by the connectionist network again if necessary or by the planning production system, which will produce a numerical solution.

The production system for elaboration knowledge uses the additional information derived from the clauses to determine which values of the problem are known, which are unknown, and their relationship to each other. The recognition of the situation uses identification knowledge about story problems, and the selection of relevant pieces of the problem uses elaboration knowledge. To illustrate what I mean by elaboration knowledge, I reiterate briefly the Change situation. One feature of a Change situation is the permanent alteration over time in a measurable quantity of a single, specified thing. The elaboration knowledge part of the model must confirm that only one thing is represented in the clauses. Three additional features are expected of a Change situation: a starting amount, an amount by which it is to be changed, and an ending amount. The elaboration knowledge part of the model must check that there are three available amounts, even if one of them is unknown. A change takes place over time, so the model looks for three distinct times to be represented in the Change situation. The production system works through the clauses, confirming that similar elements are involved and placing the values from the problem on a list that can be used by the planning production system in the model.

Thus, for the hybrid model of Figure 15.1, the identification knowledge is modeled by the connectionist network, and the elaboration knowledge is modeled by a production system. In the full hybrid model of schema knowledge, relevant elaboration and identification knowledge are used to plan a solution. Thus, the input to the planning component of the hybrid model is the output from the elaboration production system coupled with the output from the connectionist model of identification knowledge. Together, they provide sufficient information for the planning production system to set a series of goals and to call on the appropriate execution knowledge for achieving them.

Of the four types of knowledge that make up a schema, I consider execution knowledge to be the least interesting, and I have made little attempt to model how individuals learn the basic arithmetic operations. I assume that these are in place, as they are in the populations of students with which I work. A number of good production systems designed to model the acquisition and use of the algorithms of addition, subtraction, multiplication and division already exist. Hence, there is no need to duplicate those efforts.

The model here focuses instead on the selection of the appropriate values from the problem to use in carrying out necessary computations. Thus, the errors that can be modeled are those reflecting mistakes in selecting pieces of the problem or in selecting an operation to be carried out. Errors of computing are not possible (e.g., $3 \times 4 = 7$ or $3 \times 6 = 12$). The consequence of this assumption about algorithms is that we have not constructed a separate production system to make the computations, although it would be easy to do so.[2] For this reason, the execution knowledge production system is drawn in dashed lines in Figure 15.1.

The model is implemented with input to the connectionist model in the lower portion of Figure 15.1. The input consists of a single binary vector representing all information in the multistep problem (as shown in Table 15.1). Because the vector contains all the information from all the situations represented in the problem, pointers to more than one situation typically occur. The connectionist network identifies the most salient situation and passes that information to the elaboration production system. Using the output from the connectionist network together with the clause information, this part of the model determines the best configuration of problem data to represent the selected situation. The production system selects a subset of clauses to represent each configuration.

If there are multiple configurations, each one is then evaluated using the original connectionist model. For each configuration, the production system creates a new input vector that contains only the information of the selected clauses. The winning output values associated with each input vector are compared, and the input vector leading to the highest value is selected as the immediate problem to be solved. The identified situation and its subset of clauses are then passed to the planning component of the schema. Thus, the production system for elaboration knowledge and the connectionist network for identification knowledge interact to provide the necessary information that will be used to plan the solution.

A plan begins with the creation of a goal stack, and the single goal at the top of the stack is to produce a numerical solution.

Additional goals are added to the stack and removed as they are achieved. A number of different goals are addressed by the production system for planning. Some have to do with locating the unknown in the problem. Others center on carrying out the appropriate computations. Like elaboration knowledge and identification knowledge, planning knowledge is schema specific. The model uses its knowledge about the current schema to develop plans for solving the problem.

Table 15.2 contains the complete model output for the multistep problem given in Table 15.1. The first part of the table shows the output from the connectionist network of identification knowledge and the clause information used by the production system for elaboration knowledge. The second part of Table 15.2 illustrates a number of different goals developed by the planning production system and the steps the model takes to achieve them.

The model adopts a simple plan, and it does so because of the empirical results described in chapters 8 and 11. It will be recalled that students most often attempted to solve one subproblem at a time, usually the first one encountered. The model also attempts to solve the first subproblem it recognizes. If it is successful at this point, the solution is passed back to the planning component which then must determine whether the entire problem has been solved or only a subproblem. A number of things feed into this determination. First, the connectionist network is called upon to find any other plausible situations after the first one has been removed from the problem. A check is carried out to see if there are additional unknowns anywhere in the known problem structure. If potential sub-problems are discovered, their clauses and relevant input information is fed back into the model, and the entire cycle begins again. If no additional subproblems are recognized, the model produces as its answer the computed value for the last subproblem it solved.

The hybrid model is able to solve problems having more than one value initially unknown. Such problems are common in arithmetic and algebra, and they are frequently studied because stu-

Table 15.2. *The complete output for the multistep problem of Table 15.1*

Model Output	Annotated Description of Output
0.369 0.388 0.301 0.280 0.321 → GR	First subproblem identification by connectionist model.

* Combo: 1
  Combo: 2
  Combo: 3
	The possible configurations. * indicates the one that yields the highest activation value (found via the production system and evaluated with connectionist model).

owner Joe person object dollars dollars UNKNOWN decrease; toys toys UNKNOWN none time 1	The clauses that contribute to the configuration selected by the connectionist model as best. The identification of the GROUP situation and the clause information are passed to the next component of the model, which sets the initial goal and determines which values will be used in solving the problem.
owner Joe person object amount dollars 25.000000 decrease; doll toys 1.000000 increase time 1	
owner Joe person object amount dollars 28.000000 decrease; stuffed_bear toys 1.000000 increase time 1	

Table 15.2. (*cont.*)

Model Output	Annotated Description of Output
Production Rule: 25 Goal_Stack:: ID_NUMBER-SUBGROUPS SOLVE ProblemValues: UNKNOWN 25.00 28.00	IF{the top goal is SOLVE, the situation is GROUP, and the number of subgroups is not known} THEN{add a new goal of identifying the number of subgroups}
Production Rule: 26 Goal_Stack: ID_NUMBER-SUBGROUPS SOLVE ProblemValues: UNKNOWN 25.00 28.00	IF{the number of subgroups is unknown and the goal is to find the number of subgroups} THEN{count the number of subgroups and store the value}
Production Rule: 27 Goal_Stack: SOLVE ProblemValues: UNKNOWN 25.00 28.00	IF{the goal is to find the number of subgroups and that number is now known} THEN{delete the goal from the goal stack}
Production Rule: 28 Goal_Stack: ID_PART_GR SOLVE ProblemValues: UNKNOWN 25.00 28.00	IF{the goal is SOLVE, the situation is GROUP, the number of subgroups is known, and there is an unknown in the problem} THEN{set a new goal to find out which part of the problem is unknown}
Production Rule: 30 Goal_Stack: SUPERGROUP ID_PART_GROUP SOLVE ProblemValues: UNKNOWN 25.00 28.00	IF{the answer is unknown, the goal is to identify where the unknown is located, and if it is in the supergroup location} THEN{add the goal of computing the supergroup to the goal stack}

Table 15.2. (*cont.*)

Model Output	Annotated Description of Output
Production Rule: 32 Goal_Stack: SUPERGROUP ID_PART_GROUP SOLVE ProblemValues: UNKNOWN 25.00 28.00	IF{the answer is unknown, and the goal is to find the supergroup} THEN{add all subgroup values and store the result as the answer}
Production Rule: 33 Goal_Stack: SUPERGROUP ID_PART_GROUP SOLVE ProblemValues: 53.00 25.00 28.00	IF{the goal is to find the supergroup, and the answer is known} THEN{store this information in the problem values}
Production Rule: 34 Goal_Stack: ID_PART_GROUP SOLVE ProblemValues: 53.00 25.00 28.00	IF {the goal is to find the supergroup and it is known} THEN{delete the goal from the goal stack}
Production Rule: 29 Goal_Stack: SOLVE ProblemValues: 53.00 25.00 28.00	IF{the goal is to identify the missing part of a Group problem but there are no missing parts} THEN{delete the goal from the goal stack}
Production Rule: 24 ProblemValues: 53.00 25.00 28.00	IF{the goal is to solve the problem but there are no unknowns} THEN{remove the goal from the goal stack}
Production Rule: 0 Partial Answer = 53.000000	IF{the goal stack is empty} THEN{return the answer} The first subproblem has been solved.

Table 15.2. (*cont.*)

Model Output	Annotated Description of Output
0.481 0.357 0.381 0.370 0.368 → CH * Combo: 1	At this point the system reexamines the original input to determine if there are other situations containing other problems to be solved. It finds a Change situation, and there is only one possible configuration.
owner Joe person object dollars dollars 100.000000 none time 0	The necessary clauses are identified for the planning and execution components.
owner Joe person object dollars dollars 53.000000 decrease; toys toys UNKNOWN none time 1	The system recognizes that there is an unknown value for the object toy but disregards it in favor of the selected Change configuration.
owner Joe person object dollars dollars UNKNOWN none time 2	
	The production system begins a new cycle:
Production Rule: 1 Goal_Stack: ID_PART_CHANGE SOLVE ProblemValues: 100.00 53.00 UNKNOWN	IF{the goal is to solve the problem; the situation is CHANGE; and there is an unknown value on the value list} THEN{add a new goal of identifying which part of the Change situation is unknown}

Table 15.2. (*cont.*)

Model Output	Annotated Description of Output
Production Rule: 16 Goal_Stack: END ID_PART_CHANGE SOLVE ProblemValues: 100.00 53.00 UNKNOWN	IF{the goal is to identify which part of the problem has an unknown and if the last element of the value list is unknown} THEN{add a new goal of finding the end result}
Production Rule: 18 Goal_Stack: END ID_PART_CHANGE SOLVE ProblemValues: 100.00 53.00 UNKNOWN	IF{if the goal is to find the end result and the direction of change is negative} THEN{set ANSWER to the difference between the start amount and the amount of change}
Production Rule: 19 Goal_Stack: END ID_PART_CHANGE SOLVE ProblemValues: 100.00 53.00 47.00	IF{the goal is to find the end result and there is only one unknown value in the value list and if a value is known for ANSWER} THEN{replace the unknown in the value_list with the value of ANSWER}
Production Rule: 20 Goal_Stack: ID_PART_CHANGE SOLVE ProblemValues: 100.00 53.00 47.00	IF{the goal is to find the end result and there are no unknowns in the value list} THEN{delete the goal from the goal stack}
Production Rule: 5 Goal_Stack: SOLVE ProblemValues: 100.00 53.00 47.00	IF{the goal is to identify a missing part but all parts are known} THEN{delete the goal from the goal stack}

Table 15.2. (*cont.*)

Model Output	Annotated Description of Output
Production Rule: 4 ProblemValues: 100.00 53.00 47.00 Partial Answer = 47.000000	IF{the goal is to solve the problem but there are no unknowns} THEN{delete the goal from the goal stack}
Final Answer = 47.000000	IF{the goal stack is empty} THEN{return the answer}

At this point, the model has solved the relevant subproblems and returns the final answer.

dents do not solve them easily. The different components of the model pass information back and forth as necessary. For some problems, a recycling through the connectionist network will be unnecessary because only one configuration will be possible. For other problems, the model must move back and forth between the connectionist network and the production systems until it develops enough information to create a workable plan.

Thus far, the hybrid model successfully solves problems of the type illustrated in Table 15.1. Extensions of the model must now be created to deal with more complex problems, and additional comparisons of human and model solutions should be made.[3] To date, the findings are encouraging. The hybrid model presented here can solve single and multistep problems, and it produces solutions that appear similar to human subjects' solutions.

16

Some concluding remarks on schema theory

One of the foremost challenges to schema theory in the past has been its lack of specificity. This is a critical issue, of course, because to be useful a theory must provide specific and testable propositions, and schema theory has not always done so. Among the unresolved issues have been questions about schema development, about activation of appropriate schema knowledge, and about the structure of schemas in general (e.g., W. F. Brewer & Nakamura, 1984). These questions have been the focus of most of the previous chapters. The theory presented here addresses these issues and generates statistical and simulation models with which to evaluate them.

A more recalcitrant issue, which has been raised many times but never satisfactorily settled, is the extent to which any schema theory is domain specific. Is it necessary to have a specific schema theory for each domain or is there a general framework that encompasses all schema development and use? This issue, of course, cannot be resolved here, because all the research described in these chapters comes from the domain of arithmetic problem solving. It is the only one, thus far, that has been evaluated fully under the schema theory I propose. A great deal of additional research from many domains is still needed.

My opinion is that schema researchers and theorists will eventually share a common theory of structure but will require specific models of implementation. The issues about general versus specific theory coincide to some extent with the question of whether one is constructing a theory or a model. Models and theories are not equivalent. McCloskey (1991) makes the same point in his discussion of why connectionist network models should not be taken as cognitive theories. McCloskey argues that networks ought to serve as tools for the development of theories and should not be interpreted themselves as theories of cognitive functions.

It seems highly likely that the psychological mechanisms underlying schema structure, development, and access will be the same across domains in which humans operate. In the absence of strong evidence that points to different cognitive mechanisms for different domains, we can surmise that a general theory suffices. However, a model of schema instantiation within a particular domain will of necessity be highly specific to that domain, because domains differ greatly in terms of content and operations on content that are useful. Thus, for a study of schemas in any domain, I expect the need for identifying the four knowledge components to remain constant. However, the extent to which these components receive emphasis will no doubt vary from domain to domain. We can anticipate that models will be domain specific, because they will contain individualized procedures that are required only in the particular domain.

Part of the difficulty in assessing the generality of schema theory comes from the fact that schema research emerges from many different disciplines, and the questions that are asked about schemas reflect different levels of abstraction and knowledge organization. We can see this by considering the multiple levels of schema inquiry. A diagrammatic representation of this idea was introduced in an earlier chapter and is presented again in Figure 16.1. The figure depicts hierarchical levels of abstraction. In moving from the bottom to the top, we gain generality but lose specificity.

At the most specific level, we investigate the microfeatures that together constitute one small element of schema knowledge. On the level immediately above, we examine a single knowledge component of a schema. Ascending an additional level brings us to the study of a full schema, with attention to all of its specific components and how they interact. One further step up allows us to study an entire domain or area of knowledge, where it is possible to look more closely at a collection of specific schemas. And

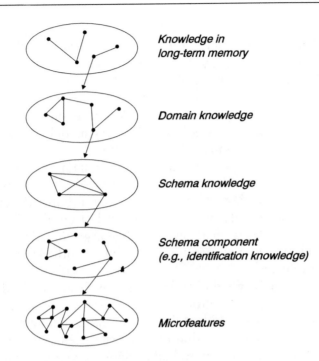

Figure 16.1. The multiple levels of schema inquiry (Reprinted from S. P. Marshall, "The assessment of schema knowledge for arithmetic story problems: A cognitive science perspective," G. Kulm (Ed.), *Assessing higher order thinking in mathematics* [Washington, DC: American Association for the Advancement of Science, copyright © 1990], p. 168)

finally, at the highest – and most abstract – level, we engage in the discussion about the nature of schemas in general, with no specific context or domain in mind.

The different levels of Figure 16.1 coincide rather closely with approaches to schema investigation taken by different disciplines.

Almost certainly, the philosophical debate about the nature of schemas belongs at the most abstract level. In general, philosophers have not been concerned with a particular context in which schemas are used but rather with whether such knowledge structures exist at all. The method of study is largely reflection or introspection.

One expects to find some of the recent cultural discussions about schemas at this topmost level of abstraction and also at the level directly below it. Cognitive anthropologists speak at times of common cultural events experienced by individuals, without focusing on particular cultures or particular events. Such high-level discussions of experience do not depend upon identification of specific schemas. The issue is whether schema development and use occur in much the same way in all cultures.

When we limit our consideration to one domain or subject area, the perspective of educators and instructional psychologists emerges. The targeting of essential schemas for instruction and assessment is a central objective at this level of inquiry. Two lines of schema-based research are evident: One is grounded in psychological and educational measurement, and the other is based on curricular reforms.

Not surprisingly, we find cognitive scientists at the third level, counting from top to bottom. Here researchers isolate a single schema, take it apart, and study how its pieces interact. At this level, an operational definition of a schema is essential, because most investigators will want to build a detailed computer model of how the schema works.

Cognitive scientists and psychologists also work at the fourth level, where the emphasis is on characteristics and concepts associated with a single schema knowledge component. Many studies of concept recognition and skill acquisition fit here.

Finally, at the ground floor, in terms of level of abstraction, one finds a large number of psychological studies. These are not necessarily represented as studies of schemas per se but as individual studies of different cognitive mechanisms or structures that can be considered to be part of a schema. Each of these pieces is examined in great detail, usually through a series of empirical studies. A paradigm may emerge for each area that is investigated, but there is relatively little sharing of knowledge among specialists in different areas. What has happened, unfortunately, is the development of a number of subdisciplines in which a great deal is understood but whose collective influence is unknown. This level is most recognized for its precision and detail in experimental investigation.[1]

Researchers in all of the aforementioned fields have, to some extent, grappled with the question of why we need schemas at all. This age-old question troubled early Greek philosophers as they tried to understand the human mind, and it continues to be a question that must be addressed by those interested in cognition. Each discipline has answered this question in its own way.

To philosophers, looking at the broad scope of human cognition and trying to understand how we know what we know, schemas seem essential because they provide the common ground of knowledge. As many philosophers have sought to demonstrate, the understanding of critical concepts is relatively similar from person to person. They reason that there must be some human characteristic that engenders this rather common store of knowledge.

The emphasis on broad similarity in human understanding is evident in cognitive anthropological studies as well. The schema can be viewed as a mechanism by which cultural experiences are preserved. If individuals do not process and use the information in relatively similar ways, they will lack this cultural sharing. Prevalent in cognitive anthropological studies are attempts to document that societies of differing levels of development share common cognitive structures, such as schemas.

The need for schemas from the educational perspective derives from a new view of competency and expertise. It comes about in part because of a loss of faith in the prevailing view of learning. In the view that has been dominant in the past (and that is now rapidly falling from favor), learning was the accretion of many small and individual pieces of knowledge. Most educators now believe that mastery of a domain involves more than this, that mastery occurs when an individual has acquired a coherent and unified body of knowledge about the domain and can use this knowledge productively. Studies of expertise suggest that most experts do have an organized knowledge store and there are indications that the organization is reasonably similar from expert to expert. Again, the schema is a plausible structure for this organization, and it can be utilized as the framework around which both curriculum and evaluation are developed.

A great deal of the existing evidence about schema acquisition and usage comes from psychological studies of cognition, either in cognitive science or in cognitive psychology. These two disciplines, and especially cognitive psychology, demand rigorous experimental verification, and the research goes well beyond mere speculation and hypothesis. Much of the evidence, of course, is indirect, because a schema is not immediately observable. The need for theory is palpable here.

Whenever a theory is evolving, two questions should be asked. First, is it plausible? That is, is it compatible with generally accepted psychological truths? And second, is it useful? That is, does embracing it move us any further either in the theoretical undertaking of understanding cognition or in the practical effort of applying psychological theory in the world? Chapter 2 can be considered a response to the question of plausibility, and the response is affirmative. Although schema theory certainly does not explain all cognitive mechanisms, it nonetheless does not oppose or contradict what is known about other cognitive phenomena.

Most of the chapters in the rest of this book address the question of usefulness, and the response is, again, affirmative. With respect to theoretical advancement, one can argue that schema theory allows new avenues of cognitive modeling as well as new theoretical studies about specific aspects of schemas, including development, access, and modification. Moreover, the advances should not be limited to a single discipline. As suggested above, schema theory has the potential for application in many fields, and theoretical growth will most likely come from many directions.

This book has a scope larger than most, and the reason is that schema theory touches so many different areas. The theory's appeal is that it serves many functions. Schemas are important in virtually all aspects of human day-to-day existence. Any aspect of human performance is likely to rely on some sort of schema use.

Schemas are inextricably bound to issues involving learning and performance. And, through these issues, schema theory extends into many fields beyond the one described here. For instance, the schema anchors anthropologist Roy D'Andrade's examination of motivation, providing the necessary linkage between culture and action (D'Andrade, 1992). Similarly, the schema is the cornerstone of psychologist George Mandler's theory of mind and body, providing the essential framework for linking emotion and behavior (Mandler, 1984). The schema also turns up in theories of language acquisition, both for the field of artificial intelligence, as in Michael Dyer's symbolic neuroengineering for natural language processing (1991), as well as for human language acquisition and reading (Just & Carpenter, 1987).

A valuable characteristic of schema research is that it promotes the convergence of theory and practice. We can observe this in a number of areas. I am especially interested in the ways that schema theory impacts learning and learning-related fields. Few learning theories move easily from the highly theoretical world of research to the practical world of modern education. Schema theory promises to be one. What could be more reasonable than that we take what we currently know and understand about how individuals learn, use that knowledge to structure what and how we want students to learn, and, further, use that same knowledge to build the test instruments that we employ to measure student learning? This notion is simple and satisfying. Where else do we have a common theory that can be used to account for the theoretical structure of a phenomenon and for the practical implementation and assessment of that same phenomenon in the real world? Schema theory and practice work together. The theory drives the practical application, which in turn provides real evidence about the theory and, hence, becomes the motivation for pursuing additional avenues of theoretical development. A further advantage of schema theory, from the educational perspective, is that it is relatively easy to understand and straightforward in its practical implementation. It also carries a high degree of face validity, which is not usually very important to theoreticians but is highly necessary for practitioners who have to explain it to diverse audiences not trained in cognitive psychology.

Schema theory has existed in one form or another for a long time. It has been tremendously important in Western culture, with roots as deep as any other psychological phenomenon. To be sure, at different times in history, theorists have focused on different aspects of schemas. What the last few decades of cognitive science have given us is a new environment in which to study schemas. New empirical methods, such as protocol analysis, and new modeling techniques, especially those of connectionist networks, allow much deeper exploration than ever before. Schema theory has continued to evolve and expand, and there is no reason to think that its advances stop here.

Notes

Chapter 1. Schema roots

1. *Penguin-Hellenews English Dictionary* (Athens, Greece, 1975), p. 710.
2. I. Kykkotis, *English-Greek & Greek-English Dictionary* (London: Lund Humphries, 1951), p. 708.
3. Plato, *Cratylus*, 423D; *Gorgias* 465B, 474D; *Philebus* 47A; *The Laws*, 2.669D. (All notes refer to the original pages of the Greek manuscripts, which are reproduced in and remain constant across different translations.)
4. Plato, *Theaetetus*, 163B.
5. Plato, *The Laws*, 4.718B.
6. Plato, *Alcibiades I*, p. 135D (in *The Dialogues*); *The Laws*, 7.803A.
7. Plato, *Timaeus*, 22C.
8. Plato, *The Meno*, 74D.
9. Plato, *The Laws*, 2.655A-B.
10. Aristotle, *Metaphysics*: 999A, 1002A, 1024B, 1042B, 1054A, 1070A, 1092B.
11. Aristotle, *The Categories of Interpretation* 1b: 4.25–30.
12. Aristotle, *The Categories of Interpretation* 1b: 4.25–30. See also *Metaphysics*: 1017A, 1026B, 1051B, 1054B as well as the footnote of translation by H. Tredennick, in the *Metaphysics*, p. 304–305.
13. There is some discussion about the correct plural form of schema in English. The Greek form is schematos, the Latin is schemata, and there is a growing tendency in English for the use of schemas.
14. Aristotle, *Metaphysics*, 1035B.
15. Aristotle, *Metaphysics*, 1032B.
16. Another example is the translation of Aristotle's κατηγορια *(categoria)* as "predicates."

17. Page numbers refer to Kant's page numbers in his second edition of the *Critique of Pure Reason*. In most translations, A refers to pages from the first edition and B to the second.
18. Kant, p. B183 and B180. Aristotle, *Metaphysics*, 991–992 and 1051–1052.
19. Sir Henry Head, *Studies in Neurology*, pp. 605–606, as cited in Bartlett, 1932, pp. 199–200.

Chapter 2. The nature of a schema

1. A second and related dichotomy can be found in Larry Squire's (1987) research on the brain, in which he defines declarative and nondeclarative knowledge.

Chapter 3. The schemas of arithmetic story problems

1. See the Appendix following this chapter for discussion about some of their research.
2. The Appendix to this chapter contains greater detail about the Riley et al. (1983) classification as well as a survey of other classifications from the mathematics education research community.
3. These quotations are taken verbatim from interviews with sixth-grade students, reported in Marshall (1981).
4. It could be argued that the surface features used by the students in Study 2 reflect knowledge about situations. However, these surface features are not pertinent to problem solving and do not reflect the basic relational situations of the problems. Noticing that several problems are about a similar topic (e.g., sports) is not the same thing as recognizing that several problems have the same underlying structure (e.g., Change).
5. One may wish to argue at this point that students should have automatically encoded the situational knowledge if it is needed for good schemas. Two points should be kept in mind: First, these students did not have particularly strong problem-solving schemas. Second, one characteristic of good instruction is that it points out to the learner what is important and what is not. If their previous instruction did not focus on situations, and all evidence suggests that it did not, then they would be unlikely to have used situational knowledge as a basis of their learning.
6. To some extent, one can consider the relationship between an object and its property as a relationship between two very different things as well.

7. One might speculate that this confusion arises in this group because of language difficulties. The Group situation requires a great deal of specific semantic knowledge about class inclusion.
8. I am not alone in making this suggestion. Baranes, Perry, and Stigler (1989) have made a strong case for the development and use of real world knowledge.

Chapter 4. Theoretical issues for instruction

1. The research is described in detail in chapter 9.
2. Lest there be any confusion that schema theory is consistent with all theories of problem solving, let me hasten to add that not all approaches to problem solving are so consistent. For instance, Newell and Simon's justifiably famous General Problem Solver (GPS) is quite different (and will be discussed at length in part V).
3. See p. 157ff. for Polya's (1945/1957) discussion of mobilization and organization.

Chapter 5. The Story Problem Solver and The Problem Solving Environment: Two examples of schema-based instruction

1. A number of technical reports have been issued about the *Story Problem Solver*, e.g., Marshall, Pribe, & Smith (1987); Marshall, Barthuli, Brewer, & Rose (1989); Marshall (1991).
2. I want to acknowledge here the important contributions to SPS of Julie Smith, Margaret Brewer, Fred Rose, Kathryn Barthuli, John Marshall, and Pam Gee. John Marshall deserves special recognition for his programming of much of PSE.
3. All pools of SPS items are described later in this chapter.
4. In this and subsequent chapters, I use the term *icon* to refer to the miniaturized version of the figures used to represent the situations. *Diagram* refers to the enlarged version used in the mapping exercises.
5. The three possible Change problems were explained in chapter 3.
6. PSE contains no Group problems having more than four subsets.
7. For many multiple situation problems there may be several correct plans. *ShowMe* displays only one of these.
8. In the mouse tutorial, students are instructed to use only the left button. The right button was reserved by password for system developers, and the middle button was set to respond in the same way as the left button.

Chapter 6. Learning and schema theory

1. This type of learning is addressed in part V.
2. More will be said about this in chapter 14.
3. I ignore here the very interesting new developments in brain scanning that define learning as the activation of specific parts of the brain. Even in these cases, we know only that something has occurred; we do not know what has been learned.

Chapter 7. Learning from schema-based instruction

1. Pilot studies indicated that students who needed more than four instances of a situation did not yet understand the situation and needed further instruction, not further testing.
2. It should be noted that the instruction was not developed under the constraint that equal abstract and specific details be contained in it. The guiding principle was to explain each situation as completely as possible, using specific and/or abstract elements as needed.
3. Due to the vagaries of collecting data on an experimental computer system, some parts of the data were irretrievably lost. This loss was purely random and affected only a small number of students on any given measure. The outcome is that the various statistics reported here are based on different numbers of students.
4. This is reminiscent of the phenomenon Lynn Reder calls "feeling of knowing" (Reder, 1992).
5. Data from one subject were incomplete and omitted from the analysis.

Chapter 8. The acquisition of planning knowledge

1. One unexplained observation of PSE is that no student ever erased an icon from the Student Work Area. Unwanted ones were simply left on the screen but never again used.
2. The exception was a young woman who always made one icon selection and then asked for *ShowMe*, demonstrating no independent problem solving on any problem.
3. The students admitted this freely in follow-up interviews. Most said that they liked the diagrams but already knew how to solve the problems and just used their own procedures.

Chapter 9. The diagram: Marker and template

1. I have been least happy with the Compare figure because it lacks the intuitive appeal of some of the others. However, students have found it quite easy to work with and to remember.
2. In retrospect, I would prefer to eliminate the "If/Then" wording and rely on the graphic display without any text at all.
3. This is the same initial task analyzed in the experiments of chapter 7.
4. This is the same task presented to the four groups of individuals as part of the validation of the situations, as described in chapter 3, and is also the same task used in the follow-up experiment described earlier in this chapter.

Chapter 10. Schema-based assessment

1. Both the items and the responses are taken from *A Question of Thinking* (California Assessment Program, 1989). A fuller discussion of these items and others used in the California assessment is provided therein.

Chapter 11. Assessment in SPS and PSE

1. See the evaluation of PSE later in this chapter for assessment of planning.
2. An earlier version of this analysis was first presented in Marshall, 1992.
3. J. Cohen & P. Cohen (1983, p. 240–241), describe the feasibility of using a dichotomous dependent variable for some studies, despite the fact that it violates the normality assumption.
4. I draw this conclusion from observing students interacting with PSE. No student ever asked whether any records were being kept, and many students made comments during the sessions such as "I think I'll try this" or "Maybe I can do that," suggesting that they felt free to explore the environment. Had they expected that the intermediate steps of their solutions were recorded, they might have done less exploring. We have observed that students of this population often tend to hide their intermediate steps of problem solving on paper-and-pencil tests (such as the pretest and posttest used in the experiments described elsewhere in this chapter), erasing all computations except the final number after they have found a solution.

Chapter 12. Production systems, neural networks, and hybrid models

1. I will discuss the generalized delta rule in chapter 14 in the presentation of the learning model.

Chapter 13. The performance model

1. These figures were originally displayed as Figures 10.2 and 10.3 in chapter 10. A full description of them may be found in that location.
2. These are not necessarily optimal values for strength.
3. In several instances the student made multiple errors on a situation and then responded correctly to one final instance of that situation. Although it is very plausible that learning also occurred in these cases, I am uncomfortable in making this conclusion based only on one response. Thus, these errors remain unexplained.
4. The similarities and differences in the two experiments are described in chapter 7.

Chapter 14. The learning model

1. In developing the learning model, I have drawn substantially from the models described in Rumelhart, Hinton, & Williams, 1986, as well as the extension of them in chapter 5 of McClelland and Rumelhart, 1989.
2. Later in this chapter I describe the results of the learning model when the additional layer is included.
3. McClelland and Rumelhart (1989) use similar rates.
4. All programs for the models in this report were written in C++ and run on a PC-80486 workstation.
5. This later use will be explained in the following chapter as part of the description of the hybrid model.

Chapter 15. The full schema model

1. In this figure and others depicting hybrid models, we do not attempt to represent all units of the model. Rather, in the interest of having simple and easy-to-understand representations, we show only a few units at each level. Likewise, we do not show all rules that are part of the production system.

2. An additional reason to omit the modeling of computational errors is that the subjects whose performance we have studied rarely make these errors. All of our subjects have been college students with poor problem-solving skills. They are proficient in computation but not in problem solving.

3. My associate David E. Smith and I have recently developed a hybrid model for decision making that grows directly from the problem-solving model (see D. E. Smith & Marshall, 1993, in press).

Chapter 16. Some concluding remarks on schema theory

1. Missing from the representation of Figure 16.1 is any reference to the neuroscience perspective. This field is absent, not because I consider it unimportant, but because there are currently very few real connections having to do with schemas between neuroscience studies and the other fields. At this point, one probably needs to construct a parallel figure to represent neuroscience research. It would be nice to imagine that the two figures would have similarities between their levels, so that one could go to a particular depth of study and cross over from one to the other to see what the corresponding neurological (or psychological) evidence is.

References

Andersen, S. K., Jensen, F. V., Olesen, K. G., & Jensen, F. (1989). *HUGIN: A shell for building Bayesian belief universes for expert systems* [Computer program]. Aalborg, Denmark: HUGIN Expert Ltd.

Anderson, J. A. (1990). Hybrid computation in cognitive science: Neural networks and symbols. *Applied Cognitive Psychology, 4,* 337–347.

Anderson, J. R. (1988, February). *Experiments with the LISP Tutor.* Paper presented at the Office of Naval Research Contractors' Meeting on ICAI and Instructional Theory, University of Pittsburgh (LRDC).

Anderson, J. R. (1983). *The architecture of cognition.* Cambridge: Harvard University Press.

Anderson, J. R. (1982). The acquisition of cognitive skill. *Psychological Review, 89,* 369–406.

Anderson, R. C. (1984). Role of the reader's schema in comprehension, learning, and memory. In R. C. Anderson, J. Osborn, and R. J. Tierney (Eds.), *Learning to read in American schools: Basal readers and content texts* (pp. 243–272). Hillsdale, NJ: Lawrence Erlbaum Associates.

Anzai, Y. (1991). Learning and use of representations for physics expertise. In K. Ericsson & J. Smith (Eds.), *Towards a general theory of expertise* (pp. 64–92). Cambridge: Cambridge University Press.

Baddeley, A. (1990). *Human memory.* Boston: Allyn & Bacon.

Baranes, R., Perry, M., & Stigler, J. (1989). Activation of real-world knowledge in the solution of word problems. *Cognition & Instruction, 6,* 287–318.

Barnett, J. (1979). The study of syntax variables. In G. Goldin & C. E. McClintock (Eds.), *Task variables in mathematical problem solving* (pp. 23–68). Columbus, OH: Clearinghouse for Science, Mathematics, and Environmental Education.

Bartlett, F. C. (1932). *Remembering: A study in experimental and social psychology*. Cambridge: Cambridge University Press.

Beland, A. & Mislevy, R. J. (1991). *Probability-based inference in a domain of proportional reasoning tasks* (Tech. Rep. ONR Contract N00014–91-J-4101). Princeton: Educational Testing Service.

Bereiter, C. (1991). Implications of connections for thinking about rules. *Educational Researcher, 20*, 10–16.

Bower, G. H. (1972). Mental imagery and associative learning. In L. Gregg (Ed.), *Cognition in learning and memory* (pp. 51–88). New York: Wiley.

Bransford, J. D., & Johnson, M. K. (1972). Contextual prerequisites for understanding: Some investigations of comprehension and recall. *Journal of Verbal Learning and Verbal Behavior, 11*, 717–726.

Brewer, M. A. (1988). *The role of diagrams in understanding the semantic relations in arithmetic story problems*. Unpublished master's thesis, San Diego State University, San Diego.

Brewer, W. F., & Nakamura, G. V. (1984). The nature and functions of schemas. In R. S. Wyer & T. K. Srull (Eds.), *Handbook of social cognition* (Vol. 1, pp. 119–160). Hillsdale, NJ: Lawrence Erlbaum Associates.

Broadbent, D. (1958). *Perception and communication*. London: Pergamon Press.

California Assessment Program (1986). *Annual report 1985–86*. Sacramento: California State Department of Education.

California Assessment Program. (1989). *A question of thinking*. Sacramento: California State Department of Education.

Carpenter, T. P., Fennema, E., Peterson, P. L., Chiang, C., & Loef, M. (1988, April). *Using knowledge of children's mathematics thinking in classroom teaching: An experimental study*. Paper presented at the American Educational Research Association Annual Meeting, New Orleans.

Carpenter, T. P., & Moser, J. M (1982). The development of addition and subtraction problem-solving skills. In T. P. Carpenter, J. M. Moser, & T. A. Romberg (Eds.), *Addition and subtraction: A cognitive perspective* (pp. 9–24). Hillsdale, NJ: Lawrence Erlbaum Associates.

Carpenter, T. P., & Moser, J. M. (1984). The acquisition of addition and subtraction concepts in grades one through three. *Journal for Research in Mathematics Education, 15*, 179–202.

Chi, M. T. H., Feltovich, P. J., & Glaser, R. (1981). Categorization and representation of physics problems by experts and novices. *Cognitive Science, 5*, 121–152.

Clement, C. A., & Gentner, D. (1989). *Systematicity as a selection constraint in analogical reasoning* (Tech. Rep. No. UIUCDCS-R-89–1558). University of Illinois at Urbana-Champaign.

Cohen, J., & Cohen, P. (1983). *Applied multiple regression/correlation analysis for the behavioral sciences.* Hillsdale, NJ: Lawrence Erlbaum Associates.

Collins, A. M., & Loftus, E. F. (1975). A spreading activation theory of semantic processing. *Psychological Review, 82,* 407–428.

Collins, A. M., & Quillian, M. R. (1969). Retrieval time from semantic memory. *Journal of Verbal Learning and Verbal Behavior, 8,* 240–247.

Cornoldi, C., & McDaniel, M. A. (Eds.). (1991). *Imagery and cognition.* New York: Springer Verlag.

D'Andrade, R. G. (1992). Schemas and motivations. In R. G. D'Andrade & C. Strauss (Eds.), *Human motives and cultural models* (pp. 23–44). Cambridge: Cambridge University Press.

De Corte, E., & Verschaffel, L. (1985). Beginning first graders' initial representation of arithmetic word problems. *Journal of Mathematical Behavior, 4,* 3–21.

De Corte, E., & Verschaffel, L. (1987). The effect of semantic structure on first graders' strategies for solving addition and subtraction word problems. *Journal for Research in Mathematics Education, 18,* 363–381.

De Corte, E., Verschaffel, L., & De Win, L. (1985). Influence of rewording verbal problems on children's problem representations and solutions. *Journal of Educational Psychology, 77,* 460–470.

Dyer, M. (1991). Symbolic neuroengineering for natural language processing: A multilevel research approach. In J. A. Barnden & J. B. Pollack (Eds.), *Advances in connectionist and neural computation theory: High-level connectionist models* (Vol. 1, pp. 32–86). Norwood, NJ: Ablex Publishing.

Ericsson, K. A., & Simon, H. A. (1984). *Protocol analysis.* Cambridge: MIT Press.

Ericsson, K. A., & Smith, J. (1991). *Toward a general theory of expertise.* Cambridge: Cambridge University Press.

Frank, O. (1971). *Statistical inference in graphs.* Stockholm: FOA Repro Forsvarets Forskningsanstalt.

Gagné, R. M. (1970). *The conditions of learning* (2nd ed.). New York: Holt, Rinehart & Winston.

Gagné, R. M., & Briggs, L. J. (1974). *Principles of instructional design.* New York: Holt, Rinehart & Winston.

Gardner, H. (1987). *The mind's new science.* New York: Basic Books.

Gentner, D. (1983). Structure-mapping: A theoretical framework for analogy. *Cognitive Science, 7,* 155–170.

Gick, M. (1985). The effect of a diagram retrieval cue on spontaneous analogical transfer. *Canadian Journal of Psychology, 39,* 460–466.

Gick, M., & Holyoak, K. J. (1980). Analogical problem solving. *Cognitive Psychology, 12,* 306–355.

Gick, M., & Holyoak, K. J. (1983). Schema induction and analogical transfer. *Cognitive Psychology, 15,* 1–38.

Goldsmith, T. E., & Davenport, D. M. (1990). Assessing structural similarity of graphs. In R. Schvandeveldt (Ed.), *Pathfinder associative networks: Studies in knowledge organization* (pp. 75–88). Norwood, NJ: Ablex Publishing.

Goldsmith, T. E., Johnson, P. J., & Acton, W. H. (1991). Assessing structural knowledge. *Journal of Educational Psychology, 83,* 88–96.

Grossberg, S. (1976). Adaptive pattern classification and universal recoding: Parallel development and coding of neural feature detectors. *Biological Cybernetics, 23,* 121–134.

Grossberg, S. (1987). Competitive learning: From interactive activation to adaptive resonance. *Cognitive Science, 11,* 23–63.

Hampson, P. J., Marks, D. F., & Richardson, J. T. (Eds.). (1990). *Imagery: Current developments.* London: Routledge.

Hebb, D. O. (1969). (Interview with Elizabeth Hall, editor of *Psychology Today*). *Psychology Today, 3,* 20–28.

Heller, J. I., & Greeno, J. G. (1978, April). *Semantic processing in arithmetic word problem solving.* Paper presented at the meeting of the Midwestern Psychological Association Convention, Chicago.

Hendler, J. A. (1988). *Integrating marker-passing and problem-solving: A spreading activation approach to improved choice in planning.* Hillsdale, NJ: Lawrence Erlbaum Associates.

Hendler, J. A. (1991). Developing hybrid symbolic/connectionist models. In J. A. Barnden & J. B. Pollack (Eds.), *Advances in connectionist and neural computation theory: High-level connectionist models,* (Vol. 1, pp. 165–179). Norwood, NJ: Ablex Publishing.

Hinsley, D., Hayes, J., & Simon, H. (1977). From words to equations: Meaning and representation in algebra word problems. In M. Just & P. Carpenter (Eds.), *Cognitive processes in comprehension* (pp. 89–106). Hillsdale, NJ: Lawrence Erlbaum Associates.

Holyoak, K. J. (1991). Symbolic connectionism: Toward third-generation theories of expertise. In K. A. Ericsson & E. J. Smith (Eds.), *Toward a general theory of expertise* (pp. 301–335). Cambridge: Cambridge University Press.

James, W. (1890). *The principles of psychology* (Vol. 1). New York: Henry Holt.

Johnson-Laird, P. (1988). *The computer and the mind.* Cambridge: Harvard University Press.

Just, M. A., & Carpenter, P. A. (1987). *The psychology of reading and language comprehension.* Boston: Allyn & Bacon.

Kant, Immanuel (1968). *Critique of pure reason* (Norman Kemp Smith, Trans.). New York: St. Martin's Press. (Original work published 1787)

Kieras, D. E. (1991). *Human learning of schemas from explanations in practical electronics* (Tech. Rep. No. 34 TR-91/ONR34). Ann Arbor: Technical Information Design & Analysis Laboratory, University of Michigan.

Kieras, D. E. (1992). Learning schemas from explanations in practical electronics. In S. Chipman & A. L. Meyrowitz (Eds.), *Foundations of knowledge acquisition: Cognitive models of complex learning* (pp. 83–118). Norwell, MA: Kluwer Academic Publishers.

Kintsch, W. (1988). The role of knowledge in discourse comprehension: A construction-integration model. *Psychological Review, 95,* 163–182.

Kintsch, W., & Greeno, J. G. (1985). Understanding and solving word arithmetic problems. *Psychological Review, 92,* 109–129.

Laird, J. E., Newell, A., & Rosenbloom, P. S. (1987). SOAR: An architecture for general intelligence. *Artificial Intelligence, 33,* 1–64.

Larkin, J. H., & Simon, H. A. (1987). Why a diagram is (sometimes) worth ten thousand words. *Cognitive Science, 11,* 65–99.

Levine, D. S. (1991). *Introduction to neural and cognitive modeling.* Hillsdale, NJ: Lawrence Erlbaum Associates.

Levine, G., & Burke, C. J. (1972). *Mathematical model techniques for learning theories.* New York: Academic Press.

Linn, R. L., Baker, E. L., & Dunbar, S. B. (1991). Complex, performance-based assessment: Expectations and validation criteria. *Educational Researcher, 20* (8), 15–21.

Loftus, E. F., & Suppes, P. (1972). Structural variables that determine problem-solving difficulty in computer-assisted instruction. *Journal of Educational Psychology, 63,* 531–542.

Mandler, G. (1984). *Mind and body: Psychology of emotion and stress.* New York: W. W. Norton.

Mandler, G. (1985). *Cognitive psychology: An essay in cognitive science.* Hillsdale, NJ: Lawrence Erlbaum Associates.

Marshall, S. P. (1981). *Sex differences in sixth-grade children's problem solving* (Final Report, NIE Grant NIE-G-80–0095). Santa Barbara: University of California. (ERIC Document Reproduction Service No. ED 200 649)

Marshall, S. P. (1985, August). *An analysis of problem-solving instruction in arithmetic textbooks.* Paper presented at the American Psychological Association Annual Meeting, Los Angeles.

Marshall, S. P. (1988). Assessing problem solving: A short-term remedy and a long-term solution. In R. I. Charles & E. A. Silver (Eds.), *The teaching and assessing of mathematical problem solving* (pp. 159–177). Reston, VA: Lawrence Erlbaum Associates and the National Council of Teachers of Mathematics.

Marshall, S. P. (1990a). Assessing knowledge structures in mathematics: A cognitive science perspective. In S. Legg & J. Algina (Eds.), *Cognitive assessment of language and math outcomes* (pp. 241–273). Norwood, NJ: Ablex Publishing.

Marshall, S. P. (1990b). Generating good items for diagnostic tests. In N. Frederiksen, R. Glaser, A. Lesgold, & M. Shafto (Eds.), *Diagnostic monitoring of skill and knowledge acquisition* (pp. 433–452). Hillsdale, NJ: Lawrence Erlbaum Associates.

Marshall, S. P. (1991). *Final report: Schemas in problem solving* (Tech. Rep. 91–01. ONR Contract N00014–90-J-1143). San Diego: San Diego State University, Center for Research in Mathematics and Science Education.

Marshall, S. P. (1992). Assessing schema knowledge. In N. Frederiksen, R. Mislevy, & I. Bejar (Eds.), *Test theory for a new generation of tests* (pp. 155–180). Hillsdale, NJ: Erlbaum Associates.

Marshall, S. P. (1993a). Assessment of rational number: A schema-based approach. In T. Carpenter, E. Fennema, & T. Romberg (Eds.), *Rational numbers: An integration of research* (pp. 261–288). Hillsdale, NJ: Lawrence Erlbaum Associates.

Marshall, S. P. (1993b). Statistical and cognitive models of learning through instruction. In A. L. Meyrowitz & S. Chipman (Eds.), *Cognitive models of complex learning* (pp. 119–146). Norwell, MA: Kluwer Academic Publishers.

Marshall, S. P. (in press). Some suggestions for alternative assessments. In S. Chipman, P. Nichols, & R. Brennan (Eds.), *Cognitively diagnostic assessment*. Hillsdale, NJ: Lawrence Erlbaum Associates.

Marshall, S. P., Barthuli, K. E., Brewer, M. A., & Rose, F. E. (1989). *STORY PROBLEM SOLVER: A schema-based system of instruction* (Tech. Rep. 89–01 ONR Contract N00014–85-K-0661). San Diego: San Diego State University, Center for Research in Mathematics and Science Education.

Marshall, S. P. & Marshall, J. P. (1991). Hybrid models of cognition. In S. Marshall, *Final report: Schemas in problem solving* (Tech. Rep. 91–01. ONR Contract N00014–90-J-1143). San Diego: San Diego State University, Center for Research in Mathematics and Science Education.

Marshall, S. P., Pribe, C. A., & Smith, J. D. (1987). *Schema knowledge structures for representing and understanding arithmetic story problems* (Tech. Rep. 87–01, ONR Contract N-000140-K-85–

0661). San Diego: San Diego State University, Center for Research in Mathematics and Science Education.

McClelland, J. L. (1986). The programmable blackboard model of reading. In J. McClelland, D. E. Rumelhart, and the PDP Research Group (Eds.), *Parallel distributed processing: Explorations in the microstructures of cognition* (Vol. 2, pp. 122–169). Cambridge: MIT Press.

McClelland, J. L., & Rumelhart, D. E. (1989). *Explorations in parallel distributed processing: A handbook of models, programs, and exercises.* Cambridge: MIT Press.

McClelland, J. L., Rumelhart, D. E., and the PDP Research Group (Eds.). (1986). *Parallel distributed processing: Explorations in the microstructures of cognition (volume 2).* Cambridge: MIT Press.

McCloskey, M. (1991). Networks and theories: The place of connectionism in cognitive science. *Psychological Science, 2,* 387–395.

Michon, J. A. (1992). Allen Newell: A portrait. In J. A. Michon & A. Akyurek (Eds.), *SOAR: A cognitive architecture in perspective* (pp. 11–24). Dordrecht, The Netherlands: Kluwer Academic Publishers.

Minsky, M. (1975). A framework for representing knowledge. In P. Winston (Ed.), *The psychology of computer vision* (pp. 211–281). New York: McGraw-Hill.

Minsky, M. (1991, Summer). Logical versus analogical or symbolic versus connectionist or neat versus scruffy. *AI Magazine,* pp. 35–51.

Minsky, M., & Papert, S. (1969). *Perceptrons.* Cambridge: MIT Press.

Mislevy, R. J., Yamamoto, K., & Anacker, S. (1991). *Toward a test theory for assessing student understanding* (Tech. Rep. RR-91–32-ONR). Princeton: Educational Testing Service.

Nelson, T. O. (1976). Reinforcement and human memory. In W. K. Estes (Ed.), *Handbook of learning and cognitive processes* (Vol. 3, pp. 207–246). Hillsdale, NJ: Lawrence Erlbaum Associates.

Nesher, P., & Katriel, T. (1977). A semantic analysis of addition and subtraction word problems in arithmetic. *Educational Studies in Mathematics, 8,* 251–269.

Nesher, P., Greeno, J. G., & Riley, M. S. (1982). The development of semantic categories for addition and subtraction. *Educational Studies in Mathematics, 13,* 373–394.

Newell, A. (1973). Production systems: Models of control structures. In W. G. Chase (Ed.), *Visual information processing* (pp. 463–526). New York: Academic Press.

Newell, A. (1990). *Unified theories of cognition.* Cambridge: Harvard University Press.

Newell, A. (1992). Unified theories of cognition and the role of SOAR. In J. A. Michon & A. Akyurek (Eds.), *SOAR: A cognitive architec-*

ture in perspective (pp. 25–80). Dordrecht, The Netherlands: Kluwer Academic Publishers.

Newell, A., & Simon, H. A. (1972). *Human problem solving.* Englewood Cliffs, NJ: Prentice-Hall.

Nisbett, R. E., & Wilson, T. D. (1977). Telling more than we can know: Verbal reports on mental processes. *Psychological Review, 84,* 231–259.

Olson, J. R. & Biolsi, K. J. (1991). Techniques for representing expert knowledge. In K. A. Ericsson & J. Smith (Eds.), *Toward a general theory of expertise* (pp. 240–285). Cambridge: Cambridge University Press.

Ortony, A. (1975). Why metaphors are necessary and not just nice. *Educational Theory, 25,* 45–53.

Pavio, A. (1975). Perceptual comparisons through the mind's eye. *Memory and Cognition, 3,* 635–647.

Peled, I., & Nesher, P. (1988). What children tell us about multiplication word problems. *Journal of Mathematical Behavior, 7,* 239–262.

Piaget, J. (1952). *The origins of intelligence in children* (Margaret Cook, Trans.). New York: International Universities Press.

Polya, G. (1945/1957). *How to solve it* (2nd ed.). Princeton: Princeton University Press.

Post, E. L. (1943). Formal reductions of the general combinatorial decision problem. *American Journal of Mathematics, 65,* 197–215.

Postman, L. (1964). Short-term memory and incidental learning. In A. W. Melton (Ed.), *Categories of human learning* (pp. 146–194). New York: Academic Press.

Reder, L. M. (1992, June). Developmental studies of metacognition. In J. Metcalf (Chair), *Theoretical, cognitive, developmental, and neuropsychological aspects of metacognition.* Invited Multispeciality Symposium conducted at the Annual Convention of the American Psychological Society, San Diego.

Reder, L. M., & Anderson, J. R. (1980). A comparison of texts and their summaries: memorial consequences. *Journal of Verbal Learning and Verbal Behavior, 19,* 121–134.

Reinke, R. E., & Michalski, R. S. (1988). Incremental learning of concept descriptions: A method and experimental results. In J. E. Hayes, D. Michie, & J. Richards (Eds.), *Machine intelligence* (Vol. 11, pp. 263–288). Oxford: Clarendon Press.

Resnick, L., & Resnick, D. (1992). Assessing the thinking curriculum: New tools for educational reform. In B. Gifford & M. O'Connor (Eds.), *Changing assessments: Alternative views of aptitude, achievement and instruction* (pp. 37–76). Norwell, MA: Kluwer Academic Publishers.

Restle, F., & Greeno, J. G. (1970). *Introduction to mathematical psychology.* Reading, MA: Addison-Wesley.

Riley, M. S., & Greeno, J. G. (1988). Developmental analysis of understanding language about quantities and of solving problems. *Cognition and Instruction, 5,* 49–101.

Riley, M. S., Greeno, J. G., & Heller, J. (1983). Development of children's problem-solving ability in arithmetic. In H. Ginsburg (Ed.), *The development of mathematical thinking* (pp. 153–196). New York: Academic Press.

Rosenblatt, F. (1962). *Principles of neurodynamics.* New York: Spartan.

Rumelhart, D. E. (1975). Notes on a schema for stories. In D. Bobrow & A. Collins (Eds.), *Representation and understanding* (pp. 211–236). New York: Academic Press.

Rumelhart, D. E., Hinton, G. E., & Williams, R. J. (1986). Learning internal representations by error propagation. In D. E. Rumelhart, J. L. McClelland, & the PDP Research Group (Eds.), *Parallel distributed processing: Explorations in the microstructures of cognition* (Vol. 1, pp. 318–362). Cambridge: MIT Press.

Rumelhart, D. E., McClelland, J. L., & the PDP Research Group (Eds.) (1986). *Parallel distributed processing: Explorations in the microstructures of cognition* (Vol. 1). Cambridge: MIT Press.

Rumelhart, D. E., & Ortony, A. (1977). The representation of knowledge in memory. In R. C. Anderson, R. J. Spiro, & W. E. Montague (Eds.), *Schooling and the acquisition of knowledge* (pp. 99–135). Hillsdale, NJ: Lawrence Erlbaum Associates.

Rumelhart, D. E., Smolensky, P., McClelland, J. L., & Hinton, G. E. (1986). Schemata and sequential thought processes in PDP models. In J. L. McClelland, D. E. Rumelhart, & the PDP Research Group (Eds.), *Parallel distributed processing: Explorations in the microstructures of cognition* (Vol. 2, pp. 5–57). Cambridge: MIT Press.

Santa, J. L. (1977). Spatial transformations of words and pictures. *Journal of Experimental Psychology: Human Learning and Memory, 3,* 418–427.

Schank, R. C. (1975). The structure of episodes in memory. In D. Bobrow & A. Collins (Eds.), *Representation and understanding* (pp. 237–272). New York: Academic Press.

Schank, R. C. (1982). *Dynamic memory.* Cambridge: Cambridge University Press.

Schank, R. C. & Abelson, R. (1977). *Scripts, plans, goals and understanding.* Hillsdale, NJ: Lawrence Erlbaum Associates.

Schneider, W., & Oliver, W. L. (1991). An instructable connectionist/control architecture: Using rule-based instructions to accomplish connectionist learning in a human time scale. In K. VanLehn (Ed.),

Architectures for intelligence (pp. 113–145). Hillsdale, NJ: Lawrence Erlbaum Associates.

Schoenfeld, A. H. (1985). *Mathematical problem solving.* Orlando: Academic Press.

Schvaneveldt, R. W. (Ed.) (1990). *Pathfinder associative networks: Studies in knowledge organization.* Norwood, NJ: Ablex Publishing.

Shepard, L. A. (1991). Psychometricians' beliefs about learning. *Educational Researcher, 20* (7), 2–9.

Shavelson, R., Gao, X., & Baxter, G. (1993). *Sampling variability of performance assessments.* CSE Tech. Rep. 361. Los Angeles, University of California: CRESST.

Shiffrin, R. M., & Schneider, W. (1977). Controlled and automatic human information processing: II. Perceptual learning, automatic attending, and a general theory. *Psychological Review, 84,* 127–190.

Silver, E. A. (1979). Student perceptions of relatedness among mathematical verbal problems. *Journal for Research in Mathematics Education, 10,* 195–210.

Silver, E. A. (Ed.) (1985). *Teaching and learning mathematical problem solving: Multiple research perspectives.* Hillsdale, NJ: Lawrence Erlbaum Associates.

Skemp, R. R. (1987). *The psychology of learning mathematics.* Hillsdale, NJ: Lawrence Erlbaum Associates.

Smith, D. E., & Marshall, S. P. (1993). Neural network models of decision-making schemas. In J. Borack (Ed.), *Applications of Artificial Neural Networks and Related Technologies to Manpower, Personnel, and Training,* pp. 137–148. San Diego: NPRDC.

Smith, D. E., & Marshall, S. P. (in press). Applying hybrid models of cognition in decision aids. In G. Klein, C. Zsambok, & J. Orasanu (Eds.), *Advances in naturalistic decision making: Research and applications.* Hillsdale, NJ: Lawrence Erlbaum Associates.

Smith, E., Shoben, E. J., & Rips, L. J. (1974). Structure and process in semantic memory: A feature model for semantic decisions. *Psychological Review, 81,* 214–241.

Smith, M. L. (1991). Put to the test: The effects of external testing on teachers. *Educational Researcher, 20* (5), 8–12.

Smolensky, P. (1988). On the proper treatment of connectionism. *Behavioral and Brain Sciences, 11,* 1–74.

Smolensky, P. (1986a). Formal modeling of subsymbolic processes: an introduction to harmony theory. In N. E. Sharkey (Ed.), *Advances in cognitive science, volume 1* (pp. 204–235). New York: Halsted Press.

Smolensky, P. (1986b). Information processing in dynamical systems: Foundations of harmony theory. In D. Rumelhart, J. McClelland,

& the PDP Research Group (Eds.), *Parallel distributed processing: Explorations in the microstructure of cognition* (Vol. 1, pp. 194–281). Cambridge: MIT Press.

Squire, L. R. (1987). *Memory and brain.* New York: Oxford University Press.

Steffensen, M. S., Joag-dev, C., & Anderson, R. C. (1979). A cross-cultural perspective on reading comprehension. *Reading Research Quarterly, 15,* 10–29.

Sweller, J., Chandler, P., Tierney, P., & Cooper, M. (1991). Cognitive load as a factor in the structuring of technical material. *Journal of Experimental Psychology: General, 119,* 176–192.

Sweller, J., & Cooper, G. (1985). The use of worked examples as a substitute for problem solving in learning algebra. *Cognition and Instruction, 2,* 59–89.

Tulving, E. (1985). How many memory systems are there? *American Psychologist, 40,* 385–398.

VanLehn, K. (1990). *Mind bugs: The origins of procedural misconceptions.* Cambridge: MIT Press.

Venezky, R. L. & Bregar, W. S. (1988). Different levels of ability in solving mathematical word problems. *Journal of Mathematical Behavior, 7,* 111–134.

Ward, M. & Sweller, J. (1991). Cognitive load theory and the format of instruction. *Cognition & Instruction, 8,* 293–332.

Weeks, R. (1924). *Boys' own arithmetic.* New York: E. P. Dutton & Co.

Wenger, E. (1987). *Artificial intelligence and tutoring systems.* Los Altos, CA: Morgan Kaufmann Publishers.

Willis, G. B., & Fuson, K. C. (1988). Teaching children to use schematic drawings to solve addition and subtraction word problems. *Journal of Educational Psychology, 80,* 192–201.

Winograd, T. (1977). A framework for understanding discourse. In M. A. Just & P. A. Carpenter (Eds.), *Cognitive processes in comprehension* (pp. 63–88). Hillsdale, NJ: Lawrence Erlbaum Associates.

Winston, P. H. (1977). *Artificial intelligence.* Reading, MA: Addison-Wesley.

Name index

Subject index

abstract knowledge, *see* knowledge
abstraction of general properties, in schemas, 50–1
accommodation and assimilation, 13–16
ACT* theory, 317, 322–5, 377
adaptive testing, 272–3, 277, 312
affective responses of students to SPS, 166
algebra word problems, 29–30, 50–1
analogical reasoning, in schemas, 55–6, 159–60, 176
attention, in schema construction and use, 47–8
automatic versus purposeful schema instantiation, 52–3

back propagation, 328–30, 368–71
basis set of schemas
  general description, 62–6
  steps for identifying: practicality check, 66, 102–7; situation description, 65, 70–6; source evaluation, 66, 84–90; status quo appraisal, 65, 76–84; theoretical verification, 66, 90–102
bias, as parameter in learning model, 367
Brewer's experiment using diagrams, 245–58

California Assessment Program, 88, 273

Change
  diagram, 135, 239
  schema components, 90–3
  situation description, 71
cognitive diagnosis, 298–302
cognitive load, 175–6
cognitive maps
  analyses, 195–200, 205–7, 301
  coding scheme for, 191
  description, 189–92, 340–4
  measures of confusions in, 193–5
  measures of specificity in, 190
  plenary map, 192
cognitive models, 317–19
cognitive science, 171–2
cognitive skills, 172–3
Compare
  diagram, 240
  schema components, 95–7
  situation description, 73
competency (*see also* expertise), 177–9, 180–1
competitive learning model, 362
computer-based assessment, advantages of, 308
connectionist models, *see* neural networks
connectivity feature of schema, 43–4
conscious versus unconscious schema implementation, 52
constructive nature of schema, 46–7
content variability of schema, 51
contexture of learning, 172–4, 179–80